TERRA NOVA

Terra Nova

Food, Water, and Work in an
Early Atlantic World

JACK BOUCHARD

Yale
UNIVERSITY PRESS

NEW HAVEN AND LONDON

Published with support from the Fund established in memory of Oliver Baty Cunningham, a distinguished graduate of the Class of 1917, Yale College, Captain, 15th United States Field Artillery, born in Chicago September 17, 1894, and killed while on active duty near Thiaucourt, France, September 17, 1918, the twenty-fourth anniversary of his birth.

Published with assistance from the foundation established in memory of Philip Hamilton McMillan of the Class of 1894, Yale College.

Yale University Press books may be purchased in quantity for educational, business, or promotional use. For information, please e-mail sales.press@yale.edu (U.S. office) or sales@yaleup.co.uk (U.K. office).

Set in Electra type by IDS Infotech, Ltd.
Printed in the United States of America.

Library of Congress Control Number: 2025931246
ISBN 978-0-300-26435-7 (hardcover)

A catalogue record for this book is available from the British Library.

Authorized Representative in the EU: Easy Access System Europe, Mustamäe tee 50, 10621 Tallinn, Estonia, gpsr.requests@easproject.com.

10 9 8 7 6 5 4 3 2 1

For Cheryl

CONTENTS

ILLUSTRATIONS

ACKNOWLEDGMENTS

I have been looking forward to writing these acknowledgments for a long time. Academic work is no less about networked labor than fishwork was in the sixteenth century, and this book has been the product of countless conversations, conferences, learning experiences, and shared cups of coffee over the years.

At Brandeis University, Govind Sreenivasan introduced me to both *Annales* scholarship and Atlantic history, which is the dual origin of this book in many ways. At the same time Cheryl Walker taught me to pay attention to words and translations (albeit in ancient Greek). At McGill University I met Allan Greer and Catherine Desbarats, who made me think seriously about Atlantic, early American, and Canadian history. It was while working with them that I became interested in the northwest Atlantic and decided to make it my PhD project. I am indebted to their early feedback and advice.

In 2012 the University of Pittsburgh accepted a PhD student who wanted to work on, of all things, the early Newfoundland fisheries (only later did the project become about Terra Nova). I am eternally grateful to Marcus Rediker not only for advising me in the work but for seeing something in it back then that I do not think I fully realized until much later. I am also grateful for his efforts to instill a passion for history from below and a respect for labor that I hope are reflected in this book. At the University of Pittsburgh I was part of a vibrant community of scholars, and this book reflects hours of conversations with people like Jake Pomerantz, Chris Eirkson,

Marcy Ladson, Katherine Parker, Patrick Manning, Bennett Sherry, Mirelle Luecke, Mari Webel, Elizabeth Archibald, Matt Drwenski, Niklas Frykman, Reid Andrews, Diego Holstein, Alex Mountain, Stephanie Makin, Leslie Hammond, Leonardo Moreno, Yevan Terrien, Jesse Olsavsky, Andrew Berhendt, and others. While completing my dissertation I benefited from an amazing committee that included Rediker, Molly Warsh, Pernille Røge, and Chris Pastore.

This book would have been very different had I not spent two years at the wonderful Folger Shakespeare Library in Washington, DC. Thanks to a generous Mellon Foundation grant, I was brought on to the Before "Farm to Table": Early Modern Foodways and Cultures project. I was lucky enough to spend my days in an office with the brilliant Michael Walkden and Elisa Tersigni. I learned to do food history talking to them and to team members Amanda Herbert, David Goldstein, Heather Wolfe, Kathleen Lynch, Jonathan MacDonald, and Julia Fine.

Since the fateful fall of 2020 I have had a home at Rutgers University, New Brunswick. I could not have asked for a better place to finish this book and to settle in as an environmental historian. A cluster of environmental scholars and friends have helped shape the final version of this project: Elaine LaFay, Hieu Phung, Victoria Ramenzoni, Archisman Chaudhuri, Toby Jones, Katherine Sinclair, Alastair Bellany, Javier Gonzalez Cortes, and Carla Cevasco. In addition I have benefited from discussions with Tatiana Seijas, Melissa Feinberg, Jennifer Jones, Camilla Townsend, Matt Matsuda, Seth Koven, Michael Opal, Lauren Rostash, Monica Katz, Paul Clemens, and many others.

At the same time, this book was shaped by my interactions with the growing environmental history movement, and I am thankful to have found a home in an energetic and generous community of scholars. Early on I got pulled into a cluster of Canadian environmental historians: Ed MacDonald, Brian Payne, Sara Spike, Peter Pope, Elizabeth Mancke, Erin Spinney, Zachary Tingley, Josh MacFayden, Matthew McKenzie, Mark McLaughlin, and others. From the ocean history movement, Helen Rozwadowski has offered endless support, and I have benefited from my collaborations with Jakobina Arch and my conversations with Daniella McCahey. Over the years I have talked with and learned from many environmental and early American historians, including Casey Schmitt, Gabriel de Avilez Rocha, Chris Pastore, Brett Rushforth, Carla Pestana, Jane Hooper, Caroline Abbott, Chris Parsons, Arianne Sedef Urus, Judith Carney, and many others.

This project and my professional career have been indelibly shaped by three scholars who have offered me encouragement, insight, and support. Molly Warsh of the University of Pittsburgh helped guide early versions of this book and quite literally introduced me to the early American community. Claire Campbell of Bucknell University welcomed me to the ranks of environmental historians and made me realize that people wanted to read my work. Amanda Herbert of the Folger Shakespeare Library and University of Durham made me understand that my work was about much more than just a fishery, and taught me how to do food history. I hope that this book repays the faith all three had in my work and the encouragement they offered.

Over the years this project has received financial support from the World History Center, the European Studies Center, and the Dietrich School of Arts and Sciences at the University of Pittsburgh; the American Society of Environmental Historians; and the Forum for Early Modern Empires and Global Interactions (FEEGI). An early version of this manuscript was workshopped in 2023 through a grant from the Rutgers Research Council. I was overjoyed when Brett Rushforth and Bonnie McCay agreed to be readers and commentators. This book was made leagues better by their generous feedback and insights. The Rutgers Center for Cultural Analysis supported my work with a yearlong fellowship as part of its "Commons" seminar, which allowed me to develop the chapter on the commons. Sometimes institutional support can be indirect, and I offer a thousand thanks to the archivists and photographers who digitized maps and manuscripts at the Folger Library, the Library of Congress, the John Carter Brown Library, and the various other archives cited in this book. I have no idea who within the corporate hegemon of Google was tasked with digitizing sixteenth- and nineteenth-century books for Google Books, or who built the incredible Google Arts and Culture platform, but I owe them a great deal.

Since 2020 I have had the pleasure of working with Yale University Press and its amazing team. My particular thanks go to my editor Adina Popescu for seeing something in this book project and for her support over the years. I would also like to thank the incredible John Greenlee for his mapmaking skills and collaboration on visually representing Terra Nova.

Much of chapter 2 previously appeared in *Annales: Histoire, Sciences sociales* as "Terra Nova: Cartes mentales de l'Atlantique du nord-ouest au XVIe siècle." Parts of chapters 4 and 6 previously appeared in the *William & Mary Quarterly* as "Beyond Bacalao: Newfoundland and the Caribbean in the Sixteenth Century."

This is a book about space, so I would be remiss if I didn't offer thanks to some of the spaces that shaped this project. The first and most important space was the home made by my parents Marc and Kathy Bouchard, and my brother Jean-Luc, who let me fill the house with history books and inane questions. The hours we spent talking about cooking food, good writing, and the value of history led to this book. Thank you to the defunct El Mundo café in Montréal; to the Tea Room in the Folger Library; to the Crazy Mocha café in Squirrel Hill, Pittsburgh; to the sunroom in my apartment in Highland Park, New Jersey, where much of this book was written; and to the patio in my backyard where it was revised. And thank you to my dogs Aethelwulf and Loz for their tireless assistance in helping me write, read, and revise in said rooms and yards.

Finally, this book would not exist if it were not for my wife, soulmate, best friend, and fiercest supporter Cheryl Leibowitz. Cheryl is the best—if you haven't met her yet, you should. She has supported my work materially and morally for years; she has often given me the best and clearest writing advice of anyone I've talked with. More than anything, though, Cheryl has filled my life with joy and love beyond measure, and what could matter more than that? This book was written during the happiest years of my life thanks to her, and I hope some of that is reflected in the text.

A NOTE ON NAMES

L anguage and names are important to the story of Terra Nova. Transla-tions are my own, unless otherwise noted. I will occasionally include original-language material when it is relevant to the point I am making. I have chosen to translate sixteenth-century English sources into modern English for readability. Dates have been modernized where necessary. As cities are so important to the story, I have made use of French urban de-monyms that do not have English equivalents: *malouin* (Saint Malo), *roche-lais* (La Rochelle), *rouennais* (Rouen), *luzien* (Saint Jean-de-Luz).

Place-names and personal names were often different in the sixteenth century from their names today. Sometimes this is merely a matter of spelling, like the use of "Jehan" instead of "Jean" in French-language docu-ments. Sometimes, though, the names we use can illuminate the more complex history of the sixteenth century. I call the navigator on the 1497 ex-pedition Zuan Caboto, a version of the northern Italian name he was known by in the early sixteenth century. The standard modern version of his name, John Cabot, deliberately reinforces an Anglocentric reading of the region's history that I find misleading. Similarly, I have chosen to call what is today Saint John's on Newfoundland by the name "Sam Joham/Saint John's." The harbor first appears on a 1519 European map as Sam Joham, and was likely known by its Portuguese, Spanish, and French names to most mari-ners before the end of the century. In other cases I hope to highlight particu-lar Iberian perspectives. I prefer to use the Portuguese Rio do Ouro and

Arguim for places in Africa that are today known in English by their Spanish names (Rio de Oro and Arguin), reflecting their role as Portuguese colonial spaces in the fifteenth and sixteenth centuries. I similarly use Española for Hispaniola and Cristóbal Colón for Christopher Columbus.

In the case of Terra Nova, I have tried to choose spellings and name variations that were more common and widely used in the sixteenth century. I use Newfoundland only to mean the island itself. Labrador signifies the northern coast of Terra Nova, not just the modern province. I will occasionally refer to the Atlantic Ocean as the Ocean Sea or Mare Oceanum, a formulation frequently used by Europeans. The reader will also find Butus for Red Bay, Isle Saint Jean for Prince Edward Island, and Isle de Sable for Sable Island. Most significant, I use River of Canada and Gulf of Canada for the Saint Lawrence River and Gulf of Saint Lawrence (see the first map). Saint Lawrence did not become the standard name for the waters of the northwest Atlantic until the turn of the seventeenth century. In the sixteenth century, Gulf/River of Canada was more common in our written sources. If the reader finds these alternative names confusing at times, that is perhaps the point. The sixteenth century was different, and names were being invented and contested at a bewildering speed, and I hope to reflect that somewhat in my writing.

MAPS

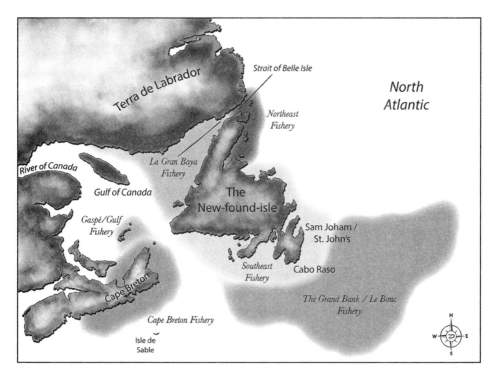

Figure 1. Terra Nova, mid-sixteenth century. (Prepared by SEH Mapping.)

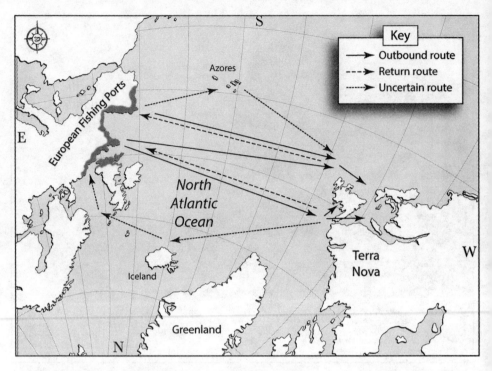

Figure 2. The far North Atlantic, showing probable sailing routes to/from Terra Nova. (Prepared by SEH Mapping.)

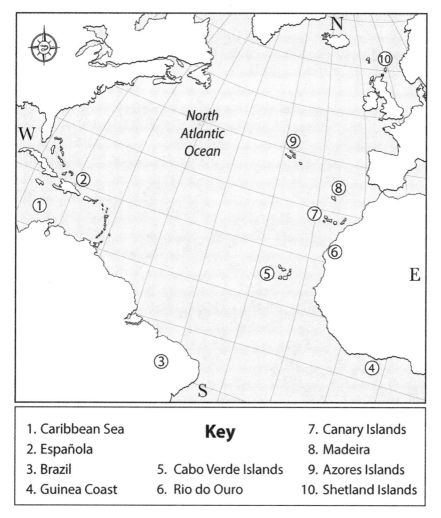

Figure 3. Atlantic basin, showing places mentioned in the text connected to Terra Nova. (Prepared by SEH Mapping.)

Key

1. Caribbean Sea
2. Española
3. Brazil
4. Guinea Coast
5. Cabo Verde Islands
6. Rio do Ouro
7. Canary Islands
8. Madeira
9. Azores Islands
10. Shetland Islands

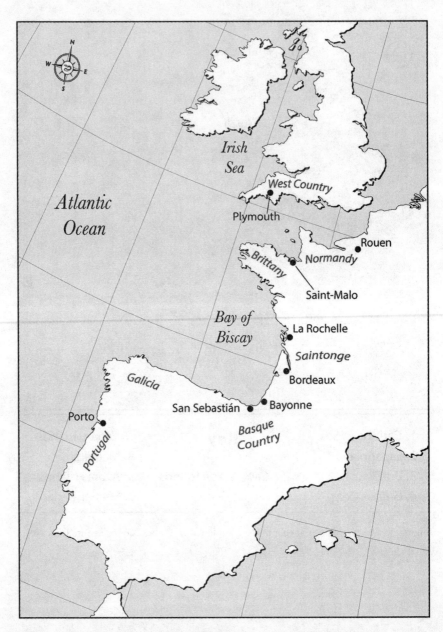

Figure 4. Fishing regions in western Europe. Major outfitting ports of the mid-sixteenth century are indicated and labeled, along with bodies of water discussed in the text. Important coastal regions are labeled in italics. (Prepared by SEH Mapping.)

TERRA NOVA

Introduction

Robert Lefant's Voyage, 1542

On a July morning in 1542 the sun broke through the overcast skies of the tempestuous North Atlantic. Rays of weak light fell upon the stony beach of the little harbor of Caprouge. Lying on the eastern, Atlantic-facing side of Newfoundland island's Great Northern Peninsula, Caprouge was, and is, a relatively isolated but picturesque harbor. At this high latitude the long daylight hours must fight fog and cloud, but that July day enough sun made it through. The rays provided energy to the sudden upswelling of humans and other-than-human beings that swarmed into Caprouge that summer, as they had every year for the past three decades.

The first thing the sun would have hit were rows upon rows of dead and drying fish lying along the stony beach. Almost all of them were Atlantic cod, a white-fleshed predatory fish that flourished in the waters near Caprouge. Though you would not have recognized them as cod if you saw them. Bundles of off-white triangles, these were fish whose heads had been lopped off and their bodies opened along the spine until they were flat as a board. Most important, the cod had been rubbed with salt—a coarse gray salt taken from marshy waters thousands of miles away to the east and carried across the sea for just this purpose. The sunlight hit the fish as the salt pulled water out of their flesh, evaporating the moisture and accelerating the desiccation process. After a few days the result was a slab of hard, dried, salty fish meat that would resist putrefaction and could be safely eaten months later. Many people in the sixteenth century called this remarkable processed food *bacalao,* a name still used all over the world.

The sunlight would have fallen on the water in the middle of the harbor, illuminating floating wooden ships, windborne machines designed to carry European laborers across the Atlantic Ocean to places like Caprouge. This summer six or so fishing ships stood anchored in Caprouge's shallow, enclosed waters. Around these bobbing vessels were a hundred or more fishworkers, teams of European mariners who were busy hauling fishing ropes, splitting fish, navigating small boats, or managing onshore stations. They shouted to each other in several languages, including Basque, Breton, French, and Spanish. Some tended to the drying fish, others did their best to find and kill more, while still others hunted birds or foraged for firewood along the beach.

Among them was a middle-aged captain by the name of Robert Lefant. A native Basque from the city of Bayonne, he was standing on the beach overseeing his crew as they went about their fishwork. That July day Lefant was idly speaking with a fellow captain, a Breton who had been hired by an Asturian ship and who had likewise found himself working in this same harbor of Caprouge. The Breton was sharing a bit of gossip, a story about the well-known pilot Jacques Cartier, who had left his home port of Saint Malo a year ago at the behest of the king of France and made for the waters of the northwest Atlantic. Instead of stopping to fish, as most mariners would have, Cartier had pushed on with his ships westward up the River of Canada, where he had found various riches and made contact with new Indigenous communities. When Cartier returned to France with his first load of treasures he left behind a settlement under the direction of the aristocrat-adventurer the sieur de Roberval. The Breton knew all this, he told Lefant, because Cartier's ship had stopped off in the same fishing harbor where the

Breton had been working the previous year. He had heard tales about the new settlement and Roberval's ambitions firsthand.

If you had asked Lefant where he was that summer of 1542, he would have used language unfamiliar to most of us. We would today say that he was working in a harbor on the island of Newfoundland in the province of Newfoundland and Labrador in the eastern part of the country of Canada. Lefant would have answered more simply: he was spending the summer in Terra Nova. The term *Terra Nova* was used by fishworkers like Lefant to describe the waters and coasts of the northwest Atlantic where they actively caught fish, a vast and malleable space that changed from year to year and season to season. Asked later what his crew was doing at Caprouge, Lefant would declare that they "were going to Terra Nova to fish for *bacalao*." That was the explanation given, and it was all the explanation that was needed.

So on that day in July the captain Lefant stood in the middle of a vast watery world he knew as Terra Nova, and listened to his Breton friend tell him about a famous captain who had decided Terra Nova was not enough and who instead sought out new lands to seize farther west. As Lefant watched his men at their profitable work, Cartier's expedition must have seemed senseless, conducted by men who did not understand this place where he had spent the past five summers. It seems clear from Lefant's later recounting of the story of Jacques Cartier that he found the whole episode little more than amusing gossip, a fact worth filing away but not something to be much concerned about. After all, there were riches enough to be had right at hand, here where ocean met shore and the water teemed with fish.

If Robert Lefant did not seem to care much about the adventures of Cartier and Roberval, others were extremely interested. The Spanish crown, the administrative center of what was rapidly becoming the largest European empire in the Atlantic basin, was deeply anxious about what these French-sponsored settlers were up to and whether their actions would threaten trade and colonization in the Caribbean. Canada and the Caribbean may seem far apart today, but they were closely linked in the sixteenth-century Spanish mind. When an attempt to dispatch a galleon to intercept Cartier fell through, the crown grew desperate. In the late summer of 1542 orders went out to local officials in the ports of northern Spain, where fishing ships returning from Terra Nova were due back soon: fishworkers should be rounded up and put to the question. That is how we know Robert Lefant's story: he was one of the mariners grabbed by Spanish authorities and interrogated about his experiences. Lefant's ship had sailed to the Spanish-controlled Basque port of Fuenterrabía, and while the crew returned home in early September Lefant was stuck behind when he became sick. He was still recovering when he was dragged in front of a notary and the questioning began. Seventeen questions were asked, some eliciting brief responses, others long explanations. The notary, Antonio de Ubilla, dutifully recorded his responses, along with those of a half-dozen other Basque mariners, and their testimonies have fortunately survived in the archives.[1]

The image of a July day in 1542 that I have conjured above is derived from Robert Lefant's testimony, although this has been enlivened at several points by my own research (which forms the basis of this book) and imagination (I do not, for instance, know exactly when his conversation with the Breton took place, or whether that day was particularly sunny) to flesh out the mariner's often curt remarks. The essence of the story is derived from his testimony, but the details and imagery reflect a more universal experience of fishwork in the sixteenth century. Tens upon tens of thousands of European mariners sailed to a place they called Terra Nova in the sixteenth century, each one contributing in some way to a vast enterprise that turned marine life into food and fuel for European markets. Robert Lefant is not significant because he was crucial to the formation of the fishery, or noteworthy to those who interrogated him, or even important because he was particularly successful at fishing. Indeed, it is quite clear that the Spanish interrogators quickly grew frustrated with the bland responses Lefant was giving them, answers that said more about rote fishwork than the struggle to colonize the western Atlantic. But Lefant is significant precisely because he was so unimportant. Lefant was representative of the innumerable ship masters and fishworkers whose quotidian labor constituted the main European experience in the sixteenth-century northwest Atlantic. It just happens that his story survived relatively intact whereas others did not.

"A Harbour and Beach alongside the Sea"

In reading the testimony of Robert Lefant, sometimes it is the most innocuous questions and replies that turn out to be the most revealing. The tenth question the authorities in Fuenterrabía asked Lefant, after learning that his fishing site was named Caprouge, was the shortest: "Was there anything there?" It had a name, and a name made it a place. Perhaps it was a place of importance? "No," Lefant replied laconically, "nothing save a harbour and beach alongside the sea."[2]

That at least was the gist of the question—according to the transcript, Lefant was literally asked "if there is *lugar* there—*si hay lugar?*" Today, *lugar* typically means "place," in the abstract sense of any kind of place. The question might well mean "Is it a place?" But in sixteenth-century Spanish, *lugar* did not just mean a place, it specifically indicated one that contained an organized, settled human community. A *lugar* implied a village, a town, even a small city—a civic settlement of some kind. *Si hay lugar? Are there settlements there?* This was the question Lefant answered in the negative.[3]

We may read between the lines and consider what the officials were really asking. Are there people? Towns? Cities? Polities? Civilization? Something to seize, to control, to exploit? In the city-centric world of sixteenth-century Spain, one might as well have asked, *Is this place of any value to us?* It was in *lugar* that civic life took place, and civic life was the basis of successful human society as they understood it. But more so, the Spanish had already found that the Americas were a world of settlements and cities. Was Caprouge like the city-states of Mesoamerica or the networked empires of the Andes? Was it a *lugar* like the many Taíno settlements of Española or the trading ports of the Yucatán? No, it was not. It was nothing save a harbor and a beach.

This book is about why those beaches and harbors matter as much as any settlement, and why the northwest Atlantic was very much a place with value in the sixteenth century. In short, it aims to put Terra Nova back in the Atlantic. By that I mean that the floating fishworkers' world of Terra Nova—not Newfoundland, not Canada, not the Newfoundland fisheries—needs to be seen as an essential part of how we research and teach early European expansion into the Atlantic basin and the deep changes this process wrought.

I am particularly interested in recovering the ways in which different people directly and indirectly experienced Terra Nova in the sixteenth century, be it through fishwork or migration or eating cod. We may then fit this into our bigger narrative of what it was like to live through and understand the creation of an integrated Atlantic system in the sixteenth century, and how Terra Nova played a part in that process.

European activity at Terra Nova represented one of the most significant—and by the mid-sixteenth century one of the largest—systems of maritime activity in the Atlantic basin. It was also one of the most stable and long-lasting structures of transoceanic commerce that Europeans established during their initial Atlantic expansion. As such, Terra Nova represents a site of permanent European occupation in the Americas, but a unique one. The continuous European presence in the northwest Atlantic was a colony without settlement, a floating seasonal entrepôt that acted as a vector for European interaction with and impact on North America and its peoples. To borrow the language used at a recent meeting of the American Society for Ethnohistory, it was both a historical root and a route for change. Terra Nova was the root cause of a permanent European presence in the northwest Atlantic as well as the route by which Europeans, their commodities, and their ideas entered the Americas. It was also a route by which American biomass was funneled back to European consumers, a development of long-term significance that continues to shape our world.[4]

To recover the fishworker's *lugar* of the sixteenth century, I focus on four things: space, food, water, and work. Each represents a basic way that people experienced Terra Nova in the sixteenth century, from the creation of new mental maps to the physical labor of fishwork to the indigestion brought on from eating too much saltcod. Space, food, water, and work are important aspects because something as vast and enduring as Terra Nova only becomes legible if we look beyond individuals and moments in time to see the patterns that underlay and shaped behavior and events. The organization of this book into short thematic chapters reflects this. Each will consider one particular facet of space, food, water, and work—such as mental geography, diets, or urban financing—and how it shaped the history of fishwork in the northwest Atlantic in the sixteenth century. Such a cross-section of perspectives and structures ultimately allows us to make sense of Terra Nova as a whole, while explaining the varied human and nonhuman experiences in the sixteenth century we see in our sources.

Atlantic Spaces

To put Terra Nova back in the Atlantic, we need to approach it as a coherent and distinct historical space. Terra Nova was a maritime space in the coastal northwest Atlantic created through the killing and processing of marine life by Europeans. At its core was a commercial fishery dedicated to mass-producing preserved codfish. I prefer to use the singular *fishery* when talking about Terra Nova, reflecting the fact that most sixteenth-century languages and sources use a singular noun (fishery, *pescherie*, *pescaria*) to describe fishing operations, and also because although the northwest Atlantic comprised many fishing grounds, they were united in the concept of Terra Nova. Terra Nova was an expansive and impermanent space that thrived for much of the sixteenth century before being undermined by a new imperial regime. Terra Nova belongs among the ranks of human-geographical spaces that a generation of environmental historians has brought to the forefront of our historical thinking: Bathsheba Demuth's Berengia, Joshua Reid's Ča•Di• Borderlands, Ernesto Bassi and Sharika Crawford's Greater Caribbeans. A history of Terra Nova, rather than Newfoundland or its variants, gives us a framework for a more expansive and inclusive history of the northwest Atlantic that treats the actions of mariners as something worth taking seriously.[5]

Was Lefant visiting a European colony when he sailed to a space like Terra Nova in the early sixteenth century? Many people, including many scholars, are likely to conflate colony with settlement and empire. In this sense a colony is a permanent installation of people in a new space on behalf of a far-reaching metropole that controls the colony as part of a larger imperial project. The sixteenth-century Atlantic had no shortage of settlements and empires. Yet this doesn't apply to sixteenth-century Terra Nova, where there were no permanent European settlements. Although various European states periodically claimed to possess all or parts of the northwest

Atlantic, none pursued sustained claims and none, crucially, established nodes of control on the ground that would have allowed them to incorporate Terra Nova into an imperial system (hence Spain's uncertainty about what was happening in 1542). And yet, for all that, I believe we should understand Lefant's Terra Nova as a colony. Continual seasonal fishing fulfilled the basic purpose of a colony, and even if it was not organized within an empire, the rise of Terra Nova benefited multiple European metropoles. Colonies are first and foremost ecological entities that exist to control space and the resources within it for the benefit of someone else. Such projects can take many forms, from the settler colonialism of the Caribbean to the *feitoria* of West Africa to the protection racket of the *Estado da India*. In the northwest Atlantic, it took the form of a floating, extractive occupation of water. Terra Nova put the biological resources of the northwest Atlantic at the disposal of the European metropole. This system of extraction was sustained over decades and then centuries, steadily drawing energy out of the northwest Atlantic and transferring it to hungry cities in Europe. The labor of fishworkers like Lefant allowed Terra Nova to be incorporated into Europe's world-ecology, creating a permanent site of resource extraction. Terra Nova was a colony without settlement, without settlers, and without empire. As such it serves as a reminder of the many different forms colonization could take in the earliest years of European extraction.[6]

Terra Nova was not the only space—human or otherwise—in the northwest Atlantic during the sixteenth century. No Mi'kmaq or Inuit or Beothuk peoples would have recognized Terra Nova. This was a distinctly European conception of space, created as an act of occupation imposed upon and eventually displacing Indigenous alternatives. A history of the northwest Atlantic in the sixteenth century about Mi'kma'ki or the Beothuk Dawnland or the southern reaches of NunatuKavut can and should be written. Yet I also believe that we need some way to describe the European colonial project in the sixteenth century, and the current candidates leave much to be desired. Calling this New France, Newfoundland, the fishery, or just ignoring the area fails to capture the reality on the ground or the place of European activity in a wider Atlantic system. Thinking in terms of Terra Nova better reflects the particular and lived history of the sixteenth century, even if that means confronting the ways in which mariners would ultimately impose their own worldview on others.[7]

To understand Terra Nova, I have deliberately taken a different approach to the problem than previous researchers. Most scholarship on the northwest Atlantic to date has been undertaken by specialists working within clear linguistic and archival boundaries. Such parameters allow for deep scholarly engagement with the surviving archival material. To this must be added the growing work of archaeologists on the ground in the northwest Atlantic, whose efforts have added detail and nuance, flesh and blood, to our image of what happened at Terra Nova. The endnotes and pages that follow will highlight the contributions and insights of these scholars: Peter Pope's study of the English; Selma Huxley Barkham, Michael Barkham, Brad Loewen, and Miren Egaña Goya for their work on Basques; Laurier Turgeon, Jacques Bernard, and Charles de la Morandière for the French; Darlene Abreu-Ferreira for the Portuguese; and many others. Each of these historians and archaeologists have offered painstakingly re-created and carefully crafted stories and data allowing us to glimpse different aspects of the early fishery, such as the numbers of French ships, the makeup of a Basque whaling crew, or the struggles of the first English settlers. I have added my own archival finds and my own interpretations of previously known sources to this body of scholarship.[8]

Yet whereas previous work has focused on deep dives, this book aims to go broad. This reflects my conviction that while we know many specifics about the sixteenth-century history of the northwest Atlantic, we lack a synthetic framework to understand the story as a whole. To create a comprehensive picture of the early northwest Atlantic, it is necessary to trade narrow dives into archives for breadth and broad patterns. This study brings together archival and printed material from across western European and the Mediterranean, along with archaeological, climatological, artistic, and cartographical evidence. (For a discussion of this, see appendix B, "Sources.") Implicit in this methodology is an argument that what defined Terra Nova as a place, an idea and a lived experience was, in many ways, its bigness. It was physically expansive and complex, a watery world home to all manner of marine and terrestrial life and tens of thousands of human beings. It was common for observers to find Breton, Basque, Norman, and Innu or Mi'kmaw fishworkers all laboring alongside one another in the same harbor, creating a plethora of multiethnic historical sites that defy simple study within linguistic or national frameworks. It was also common for these visiting communities to turn on one another, making these sites of violence and competition as well as fishwork. Beyond the beach, the activities of Europeans at Terra Nova were shaped by events far across the Atlantic, not just in Europe but in Africa, the Caribbean, and Brazil. To study and appreciate so vast and dynamic a world, then, we must go broad in the scope and nature of the sources we use.

Food

With this reframing of Terra Nova in mind, we can return to the story of Robert Lefant and better appreciate what he was doing in 1542. Sitting in a seaside room, Spanish officials began their questioning by asking how Lefant had found his way to Terra Nova, and he responded clearly and succinctly. Lefant was from the French-controlled Basque province of Labourd (Basque Lapurdi), and was a Catholic. He was aged fifty years, "more or less," meaning that his lifetime encompassed the entire history of the Terra Nova fishery. Born around the time that Cristóbal Colón made contact with the Caribbean, Lefant would have been a young teenager when the first fishing voyages left Brittany, Portugal, and England for the northwest Atlantic. Now middle-aged, he was himself leading a crew to the other side of the Ocean Sea in search of food. His voyage formed part of a new wave of Basque involvement in the fishery at Terra Nova. By 1542 more and more ships were sailing from Basque ports, challenging Norman and Breton dominance in the northwest Atlantic.

Lefant told the authorities that he was the master of a ship from Bayonne, which lay just over the Franco-Spanish border. He had been hired by a merchant named Garcia de Soto to command a fishing voyage that summer as the ship's master. This was a typical arrangement: the master was expected to run the entirety of the fishing voyage, including its outfitting, in exchange for ample payment, while the shipowner claimed a large cut of the profits (and risk). In the summer of 1542 Lefant was responsible for the lives of thir-teen men and four *grumetes,* teenagers serving a kind of apprenticeship. Per-haps Lefant had started his own career at sea as a *grumete,* and perhaps in a few years these four boys would be leading voyages of their own. All the crew members were engaged in fishwork, the activity of converting marine life into processed food and oil. Fishworkers at Terra Nova focused their efforts overwhelmingly on one species, the Atlantic cod, which Lefant called *baca-lao* in his deposition. Most Europeans would know the *bacalao* well as a sta-ple of their weekly diets, even if they were unaware of the kind of labor Lefant and his crew were doing across the Atlantic Ocean.

Writing of wolves, violence, and colonization in the early Americas, the historian Jon Coleman has vividly and accurately observed, "Any story of colonization must account for the flesh in the human's teeth as well as the thoughts in their heads" in order to preserve the "physicality of the colonial experience." Fish was flesh, eagerly chewed by humans after being pulled from waters rather than land. Before the year 1600, most Europeans inter-acted with the northwest Atlantic through their stomachs. Across the six-teenth century households from Portugal to Holland ate thousands upon thousands of processed codfish pulled from the waters of Terra Nova. To put Terra Nova back into the Atlantic, then, we must follow how the commodi-ties produced there were ultimately used and consumed in the Atlantic ba-sin. Sixteenth-century fishwork at Terra Nova linked European consumers to North Atlantic waters, and this set in motion deep processes that would lead to long-term collapse and disaster. Food allows us to make sense of what Terra Nova was and why it was important for the sixteenth century and beyond.[9]

Terra Nova's consumable history is its most enduring and impactful leg-acy, especially to coastal communities in Europe. To give one example, a 2011 cookbook showcasing regional recipes from across all of France's ninety-five metropolitan and five overseas *départments* featured four recipes for cod, the most of any fish. They included saltcod from Réunion (*rougail de morue*) and hashed stockfish from the mountains of Aveyron (*estofinado*). This culinary legacy has nonetheless been affected by the collapse of cod stocks in the northwest Atlantic at the end of the twentieth century, and the

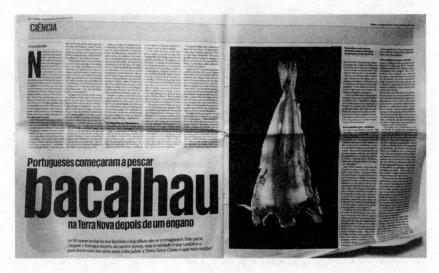

Figure 5. A Lisbon newspaper celebrates the return of *bacalhau* from Terra Nova, July 10, 2017. (Photo by author.)

realization that there was no inexhaustible supply of fish under the sea. Mixing nostalgia with regret, in the spring of 1996 the Norman regional journal *Patrimoine Normand* ran an article entitled "The Great Trade: Fishing at Terra Nova, a Lost Heritage." The text bemoaned that "Fécamp has for many years sent ships to fish for cod, and the fishery at Terra Nova has made its fortune. But there are no longer '*terre-neuvas*' at Fécamp." A transatlantic loss was framed in very local, nostalgic ways. By contrast, in 2017 the Lisbon newspaper *Público* celebrated the story of fishing at Terra Nova with a full centerfold spread declaring, "The Portuguese began to fish for *bacalhau* at Terra Nova after a mistake" (see figure 5). The upbeat tone and talk of mistakes may feel misplaced in an age of collapse. Nonetheless, the image of dried *bacalhau* and the reference to Terra Nova's long, troubled history would have been instantly recognizable to most people in Lisbon. The article declared, "If anyone has a history with *bacalhau*, it is the Portuguese" before launching into a description of a six-century history emphasizing a special Portuguese relationship with Terra Nova. The memory of sixteenth-century fishwork and fish food is still very much alive.[10]

We must take this legacy of fish eating seriously, studying food from both the producer's and the consumer's perspective. Like the cod itself, we will begin in the cool waters of the northwest Atlantic and end on a European plate. This book owes much to Jakobina Arch's pioneering work on the Japanese whaling industry. Arch demonstrated the importance of linking sea to land, following marine life as it was taken out of the ocean and consumed by terrestrial communities. Richard Hoffmann has more recently done the same for medieval European societies, showing that the interplay of marine harvesting and cultural ideas about seafood cannot be separated. Following Arch's and Hoffmann's work, we will also see how people thought about codfish in ways both abstract and practical. This is an essential step toward putting Terra Nova back into the Atlantic, seeing how people envisioned the northwest Atlantic's place in their alimentary world.[11]

Water

All mariners experienced Terra Nova as part of a voyage, the cyclical movement from a European port to the coasts of the northwest Atlantic and back. A seasonal venture typically took around four to five months. In April 1542 Lefant's voyage began with a city when his ships sailed north from Bayonne to the port of La Rochelle. This marsh-adjacent city was amply stocked with essential supplies like salt, wine, and dried provisions. After eight days onloading supplies and raising funds, Lefant sailed along the coast toward Brittany and the jumping-off point for a transoceanic voyage to Terra Nova. Lefant told his interrogators that he sailed outward from Ushant at the tip of Brittany, heading "directly to Terra Nova." He obviously assumed that his audience would know what this meant, due to broad familiarity with the fishery, but today we can't be sure exactly what route he took. The ship left Brittany on May 1, and the outbound voyage took around one month, with no hope of stopping en route. A mere sixty tons,[12] Lefant's ship was around the size of Cristóbal Colón's more famous *Pinta* and may have been only sixty-five feet (twenty meters) long, and perhaps fifteen to twenty feet (five to six meters) across. Within this cramped space were the eighteen crew members and everything they needed for a voyage of several months: dozens of barrels of biscuit, cider, and salt pork, sacks of rough gray bay salt, ropes and hooks for fishing, disassembled barrels ready for the catch, iron nails to build drying racks, metal axes to trade or to chop down trees, and a small boat or two on deck. While later fishing ships would sail well armed with cannon, muskets, bows, and pikes, Lefant claims to have brought only three swords with him to Terra Nova, an indication that he expected few violent encounters with either the Indigenous communities of Terra Nova or European mariners, but still came prepared.

For the summer season of 1542, Robert Lefant chose a harbor he called Carruje in Spanish, a translation of French Caprouge. According to his testimony, five years previously Lefant had served on a voyage that had sailed northward through the Straits of Belle Isle and into La Gran Baya. A name used by fishworkers for the south coast of Labrador, La Gran Baya was fast becoming the center of Basque fishing activity in the northwest Atlantic, and would soon be the site of the world's first commercial whaling industry. Despite its popularity and his own familiarity with the region, this year Lefant had chosen instead to bring his crew to Atlantic-facing Caprouge. The harbor was enclosed by two arms of forested land sheltering it from the Atlantic Ocean, with an inward-facing set of beaches. Archaeologists have come to identify what Lefant knew as Caprouge with a beach site known as Champs Paya, a later Breton name for the area, or the Dos-de-Cheval archaeological site. In the sixteenth century it was one of the many communal fishing sites that dotted Terra Nova. Photographs taken in 2013 by archaeologists show the topography of Caprouge harbor, including a rocky beach near Dos-de-Cheval (see figure 6). This is likely the very beach on which Robert Lefant lived and worked during the summer of 1542.[13]

The floating world of Terra Nova belonged to no one community. In previous years Lefant had found himself working alongside Indigenous communities in La Gran Baya. He even remarked to his interrogators that relations between fishworkers and the Innu in southern Labrador had become so close that the latter spoke several European languages. In 1542 Lefant gave no indication that First Nations (in this case the Beothuk of Newfoundland) had settlements nearby at Caprouge. If there were no Beothuk at Caprouge, nonetheless Lefant and his crew were certainly not alone. On

Figure 6. Caprouge harbor, 2013, showing the harbor mouth looking east over the fishing beaches. (Courtesy of Bryn Tapper.)

the voyage to Terra Nova Lefant had already run into fishing ships from several Basque and Breton ports. When they arrived in the harbor, they found ships from French and Spanish Basque Country, Brittany, Asturias, and Normandy. Perhaps a hundred Europeans in half a dozen ships in all fished in Caprouge harbor during the summer of 1542. Harbors like Caprouge functioned as a kind of aquatic commons, a space whose resources were accessible to all fishworkers who agreed to abide by a shared set of customs. If they did not work together, they at least worked alongside one another in the multinational, multilingual, and space-sharing arrangement that typified the sixteenth-century fishery.

In the age of sail and oar, water served as a connector between different human and nonhuman communities, and we cannot fully understand Terra Nova without addressing its place in the wider Atlantic basin. One of the other mariners interrogated in 1542 gives us a glimpse into how water connected Terra Nova and those who worked there. Though his testimony was not as illuminating as Lefant's, Martin de Artalecu was typical of the urban merchants who drove the sixteenth-century fishery. Artalecu was a citizen of Fuenterrabía, but unlike Robert Lefant he was a shipowner rather than just a captain for hire. He is the kind of person French notaries at the time would have described as *bourgeois*, a many-layered term we will return to later. In 1541 a merchant of Saint Jean-de-Luz (in French Basque Country) had chartered Artalecu's one-hundred-ton *San Salvador* on a voyage to La Gran Baya, with Artalecu serving as master. The following year, before being interrogated, he had returned to Terra Nova yet again to fish. A few years later, in 1549, Artalecu and his ship appear in records again; he hired a crew to sail to Terra Nova. Years went by, then suddenly Martin de Artalecu met his end in 1555 when the venerable *San Salvador*, on which he was serving as ship master, was lost at sea. It was returning from San Juan in Puerto Rico, thousands of miles south of Terra Nova. This is clear evidence that Artalecu was among those mariner-merchants who did not just fuel the fishery but also traded to the Caribbean. The men whom Lefant worked alongside at Caprouge sometimes found themselves sailing to many different corners of the Atlantic basin.[14]

As the lives of mariners like Lefant and Artalecu suggest, the "Terra" in Terra Nova is misleading—as sixteenth-century fishworkers were well aware, this was a watery world, a floating colony designed to harvest beings swimming below the ocean's surface. To reconstruct Terra Nova, we must put water at the center of our history, exploring the nature of coastal and ocean spaces, and how humans and animals interacted in these unusual and important maritime worlds. This book is offered as a contribution to the growing scholarship that attempts to think with water, and in particular I follow Renisa Mawani's belief in the "Ocean as Method" approach to history: a way of "reading, writing, and thinking with the sea as metaphor and materiality" that allows us to understand the watery world of Terra Nova through the eyes of our historical subjects.[15]

I combine this ocean-centric environmental scholarship with an Atlantic studies perspective. As intuitive as an Atlantic framework may seem for a "transatlantic" fishery, historians have shied away from using this model for the sixteenth century. Atlantic history is typically applied to cultural contact zones like the Caribbean, European settlements, systems of coerced labor, one-way migrations, and above all to empires and colonization. These features were largely absent, or at least moderated, at Terra Nova. Because early European activity in the northwest Atlantic was structured so differently from other contemporaneous Atlantic systems, historians of both the fishery and the early Atlantic have been hesitant to grant it more than quasi-Atlantic status as a minor branch of commerce, despite its scale. Even when Peter Pope broke ground by applying an Atlantic approach to the history of Newfoundland's fishery, his work was confined to English commerce in the seventeenth century. We are therefore faced with a question: how can a maritime system that is, at face value, both transatlantic and successful also diverge so drastically from the experience of Europeans elsewhere in the Atlantic? I believe an Atlantic history framework offers the most useful model for understanding the early history of European activity at Terra Nova. Atlantic history at its core is a recognition of connection and transformation within a shared system. In the sixteenth century Europeans saw Terra Nova as connected to and growing out of experiences and ongoing projects elsewhere in the Atlantic basin, from Madeira to Iceland to Española to Brazil. At the same time, experiences at Terra Nova had repercussions elsewhere, shaping how Europeans interacted with the rest of the Atlantic basin. There has been a push of late to make Atlantic history more "messy," to confront the variability of experiences and improvisational nature of early European expansion. The history of Terra Nova must be a major part of this revision.[16]

Important recent shifts in the field of history have shaped how I approach an Atlantic, ocean-centered framework. Several overlapping changes in the scholarship covering the history of the colonial Caribbean point toward potential ways to write a regional history within the framework of wider Atlantic studies. "New Conquest History" has advocated for a messier and bottom-up reframing of early European arrivals. A new generation of scholars has challenged our spatial understanding of the Caribbean, offering alternative visions of the Greater Caribbean, Turtlemen's Caribbean, or the Creole Archipelago. New work in Indigenous and African histories has shifted the focus from settlers to Taíno, Kalinago, and African-descendant communities. Finally, there has been a renewed push to explore the transatlantic dimensions of early Caribbean history. In many ways, this book is an attempt to apply some of these new approaches to the history of the northwest Atlantic. Another historiographical shift has been the rise of environmental history as a robust field. Environmental history has always been particularly important to histories of the far north, including Canadian history, which often subsumes Terra Nova. But now, as the world burns around us, historians of the environment have been galvanized to better explain the long history of human interactions within an other-than-human natural world. The northwest Atlantic is a perfect case study for these new approaches. Drawing on environmental history's vibrant subfields, I combine approaches from ocean history, coastal history, food history, and animal history. The surge in work on climate history is less reflected in this study, if only because much more work needs to be done before we properly understand the relationship between the Little Ice Age and fishwork. I am also concerned with many of the larger projects of historical ecology that come out of the works of Jason Moore and others who are interested in the intersection between capitalism, colonialism, and environmental change. Such approaches, from the grand level of global upheaval and climate to the historical disruptions of localized ecologies, are woven throughout this book.[17]

Work

After arriving at Caprouge in June 1542, Robert Lefant's crew would have quickly adopted the work rhythm of Terra Nova. Every day teams got into small boats (called *txalupa* in Basque, shallop in English, *chalupa* in Spanish) to catch fish by hand, one line and hook at a time, baited with old pieces of cod, seabird, or fresh capelin. Bait the hook, drop the line, wait for the bite, haul up the fish—this was the way food was made, a process repeated endlessly as long as there was daylight and space in the boats to store the fish. Catches were then turned over to shore-bound crew for processing. These men swiftly turned the fresh-killed cod into a commercial product ready to be dried: head lopped off, guts removed, liver tossed into an open barrel, body split and spread out. Finally, the fish was rubbed with salt and placed on racks made of wood or flat stone to dry in the sun. After several days in this state (depending on weather and salt) the now-desiccated fish would be ready to be stored aboard the main ship to transport home. A ship like Lefant's might catch and process ten thousand to twenty thousand codfish over the course of the season.

What was Lefant doing at Terra Nova? For a language nominally born of an island peoples, English is remarkably impoverished in how it describes the making of marine food. We might say that he was a *fisherman* doing *fishing*. This does not quite capture the nature of the labor involved, and makes it hard to distinguish between Lefant's travails and those of a coastal angler or fishpond tender. I prefer to say that Lefant was one of many mariners undertaking *fishwork*, the labor of processing marine life for markets. We will explore this term more later, but we should understand fishwork as a kind of labor marked by two important features. First, fishwork was the act of killing and processing marine life into exportable commodities—of turning living cod into salty *bacalao* for a distant market in Europe. Second, fishwork was always networked with other kinds of labor that were essential to its success. For every fishworker like Lefant, there were legions of supporting laborers who contributed to the success of the venture. Farmers grew wheat for his ration of biscuit, day laborers onloaded and offloaded his ship, merchants gave him credit to buy supplies, saltpan workers provided the salt he needed for *bacalao*, and eventually fishmongers would sell his catch. Fishworkers like Lefant and his team never worked alone, and their seasonal efforts at Terra Nova were part of a much wider expansion of commercial fishwork in the early Atlantic.

To understand the northwest Atlantic in the sixteenth century, we must tell the stories of people like Robert Lefant, described by the sixteenth-century

French geographer André Thevet as "those who go there to fish for the cod we eat over here." Many of the chapters in this book will start with a very brief story and example, partly because these episodes are important and engaging, but also to remind us that we must see the sixteenth century not as a fleshed-out world but as a series of incomplete, if tantalizing, snapshots. As Brian Fagan has noted of fishwork more broadly, "Fisherfolk and their communities have almost entirely escaped notice. They held their knowledge close to their chests and seldom gave birth to powerful monarchs or divine rulers. Because they lived and died in quiet obscurity, writing their history means drawing on a wide range of esoteric and specialized sources." In an attempt to grapple with these issues, as much as possible I have tried to write this story "from below," taking the perspective of fishworkers.[18]

When we try to make sense of the work Lefant and others did, we immediately face a host of thorny conceptual questions. What language should we use to describe Terra Nova? Was it modern or medieval? Capitalist or pre-capitalist? Part of a new world or an extension of Europe? A colony, a fishery, or both? These are difficult questions to answer, for Terra Nova looked forward and backward, and often side to side. One could find fourteenth-century fishing techniques paired with seventeenth-century financial systems. The trade ruthlessly harvested natural resources without being capitalist. But it was these contradictions and complexities that made Terra Nova an unusual and enduring space of human activity—even as they make our job as historians difficult.

Consider the question of whether or not fishwork at Terra Nova was capitalistic. I understand capitalism as a social, economic, and ecological system. It organizes labor into a hierarchy for the extraction of natural resources to transform them into commodities for consumption within a market economy. Capitalism was a system that had to be created, and much of that act of creation took place on the water. Liam Campling and Alejandro Colás have rightly argued that the sea is central to the historical development of capitalism. It is the connective tissue that makes global commerce possible, but is also itself a site of resource extraction and proletarianization. We could ask whether the Terra Nova fishery was "capitalist" in the sense of being part of this emergent system and evincing the kinds of labor relations and extractive regimes we see elsewhere.[19]

Here we run into a contradiction at the heart of Terra Nova. Viewed one way, fishworkers look like wage laborers processing commodities for market consumption; viewed another way, they seem more like hunter-foragers obtaining food within seasonal migratory kinship networks. The sixteenth-century fishery at Terra Nova extracted resources and expanded Europe's world-ecology outward. Yet fishworkers did so without embracing capitalist modes of production and while lacking control over resource production. Consider that Robert Lefant was hired by a minor urban merchant to procure food using little more than hooks, salt, and sun, and yet the *bacalao* he produced was a valuable, processed, alienated commodity that might appear in marketplaces on the other side of the ocean. The floating colony he visited was certainly part of the emerging capitalist world-ecology in the Atlantic basin, yet his own role was marginal and obscure.

How do we make sense of this? As places like Terra Nova can show us, distinctions between capitalist and noncapitalist are not as clear-cut as we would like them to be. The anthropologist Anna Tsing's revelatory *The Mushroom at the End of the World* introduces the concept of "salvage accumulation," a mode of production that captures what happened at Terra Nova. She describes "the process through which firms amass capital without controlling the conditions under which commodities are produced." Under such processes, noncapitalist modes of production are linked to and embedded within capitalist systems of circulation and consumption. This is fishwork: producing marketable fish for resale using relatively simple techniques without having any control over the undersea ecology that creates cod in the first place. For consumers separated by distance and market forces from Terra Nova, processed fish arrived as a pre-packaged commodity alienated from its site and method of production. Consumers saw a marketable commodity; fishworkers saw an age-old process of food harvesting. Yet, noncapitalist production techniques could and did contribute to emergent capitalism.[20]

As this reasoning suggests, my argument about what Terra Nova was — and therefore how we should interpret it — does not fit neatly in any one framework. It was not capitalist or pre-capitalist, modern or medieval, New World or Old. If anything, my argument is that in the sixteenth century the mariners' Terra Nova was deeply ironic. It was built upon and embodied a series of contradictions and cross-purposes, some that were outright funny, most that are hard for modern historians to make sense of. Fishworkers used a phrase meaning "New Land" to describe old waters. Fishwork at Terra Nova was outside capitalism but drove capitalist growth and the commodification of fish. Terra Nova was a permanent colony that lacked settlements or imperial claims. Fishwork lay the long-run groundwork for disaster in the form of overfishing, and yet sixteenth-century mariners themselves eschewed the fur trade and were incapable of overfishing. The fishery was marked by a tension between legal incoherence (an absence of overarching state control) and social coherence (fishworkers all followed remarkably similar patterns of behavior). Mariners from a dozen regional communities and four kingdoms somehow all did the same things at the same places every summer.

The point is that even if it was built on a series of strange contradictions, Terra Nova worked, and worked well, in the sixteenth century. Its weirdness was a feature, not a bug, and it provided a certain flexibility to European mariners that proved to be a strength in the tumult of the sixteenth century. Most important, the unusual social and economic approaches Europeans used allowed them to work within the ecological limitations and opportunities of the northwest Atlantic. Rather than try to resolve the conceptual ironies underlying the history of Terra Nova, then, I think we ought to embrace them, much as sixteenth-century mariners did.

Endings and Beginnings

Robert Lefant and his crew spent only around two months at Caprouge during the summer of 1542. By September they were back in Europe, their catch sold in cities like San Sebastián, Fuenterrabía, and Bayonne. The fish caught and brought back from Terra Nova were only just beginning their journey and might have been eaten by households anywhere in Europe and the Mediterranean that winter and spring. Some of the *bacalao* may even have been carried as provisions on a ship returning to Caprouge to fish the following season. But by October the seventeen mariners and their master were safe at home, having received their wages in a mixture of cash, credit, and fish. Only Lefant followed a different path, having been brought in to testify before he could return home to spend his share of the wages.

At the end of his testimony, the last thing Robert Lefant attested to was that everything he had said was the truth. He confirmed to the interrogators that he "knew nothing else," and was then asked by the notary to sign his name. But there was a catch. Lefant could not write. A mariner with years of experience who had successfully commanded a fishing voyage to the other side of the vast Ocean Sea, Lefant could not leave his own name in his own hand for posterity. Yet his testimony was accepted in the end because of "the truth under the oath which he had sworn": Lefant had given his word on the sign of the cross, and that was proof enough of his honesty. It is a reminder that even though we are often reliant on written sources, the sixteenth-century fishery at Terra Nova was made by an oral culture, one in which verbal oaths and agreements still held major purchase. So much of the story was unwritten, and so many key moments were shaped by experienced mariners who did not know enough writing to sign their own names.

This is all we can glean from Robert Lefant's responses. What he did after he left Fuenterrabía is unknown, and we cannot tell if the summer of 1542 was the end of his career at sea. His interrogators subsequently interviewed half a dozen other mariners, all Spanish Basques, whose experiences were not much different from Lefant's. The responses get shorter over time, and there is no indication that the authorities were finding what they were looking for. After this day in September the matter was largely dropped. The small settlement planted by Roberval and Cartier near Québec was put to the torch and abandoned the following year, France never followed up its attempt, Spain never tried to challenge it, and the fishworkers went back to their yearly cycle of fishing voyages. Lefant's testimony was filed away and forgotten.

Almost five centuries later, the story of Robert Lefant offers us a glimpse into how a yearly fishing voyage to the northwest Atlantic might be experienced in the sixteenth century. More than that, Lefant's testimony presents us with many of the themes and problems that will be explored in this book. We have seen him articulating issues of space and place-naming; the nature of fishwork and the business of fishing; the relationship between fishery and empire; contact (or absence thereof) between Indigenous groups and European mariners; the multi-communal and flexible nature of the early fishery; and the ways that Europeans worked within and shaped the environment of the northwest Atlantic.

PART I

Terra Nova

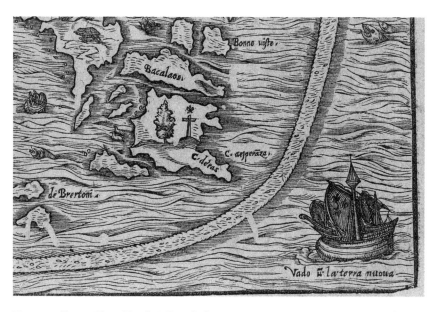

Figure 7. "I go to Terra Nova": A French ship announces its intentions as it approaches the Grand Banks. Detail, map of Terra Nova by Giacolmo Gastaldi, 1606 edition of 1556 map. (Courtesy of the John Carter Brown Library, Creative Commons license CC by 4.0, https://creativecommons.org/licenses/by/4.0/.)

Before the name: What was the place like before it was named?
— *Paul Carter,* The Road to Botany Bay, 1987

Tri martolod yaouank . . . la la la . . .
O voned da veajiñ, gê! . . .
Gant 'n avel bet kaset betek an Douar Nevez
Betek an Douar Nevez, gê!

Three young mariners
They went on a voyage!
Pushed by the wind towards Terra Nova
Towards Terra Nova!
— *"Tri Martolod," nineteenth-century Breton folk song*

ONE

Stories

Let us start with the story of what we think happened in the northwest
Atlantic in the sixteenth century. While we know many details about
what occurred before 1600, turning this into a complete narrative presents
problems for modern historians and archaeologists. When the fishery and
the mariners' world of Terra Nova appear in our earliest sources, they are already fully formed and active. Specifics about Terra Nova's origins are often
lost to archival degradation or were never written down. Modern historians
might well sympathize with members of the city council of Bayonne in the
early 1710s, who received letters from the mayor of Saint Malo asking if they
knew anything about the history of Terra Nova. This question was suddenly
of considerable importance at a moment when England was trying to negotiate exclusive control of the fishery in a peace treaty, raising the *malouins'*
ire by "saying that they were the first to have discovered it." Missives sailed
back and forth as the two ports tried to determine whether their own mariners had reached the northwest Atlantic before the English, and the council
of Bayonne promised to "do some research into our memorials and to also
ask at St. Jean-de-Luz and Ciboure." The earliest years were already hazy to
Europeans barely two centuries after we think the fishery was first created.[1]

If our eighteenth-century Bayonne councilmen could have seen what
historians now understand to be the early history of European fishing in the
northwest Atlantic, they would have understood that there was no sudden
European discovery followed by a stable fishery. Instead, there was a long

arc of growth and change over the first eighty years of the sixteenth century. There is a confusing early period of European activity around the northwest Atlantic in the first decades of the sixteenth century; a messy but steady expansion of the fishery in the 1520s–30s; an explosion in growth after 1540, rising to a steady and mature fishery in the 1560s–70s; and finally, a shift toward transformation after 1580 that fundamentally changes the nature of Terra Nova. It is worth sketching out this general narrative before we dive into the waters of Terra Nova.

Starting Points

In June 1497 the Venetian-born navigator Zuan Caboto guided a ship outfitted by the merchants of Bristol into the waters of the northwest Atlantic. He made landfall somewhere—we do not know where exactly—in what is today eastern Canada, probably on the east coast of the island of Newfoundland. Caboto brought back vague word to England of newly found islands and waters filled with codfish. Contemporary Europeans certainly reacted to Caboto's report as if he was the first to encounter new islands to the far west, even if later generations of scholars have concocted countless visions of pre-Colón voyages to the northwest Atlantic. So it was something new; but how new? Scholars, educators, and the public are used to imagining this moment in 1497 as a starting point for many kinds of history: of transatlantic fishing, of empire in North America, of the fur and whale trades, even of Canada itself. Where better to begin our stories of the New World than in the New Found Land? The very name is so forward looking, "redolent of late-medieval promise," as one author has put it. Such a view is misleading, and not how mariners at the time viewed things. Rather, the voyages of Caboto and those who followed were a midpoint for some and an endpoint for others as much as a starting point for many fishworkers.[2]

In one sense, this history of the northwest Atlantic cannot have a starting point. The coasts and islands and seas have been there for millions of years. The present geography only formed well after the Mesozoic era, as continental migrations caused the Gulf of Canada to open up and Newfoundland to become an island. The region as we know it today was heavily shaped by the glacial movements of the Pleistocene. Shortly after the last Ice Age the region was recolonized by plants and animals from the rest of North America and the North Atlantic, the first of many migratory waves to shape the area's story. For the most important and enduring actors in the northwest Atlantic—cod, whales, birds, seals—human scales of history hold very little meaning.[3]

Nor could 1497 mark the beginning of the human history of the region. Before it was Terra Nova it was the Dawnland, the far northeastern edge of the Algonkian-speaking world that stretched south into coastal New England. Over ten thousand years before Europeans developed a seasonal fishery, human beings arrived along the coasts of the northwest Atlantic, migrating from western and southern parts of the continent. They were there not long after the retreat of glaciers, following in the wake of recolonizing plants and animals, and First Nations rightly claim to be the original, continuous, and autochthonous inhabitants of the region. The ancestors of Mi'kmaq, Innu, and Beothuk communities went through many changes over these millennia, and modern archaeologists categorize their history into different phases like Archaic and Woodlands periods. Migration within the northwest Atlantic was common, while exchange and language maintained connections between the different peoples who would encounter Europeans at the turn of the sixteenth century. In the centuries immediately before 1500 First Nations coalesced into the major communities who would be living in the northwest Atlantic at the moment Europeans arrived: Beothuk, Mi'kmaq, Innu. For most of these communities the year that Christians reckoned as 1497 would have passed with little fanfare, and even if some saw a solitary wooden ship floating offshore it is not clear that it would have been seen at the time as a momentous inflection point.[4]

The summer of 1497 was not even the beginning of European interactions with the northwest Atlantic. Some five centuries earlier small parties of Norse, voyaging out from their colonies in Greenland, had explored and briefly settled the region that became Terra Nova. At least one camp was established on Newfoundland island, but more extensive exploration and resource harvesting may have taken place further south. That said, there is a tendency to make too much out of this. The Norse did not stay long and had only fleeting contact with Indigenous communities. These early voyages preserved little usable information on the region for later generations of Europeans, who were largely unaware of the Norse achievements. Far more significant in the long run (but often overlooked in popular accounts) was the parallel eastward migration of Inuit peoples around one thousand years ago. By the thirteenth century the Inuit had arrived in northern Labrador and Greenland, rapidly displacing the earlier Dorset peoples to become the dominant community in the High Arctic. In the sixteenth century they would venture southward and link up with First Nations and European mariners. The human history of the northwest Atlantic offers old and ever-changing patterns.[5]

But the history of Terra Nova must have a different starting point, because something distinct happened in the early sixteenth century when a permanent floating European presence coalesced very rapidly in the waters of the northwest Atlantic. The northwest Atlantic was a place where different strands of Atlantic history met and were woven together by a diverse group of maritime actors: the late medieval expansion of commercial fisheries, the Iberian conquest and colonization of islands, the European search for new sources of food and resources in a widening Atlantic basin. Terra Nova was part of this project, but hardly the inception. To see the strands of history that would coalesce at Terra Nova, we must look further afield.

Consider that the earliest reports about islands and codfish in the northwest Atlantic were brought back by voyagers sponsored by the English and Portuguese crowns. Both of these would-be colonial powers were drawing on almost a century of overseas experience by 1500. The successful capture of Ceuta in North Africa in 1415 marked the starting point for Portuguese expeditions, compelling more and more voyagers, settlers, and warlords to head south and west. Portuguese navigators and merchants soon began moving down the western coast of Africa and into the mid-Atlantic Ocean in a series of exploratory and trading voyages. Hundreds of miles to the north in 1415 the king of England, Henry V, declared a ban on all English fishing vessels sailing to Iceland as part of a long-running dispute with the Danish crown (and soon with Hanse merchants as well). We know, however, that Iceland was far from the only commercial fishery experiencing growing pains in 1415, and similar disputes would soon overtake fishworkers in the Irish Sea, North Sea, Algarve, and elsewhere. This would soon spiral into a dispute, often a violent one, between English, Danish, and Hanse mariners over the fishing grounds. Over time these ventures, both north and south, took on lives of their own. By the 1440s Portuguese ships had rounded Cape Bojador and were at Cabo Verde and the Guinea Coast, and thereafter the first *feitoria* trade posts would be planted on the West African shore. Soon Castilian adventurers would follow suit, attacking and seizing the Canary Islands in a series of brutal wars. Concurrently, there was a parallel and often invisible effort by European mariners to seize and exploit new coasts and open waters in the eastern Atlantic. By the end of the fifteenth century, they had blanketed the eastern Atlantic from northern Norway to the Sahara with commercial fisheries. This resource frontier would eventually be pushed to the northwest Atlantic, but the tide of expansion began much earlier. Terra Nova was born out of, and embedded in, this vibrant early Atlantic world, already several generations old.[6]

We are therefore presented with a surfeit of starting points for the story of Terra Nova, from glaciers to Indigenous migrations to the fall of Ceuta and rise of an Iceland fishery. These many threads were constantly weaving together across the sixteenth century. A key turning point would be the very first decade of the sixteenth century, when the legacies of Iceland, Ceuta, and Indigenous migrations all came together on the shores of the northwest Atlantic. The surviving evidence points to the years around 1505 as the moment when a permanent fishery coalesced in the northwest Atlantic, and though it would be some time before Europeans committed fully to the idea that a fishery was the only way to interact with this space, it is probably from 1505 that we can speak of a fishworkers' world of Terra Nova.

The Shore Gazes Back

Wherever we start our stories in time, at Terra Nova they almost always begin on a coast. This physical setting helped shape the way sixteenth-century history subsequently unfolded. Rocky, fog-shrouded, complex geographies of cliffs, beaches, and sandbanks greeted explorers and fishworkers alike at the end of their monthlong outbound voyage. And yet on some fundamental aesthetic level there must have been something inescapably familiar about the color palette and sensory experience of these sea-etched landscapes to mariners raised along Europe's own rugged littoral. Such impressions are hard to quantify or interpret, but the arrival of European mariners along the coasts of the northwest Atlantic was perhaps more a moment of déjà vu than of novelty.

The beaches and coasts of the northwest Atlantic were unsettling in another way, thanks to a historical quirk of the Atlantic basin. The far North Atlantic arc demonstrates remarkable east-west continuity in biology, climate, and geology. In some ecological ways eastern Canada is closer to northwestern Europe than other parts of the Americas. This is especially true of the seas, and a variety of marine animals—cod, herring, salmon, seals, whales—can be found on both sides of the far North Atlantic. This was part of the essential logic of the Terra Nova fishery, which allowed for the transfer of European commercial fishing patterns across the Atlantic, something possible only because the fish were the same in both cases. On land the plants and animals fishworkers found were variations on the flora and fauna of northwest Europe: pine and maple trees, deer and bears, seabirds and hawks. In these newfound lands far away, mariners encountered echoes of home, such that European mariners interpreted the coastal northwest Atlantic through the lens of their own homelands. Fishworkers carried ideas with them from one Atlantic coast to another, including names for living things and coastal places.[7]

What was this coast? It was rocky shoals and sandy banks, waves crashing on rock and the stink of seaweed. It was all the complexity of a coastal ecosystem stretched for thousands of miles; it must have seemed overwhelming and endless. Europeans experienced the shores of the northwest Atlantic only during the warmest part of the year, so theirs was a hot and bright coast. Summer at Terra Nova was a strange thing, a study in extremes. A place like Robert Lefant's Caprouge was on the same line of latitude as Brussels and Exeter but had none of the same mild weather. One Basque mariner interrogated after Lefant reported that a ship would not dare brave the Straits of Belle Isle until June, for it was not "possible to navigate or to enter by La Gran Baya because of the cold and snow and ice, and the mountains of ice which touch the bottom of the sea, though 100 fathoms deep." Later visitors commented on the great icebergs that traveled south along the coast, reaching the Grand Banks well into May. The days were long, for at this latitude in June the sun rises at 5 a.m. and sets at 9 p.m. Mariners could expect fifteen-hour workdays, catching and processing cod as long as there was light. More often than not, though, the sun was hidden behind storm clouds and fog. The thick fog banks of Terra Nova were the stuff of legend—and the cause of many a mishap and disaster. Rocks and coasts wreathed in mist stood ready to sink any passing ship or boat, and some fishing crews were known to ambush unsuspecting vessels they surprised in the fog. As the Atlantic Canadian historian Sara Spike has observed, later European colonizers speculated that the fogs were made from the exhalation of sea creatures and living organisms: the water made life, which made fog. If they were wrong in the science perhaps they were right in a way that sixteenth-century fishworkers would have understood: the sea created the coast, and that coast was alive, impermanent, and mysterious.[8]

Nor were the coasts of Terra Nova a place the Europeans could call their own. Even as they encountered reflections of Europe, fishworkers worked along shorelines that were already occupied and well known to the Indigenous peoples of the northwest Atlantic. There were already Algonkian place-names along the coast, though Europeans learned or preserved very few of them, preferring to substitute place-names from their homelands. French visitors rapidly repurposed Algonkian names for seabirds, adding *apponatz* (great auk), *margaulx* (gannet), and *godez* (guillemot) to their fishwork vernaculars. This is a sign, perhaps, that they were learning about foraging and hunting from communities that already lived there. The Indigenous coast of the northwest Atlantic was also unusually expansive. Most First Nations made more extensive use of rivers than Europeans did, linking riverine ecologies to coastal ones. They moved freely on open water to connect different coves, harbors, shoals, and beaches. Theirs was not a coastal world in the same way that Terra Nova would be for Europeans, but something different, more ecologically complex.[9]

The coast of the northwest Atlantic was ultimately not merely a site of work but of contact: a place of meetings, exchanges, and clashes between

First Nations and fishworkers. The northwest Atlantic has many beaches and harbors, but not all of them are suitable for summer living and fishwork. European and Indigenous populations would often concentrate in the same areas during the summer months as both groups of communities came to find food. We know that explorers and possibly even fishworkers captured First Peoples and brought them back to Europe, especially in the first three decades of the sixteenth century. Which communities these unlucky captives came from is unknown, as is their fate in many cases. Beaches themselves were only sometimes the site of contact, despite how much they retain that place in popular memory. European voyagers often encountered Mi'kmaq or Saint Lawrence Iroquoians at sea, sailing the coasts, rather than on shore. The majority of these moments are lost, victims of archival degradation and the inherent obscurity that surrounds the early efforts of mariners. But this haphazard process of contact is of considerable importance. In the sixteenth century there would be no destabilizing shock—no sharp demographic collapse or biological upheaval—to alter the local ecology. This would come later, closer to the turn of the seventeenth century. The earliest points of contact were consistent but circumscribed, confined to coasts and coastal waters. Where contact between First Nations and fishworkers took place, it appears to have been in small groups and usually on the water. Encounters took place when both sides were arranged in similar-sized groups and both were on the familiar ground of beach or boat. For brief moments, Indigenous and European coasts overlapped and interacted before pulling apart again.

The Tale of Terra Nova

This was the littoral world Zuan Caboto found in 1497 and reported back to Europe. A little over a decade of intensive exploration followed Caboto's voyage, as ships from England, Normandy, and Portugal all swept the northwest Atlantic searching for opportunities. Around a dozen voyages (some sponsored by states but others by opportunistic groups of merchants) are recorded in this short span of time, seeking trade and settlement opportunities. Of particular importance were a series of voyages by the Portuguese-sponsored Corte Real brothers, who would get credit for many decades for "discovering" the northwest Atlantic. Alongside these ventures, several attempts to permanently settle the region were undertaken in the first four decades of the sixteenth century, including a series of aborted attempts by the English and more sustained but fruitless efforts by the Portuguese. The Norman shipping and fishing magnate Jean Ango dispatched ships to follow in Caboto's wake around 1508–9, even as he was also sending voyages to Sumatra and other tropical locales. In general, there are strong parallels in the northwest Atlantic to the wave of voyages that swept the post-Colón Caribbean. Both were marked by a flurry of overlapping exploratory and trading voyages operating for a variety of European kingdoms in the 1490s–1500s.[10]

Against this backdrop of exploration and attempted settlement, other actors were taking the initiative. As early as 1502 English ships were bringing back barrels of "saltfish" from the northwest Atlantic, though whether these were ad hoc ventures or a sustained fishery is unclear. The evidence nonetheless points to a commercial multinational fishery in operation by around 1505, less than a decade after Caboto's voyage and just as the first wave of exploration was waning. A text written decades later asserted that Breton and Norman fishworkers were working the waves of Terra Nova by 1504. In 1506 the Portuguese were already describing a "fishery [*pescaria*] of Terra Nova," and in 1508 the first named ship appears in our records. The documentary evidence indicates that Bretons, Normans, Portuguese, and English ships were involved in this early fishery. In the second decade the records are more consistent, indicating that Bretons were carrying cod to Rouen and Bordeaux by 1515–17. By the 1520s the pace and scope of operations seems to have increased, and while the scale of the fishery at this point is difficult to assess, it may have been between fifty and one hundred ships per year. In 1521 the English were writing of a "fleet" of fishing ships, while a few years earlier one author had guessed that a hundred "French" ships crossed to Terra Nova each year. The Bretons appear most consistently in surviving records, and their active role as exporters of Terra Nova cod meant that they were closely associated with the region. The size and intensity of the fishery probably expanded and contracted with cycles of war in western Europe, causing frequent fluctuations in scale.[11]

In his 1527 letter to the king of England, the explorer John Rut gave a glimpse of the early fishing fleet in Terra Nova. On August 3 of that year the expedition entered Sam Joham/Saint John's harbor, the natural cove that remains today the central feature of the capital city of Newfoundland. He reported, "There we found eleven Norman ships, and one of Brittany, and two Portuguese barques, all fishing." The fifteen ships from three different regions (and likely many more ports of origin) all seem to be working side by side, in a pattern repeated across the century. Returning via the Caribbean, Rut's expedition stopped in ports owned by the Spanish crown, whose officials took great interest in the English ships. A report back to Madrid noted that the English vessel encountered troublesome waters and, faced with this, the ship "turned about and came to reconnoiter the *Baccalaos* [Terra Nova], wherein they found around fifty ships, Castilians and French and Portuguese, fishing." This report suggests that in 1526–27 some fifty fishing vessels operated around Terra Nova.[12]

By the mid-1530s, when the writings of Jacques Cartier shed some direct light on the northwest Atlantic, the fishery was already a well-established and widely known operation. In March 1534 the town of Saint Malo had even tried to stop ships from sailing to Terra Nova so that Cartier himself could recruit from among local fishworkers to take advantage of their experience and knowledge. When his ship arrived along the southern coast of Labrador, Cartier found most of the harbors already named and worked by fishing crews. Brest, Blanc Sablon, Butus, and Chasteaulx were all busy ports named by fishworkers before the 1530s, as well as more notable landmarks like Cape Breton, the Isle of Birds, and the Grand Bank. According to his 1542 testimony, Robert Lefant himself first voyaged to southern Labrador, already being called La Gran Baya, in 1537. He claimed that he knew of five Spanish (two from Corio, three from San Sebastián), seven Portuguese, and one English ship also at work that summer. More broadly, by the 1530s the use of the nomenclature Terra Nova—and the idea of Terra Nova as a distinct space—seems to have become common among mariners.[13]

The 1540s were the turning point. The amount of surviving archival records related to the fishery explodes (relatively speaking) after this date, and our ability to trace changes improves dramatically. The scale and complexity of the fishery grew steadily from 1540 onward, reaching a mature stage around the mid-1560s. The size of the European fishing fleet may have doubled between the 1530s and 1540s, and then doubled again by the 1560s. Growth was uneven, and the scale of the fishery could fluctuate significantly—Norman ports outfitted almost no ships in 1545, only to set a record for number of voyages in 1549. In general, the evidence points to a handful of major years for fishworkers in the mid-sixteenth century, so that 1542, 1549, 1555, 1559, and 1565 all appear as prosperous moments. The records for the 1560s are the most consistent in showing a high tempo of operations, and the year 1565 is a benchmark for the height of the fishery. At least 300 ships (including 156 for which we have direct evidence from just three outfitting ports) carrying perhaps ten thousand to fifteen thousand mariners sailed to the northwest Atlantic. This was clearly not a small fishery.[14]

This period of growth defines how we remember the Terra Nova fishery in the sixteenth century. It was an era of remarkable coherence, as most fishing operations across communal lines followed very similar patterns of how voyages were organized and how preserved fish was produced, sold, and consumed. Most ships carried their catch directly back to home ports in western Europe, where it was sold to urban merchants. Ships tended to be small, sometimes as small as sixty tons but often in the range of eighty to one hundred tons, with crews of fifteen to thirty fishworkers. In this heyday of 1540–80, the Terra Nova fishery was a distinctly multinational institution. We have evidence of ships sailing to Terra Nova from (north to south) Normandy, the West Country and southeastern England, Brittany, the coast of Biscay in France (including Saintonge), Basque Country, Asturias, Galicia, and northern Portugal. At the end of the century, Hollanders would get involved. In the 1540s Norman communities predominated in the fishery, while from the mid-1550s onward Basques (both French and Spanish) rose in prominence. Sometimes different communities clustered together (the Basques at La Gran Baya, the Normans on the Grand Banks), but there is quite consistent documentary evidence that ships from different ports worked in the same harbors.

Throughout the mid-sixteenth century, the growth in the scale and tempo of operations in the northwest Atlantic was dependent on the salt produced in the Bay of Biscay. Access to the southern Portuguese salt town of Setúbal was limited to Portuguese, Galician, and some Basque mariners, whereas the many towns along the marshy coast of the Bay of Biscay in the kingdom of France were open to ships from across northwest Europe. Mariners from Normandy, England, Brittany, and northern Iberia all relied on access to the marsh salts of the bay to provide the crucial ingredient in saltcod production. By mid-century the city of Rouen organized regular December-January runs to La Rochelle and Brouage to procure enough salt for the spring fishing fleet. A large number of Norman ships left their ports early to ensure that they had time to visit "La Baye, La Rochelle or Brouage to take salt" before sailing directly to Terra Nova. Biscayan salt would fuel the growth of the sixteenth-century fishery.[15]

As the fishery expanded, European activity in the northwest Atlantic diversified. From the 1550s onward Spanish Basques regularly hunted whales in Terra Nova in a sustained effort, establishing a parallel industry to the cod fishery. The Basque whaling industry is now famous, thanks to some incredibly preserved archaeological finds, and was the progenitor of all later forms of Atlantic whaling. This operation, small but intensive, slaughtered thousands of whales in a few decades and peppered the coast of La Gran Baya with smoke-belching ovens that turned blubber into oil. Walrus and seal were occasionally hunted as well. A low-level fur exchange between fishworkers and Indigenous communities was common in the sixteenth-century fishery, but from the 1580s onward an independent and systematic fur trade was undertaken by European merchants. More and more of Terra Nova's biology was incorporated into European consumption, although cod remained the primary product.[16]

The 1580s marked a final turning point in the history of Terra Nova. Rather than a disruptive, clean break, change came as a slow pivot toward new ways for Europeans to interact with and change the northwest Atlantic and its people. The number of Spanish Basque, Galician, and Portuguese fishing ships visiting the northwest Atlantic declined from the 1580s onward. In turn, the number of West Country English vessels present at Terra Nova began to increase rapidly, soon joined by Hollanders. Concurrently, some Inuit communities began to move southward from the Arctic toward the south Labrador coast, both creating conflict with Innu and European communities and offering new opportunities to trade. These changes would ultimately drive the slow emergence of a division within the fishery. West Country and Hollander mariners were prone to carry their catch directly from Terra Nova to ports in southern Iberia and the western Mediterranean. Merchants trading to the western Mediterranean would receive larger returns, and came to connect the northwest Atlantic to new markets in Iberia, the Mediterranean, and eventually the Caribbean. Most Breton, Norman, and Biscayan ships, by contrast, continued to bring their codfish back to northwest European ports. Increasingly, some ships came not to fish at all, but to trade. The result was a divided fishery, with sixteenth-century operations continuing alongside a new commercialized export-oriented fishery and a growing fur trade.[17]

Meanwhile, new efforts to explore, colonize, and claim the northwest Atlantic were sponsored by the English and French crowns after the 1580s. English navigators explored the north toward the Arctic, and French explorers charted south toward the Gulf of Maine and down the River of Canada. Most failed, but unlike earlier efforts these did not slacken and would ultimately lead to permanent settlements around the Gulf of Canada. French-sponsored settlements were placed at Acadie in 1605 and Québec in 1608. English adventurers made the first successful attempt to plant a settlement on Newfoundland island in 1610, though it would take many decades for the settlement to stabilize and gain a foothold. Land, both as a site of colonial control and as a source of wealth through animal pelts, became a new focus of European imperial interests. These shifts did not just mark a break in how the fishery operated, they changed the idea at the center of the sixteenth-century maritime experience. The idea of Terra Nova was predicated on an open, multi-communal, and water-centric fishery that had lasted most of the sixteenth century as the main way in which mariners understood and interacted with the northwest Atlantic. But throughout the 1580s–90s communal identities hardened, settlements became a reality, and a common resource was more intensively exploited by competing mariners.[18]

When does our story end? Terra Nova never quite died; rather, it changed and was supplanted over time. But a revealing moment in that transformation and a useful endpoint for the tale of Terra Nova might be May 12, 1604. On that date, according to the famed navigator-settler Samuel de Champlain, as his ship cruised south through Terra Nova, "We entered into another port, five leagues from Cap la Hève, where we came upon a ship which was in the act of trading furs against the King's laws." Champlain was charting the coast of Nova Scotia on behalf of his patron, the sieur de Mons, who had been granted a monopolistic privilege by King Henri IV of France on the region encompassing much of what was once Terra Nova. That day in May, entering a small harbor (now Liverpool, Nova Scotia), Champlain came upon a small ship, the *Levrette*, manned by a Norman crew and hailing from Le Havre. The captain, Jean de Rossignol, appeared to be conducting a spirited trade in furs with the local Mi'kmaq. This was deemed by Champlain to be illegal under the terms and privileges accorded to de Mons by the French crown, a fact later confirmed by legal proceedings in France. Rossignol and his ship were seized, and the cargo added to de Mons's assets. To commemorate the incident and the successful prosecution of the Norman vessel, Champlain would later name the harbor Port au Rossignol.[19]

There is a world of difference between this moment in 1604 and the story of Robert Lefant in 1542. For most of the sixteenth century mariners like Rossignol and Lefant moved freely through the waters of what they understood to be Terra Nova, catching cod and circulating goods and ideas. There was no expectation that they might encounter an armed ship bearing royal authority or monopoly rights to the region, for colonial and commercial control of the fishery was outside the interests of any European state. That Champlain could impound and punish Rossignol for fishing in Terra Nova rests on a legal and geographical understanding of the northwest Atlantic that was unthinkable a few decades earlier. The very idea that it would be wrong for the crew of the *Levrette* to trade with the Mi'kmaq must have seemed farcical to the bemused crew, and we may imagine their bewilderment as Champlain was able to force his version of events through the legal world of the kingdom of France. Decades earlier, when Lefant had been brought before state officials and put to the question, they were content with his description of fishworkers' world of harbors and beaches. In 1542 that world had not been worth the trouble of states and empires; now, in 1604, monopoly was here to stay.

This is a story about the years before these changes, the world of Lefant and Rossignol rather than Champlain. It is a story about the earliest years of European activity in the northwest Atlantic, not quite the "long century" of 1497–1604 but a shorter one of 1505–80, and the glimpses we have of what that world looked like. The pre-1580 part of Terra Nova's history is the least well understood, a nebulous time before the region was transformed by competition and empire. This was the world of Terra Nova, of a mariner's space in the northwest Atlantic, one that shaped the very nature of European occupation in the region for nearly a century. What that looked like, and how it was created, is the subject to which we now turn.

TWO

Names

"Having prepared a fine ship . . . to be sent to Terra Nova for cod fishing, which was his usual trade, he became wrapped up with the fantasy of going along on the voyage." In his 1599 collection of sea stories, Captain Bruneau de Rivedoux tells this tale of the hapless mariner Pierre Houé and his fishing voyage as a warning against being too enamoured of dangerous transoceanic trips. But there is something about that phrase "his usual trade" that captures the familiarity, the appeal, and the longevity of the northwest Atlantic fishery, an enterprise that even in Rivedoux's time was several generations old.[1]

Usual too was the language Rivedoux imagines Houé employing to describe his destination, when he says he sailed *aux terres neuves*, a pluralized French version of Terra Nova. Put simply, *Terra Nova* was used by mariners to signify the places in the northwest Atlantic they went to do fishwork: where one fished, that place became part of Terra Nova. Localized variations of the nomenclature Terra Nova are found in surviving European records across the sixteenth century as the most consistent way mariners described the places they visited in the waters of the northwest Atlantic. Although its popularity has been acknowledged in some of the historical literature on the early fishery, the transnational use, origins, and meaning of *Terra Nova* to sixteenth-century Europeans have not received proper attention. The idea was both expansive and malleable and confusingly imprecise at the same time, but it reflected the unique experiences of mariners in the sixteenth century. Terra Nova was an idea as much as a place, one bound up with the activity of fishing. Examining the history of the term and how its use intersected with ideas about work and the environment enables us to see the northwest Atlantic as Europeans did in the sixteenth century: not as Newfoundland but as Terra Nova.[2]

Geography is as much a matter of mentally constructing worlds as it is of describing physical features on the Earth's surface. We may call these constructions mental maps, the subjective geographies and experiences of place that all of us carry within our heads. Yet mental maps reflect not just personal but collective experiences and shared knowledge, and this is what makes them such powerful tools for understanding the past. The words and images historical actors used to represent places like the northwest Atlantic reflect not an objective reality but the assemblage and translation of people's mental maps, their subjective understanding of different spaces. To understand a historical space like Terra Nova, then, we must work our way up from the bottom, following the behaviors and actions of mariners to see how these formed concepts of space, and how these mental maps in turn informed wider European understandings of place and geography in the northwest Atlantic.[3]

Names exist not to describe space but to create it. This was the lesson Paul Carter and Yi-Fu Tuan have hammered home in their studies of the power of place-names. Names and descriptions reflect human activity and interactions with an environment, such that, as Timothy Ingold has put it, "Places do not have locations but histories." We must therefore be careful in the words we choose, considering whether or not they match the concepts of mental space deployed at a particular moment by a particular community. The use of a single name like Terra Nova across several languages suggests that maritime communities shared information and histories of place. In the sixteenth century mariners did speak, and we have the ability to hear their voices. "Terra Nova" appeared most regularly in bureaucratic writings, including notarial records, port registers, court cases, municipal council records, government interrogations, and royal edicts. Here sailors or fishworkers stood before a notary to declare their intentions and experiences, creating textual records that were mediated but nonetheless reveal significant truths.

When we look and listen, we can see that mariners were fully capable of vocalizing a kind of mental map-from-below.[4]

We can see the relationship between word use and mental maps in the masses of legal sources produced through fishwork, but we can also see points of contention and alternative names when we compare them to other written and cartographic evidence. No one group of sources can give us a complete insight into the mental world of sixteenth-century European mariners. Instead, it is through a broad comparative approach that we can tease out patterns of thought and experience. The surviving notarial records, for instance, offer a chance to see patterns in language use across a wide breadth of time and space, from Lisbon in 1506 to Amsterdam in the 1590s. It is telling that business documents are very consistent in their use of variations of *Terra Nova*. Yet we can learn much from moments when elite authors or navigators feel the need to explain terms like *Terra Nova*, *Newfoundland*, or *Bacalaos* to their audiences. We can learn more from maps that use place-names (Cortereal Land, Norumbega) that rarely if ever show up in our business contracts and court cases. And most tantalizing of all are snippets of thought—about birds, about festivities, about space—that shine through in miscellaneous accounts and notes that have been preserved in archives across Europe. Through these patterns and comparisons we can arrive at a better understanding of how mariners talked and thought about space and work in the sixteenth century.

What's in a Name?

In 1510 the vessel *La Jacquette* from the small Breton port of Dahouët was sailing down the Seine River in Normandy when a serious altercation took place: a mariner, Guillaume Dobel, pushed a second mariner into the river, killing him. In 1513 a petition was submitted by Dobel's friends to a court in Nantes to defend his conduct, which revealed that they were in Normandy: "Coming from the city of Rouen, where the aforenamed [the shipowners] had sold the fish that they had sought and caught in the region of La Terre Neusfve." "Terre Neusfve" was the standard French variation of "Terra Nova," here used to describe a place ("the region") linked to fish. The petitioners gave no other details, perhaps assuming the meaning was clear to their fellow Bretons.[5]

The use of Terre Neusfve by the crew of *La Jacquette* is an early surviving usage of Terra Nova to describe space in the northwest Atlantic. The usage would be repeated by countless mariners across Europe during the sixteenth century. Though the name defied precise boundaries, by examining where mariners gave details about their activities we can have some sense of what Terra Nova looked like to these mariners (see figure 1). In a broad sense, Terra Nova seems to have encompassed what is today the Grand Banks, the coast of the island of Newfoundland, southern Labrador, and the entire Gulf of Canada. Terra Nova certainly included the whaling and cod-fishing grounds of southern Labrador and the Strait of Belle Isle, known to Basques as La Gran Baya. Beginning in the late sixteenth century, some notaries in Biscay and Normandy clarified where their fishworkers were headed with an important emendation: "Terra Nova on the Bank." The text indicates that the space of Terra Nova included the vast offshore fishing grounds that we would today call the Grand Banks. In the early seventeenth century some contracts went even further, specifying "On the Bank, Banquereau, or Sable Island." Sable Island is a small sandy islet a hundred miles east of what is today Nova Scotia, and the Banquereau is an offshore coastal shelf near Cape Breton. This implies, then, that the concept of Terra Nova eventually stretched far south and southeast to include much of the modern maritime provinces of Canada. Altogether, Terra Nova at its greatest extent could extend perhaps 1,200 miles west to east and another 960 miles north to south. The distance from the easternmost tip of the Grand Banks to the Saguenay River (1,200 miles) was only slightly less than the distance from the outer Grand Banks to western Ireland (1,400 miles). This made Terra Nova a potentially vast region, a substantial portion of the Atlantic basin, even if its yearly boundaries fluctuated.[6]

We can see this in hindsight, but in 1513, when the crew of *La Jacquette* filed their petition, it was far from clear to most Europeans what the northwest Atlantic looked like. Between Zuan Caboto's voyage of encounter in 1497 and the expeditions of Miguel Corte Real and various Bristol-Azoreans around 1500, European navigators established that something, some combination of land and fish-rich sea, existed well to the west of the British Isles and Iceland. To become a place, this agglomeration of experiences and sightings would need a name. A place can have many names over time, and many names at once. The northwest Atlantic could have been Terra Nova, the New found island, Newfoundland, Bacalao, Norumbega, or Cortereal Land. At some point it was each of these to someone, especially to various mapmakers who had never even visited. We tend to erase such complexity when we use Newfoundland as a term, for it was not self-evident in the early sixteenth century that Newfoundland island would become the central point to describe the fishery. Indeed, for much of the sixteenth century it was unclear to Europeans if Newfoundland was even a single island or an archipelago. To hedge their bets, some record keepers pluralized Terra Nova to Terres Neufves or a different variant, sometimes alternating within the same text.[7]

Understanding the genesis and lineage of the name Terra Nova is an important step toward recognizing its distinct meaning and usage in the sixteenth century, as well as the key role played by mariners in defining and using this watery space. Terra Nova, written as a noun-adjective combination, appears in slightly different forms in different languages. French Terre Neuve (typically spelled Terre Neufve or Terre Neusfve in sixteenth-century sources), Spanish Tierra Nueva or, more commonly, Terranova, Gascon Terre Nabe, and Italian Terra Nuova were local variants used in the sixteenth century, most of which are still used today. As they are all modified versions of the same phrase, Land-New, and etymologically the same, I treat them as interchangeable: Terre Neuve is Tierra Nueva is Terra Nuova. The fact that the name is only slightly different in spelling across several languages is itself interesting, suggesting that it spread rapidly from a common source. An alternate phrasing, Nova Terra, appears extremely infrequently in surviving records, and only at the start of the sixteenth century.[8]

Although Terra Nova could be both Latin and Portuguese (the forms are identical when written), there is reason to believe the usage originated in Portugal. We know that Portuguese mariners from the Azores and the mainland were actively visiting the northwest Atlantic at the turn of the sixteenth century. Between 1500 and 1502 the Azorean brothers Gaspar and Miguel Corte Real explored the region, bringing useful information back to Lisbon, a hub of geographic knowledge. Further, the use of Terra Nova in a surviving record first appears in Portugal just after the turn of the sixteenth century. In 1502 the crown of Portugal confirmed the discoveries made by Gaspar Corte Real, describing them as "Terra Nova." In 1506 a Portuguese decree relating to the taxation of fish described "The fisheries of Terra Nova." In general, Terra Nova appears more frequently in Portuguese than Latin, and there was a clear connection between the northwest Atlantic and Portuguese mercantile activity during this crucial formative period. It seems likely, though not definite, that what was originally meant to denote the coast explored by Corte Real became, by 1506, the standard Portuguese label for the northwest Atlantic.[9]

Even if the name Terra Nova had Portuguese roots, it very quickly spread outward from Portugal. Terre Neufve appears in 1508 in a Norman court case, the same year Terra Nova appears on a map made by a German cartographer in Rome. We find Tierra Nova in a 1511 Aragonese document, quickly followed by Terre Neufve in Breton records in 1513–14. Basques were talking about Terres Nabes in 1512, soon joined by Galicians sailing for Terra Nueva in 1517. In the following decade even English sources often replaced the familiar New-found-land with Newland, a direct translation of Terra Nova, and from as early as 1520 preserved cod was widely known as "Newland fish" in England. It is possible that mariners from Brittany were the main vector for adopting and spreading the term *Terra Nova* in northwest Europe. Bretons were known as active fishworkers in the northwest Atlantic, and they are prominent in many of the records noted above. They may have learned the name from Portuguese mariners and then adopted it in the first decade of the sixteenth century as they themselves became the preeminent fishworkers. However it spread, from the 1520s Terra Nova was the most common way to describe the northwest Atlantic in all the surviving records. Even in Bristol, the city credited with "discovering" what they called New-found-islands, port records from 1516–17 record two fish-carrying ships (one Breton, one Norman) coming not from Newfoundland but from Terra Nova.[10]

Why a New Land? Variants of New Island and New Land were used in the earliest written records to describe encounters with land in the northwest Atlantic. The original meaning was aspirational, and in royal documents it is used to mark new islands and lands, both discovered and as yet unfound, that might be seized and exploited. Perhaps intended as placeholders until more sense could be made of the northwest Atlantic, New Land stuck. As Stephanie Pettigrew and Elizabeth Mancke have pointed out, variants of New Land would occasionally appear elsewhere in the Atlantic in the late sixteenth and seventeenth centuries, including Nova Zemlya in the Arctic. In none of these places, however, did it become entrenched as it did in the northwest Atlantic. Nor was it applied to maritime spaces as it would be in the northwest Atlantic. The sixteenth-century use inverts how New Land was employed elsewhere, shifting Terra Nova from island and continent to coast and sea. It is possible (though we are unlikely to ever know) that New Land was even meant ironically: once a shorthand phrase to mark the land-locked dreams of explorers, later appropriated by mariners to describe familiar waters.[11]

Once it was adopted by mariners, Terra Nova was used consistently throughout the first century of the fishery. One of the earliest records to name a ship sailing to the northwest Atlantic, a 1508 court case from Normandy involving a ship from Brittany, used a form of the name rendered as "for a voyage to Terra Nova [*à* La Terre Neufve]." This was virtually indistinguishable from how the term was used nearly a century later by notaries in La Rochelle, "Voyage to Terra Nova [*à* La Terre Neufve]," and Honfleur, "A Terra Nova voyage [*de* La Terre Neufve]." In between we find thousands of cases of this same formulation in loan contracts, charter parties, court cases, sales agreements, tax records, and the like. Such texts reflect official statements made by merchants and mariners regarding their operations in the Atlantic. This was the term used by Robert Lefant and his fellow Basques in their 1542 testimonies. It is telling that in the 1590s, as Hollander merchants and mariners began to engage with the northwest Atlantic fish trade, references to the region started to appear in Amsterdam's notarial records. The Hollanders were latecomers to the trade, jumping into a fishery that was almost a century old. When Amsterdam notaries had to record the name of the place where fishworkers were headed, here in a city many miles from Lisbon and far removed from the confusion of the early sixteenth century, the scribes used the phrases Terre Neufve or Terra Neuf to describe the northwest Atlantic—the French name was sometimes copied verbatim. Hollander merchants were learning of the region from French-speaking mariners, who of course used the name they were most familiar with, Terra Nova.[12]

Two records show that the term *Terra Nova* was not used just by scribes but by the fishworkers themselves. In the 1540s an anonymous Norman mariner recorded a brief memo on the last page of a navigation guide. In two short paragraphs, scratched out in a hasty script, the sailor left himself a note "for Terra Nova [La Terre Neufve]" in which he stated that the best way to tell when you were near the offshore coastal shelf known then, as now, as the Grand Banks (look for the birds) and in which harbor he had left his ships from the last season (sunk underwater for safekeeping in Renews harbor). A decade later, in 1559, an anonymous Breton merchant jotted down in a small notebook reserved for his accounts the "names of the mariners for my ship for Terra Nova [Terre Neuffve]." Both of these records, made by mariners familiar with the fishery, were hasty notes meant for their own use, not intended for official record keeping.[13]

Such instances prompted the geographer André Thevet to describe in one of his many works "the country which is vulgarly known as Terra Nova, which from the time of its discovery until today has borne and still bears this name." Thevet frequently insisted that his own writing was based on interviews with mariners, especially Bretons, and his use of "vulgarly" reflects mid-sixteenth-century modes of describing popular or common modes of speech and thought. In the 1570s Anthony Parkhurst described the fishery in a famous letter to Richard Hakluyt, carefully noting that it was also called Terra Nova. His text described "the sundry navies that come to Newfoundland, or Terra Nova, for fish," implying that while geographers such as Hakluyt might know it as Newfoundland, most others would be familiar with Terra Nova. There are thus records that indicate Terra Nova was in popular usage by fishworkers, not just scribes.[14]

While texts recorded the consistent use of Terra Nova by mariners, sixteenth-century cartographers did not regularly employ the concept of Terra Nova in their maps. When they did, it was applied haphazardly to different pieces of land or islands. The term appears only on a handful of maps, including those by the Venetian mapmaker Giacolmo Gastaldi, whereas alternative labels and configurations of space are the norm (see figure 7). Cartographers and geographers in the sixteenth century generally organized and labeled the northwest Atlantic in one of two ways. The first was to label different parts of the region with titles bestowed by officially sanctioned navigators, in particular labels of possession. Thus Jacques Cartier's voyages gave rise to New France, while the efforts of Verrazano created the realm of Norumbega. The earliest maps of the northwest Atlantic label it variously as the Land Discovered by the English, Land of the King of Portugal, or the Land of Labrador. By contrast with the popularity of the term *Terra Nova*, the use of *Newfoundland*, or the use of the island itself as a marker for the fishery, was unknown outside of English writings and maps.[15]

These conflicting ways of portraying space could sometimes appear on the same map. In 1511 the celebrated Genoese cartographer Visconte de Maggiolo completed a portolan atlas that encompassed the entire globe. In the northwest corner of the Atlantic, Maggiolo drew his viewer's attention to the "Land of the English," the "Land of Labrador of the King of Portugal," the "Land of Corte Real of the King of Portugal," and the "Land of Fishery." Four terms to describe what that same year Guillaume Dobel would sum up as "Terre Neufve." The descriptors used by Maggiolo were typical of how Mediterranean, German, Iberian, and French mapmakers came to identify land in the northwest Atlantic in the sixteenth century: a combination of names derived from exploration, royal territorial claims, and commodity production.[16]

A second approach, increasingly common as the century wore on, was to simply label the entirety of the northwest Atlantic according to its chief export, codfish. Most popular was *Bacalaos*, the Iberian term for dry saltcod, which was extended to cover the whole of the northwest Atlantic. For many European and Mediterranean consumers, codfish came from, quite literally, a place called Saltcod on their maps. The name appears around 1508 on a German-Italian map, and possibly as early as 1504 on a Portuguese chart. In both cases Bacalaos originally designated an island, but for Iberian and Mediterranean geographers it sometimes meant the entire coast of the northwest Atlantic, and sometimes a small subset of the region. The atlas maker Alonzo de Santa Cruz, for instance, labeled the whole coast of the northwest Atlantic as "Tierra de Bacallaos" in his mid-century book of islands. Naming such a large region of the Atlantic for a single commodity may find parallel only in Brazil, named by the Portuguese after the dyewood. The term *Bacalaos* lived a kind of parallel life to Terra Nova, appearing on maps across the century before fading in the seventeenth century. Yet it was never as consistently used or embraced as widely as Terra Nova. Nor was it clear that Bacalaos described a coherent place like Terra Nova — cartographers and geographers tended to apply it haphazardly to different coasts and islands, and mainly to land rather than water. Importantly, Bacalaos rarely appeared in written accounts related to mariners, and it seems that few fishworkers thought of themselves as catching cod in Bacalaos. This is further evidence of the competing ways of thinking of new spaces that existed in the sixteenth century.[17]

These alternative names rarely caught on among mariners, and few had the purchase achieved by Terra Nova in our records. The reverse was sometimes true, and Bacalaos or Newfoundland (the latter still only ever in English documents) were sometimes used by state officials or navigators in the nebulous and expansive sense of Terra Nova. I would argue that this is because Terra Nova was not just a different way of naming the northwest Atlantic, it was a different idea about what that space was. Cartographers wanted to assign labels to lands, places that could be claimed, seized, and exploited. Mariners seem to have preferred a term malleable enough to apply to the kind of mobile, floating work they did in the northwest Atlantic. Terra Nova was a place for fishwork, not fixed land claims, making it useful for mariners but less so for cartographers.

Place and Space

What, then, did it mean to visit Terra Nova? An anonymous Norman mariner, writing in the 1540s, tells us that you knew you had reached Terra Nova when you saw birds. As the ship approached the northwest Atlantic after a month or more of sailing, the experienced mariner looked for "great flocks of *faulqnetz* and also great flocks of a small bird called *marmyons*, then you are forty leagues from the bank." When the birds disappeared, he advised, you had at last reached the Grand Banks and could drop your line to take soundings. Stephen Parmenius, a Hungarian poet shipped to Terra Nova in 1583 to memorialize Sir Humphrey Gilbert's voyage, likewise associated the region with animals, weather, and climate. You were at Terra Nova when you found endless fog and rain and fierce winds, when it was so hot during the day that your fish scorched in the sun if you left it out too long to dry, and when you saw your first icebergs, even in the month of May. "Some of our company have reported," he advised his English audience, "that in the month of May they were stuck for sixteen whole days on end in so much ice that some of the icebergs were sixty fathoms thick; and when their sides facing the sun melted, the entire mass was turned over, as it were on a sort of pivot, in such a way that what had previously been facing upwards was then facing down, to the great danger of any people at hand, as you can well imagine." For other mariners it was the people who made Terra Nova. Alayn Moyne, a Breton pilot hired to guide the English adventurer Richard Hore's ships to Terra Nova in 1536, knew he had reached Terra Nova when he was once more among his countrymen from Brittany. While the English crew spent their days in small boats offshore catching fish, Moyne left them to wander the beaches, where he "went on land among the Bretons his countrymen and made merry with them for a day or two." Breton mariners were found in Terra Nova every year from May to August without fail, a comfort to Moyne—which nonetheless cost him quite a bit when he was charged with dereliction of duty back in London. Many mariners knew that they had arrived at Terra Nova when they caught their first sight of Mi'kmaw trading parties, Innu fishing camps, or Inuit kayaks. Terra Nova was a place that mariners understood not just as a point on a map but as a series of experiences: certain birds, particularly unpleasant weather, one's fellow countrymen, and an ever-present Indigenous community. These experiences in turn shaped what could and could not be part of Terra Nova.[18]

Terra Nova was something artificial, a map of the mind made through human actions and tied to the behavior of mariners in the sixteenth century. That is, after all, what a place is—an idea about space and spatial relationships that we create through our actions and words. Terra Nova had to be made and imposed on the world, but in so doing mariners had created some-thing useful and intelligible to other mariners. People, birds, coasts, fog, sea ice, memories, and experiences: these were the constituent elements by which Europeans constructed a sense of place. For Terra Nova was definitely a place, a discrete space on the mental map of many Europeans. Terra Nova was a destination to be visited, a fishery distinct from Iceland or Ireland or countless others. But places are subjective, shifting things. Terra Nova was not fixed, not a point or carefully bounded area on a coordinate map.

The ways by which mariners in the sixteenth century thought about Terra Nova corresponds with how anthropologists and archaeologists under-stand the making of space and place by humans. A place is a thing to be cre-ated, and we create by doing—actions produce knowledge, which produces place. The unifying elements are movement and work. As Timothy Ingold has put it, "*We know as we go*, from place to place . . . people's knowledge of the environment undergoes continuous formation in the very course of their moving about in it." We use our experiences, our memories of move-ment, to create concepts of place and mental maps to navigate between and within those places. Sometimes these mental maps survive in written or car-tographical form, but sometimes not. As Ricardo Padrón has shown, this ex-periential and itinerary-based approach to mapping and navigation was essential to how the Spanish understood colonial spaces in the Americas. This helps explain how Terra Nova functioned, as a human mental map in-separable from the "image-based practical mastery" of mariners working the northwest Atlantic.[19]

These mental images made by movement and actions become a place. But how does movement become space that can then be articulated as a men-tal map? We will have to turn to theories of landscape. María N. Zedeño has compellingly argued for seeing the world as a landscape comprising land-marks, the latter being particular points of human-natural interaction (trees, roads, beaches, and so on). Landmarks are the " 'pages' in the history of land and resource use," such that "landscape may be defined as the web of interac-tions between people and landmarks." Although the language is terrestrial—landscape—the process is that of experience (landmarks) shaping an image of space (landscape) that forms our mental maps. This certainly reflects how

Terra Nova functioned: as a maritime landscape comprising experiences, of landmarks, like the beach at Caprouge or the birds of the Grand Banks. Zedeño's work complements Christer Westerdahl's pioneering insight that understands maritime space as constituting a maritime cultural landscape that *"signifies human utilization (economy) of maritime space by boat."* The concept of the maritime cultural landscape, an attempt to synthesize material and cultural evidence into a comprehensive tool for archaeologists, especially underwater archaeologists, helps us to understand these spaces as analogues and contrasts to terrestrial landscapes. Like Zedeño's landscape, Westerdahl's comprises landmarks and memories, each tied to a maritime action. We will go one step further, for such a maritime culture landscape—a collection of maritime landmarks—was the foundation of mariners' mental maps of space in the northwest Atlantic.[20]

The sites and experiences comprising Terra Nova were all tied to fishwork. Drawing on later experience, Peter Pope has suggested that the maritime cultural landscape of the fishery was composed of fishing booths (shore camps), but this ignores the multiple and varied sites of fishwork in the sixteenth century. There were the harbors and banks, the shoals and islands, the beaches and cliffs, the bird nests and freshwater streams that were used by European mariners each summer. These sites could be used in many ways, for fishwork constituted many kinds of labor requiring many kinds of space. Rocky areas were used to sun-dry salted cod, beaches were used to launch fishing boats, and camps were set up beyond the shoreline. For those who worked the Grand Banks in pursuit of pickled "green cod" (*morue verte*), the sea itself was a site of fishwork, and crews here might never set foot on shore. Because of this close association between fishwork and the northwest Atlantic, across the sixteenth century the name Terra Nova appears in writing paired with a variation of the verb "to fish": "Terra Nova-Fishing." The most usual formulation in notarial records from French-speaking ports, for instance, was "to travel to Terra Nova to fish," but after mid-century the phrase "voyage de La Terre Neufve à la pescherie" appears, which implies roughly "a Terra Nova voyage for fishing." The Terra Nova voyage had become a recognized bureaucratic trope. To declare, "I am going to Terra Nova" was functionally equivalent to "I am going fishing." This linguistic pattern reflects an understanding that space was mutable, deter-mined by the ability to perform a certain action there. Where there were fish to be caught, there was Terra Nova. A harbor became part of Terra Nova not because of where it was located but because it was used for fishing.[21]

Such a conception of space, so rooted in experience and work, could be created only by the European mariners who ventured to the northwest At-lantic every summer. Many fishworkers served at Terra Nova for multiple seasons, and families and entire port towns became tied to the seasonal fish-ery, allowing them to develop intimate understandings of the maritime spaces in which they worked. Through such hands-on training, word of mouth, and the circulation of information within port towns, mariners could cultivate, transfer, and preserve knowledge of work and place in the northwest Atlantic. Ecologist Fikret Berkes has argued that the kind of local-ized, detailed knowledge that comes from spending so much time working a particular landscape forms a "sacred ecology" that allows communities to more effectively manage natural resources. This process of familiarization was essential to the history of Terra Nova. One who understood this was the anonymous Norman mariner who in the 1540s wrote about the boats he had left in Terra Nova, specifying that they were in "the harbor of Jean Denys called Rangoust." This most likely meant what is today Renews harbor, named after a Norman navigator who had visited the area some three dec-ades before our anonymous mariner. The same mariner wrote about leav-ing some boats in a "cul-de-sac" and others in an "anse-a-main" of the river that flowed into the harbor, both terms used to mean particular kinds of bends in the waterway. Work brought familiarity, and familiarity shaped conceptions of space.[22]

This knowledge about the sacred ecology of Terra Nova was a powerful advantage for mariners. It gave them access to space in the northwest Atlan-tic in a way that conferred exclusivity and even a kind of authority. In 1521 merchants in London wrote of the potential to hire mariners for a trade ex-pedition to Terra Nova. They were specifically interested in those who had "experience, and exercised in and about the aforesaid land, as well as knowl-edge of the land, the correct routes by sea, there and back, and knowledge of the havens, roads, ports, creeks, dangers and shoals upon that coast." The appeal rested on the idea that a pool of fishworkers had spent enough time in the northwest Atlantic by 1521 that they had developed, shared, and internalized all the important information necessary to sail and work there safely. They sought expertise and finely detailed knowledge that could come only through maritime work; without it, the merchants could do nothing. Often such knowledge about space in Terra Nova was possessed by pilots who might hire themselves out to prospective captains. These pilots, acting as a transnational link between different fishing communities, could demand high wages. Breton mariners appear consistently as pilots, such as the one Robert Lefant encountered at Caprouge serving aboard an Asturian fishing vessel. If you did not know what you were doing, and had not hired a good pilot, the voyage became very difficult. After failing to procure a proper pilot, Sir Humphrey Gilbert's hapless flotilla left England on June 11, 1583, but did not reach Sam Joham/Saint John's harbor until August 3. The ships had taken a roundabout route southward searching for winds to carry them northwest to the fishery, not knowing the right way, with the result that their sailing time was nearly doubled. A letter written by Stephen Parmenius makes clear that many of the crew members were in bad shape (including an outbreak of dysentery) and desperately unhappy until they finally found dry land. The same flotilla encountered disaster and the loss of a ship on its return voyage, further evidence of the need to follow experienced pilots who had themselves seen and worked in Terra Nova.[23]

It is not surprising, then, that the first proper sailing guide printed in Europe that described Terra Nova in detail was written by a pilot who had experienced fishwork in the northwest Atlantic. Martin de Hoyarsabal, a Basque captain from Ciboure in French Basque Country who had served in the fishery, published his *Voyages avantureux* in 1579 in Bordeaux. Modern historians have used his guide to reconstruct sixteenth-century geographic names and to understand which harbors were most actively used by fishworkers. It is telling that Hoyarsabal's guide appears late in the century, many decades after Terra Nova had been created. It was a text that codified what was already known, rather than blazing a new path. Whether most mariners sailing to Terra Nova actually used the *Voyages avantureux* is questionable; most would already have known what to do through their own experience. The text is nonetheless useful as a glimpse into the kinds of sacred ecologies that had become well established by 1579.[24]

One important thing Hoyarsabal's sailing guide shows us are the place-names that were used in the sixteenth century. As they created Terra Nova, fishworkers wrote themselves into the coastline in fundamental and enduring ways. Naming things was the first weapon in the European arsenal to control the Atlantic basin, and one of their most enduring legacies. Craig Colten's work on the Gulf Coast has noted that European names were most easily applied to river mouths and coastal sites in the sixteenth and seventeenth centuries. Indigenous names, by contrast, tended to be more durable along rivers and other interior spaces. At Terra Nova, where fishworkers rarely ventured beyond the shoreline, this pattern held true, and European names became entrenched along the coastal northwest Atlantic. To replace Indigenous words, Europeans first deployed their own language of geography to describe the northwest Atlantic's coasts for Europeans back home. Mariners and cartographers applied the precise terminology developed over centuries in the eastern Atlantic, carefully delineating *bayas* from *cabos*, rivers from roads, banks from shoals, *insulae* from *terra*, *destroict* from *havre*. They created a utilitarian coast-scape, a way of differentiating the nature and usefulness of every landmark with a single word. Some places were named for their geography, like Cabo Raso (Cape of Shoals/Shallows) or Belle Isle, or for a salient biological feature, such as Penguin Isle. But to name places in the northwest Atlantic, Europeans often turned to their own coasts. Cape Breton was named for Breton mariners just before 1519, an entire island named for a community in a coastal corner of western Europe. Brest, a major port along the south coast of Labrador, was named for a noteworthy port town in western Brittany. Scholars have long noted the large number of Basque-derived place-names in the northwest Atlantic, some of which were used only in the sixteenth century while others have endured. Fishworkers wanted to see and hear echoes of their own countries, to be reminded of home while on the other side of the Atlantic. Even the name Terra Nova makes no sense without Europe—there can be no new without old. It is precisely the absence of novelty that is so striking about the legacy of place-names Europeans have left in the northwest Atlantic.[25]

Sometimes these sacred ecologies could be quite explicitly sacred. Fish-workers were all good Christians, mostly Catholics, and so too were various navigators and would-be settlers who flocked to the northwest Atlantic. The mysterious third voyage of Zuan Caboto in 1498 might have included an explicitly missionizing motive and even a delegation of priests. As a result, Terra Nova always conveyed a religious connotation as part of its fishwork geography. Consider the famous harbor of Sam Joham/Saint John's, an explicitly Christian toponym. Though only the English name has survived, most mariners probably knew it as San Juan or São João, and it offers a parallel to a place like San Juan in the Caribbean, which was named around the same time. To confuse matters, there was also a San Juan island off the north coast of Newfoundland island on some sixteenth-century maps, a Saint John's harbor on the south shore of Newfoundland, and a large Isle Saint Jean island in the Gulf of Canada. Yet John was hardly the only saint to pop up in the northwest Atlantic coastline. A small inlet near Anticosti Island was christened the Baie de Sainct Laurens by Cartier in 1535, and toward the end of the century the name was upscaled by some geographers to describe the Gulf of Canada as a whole. Generations of fishworkers, trappers, and settlers carefully worked their way across Saint Lawrence's gulf and up his river in pursuit of fish, fur, and fortune. Then there was Isle Saint Pierre, today still part of France, a popular fishing camp by the late sixteenth century. When the king of Portugal granted João Fagundes permission to settle the coasts he had recently explored in 1520, he cited the various islands and harbors the Portuguese mariner had already christened: Saint John, Saint Peter, Saint Anna, Saint Antonio, Saint Pantelion, and Santa Cruz islands, along with the Archipelago of the 11,000 Virgins. To navigate the strait between Newfoundland and Cape Breton meant running the gauntlet of sanctified archipelagos and inlets. We know that if a fishworker met his end at Terra Nova, he was given a proper Christian burial, the ground itself hallowed by the internment. Lori White's fascinating study of the Basque whalers' cemetery on Saddle Island, in Butus harbor, has recreated the last rites of several dozen deceased mariners. The cemetery, White makes clear, followed explicit Christian burial practices, including how bodies were oriented and marked. Egaña Goya has found evidence of early seventeenth-century Basque burials in Terra Nova. As she and others have pointed out, this practice dates back further, and there is reason to believe that fishworkers' burial grounds existed at major fishing harbors in the sixteenth century. Selma Barkham has found evidence of at least three priests traveling aboard Basque whaling vessels in the 1560s as well as a priest at Placentia among the cod-fishing ships in 1585. In all this, mariners were treating Terra Nova as an extension of Christendom, their imagined community of believers, and transplanting religious practices from coastal Europe to the other side of the Atlantic.[26]

If it was created from experience, observation, and a dash of faith, Terra Nova was nonetheless entirely a product of European perspectives. The sites of fishwork that composed Terra Nova were all places where Basque, Breton, Norman, Portuguese, and other mariners from across the sea labored. Instead of being at the center of how Europeans interacted with space, as was and would be the case in the Caribbean, Mesoamerica, North America, Brazil, and elsewhere, Indigenous communities in Terra Nova were peripheral to the main activity of harvesting marine life. The relationship was a complex one in which both parties carefully balanced a mutual interest in the exchange of goods (typically metalwork for furs) while maintaining a deliberate distance. Even so, Zoe Todd has persuasively argued that Indigenous conceptions of space were fundamentally different from those employed by Europeans. If European mariners saw space as constructed through fishwork (a human act of harvesting a passive nature), then Indigenous peoples viewed "land and places as sets of relationships between human and nonhuman beings co-constituting one another." Indigenous mental maps were not constructed through the use of fishwork landmarks, as were those of mariners, and this led to different names and geographies. The geographic knowledge and territorial claims of the Beothuk, Mi'kmaq, Innu, and Inuit were all suppressed through the imposition of the worldview of European mariners, for if there could be no New France in Terra Nova, then neither could there be Ktaqmkuk or Akami-assi. In a rightfully scathing essay, Susan Manning has drawn attention to how seventeenth-century settler colonialism on Newfoundland island has intentionally hidden Indigenous place-names and concepts of place. I would suggest this process began even earlier, and the very language that Indigenous peoples used to describe and label the northwest Atlantic was often lost or misrecorded by mariners, so that relatively few place-names of Algonkian origin survive in Newfoundland and Labrador along the coast. Much as it competed with cartographic conceptions of the northwest Atlantic, Terra Nova denied Indigenous conceptions of space.[27]

The Secrets of Terra Nova

More than anything, thinking with Terra Nova encourages us to move away from rigid conceptions of geography to embrace more nebulous and dynamic (if confusing) frameworks that better reflect the lived experience of humans in the premodern world. As *Terra Nova* was a vague term whose complexities were probably understood only by those who had actually visited, it was a useful label to be deliberately deployed in bureaucratic documents by mariners. In the majority of cases where mariners reported they were traveling to Terra Nova, they were often (but not always) careful to avoid describing exactly where they were going. When one mariner reported he visited the "north part of Terra Nova," this could have meant anywhere from southern Labrador to the Strait of Belle Isle to the entire north coast of Newfoundland island. Perhaps he was trying to conceal his movements from an inquisitive state or from competitors. Anthropologists, archaeologists, and historians have long tried to come to grips with what scholars have called the "secrecy" of fishworkers. Control of information is essential to fishwork. As Thorolfur Thorlindsson has noted, "A skipper is in many ways like a researcher looking for patterns which may help him understand his environment and make him more successful in catching fish." To preserve advantage, given the finite amount of marine biomass in a given fishery, that information can be withheld—from competitors, but also from state actors who would seek to tax and control fishwork. Global fishworkers have long practiced the art of concealing information about fishing grounds, much to the chagrin of historians wishing to reconstruct their voyages. To this might be added the tendency of most sixteenth-century European coastal populations to evade state inquiry and deliberately hide their business. "Terra Nova" was a useful tool in this careful dance between fishworkers and the state. It was descriptive enough to denote a real destination in the Atlantic basin, but vague enough to avoid giving away too much information.[28]

The expression "Terra Nova" conveyed a complex set of experiences and patterns of human labor that in turn constituted a shared mental map of the northwest Atlantic that was charged with meaning for those who visited in the sixteenth century. This meaning derived from two elements. First, the term *Terra Nova* was tied to the practice of fishwork, so that to go to Terra Nova was in effect to go fishing, allowing the word pair to express mental maps shaped at a personal level by the activity of seasonal fishwork in the northwest Atlantic. It was not a label of possession like many other names bestowed in the sixteenth century—Terra Nova did not connote an aspiration to control in the way that New France did, for instance. Rather, it was a label of practice, a name created through movement and labor. Second, the nomenclature Terra Nova was sufficiently vague and malleable to be useful to mariners who wished to keep their movements hidden from outsiders (whether state or church officials, or competitors), but who also might have to move their operations around as seasons and weather shifted in the tempestuous and ever-changing northwest Atlantic. Terra Nova, in short, had the virtue of expressing the lived experience of fishwork while also being practically useful to mariners.

What the two words *Terra Nova* could never quite express, and what maps could never capture, was the movement and vitality of the northwest Atlantic as mariners experienced it. Terra Nova was not static, not a fixed point on the surface of the Earth. It was a space that lived, breathed, shifted, and grew over time. Every autumn Terra Nova evaporated, disappearing as the last European fishworkers left for home and the first waves of sea ice moved south with the changing of the seasons. Every spring it was born anew, imposed on the northwest Atlantic as European mariners, codfish, and warm weather returned. How people moved to and through Terra Nova, and how their movements were shaped by climate and ecology, will be explored next.

THREE

Rhythms

S tanding before the city council of Bayonne on the last day of March in 1521, Pes de la Lande and Mathiu de Biran were nervous. A pair of local merchants, they had come to present their "humble remonstrance" asking permission to unload a cargo from their jointly owned ship. The *Marie* was filled with pounds of metal ore ready for market, but sat floating at the port of Bocau farther down the River Adour from Bayonne. The currents, the merchants claimed, were too strong to bring the ship up to Bayonne directly. Instead, they wanted permission to offload the cargo at Bocau and ferry it up later by barges to Bayonne, freeing the ship's hold for other uses. The reason for their haste was that de la Lande and Biran had suddenly decided to use the *Marie* for a new purpose, even though the metal venture was not yet finished. They wanted to outfit the ship for a voyage to Terre Nave to go fishing. De la Lande and Biran made clear that their haste came from the pressing realization that it was already the end of March, and if they waited too long, "the voyage will be lost for the whole year." The crew was complaining about delays, the biscuits were already baked and loaded, all that was needed was to clear some space for the intended fish catch. Perhaps they shouldn't have waited so long to decide on a Terra Nova run, but having done so it was a race to get under way before they faced "a very great loss" if they missed their window.[1]

The anxious request of Pes de la Lande and Mathiu de Biran reflects something that European merchants and mariners had already grasped by the 1520s. Terra Nova required careful timing, for it was a moving target. The northwest Atlantic moved, was alive, was ever-changing over the course of the year. Terra Nova could not be a fixed space, neatly bounded. This is why the relationship between mental maps and fishwork was so important. Where one did fishwork, and therefore where one found Terra Nova, could fluctuate from year to year or even from month to month. The northwest Atlantic was a place defined by rhythms. These operated at multiple levels, some defined by humans, some by other-than-human animals, some physical. All, however, contributing to shaping how humans—both Europeans and First Nations—moved through and within the northwest Atlantic each year. Terra Nova was a world of opportunities for those in search of food and profit, but those opportunities followed a strict timetable.

A Kingdom of Water and Fish

In her pathbreaking *The Sea Around Us*, the environmentalist Rachel Carson captured in words the essential rhythm of seascapes:

> For the sea as a whole, the alternation of day and night, the passage of the seasons, the procession of the years, are lost in its vastness, obliterated in its own changeless eternity. But the surface waters are different. The face of the sea is always changing. Crossed by colors, lights, and moving shadows, sparkling in the sun, mysterious in the twilight, its aspects and its moods vary hour by hour. The surface waters move with the tides, stir to the breath of the winds, and rise and fall to the endless, hurrying forms of the waves. Most of all, they change with the advance of the seasons.

Her lyrical invocation of seasonality and change would have resonated on a deep level with humans who had experienced life in the waters of the northwest Atlantic in the sixteenth century.[2]

Every year a cycle of water, wind, and cold air moved through Terra Nova, pushing and pulling living organisms large and small. This dance of ice and fish in turn called forth humans both near and far to its shores every year. Each spring came Beothuk, Mi'kmaq, Innu, Inuit, and Saint Lawrence

Iroquoian communities to the coasts and waters of Terra Nova. Hard on their heels were the first European fishworkers, appearing with the dawn over the eastern horizon as the weather turned warm. They dodged icebergs and picked their way across rocky islands in pursuit of seabirds, or carefully navigated through the thick fog banks that hid treacherous shoals and cliffs. Mi'kmaq in canoes sailed to Miquelon and southern Newfoundland to find fish, seals, and walrus. Breton mariners might barricade themselves in a harbor all summer, while Normans crisscrossed the vast Grand Banks as they followed the codfish. By August and September European ships moved away, sailing back home, as the First Nations began preparing to migrate across the interior in search of new sources of food. Come October, the coasts of Terra Nova were quiet, the human tide having receded once more. One English visitor, thinking of the feasts of salmon and lobster he had enjoyed one summer at Sam Joham/Saint John's harbor, marveled that "at other times of the year, only wild beasts and birds have the run of all this country, which now seemed a place very populated and much frequented." The aquatic rhythms of Terra Nova created a world of floating, transient populations that seemingly produced abundant, human-filled summers and barren winters left to the beasts.[3]

When we pay attention to the rhythms of water in the northwest Atlantic, we can see how they shaped the essential nature of Terra Nova in very different ways at different scales. At the scales that humans experienced it, such as a five-month voyage for fishwork or a summer in a seaside Mi'kmaw village, Terra Nova seems unstable and ever-changing. It was bound to the movements of marine life and weather systems, following the yearly rhythms of fish, ice, and cold temperatures, which themselves moved every few months. The boundaries of Terra Nova expanded and contracted with the seasons and movements of human beings. Yet at the other end of the spectrum, across the sixteenth century, we can see how this rhythm imbued Terra Nova with a consistency and immutability that allowed it to endure. The cycles of fish and ice, of cold fronts and whales, were predictable, repeating, reliable. If Terra Nova expanded and contracted with the seasons because of the rhythms of nature, it nonetheless persisted year after year after year in a recognizable form. It was both these scales—the short-term need to access fish and the long-term reliability—that brought different migratory communities together each year.

The short-term rhythms of the northwest Atlantic were shaped by the peculiarities of a subarctic environment. Terra Nova encompassed a series of lateral biome bands sandwiched between the High Arctic and temperate Northeast Woodlands. The polar historian Adrian Howkins has noted the importance of the nutrient-rich polar regions: "The seas and oceans of Antarctica and some parts of the Arctic are sites of high biological abundance; polar lands are often areas of biological scarcity. . . . In some parts of the Arctic and in nearly all of Antarctica, so stark is this contrast that much terrestrial life is dependent in one way or another on the productivity of nearby seas and oceans." The islands and coasts of Terra Nova offered a moderated version of this basic dichotomy. Whereas coasts and inland areas faced harsher climate swings and more limited biological resources, as the waters of the northwest Atlantic changed across the year they encouraged a surge in marine life and allowed for rapid movement. As Donald Holly Jr. has pointed out, in the subarctic "there is an inverse relationship between species variety and abundance." A narrow range of species offers a huge number of individuals to harvest. The land was sparse, but not as barren as European visitors thought. Todd Kristensen's work on the Beothuk, for instance, has drawn attention to the intensive exploitation of birds during the warm months. Starting with land birds like ptarmigan and grouse, Beothuk shifted to seabirds partway through the summer. As Kristensen has observed, "Food availability in Newfoundland occurred in pulses of relatively dense animal congregations." One had to know these seasonal rhythms, and to know where to find their concentrations. Innu, Beothuk, and Mi'kmaq knew these rhythms precisely, and by moving from one site of concentration to another—both spatially and temporally—enjoyed sustained access to food. Europeans, less familiar with the environment and its intricate rhythms, saw only emptiness.[4]

Even so, the climate swings and breeding cycles of the subarctic did affect life on land more than sea. Cold weather, high winds, extreme temperature swings, and thin soils suppress flora and fauna more than fish and whales. The underwater currents around the Gulf of Canada provided favorable conditions for marine life and allowed humans to move quickly between the numerous fishing shoals and islands. The result was that the most easily accessible and important biological abundance of the northwest Atlantic was concentrated in the water. In the mid-seventeenth century a Jesuit missionary would accurately describe the lands along the River of Canada, then slowly being settled by French colonizers, as "the Kingdom of water and of fish." Such a royal title could have been applied to the whole of Terra Nova.[5]

The water that made Terra Nova valuable also moved, and in so doing acted as the main driver of seasonal rhythms. Several major currents came together in the seas and coastal shelves of the northwest Atlantic. Down from the Arctic rushed the Labrador current, moving cold saltwater through northern Terra Nova and into the Gulf of Canada and Grand Banks. This was the key to Terra Nova, the frigid submarine thoroughfare that brought from the polar regions nutrient-rich water that allowed marine life to bloom. Up from the south coursed the mighty Gulf Stream, well offshore but picking up anything that came its way and carrying it in warm waters across the Ocean Sea toward Europe. Currents ran at cross-purposes: if the warm Gulf Stream moved northeastward far offshore, then inshore along Nova Scotia ran a southward Scotian Current. The heart of Terra Nova, the great engine of movement, was the Gulf of Canada. Into the gulf came the waters of the River of Canada and its tributary lakes, the long aquatic highway that cut through the heart of the continent to connect the Great Plains with the Atlantic Ocean. Through the Cabot Strait and the Straits of Belle Isle came the frigid Labrador and Scotian Currents. In the wide Gulf of Canada these different flows mixed together to form a series of gyres, which in turn pumped water outward, through the straits and back into the sea, where it joined with the Gulf Stream. The continuous movement, countermovement, gyration, and expulsion of saltwater kept things moving and ensured favorable conditions for marine life in the region.[6]

Even as the waters of Terra Nova flowed and coursed with the seasons, there were deeper movements at work. The climate of the Northern Hemisphere was caught in the tumultuous grip of the Little Ice Age, producing gradual shifts in temperature and weather across the sixteenth century. The earliest decades of the century, when European ventures to the northwest

Atlantic began in earnest, may have been relatively warmer and more stable than in later years. This allowed mariners to move more freely about Terra Nova from an earlier date. After the 1550s average temperatures were increasingly lower, and the weather more erratic. In 1610 Samuel de Champlain arrived at Tadoussac, at the confluence of the Saguenay and River of Canada, where he found a group of fishworkers and traders. Some among the "old mariners" there commented that the ships "had arrived as early as the eighteenth [of April]," but they were astounded because "such a thing had not been seen for sixty years." Their testimony indicates that in the 1550s it was normal to arrive in early April or earlier, but that for the rest of the sixteenth century this was impossible. This points to the consequences of cooling temperatures after the 1550s, such that Terra Nova was probably smaller than it had been in earlier decades. The seasonal cycles of water, ice, and cold were consistent, but their limits could vary in subtle ways over time.[7]

These were the rhythms, large and small, that shaped Terra Nova and that set the basic conditions for human life and work in the northwest Atlantic. These rhythms posed important challenges for both Indigenous and European actors. The seasonal abundance of marine biomass—cod for the Europeans and a variety of animals for First Nations—was an alluring source of food and energy for hungry communities. Harvesting required labor, however, and it made little sense to concentrate and sustain labor along the coasts of Terra Nova year-round if there was nothing to gather and process. Nor was it advisable to move that labor away from shores and open seas during the warmest months, when the interior had less to offer. In the face of these basic constraints, the most sensible solution was adaptation.[8]

Adaptation

In the kingdom of water and fish, timing mattered a great deal. There was a clear, consistent, and narrow window of time in which the weather and winds cooperated, the ice flows receded, and the fish were abundant. Seafaring Europeans thought this began toward the end of April and lasted until late August, perhaps four months at most (see figure 8). When one factored in the monthlong voyages to and from Terra Nova, the time frame

Figure 8. The slow change of the seasons. Terra Nova as viewed from space on April 7, 2008. The darker colored landscape of Nova Scotia is where warmer weather brings spring conditions, while everything else remains frozen. (MODIS Land Rapid Response Team, NASA GSFC. Courtesy of the Visible Earth Project.)

could be dauntingly narrow. A Spanish author in 1574 wrote simply but clearly of "the ships that go to [Terra Nova] at the end of March and the beginning of April and return from it in the middle of September and in October." If one waited too long and missed the departure date, one's investment and plans were indeed (as de la Lande and Biran put it) "lost for the whole year."⁹

To survive a subarctic edge zone of wild temperature swings and undiverse abundance, one had to live near the ocean, the source of both food and movement. In the sixteenth century, the coasts of La Gran Baya and elsewhere in Terra Nova were sites of encounter between different maritime peoples, human communities oriented and accustomed to working, living, and moving on ocean water. Centuries of settler-colonialist historiography had long cast Indigenous America as land-locked, making Indigenous history sit awkwardly in Atlantic studies and encouraging a contrast between seaborne (and implicitly "modern" Europeans) and land-bound (and implicitly "backwards") Indigenous groups. Only slowly has scholarship recognized that evidence of the maritime activity of Indigenous groups across the Atlantic littoral is abundant and clear. The northwest Atlantic led the way, and Charles Martijn's pioneering work on the Mi'kmaq laid out an early argument for viewing the community as a maritime society whose members roamed the sea. Decades later, Jack Forbes made the case more broadly for Indigenous and Inuit seafaring, and even the potential of contact with Europe. A surge in recent work by historians (like Andrew Lipman's revealing *Saltwater Frontier*) has done much to raise our awareness of Indigenous American communities as maritime peoples accustomed to using and traveling over ocean spaces. Across the northeast of North America, communities made extensive use of seaways to travel, extend political and economic power, and find food.¹⁰

Recent archaeological and historical work has confirmed that Algonkian-speaking, Iroquoian-speaking, and of course Inuit communities in the northwest Atlantic were seafaring, coast-exploiting, maritime peoples first and foremost. Matthew Bahar has argued that the Mi'kmaq were the preeminent naval power in the region until the mid-eighteenth century. The Mi'kmaq regularly sailed across the Gulf of Canada to the Magdalen Islands and southern Newfoundland island. Their political and economic world stretched across the waters from what is today Nova Scotia and New Brunswick to southern Newfoundland and the many islands of the Gulf of Canada. The Beothuk may not have been seafarers, but they lived along coasts and made extensive use of maritime resources. All were embedded in and a product of the environmental rhythms and structures of Terra Nova, the ebb and flow of fish and seasons. Much as the Bretons, Basques, Saintongeois, Galicians, and others were first and foremost communities of the Atlantic rim, so too were First Nations at Terra Nova Atlantic coastal peoples.[11]

The three Indigenous communities permanently living in what became Terra Nova—Beothuk, Innu, and Mi'kmaq—all practiced seasonal migration as a food-production strategy. Archaeological, ethnographic, and oral histories do not point to long-term, year-round settlements or agriculture. As Charles Martijn has observed of the Mi'kmaq, migratory routes and seasonal settlements probably varied considerably from year to year as other-than-human populations and local ecological conditions changed. Such seasonal migrations and variability do not preclude deep connections with land and sea that we often associate with settled communities. Surveying millennia of changing occupation at the Port aux Choix site on northwest Newfoundland island, archaeologists have described successive layers of the cultural landscape at this important harbor. Such cultural landscapes change with each new occupying community, but each "has a life history comprised of layers of different kinds of meaning, for example pertaining to resources, topography, routes of movement, events, stories, myths and rituals. These life histories evolve as meanings accumulate over time." Such cultural landscapes and connections to place are essential to seasonal migrations, allowing Beothuk, Mi'kmaq, and Innu communities to make sense of the seasonal rhythms and opportunities around them.[12]

The First Nations of Terra Nova were well aware of the maritime abundance of the region and oriented themselves toward water during the summer months. For the rest of the year they moved between forest, riverine, and open biomes in search of game and forage. The Mi'kmaq peoples may have numbered several thousand in the sixteenth century, but most individuals experienced life as part of a smaller community that moved between coast and forest season after season. The anonymous *gran capitano*, writing in the 1530s, noted of the Beothuk: "When the fishing season ends with the approach of winter, they return with their catch in boats made of the bark of a certain tree called *Buil* [birch], and go to warmer countries, but we know not where." This approach was successful, at least in the eyes of European visitors. Interestingly, as Matthew Betts and M. Hrynick summarize in their recent work on the Atlantic Northeast, this may have been a relatively (for 1500) novel adaptation by Algonkian-speaking communities. "Recent archaeological work has begun to suggest that the Protohistoric period may have been marked by rapid shifts in seasonal occupation of the coast. . . . In contrast to year-round coastal and interior populations . . . [recent work] suggested coastal-interior transhumance, with summers on the coast." There is archaeological evidence indicating that communities further south, around the Gulf of Maine, eschewed marine food sources compared to terrestrial ones in the centuries before 1500 but shifted to the coast around this time. Within Terra Nova, embracing the rhythms of seasonal migration may have taken place not long before Europeans themselves adapted to the cycles of the northwest Atlantic.[13]

Many later European authors stressed the cyclical, seasonal nature of First Nations foodways. The Jesuit missionary Pierre Biard observed of the Mi'kmaq around 1610: "In the month of February and until the middle of March, is the great hunt for beavers, otters, moose, bears (which are very good), and for the caribou, an animal half ass and half deer. If the weather then is favorable, they live in great abundance, and are as haughty as Princes and Kings; but if it is against them, they are greatly to be pitied, and often die of starvation." Later he noted, "From the month of May up to the middle of September, they are free from all anxiety about their food; for the cod are upon the coast, and all kinds of fish and shellfish." Earlier generations of historians and archaeologists often took these Jesuit descriptions of plenty and dearth at face value. As the work of Carla Cevasco has at last made clear, European perceptions of Indigenous hunger and dearth tended to badly misinterpret actual experiences by Indigenous peoples. First Nations did not experience hunger, scarcity, or seasonality as Europeans often did, and were socially, physically, and psychologically prepared to endure changes in food supply that would have evoked horror in colonizers. Mi'kmaq communities were well adapted to natural food cycles, and rarely suffered in the way that visiting Jesuits claimed. They thrived on seasonal rhythms, maintaining through their mobility a relatively large population and strong hold over the coastal northwest Atlantic.[14]

The mobility of First Nations within Terra Nova helped shape the nature of encounter and exchange with European mariners. In the absence of Indigenous or European permanent settlements, encounters tended to take place haphazardly on the coast. Many Mi'kmaq and Innu, and later the Inuit and Saint Lawrence Iroquoians, actively sought out fishing harbors and visited fishing camps. Yet because of their mobility, these meetings could be brief or even altogether avoided, and while fur-for-metal exchange was common, sustained contact between European and Indigenous communities seems to have been rarer. The Beothuk, in particular, were notorious for avoiding contact altogether, especially as the century wore on. Archaeologists have noted the preferred Beothuk strategy of raiding fishing camps at the end of the summer for metal and other goods Europeans left behind. Exchange with Europeans (or, in the Beothuk case, foraging for metal) was worked into the seasonal rhythms of abundance, a cyclical opportunity treated like seal hunting or gathering auk eggs rather than a sustained economic strategy.[15]

Alongside the seasonal migrations of First Nations, mariners from across the Atlantic embraced a similar kind of mobility. The European fishery in the northwest Atlantic originated and developed independently of permanent settlements and remained in a kind of constant flux as Terra Nova expanded and contracted in different ways each year. Sometimes fishworkers returned to the same harbor or shoal several seasons in a row. Other times they moved between fishing sites over the course of a single summer. Although some sites, like Brest in Labrador and Sam Joham/Saint John's in Newfoundland, were well-known centers of fishwork, none saw permanent infrastructure or year-round settlement. Mobility was the hallmark of the fishworkers; they were more nomads and migrants than settlers. Historians have tended to focus on the fishery as a set of discrete voyages. This is partly a product of the sources, the notarial and court records that focus on individual ships and their business arrangements. Yet I would suggest instead that we view the transatlantic fishery as a whole as a seasonal, cyclical migratory system. The aggregation of hundreds of ships moving to Terra Nova every spring and back every autumn allowed harvesting without necessitating permanent settlement. At the same time this migratory system made a permanent European presence, and thus a de facto permanent colony, possible. This migratory logic was essential to the formation and sustainability of the northwest Atlantic fishery in the sixteenth century. Migration neatly sidestepped the problem of settlement, providing abundant European labor when and where it was needed without having to deal with the costs of year-round habitation.[16]

The Atlantic basin had seen long-distance fisheries before, but never on this scale or duration. European fishworkers could easily spend half a year away from their homes, traveling to, from, and around the fishery. As they did so, their social organization shifted. European fishworkers experienced life as small teams of mariner-laborers under the rule of their shipboard master. City-dwelling Basques and Normans suddenly became migratory hunter-gatherers, harvesting fish, whales, and seals by moving with the rhythms of nature. One reason for the success of a transoceanic migratory system like the early fishery was that it took place within a surprisingly coherent biome that stretched across the far North Atlantic. Like Algonkian-speaking communities, Europeans were seasonally migrating within a single subarctic zone. If nothing else, these European mariners had to adapt to the reality of being separated from their home communities for five months straight. This long-term dislocation was more than just a simple voyage, and it took place at a scale that involved tens of thousands of mariners every year.

In the sixteenth century migration was facilitated by technology, then as now. For Europeans this meant the sailing ship, while for Indigenous groups in might be the canoe, snowshoes, and kayak. Europeans were, however, particularly dependent on their wooden vessels to make such long-distance migration possible. What was this ship technology? It was more than just a means of transport and movement. It was a technology to facilitate climatological equilibrium. The ship brought Europeans from relatively temperate coastal regions to a temporarily temperate Terra Nova. It allowed them to avoid the weather and ecologies of the subarctic northwest Atlantic at their fiercest. Summer at Terra Nova was never as temperate as Europeans wanted, as they constantly complained, but in their cyclical movements around the Atlantic European mariners arrived just when things became manageable and left before they became threatening. One might say that the ship technologies allowed Europeans to enjoy a kind of artificial, hermetically sealed climate experience during their seasonal migrations—from temperate ports to temperate coasts and back. Sailing ships have often been viewed as technologies of movement, violence, and commerce. So too could they be technologies of climate control in the premodern world, as Europeans discovered early in the sixteenth century.

Nor was it the kind of migration that historians usually attribute to the early Atlantic, the movement of populations from one side (forcibly in most cases, voluntarily in others) of the Atlantic to another, or from one part of the Americas to another. Instead, we see a cyclical movement that is repeated across the decades of the sixteenth century, a pendulum of labor swinging back and forth from Brittany to Cape Breton, from Vizcaya to La Gran Baya. Rarely do we hear from those like the "old mariners" (*vieux mariniers*) Samuel de Champlain met at Tadoussac in 1610, but we can imagine what they experienced. A lifetime of fishwork, marked by the regular rhythm of warming waters that brought forth codfish like clockwork and called to them across the sea each spring. For those old enough to remember the days before the River of Canada iced over, how many times had they crossed the Atlantic in pursuit of cod? How much of their lives had they spent on the shores of Terra Nova? What does that do to someone?

Convergence

Robert Lefant, the French Basque captain with whom we began this book, was not the only fishworker subject to Spanish inquiries in 1542. Among those taken was a resident of Fuenterrabía named Clemente de Odeliça, who had spent the summer along La Gran Baya. Inquiring authorities were much less interested in this labor than in what he knew of Indigenous populations in the northwest Atlantic—and what the French knew of them.

"Asked who are the inhabitants of this land of La Gran Baya, and farther up the river [Odeliça] said that many Indians came to his ship in La Gran Baya, and they ate and drank together, and were very friendly, and the Indians gave them deer and wolf skins in exchange for axes and knives and other trifles; and for Indians dressed in skins they are men of skill." Odeliça was likely describing an encounter with the Innu, an Algonkian-speaking First Nation we believe lived along the southern coast of Labrador in the early sixteenth century. The mariner's description of metalware-for-furs exchange and fraternization on board ships points to a close relationship between Indigenous communities and fishworkers that is otherwise obscure in the surviving records.[17]

His comments were corroborated by something Lefant stated earlier in the deposition, when he casually remarked that "the [Indigenous] people trade in marten skins and other skins, and those who go there take all kinds of ironware. And that the Indians understand any language, French, English, and Gascon, and their own tongue." Odeliça and Lefant took it for granted that they would encounter First Nations along the shores of Terra Nova when they arrived in the summer. The Innu whom Odeliça encountered had come to the coast in search of abundant marine food, migrating from inland biomes as weather and breeding seasons shifted. That they ran into a Basque crew catching cod reflects the fact that Europeans had come for much the same reasons, migrating across the Atlantic for a season to take advantage of shifting abundance.[18]

Writing of the place of winter in shaping modern Canada, Ken Coates and William Morrison have reflected, "Some newcomers did adapt to winter, adopting indigenous clothing and learning to adjust to the seasonal rhythms. But for the most part, people who lived in the North did so only temporarily, so few felt the need to make the necessary adaptations. Most who came to the North brought southern things with them." In the sixteenth century, European fishworkers found a kind of middle ground between these approaches. They avoided true winter in the north through their cyclical migrations. Yet in so doing they inadvertently adapted themselves to the climate and ecology of the subarctic Atlantic. Mariners sought solutions that allowed them to work within seasonal cycles to harvest marine life. At the same time, the sixteenth-century experience at Terra Nova should be situated contra the wider history of European terraforming from the fifteenth through the nineteenth centuries. This process of ecological disruption is central to European expansion, settler colonialism, and the origins of our present environmental crises. From the top of Turtle Island to the tip of Tierra del Fuego, European settlers unleashed changes in the land and plagues of sheep in pursuit of their neo-Europes. The collective psychosis that propelled this project, the belief in humans-beyond-nature and the imperative to subjugate and "improve" a "natural" environment, is increasingly being seen as a key driver of European expansion and long-term environmental and economic change. But not at Terra Nova. The ecological impact of a European presence in the sixteenth century was not insubstantial, and it produced a significant amount of food resources for Europe and the wider Atlantic basin. But in shifting toward seasonal migration, European mariners found a path that required neither total transformation (the bringing of "southern things" with them) nor total adaptation. In crucial ways they changed themselves—abandoning certain forms of social organization to embrace others, adapting to seasonal rhythms and mass migration instead of planting agricultural settlements—while still limiting themselves to a temperate, seasonal experience in the coastal northwest Atlantic.[19]

Thus European fishwork at Terra Nova resembled, to a surprising degree, the kind of environmental thinking and socioeconomic organization we see in First Nations at Terra Nova at the same time. Indeed, fishwork at Terra Nova resembles Indigenous practice more than most kinds of social organization within coastal Europe—a Norman wheat farmer or urban merchant would scratch their head at the odd life of Odeliça and Lefant. If it is true that Mi'kmaq, Beothuk, and Innu communities adapted seasonal migration only just before 1500, then these processes happened at nearly the same time and at nearly the same place. In short, there seems to have been convergence around 1500, with European fishworkers and First Nations moving toward the same migratory, seasonal social models in the northwest Atlantic.

In recognizing the significance of convergent seasonal migration in shaping the fisheries, we may move toward Jason Moore's call to write histories of humans in the "web of life"—that is to say, not histories of humans outside of a thing called "nature," acting upon and something being acted upon by an environment that is other-than-human. Instead, "*nature* with an emphatically lowercase *n*. This is nature as us, as around us. It is nature as a flow of flows. Put simply, humans make environments and environments make humans—and human organization." Such a task is difficult, as Moore and others acknowledge, because many historians are heirs to a worldview and a language that separates humanity from the "natural." Yet sometimes people did find ways to adapt, move, and labor in ways that suggest they recognized their own limits and relationships with other living and nonliving entities. At Terra Nova, we can see this in practice, how humans from both sides of the Atlantic found ways to work within the ecological and climatological web to take advantage of abundant resources. What they did with those resources would be different, but divergent approaches to exploitation rested on adaptation. Ecology drove convergence; seasonal rhythm fostered encounters between seemingly divergent communities, which ended up adopting similar approaches to what each viewed as survival and prosperity in the subarctic northwest Atlantic.[20]

PART II

Water

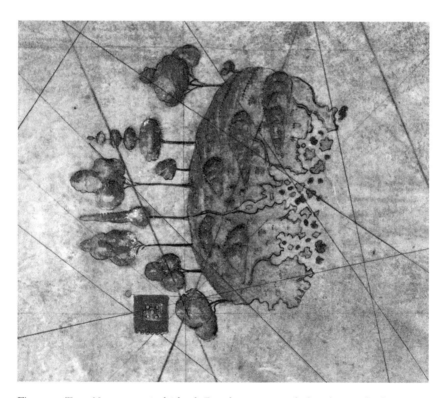

Figure 9. Terra Nova as tropical island. Detail, 1504 nautical chart by Nicolo di Caverio. (Courtesy of the World Digital Library.)

It is ill fishing before the net
Worse fishing behind as nets are set.
—*John Haywood, "Of Fishing," 1555*

Also some months ago his Majesty [the king of England] sent out a
Venetian, who is a very good mariner, and has good skill in discovering
new Islands, and he has returned safe, and has found two very large and
fertile new islands.
—*Letter from Raimondo di Soncino to the Duke of Milan, August 24, 1497*

FOUR

Islands

In the summer of 1511, the Catalan navigator Juan de Agramonte was given a special mission by the Spanish crown: to discover "the secret of Terra Nova." A written warrant instructed Agramonte to gather a crew and ship, hire a proper Breton pilot, and sail to the northwest Atlantic to find islands that might be of value to the Spanish imperial project. In the eyes of the crown, the timing was right. By 1511 the colonial project in the Caribbean was still in its infancy, and the European presence in the Americas faced a multitude of futures. Fourteen years earlier the Spanish crown had learned of the presence of a landmass in the far northwest Atlantic, thanks to a clandestine letter sent from England to Cristobal Colón that reported on the voyage of Zuan Caboto and his "new-found-isles." In the ensuing decade and a half, a wave of English, Azorean, Portuguese, Norman, and Breton ships had fleshed out the Venetian's initial encounter, bringing back news of various islands and mainlands of potential value as well as fish-rich seas. Over the same period Spain's commitment in the Caribbean had grown, now extending to permanent settlements in Española, Cuba, and Puerto Rico, as well as initial forays toward the mainland. With attention and resources not yet absorbed by adventures in Mesoamerica, the crown was willing to consider adding the insular world of Terra Nova to the already impressive array of islands that it claimed to possess, settle, and exploit across the Atlantic basin.[1]

To that end, Agramonte was given one particularly noteworthy charge in his instructions. Any islands he found were to be "settled in our [the crown's] name, as has been done in the said island of Española." The patterns of imperial territorial claims, forcible seizure of island spaces, land distribution, and intensive agriculture that marked emerging Caribbean settlements (and that themselves had a much older lineage) were to be transplanted to the subarctic Atlantic. In hindsight this seems almost laughable, as if subarctic Newfoundland could ever be like tropical, densely settled Española. Yet we know that the Spanish plan for a New Española was not an isolated ambition. Between 1499 and 1521 the Portuguese crown made similar requests of its own subjects, merely substituting Madeira for Española. Their aspirations for the North Atlantic were of Nueva Española and Nova Madeira, not of New-found-lands.[2]

This was a vision of the western Atlantic that the enigmatic Irish-born cartographer Hercules O'Doria enshrined in a map at the end of the century (see figure 10). Though made in the 1590s, it clearly echoes much earlier Spanish cartography and conceptions of space in the western Atlantic. In an otherwise sparse portolan chart of the American coastline, the mapmaker opted to mark in bold colors two regions: the islands of the Caribbean and the islands of "Tera Nova." In this composition, an orange Española acts as the southern complement to a large green Terra Nova, with only a thin and largely blank coast between them. This was the Spanish Atlantic, anchored on two insular poles, which Agramonte had been tasked with making real.[3]

Yet with hindsight O'Doria's map feels naive, even fanciful. At the time it was drafted in the 1590s, it would have looked anachronistic and out of touch with reality. Historians think it likely that Agramonte's ambitious 1511 voyage never departed from Spain, and no Spanish settlers landed in Terra Nova. Portuguese attempts to colonize were more serious, but in the end proved failures. In historical memory Terra Nova would remain a realm dominated by various fishing communities, and neither Agramonte nor his Portuguese rivals have passed into history among the notable navigator-colonizers of the sixteenth century. The allure of islands had proved to be a siren's song.[4]

Although by the mid-sixteenth century the northwest Atlantic was dominated by a commercial fishery, in the first decades after Caboto's voyage

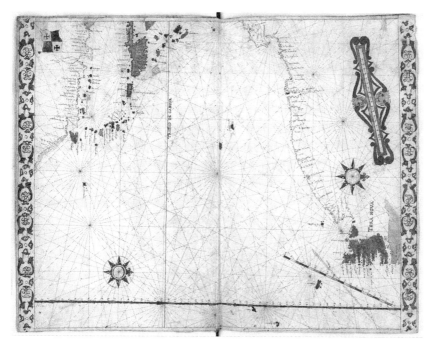

Figure 10. Map of the western Atlantic by Hercules O'Doria, 1592. (Courtesy of the John Carter Brown Library, Creative Commons license CC by 4.0, https://creativecommons.org/licenses/by/4.0/.)

many European navigators, geographers, and state actors had very different visions of what they could do with this new (to them, at least) island world. This chapter aims to change how we think of the historical trajectory of Terra Nova by reminding us of the ways in which Europeans saw the Atlantic in the earliest decades of the sixteenth century. Europeans first understood the northwest Atlantic as a world of islands, bringing with them mental baggage that had been shaped at mid-Atlantic and Caribbean archipelagos like Madeira and Española. This insular vision inspired many Europeans to see island colonies incorporated within an Iberian Atlantic as the fate of Terra Nova. If we take this perspective, it is possible to better understand how it was that fishworkers surpassed settlers as the drivers of change at Terra Nova.

Insulamania

Although we now think only of New-found-land, the earliest reports to come out of the voyages of Caboto, Corte Real, and the Azoreans spoke of islands rather than land. The very earliest English record related to Caboto in 1497 referred to "the new Isle." That same year, reports on Caboto's voyage sent by Italian diplomats in England to Venice and Milan spoke of *ixole nova* and *insula nova*, respectively. A clandestine letter written shortly thereafter by the Englishman John Day to Cristóbal Cólon alluded to Caboto's encounter with the "Island of the Seven Cities," and Day believed he had found the Isles of Brasil. Most of the early English texts refer to the "New found ilondes," and the Portuguese navigator Miguel Corte Real was initially tasked with finding "various islands [*algumas ilhas*] and mainlands" that lay in the northwest Atlantic around 1500. The first Europeans to reach the northwest Atlantic were more excited by the presence of islands than anything else.[5]

With that in mind, let us approach Terra Nova as they did, from the east, not looking outward from the looming mainland to its west and the long history of settlement that followed. This is the view O'Doria presents us with in his map, a panorama of the islands and coasts gazing inward from the eastern Atlantic. From the east the waters of the northwest Atlantic appear as island-filled worlds of opportunity and familiarity. There appears a great bay—the Gulf of Canada—stoppered by islands, Newfoundland and Cape Breton, each surrounded by its own satellite archipelagos. These island worlds are linked by the northward flow of the Atlantic Ocean itself, the Gulf Stream that shrinks the otherwise substantial distance between the tropical Caribbean islands and frigid Terra Nova. Our modern usage of Newfoundland to denote the northwest Atlantic, a large island standing in for a region and its history, has collapsed and erased the multiplicity of islands. Not just the large ones like Newfoundland, Cape Breton, Isle Saint Jean, or Anticosti, but the countless small islands like the Isle of Birds, Fogo, Bacalao, Miquelon, or Belle Isle, where Europeans found the food, forage, beaches, and fishing grounds that made the fishery successful every year. Early cartographers and geographers stressed the multiplicity of archipelagos in their

Terres Neufves, sometimes portraying Newfoundland itself as a collection of smaller islands.[6]

Christina Gillis has described islands as "the most 'edged' of spaces," even though those edges "neither confine nor contain." At the place where sea encircles land, islands are sites where many kinds of edges meet and clash, and boundaries shift with natural and human time in ways that excite and confound those who live there. The island worlds of the northwest Atlantic would be the social and cultural edges between different realms where Mi'kmaq, Beothuk, Innu, and others collided with Europeans. Its place at the edge made Terra Nova a crucial jumping-off point for European interactions with and settlement in the mainland Americas. In this it resembled the Greater Antilles to the south, as O'Doria tried to show on his map. Island worlds like Terra Nova and the Caribbean were sites of provisioning, outfitting, and support for later ventures to the west. Hernán Cortés made his leap to Mesoamerica from Cuba. The sieur de Roberval, and later Samuel de Champlain, relied on the Terra Nova fishery to feed their settlements along the River of Canada. It is hard to imagine the subsequent history of the Americas in the sixteenth and seventeenth centuries without their archipelagic springboards at the edge of the western Atlantic. In this way the islands of Terra Nova are not unlike Gary Okihiro's Hawai'i: "The island acts upon and moves the continent."[7]

The difference between new-found-lands and new-found-isles is a crucial distinction. The early Atlantic was an insular space, literally a world of *insulae*, one shaped by and in turn shaping a Euro-Mediterranean preoccupation with islands and archipelagos. As John Gillis has brilliantly demonstrated, islands had a particularly strong hold on the late fifteenth-century imagination of many Europeans, and islands were seen as crucial to the early development of the Atlantic world. Gillis and later Stefan Halikowski Smith have described fifteenth- and sixteenth-century Europeans as possessed by "insulamania," a manic obsession with islands, that produced a series of utopian projects for their development. So powerful was this mania that it spawned an entire literary genre, the *Isolario*, or "island books," in sixteenth-century Venice. This obsession with island atlases reflected practical experiences. As modern historians have argued, it was on the mid-Atlantic archipelagos that a framework for understanding, annexing, and exploiting the Atlantic was born. In the fourteenth and fifteenth centuries Europeans found the Canaries and Cabo Verde off northwestern Africa, the Azores and Madeira farther out to sea off Portugal. These were swiftly joined by the myriad of insular spaces large and small in the Caribbean, a veritable sea of infinite archipelagos and islands. They had recent experience to draw upon: Colón first encountered his "New World" as a realm of islands, crashing into the archipelago of the Bahamas and coursing the length of Española. The answers Europeans developed to new and unexpected questions about culture, nature, religion and the use of violence, and the colonial and imperial structures they produced, were the product of island encounters with peoples like the Guanches of the Canaries or the Taíno of Española. These answers then set a template for the rest of the Atlantic world.[8]

It was the shared experience of Madeira, the Canaries, Española, and elsewhere that encouraged the idea that Juan de Agramonte and others could turn the islands of Terra Nova into a new Spanish or Portuguese colony. This was particularly true of the ecological experience, the ways in which Iberians had encountered and understood island environments. Such Iberian mariners and would-be settlers, drawing on the lessons of the fifteenth century, often overlooked environmental realities on the ground and instead projected expectations of island spaces shaped by the Canaries, Madeira, and elsewhere. Islands were, in this worldview, destined for a mix of European-style agriculture, food production, mineral extraction, and permanent settlement, including urban centers. If Terra Nova was filled with islands, then it could be treated like the other archipelagos that had already been incorporated into the European Atlantic. Early reports stressed what was on land as much as at sea. The Day Letter, a missive written from England to Cristobal Colón after Caboto's voyages, noted the presence of tall trees for masts and that the land was "rich in grass," observations echoed in Italian correspondence about Caboto's voyages that predicted Terra Nova could sustain Brazil wood trees. According to reports written after their return, the Corte Real brothers found "pines and other excellent woods" for shipbuilding. Following these early reports, one Italian map made in 1504, copying an earlier Portuguese chart, depicted Terra Nova as a lush tropical island complete with big green trees (see figure 9). For many Europeans in the very early sixteenth century, it was insular land more than sea that seemed to beckon.[9]

An Iberian Atlantic

As the experiences of navigators like Agramonte and cartographers like Hercules O'Doria indicate, in the very early sixteenth century, European expansion into the western Atlantic basin, including Terra Nova, was driven in large part (though not exclusively) by Spanish and Portuguese actors. In turn, there was an expectation that an island sea like Terra Nova might be incorporated into either or both of these Iberian empires. In this way Terra Nova would be like the Caribbean islands, which already followed this path. This framework helps us make sense of what took place, but also allows us to make comparisons and connections within an Iberian Atlantic by seeing how Terra Nova developed alongside projects in the mid-Atlantic islands and the Caribbean.

It remains fashionable to implicitly divide early European expansion into a southern and a northern branch, one aimed at the Caribbean Sea (and from there the various American mainlands) and the other at what is today Canada. Each narrative has its own cast of quasi-heroic explorers and founders whose actions and personalities have attracted (until recently) disproportionate attention: Colón, Vespucci, de Soto, Cortes, Pizarro in the south, and Caboto, Verrazano, Cartier, Gilbert, and Champlain in the north. This is often framed as an ethno-imperial division as well: a Luso-Spanish southern wing against an Anglo-French northern arc. Such a separation sits well with modern national histories and serves the nationalist-political goal of isolating the history of a perceived Anglo-French North America from a wider Latin American experience. Such a division is deeply misleading. European interaction with the northwest Atlantic, through the creation of major commercial fisheries, was driven in large part by Iberian actors. In this way the history of early Terra Nova from roughly the 1490s to the 1520s mirrored that of the contemporary Caribbean.[10]

Historical research into early Terra Nova has often stressed French and English perspectives. Where the Spanish are addressed, it is overwhelmingly

WATER

in terms of Spanish Basque whaling and fishing from the mid-century onward. Portuguese activity has not received much attention beyond the work
of Darlene Abreu-Ferreira, though as she points out this is partly because of
the limited archival material. I am asking for a more balanced perspective
that acknowledges an early Spanish and Portuguese importance to the European occupation of the northwest Atlantic, concurrent with their efforts in
the Caribbean and Brazil. This pairs well with concurrent efforts by Carib-
beanists to put the French and other non-Spanish European powers back
into Caribbean history. Some years ago, Ernesto Bassi wrote of the potential
for understanding Atlantic history as an essentially Spanish system and experience. His call to "embrace the Atlantic from Spanish American shores"
can apply to Caribbean islands but also to Spanish-dominated fishing ports
in La Gran Baya or Cape Breton before 1600. In adopting this approach to
the study of the early sixteenth century, of putting the Iberian back in
both Terra Nova and the Caribbean, we can begin to bridge the north-south
historiographical divides.[11]

Spanish and Portuguese state-backed exploration in the greater Caribbean
is well documented, but there were northern analogues. Though generations
of scholars have given pride of place to the Venetian Zuan Caboto and English claims to discovering Terra Nova, of greater significance were the actions
of the Portuguese-backed Corte Real brothers and several Azorean mariners
employed by English merchants. In 1500 Gaspar and Miguel Corte Real,
members of an Azorean family long associated with trade and exploration in
the Atlantic, made an extensive survey of the northwest Atlantic, including
the coast of Greenland, Labrador, and Newfoundland island. The northwest
Atlantic experienced a kind of double discovery, with Caboto bringing news
to England (where it was soon passed on to Spain and Italy) and the Corte
Reals bringing more concrete information to Portugal (where it was passed to
Spain, Italy, Germany, and elsewhere). In the 1520s these early efforts were
followed by exploratory voyages led by Estavão Gomes (sailing for Castile)
and João Fagundes (sailing for Portugal). As a consequence, most sixteenth-
century cartographers, geographers, and state actors understood Terra Nova
to have been "discovered" by the Portuguese, often giving full credit on maps
and in writings to the Corte Real brothers.[12]

This is not to say that only Spanish and Portuguese navigators and states were active at Terra Nova in the first few decades of the sixteenth century. Far from it—we know that Breton, Norman, English, and other voyagers were visiting well before the 1540s. A set of Norman voyages around 1508–9 brought back important information (and possibly captives), while as early as 1517 English adventurers were advocating for outright settlement. In the early 1520s France would establish the physical relationship between Terra Nova and the North American continent. Yet the Iberians had an outsized impact in three important ways. First, Iberian exploits in the fifteenth century influenced wider European thought, cartography, and approaches to colonization on islands like Newfoundland and Cape Breton. We have just seen some of that legacy in examples like O'Doria's map, or the prevalence of Luso-Spanish place-names in Terra Nova (Cabo Raso, La Gran Baya). Second, Spanish and Portuguese maritime communities were among the most active navigators and settlers in the crucial first few decades of the sixteenth century. English adventurers and state actors occasionally proposed settlement schemes, but Spain attempted settlement in 1511, and the Portuguese actually achieved it in the 1520s, as described below. This took place even as Portuguese and Spanish fishworkers maintained a strong presence at Terra Nova throughout the century. Even if they never dominated, they were an early and continual presence.

Third, the two Iberian crowns and their would-be settlers most explicitly connected their experience in the mid-Atlantic to the potential exploitation of islands in the northwest. In the year 1499 the king of Portugal granted a series of letters patent to João Fernandes, who would go on to discover Labrador. The crown rewarded Fernandes for his "effort to seek out and discover at his own expense some islands lying in our territory" by granting him "the governorship of any island or islands, either inhabited or uninhabited, which he may discover and find anew, and this with the same revenues, honours, profits and advantages we have granted to the governors of our islands of Madeira and the others." In the eyes of the Portuguese crown, Terra Nova was to become the Madeira of the north. When Gaspar Corte Real returned from his voyage in 1501, he reported that "he will be able to secure without difficulty and in a short time a very large quantity of timber for making masts and ships' yards, and plenty of men-slaves, fit for every kind of labour, inasmuch as they say that this land is very well populated and full of pines and other excellent woods." What attracted Corte Real's attention was the presence of terrestrial resources, in this case hardwood trees, and the prospect of slaves. This represents an attempt to fit Terra Nova into the southern Atlantic model of conquest and exploitation that emphasized the use of land, especially on islands. These different records suggest that during the first two decades after the discovery of islands in the northwest Atlantic a conscious effort was made by navigators to replicate the successful model of island-based expansion that had been pioneered in the south Atlantic.[13]

Yet attempts to model the far North Atlantic on the emerging Iberian Atlantic swiftly proved untenable in the face of the ecological and climatological realities on the ground. Though several attempts were made to settle the northwest Atlantic, Europeans repeatedly found the temperatures too cold, the soil too barren, and the region too sparsely populated to make settlement practicable. European settlers throughout the sixteenth century had difficulty overcoming Terra Nova's climatic and seasonal barriers, and indeed seem to have been deeply confused as to why a region that was on the same latitude as southern France experienced such dreadful winters. A century after these early voyages the English promoter John Mason was still complaining of Terra Nova that "it is thus cold in the winter season by accidental means, contrary to the natural position of [Terra Nova] on the sphere." How dare the island not be as warm as they wanted! But Terra Nova was not Madeira, and certainly not Española, Europeans quickly discovered.[14]

This lesson was learned the hard way through the most overt attempt by the Iberian crowns to settle the northwest Atlantic. According to surviving royal letters and later writers, in 1520 an expedition was organized by João Alvarez Fagundes to plant a Portuguese settlement in the northwest Atlantic. Having already explored the region in previous years, he was now tasked by the king of Portugal to explore and lay claim to whatever islands and lands he could find. Most important, the royal letters patent specify the terms by which Fagundes could exercise power: "which lands and islands we give and grant him [Fagundes] the governorship in the same form and manner that we have granted the governorship of our islands of Madeira and the rest." It appears that Fagundes promptly acted on his grant and tried to establish a settlement in the areas he claimed to have discovered, possibly near Cape Breton. Thus for a moment in the 1520s, the Portuguese maintained a settlement in Terra Nova.[15]

But only briefly. Previous experience in the Azores and Madeira, then in Africa, Brazil, and India, showed the Portuguese that permanent outposts were crucial to developing economic interests. Not so, as Fagundes and his settlers were discovering, in the northwest Atlantic. Many a fishing vessel simply bypassed Fagundes and his settlers. For a few years the settlers struggled on, failing to capitalize on the emerging fishing industry, trapped ashore for the long winters, slowly succumbing to irrelevance in a place that turned out to be very different from Madeira. The fate of the Portuguese settlement is not known, but some clues from French-language sources suggest that it did not last long. In his important 1550s sailing rutter called the *Voyage avantureux*, the Saintongois mariner Jean Alfonse remarked: "At one point the Portuguese had wished to settle the land surrounded by shoals, but the men of the land caused them to fail in their enterprise, and killed all those who came there." A poem by Jehan Mallart, based on Alfonse, is even more to the point in its rhyming couplet: "Les portugays l'ont quelque foys peuplée / Mais ceulx de l'isle ont ceste gens tuée [The Portuguese once tried to settle there / But those of the island killed them]." Both authors are vague about who "the men of the land" might be, but it likely refers to Mi'kmaq communities. A fundamental misreading of the environment and Indigenous communities had ended the first multi-year European settlement in North America.[16]

Atlantic Colonies

Even if Fagundes's settlement (or Agramonte's or that of any other would-be settler) had somehow succeeded, the nature of colonization in the Americas was about to radically change. In 1521 Hernán Cortés succeeded in taking the city of Tenochtitlán; suddenly, the potential for conquest and settlement in the Mesoamerican mainland presented itself to the Spanish and their rivals.

In the 1530s Spain would add the Andes, and Portuguese settlement in Brazil intensified. Even when the French invested in exploration and colonization projects in the north led by Jacques Cartier, their focus was on bypassing Terra Nova and heading for the mainland. The sieur de Roberval's settlement of 1541–43 was located near present-day Québec, not in Terra Nova, closer to Saint Lawrence Iroquoian communities. The settlement seems to have been deliberately designed to bypass the fishery of Terra Nova and to find access to potential Indigenous settlements deeper in the heart of North America. After 1521 the quest was on for a northern complement to the settled peoples and riches of Spanish America, for *lugar* rather than islands.[17]

With hindsight, we can see that the 1520s were a kind of inflection point in the settlement of the Americas. Spanish involvement in Mesomaerica and beyond set a new template for colonization that seemed far more alluring. The Caribbean began its shift from the center of colonial activity to a logistical appendage to activity on the mainland. Spanish forays into Florida and the Carolinas in the early 1520s were never followed up, and Gomes's voyage up the east coast of North America was an isolated affair. Europe was soon flooded with printed materials about the mainland Americas; islands were increasingly relegated to a mental backwater. This is not to posit a set of counterfactuals about the potential for an imperial northwest Atlantic. Rather, it is meant to try to take seriously and explain the behavior of Europeans in the first two decades of the sixteenth century. Looking forward in time from 1511, it was not obvious that Terra Nova wouldn't allow for permanent settlement or agriculture. Agramonte, Fagundes, and others thought they were doing the smart thing. We should not dismiss these early attempts as foolish, but rather as reflecting widely held beliefs and experiences about the nature of the Atlantic basin.

I also think that we must read subsequent European attitudes toward and actions in the northwest Atlantic as taking place in the shadow of this early infatuation with and then rejection of island worlds. Nothing else really makes sense without it. The failure to plant permanent settlements in the northwest Atlantic was potentially the single most important feature of European activity at Terra Nova in the sixteenth century. The consequences of this absence run throughout this book, and touch upon every level of the fishery. The repeated failure of empire in the northwest Atlantic likewise has its roots in these early attempts and their collapse in the 1520s. The Spanish and Portuguese crowns were the only European states with anywhere near the capabilities to incorporate the northwest Atlantic into a wider imperial system in the early to mid-sixteenth century. Half-hearted English and French voyages of exploration or settlement cropped up every now and then, but serious attempts to colonize Terra Nova did not return until much later in the century.

Why was this? I suspect that the failure of colonization in the early sixteenth century had more subtle repercussions in the European mind than we can imagine. Europeans, we have seen, brought strong preconceived notions about the nature of islands and insular environments to Terra Nova. Reality proved them wrong. Plans were foiled, people died. The result was a kind of denial about the northwest Atlantic on the part of many Europeans. Having been burned, the Iberian empires responded by turning their backs on the northwest Atlantic. To consider a telling example, Iberian maps for several decades after 1520 either did not show islands in the northwest Atlantic or minimized them. Diogo Ribeiro's important 1529 map shows an unbroken coast in the northwest Atlantic devoid of islands. Lopo Homen's celebrated 1554 map shrinks Newfoundland into a tiny set of islands next to a large mainland, and leaves open whether Cape Breton is an island or a large peninsula. Even Alonzo de Santa Cruz's otherwise thorough *Isolario general de todos las islas del mundo*, which includes a section on Terra Nova, shows a remarkably smooth and straight coastline (see figure 11). He quite literally presents an islandless map in his island book. Maybe cartographic thinking had changed. Or maybe there is a degree of petulance in the post-1520s Iberian generation's mental geography of the northwest Atlantic: if Newfoundland was going to be the wrong kind of island, then it didn't get to be an island at all. It would not be until much later in the century, by the time that Hercules O'Doria was making his colorful map in a new wave of imperial expansion, that Spain was willing to see Terra Nova as a world of islands again.[18]

If Fagundes and his fellow navigators had found the northwest Atlantic singularly unsuited to their island-centric approaches, the anonymous

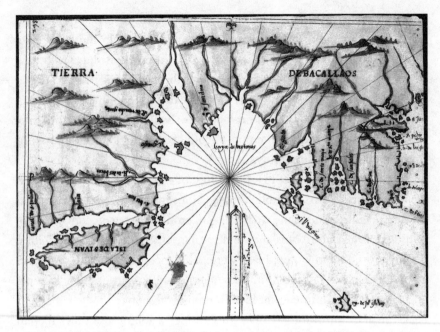

Figure 11. Terra Nova without Newfoundland Island: "Tierra de Bacallaos" in Alonzo de Santa Cruz's *Isolario general*. (Courtesy of the World Digital Library.)

fishworkers who lurked in the background of this story were not dissuaded from visiting the region. Much as Agramonte, Fagundes, and O'Doria had brought the baggage of Atlantic experience to the island worlds of Terra Nova, so too would fishworkers bring the legacy of maritime labor in the eastern Atlantic to this new expansion of Europe's fishing frontier.

FIVE

Frontiers

In the depths of the winter of 1514, the monks of Beauport, a small monastic community hugging the rugged north coast of Brittany, had reached
a breaking point. In recent years war had swept northwest Europe, English
rovers had pillaged the coastline during the summer, and successive seasons
had proved to be colder and wetter than normal. Yet instead of venting
themselves on war and weather, the monks' ire was directed against a group
of "wicked men" who inhabited the nearby Île-de-Bréhat. The abbey of
Beauport claimed control over the island and its residents, and the monks
were increasingly frustrated by the recalcitrant behavior of these "wicked
men from the said island who exceed the age of eighteen years and who
fish on the ocean using rods, nets or other methods to take fish, whatever
sort of fish they can, such as conger eels, cod, hake as well as other fish,
in whatever places they can, such as the coast of Brittany, Terra Nova [La
Terre Neuffve] and Iceland, among others." The core of the dispute was
over the payment of tithes by the residents. But the complaint made clear
their frustration with the practice of Bréhat fishworkers sailing to distant
waters, including what they called Terra Nova, to catch fish. The document is remarkable both for its extremely early date and for the fact that
it indicates that the otherwise obscure Île-de-Bréhat, a tiny island port in a
sea-swept corner of Brittany, was at the leading edge of European expansion
into the Atlantic basin. Indeed, we know that as early as the summer of 1508
the master Jacques de Ruffosse of this same Bréhat sailed a ship called *La*

bonne avanture to Terra Nova. Ruffosse had outfitted and financed his ship by making a deal with merchants in Rouen, Normandy, who later brought suit against him after he refused to honor the terms of their deal. Having paid 352 *livres*[1] to outfit the ship, the Rouennais merchants were upset that Ruffosse sailed home to his native "harbour of Bréhat in Brittany" instead of Honfleur as agreed. The Norman merchants may have sympathized with the monks of Beauport as to the trustworthiness of the people of Bréhat.[2]

Ruffosse and his fellow "wicked" mariners were participating in a project far greater than they or their monastic overlords would have appreciated, and one that was more important than just the creation of a fishery at Terra Nova in the northwest Atlantic. Tellingly, in their 1514 complaint the Beauport monks describe the fishworkers as visiting many different places, from the coastal fisheries of Brittany to the Americas, from Iceland to unnamed waters ("among others"). The men of Bréhat ranged widely in pursuit of their catch, a fact that should remind us that Terra Nova did not emerge in a vacuum but rather as part of a network of fisheries and food-production enterprises in the Atlantic basin. The creation of these fisheries long predated the first encounters with Terra Nova, compelling us to reach back into the fifteenth century to find the origins of European activity in the northwest Atlantic. When we do so, we can see that such voyages changed the European relation to, and role within, the ecology of the Atlantic basin. A fish was a battery, a source of energy that could power a human body and human labor. That energy was stored in the flesh and fat of seafish as calories, unleashed through the cooking and eating processes. Often this energy was used indirectly, in the form of oils that were burned to light homes or to lubricate industrial equipment. Fisheries, then, formed a kind of floating energy frontier.

This chapter reconstructs and contextualizes the rapid expansion of commercial oceanic fishing in the fifteenth and sixteenth centuries. The environmental scholar Jason Moore has argued for the role of a resource frontier as the driving force behind European colonial and capitalistic expansion from the fifteenth century on. In expanding their resource frontier, Europeans incorporated new biomes into their world-ecology. As Moore has summarized: "With the rise of capitalism, varied and heretofore largely isolated local bun-

dles of socio-ecological relations were incorporated into—at the same moment becoming constituting agents of—capitalism as ecological regime. The
geography of the commodity frontier, driven forward by the time-discipline of
an emergent capitalist order and the contradictions of its peculiar socializa-
tion of nature, was fundamentally globalizing. Hence the hyphen [in world-
ecology]: we are talking not necessarily about the ecology of the world
(although this is in fact the case today) but, rather, a world-ecology." I am trying to add fish—as both food and fuel—back into that model. Europeans'
world-ecology was a wet one, and it was on the seas of the eastern Atlantic that
they were able to achieve early and enduring success.[3]

Facing the Frayed Atlantic Edge

The Ocean Sea meant food, which meant life, for countless thousands of
Europeans along its northeast rim, as for the millions of people who lived
around its many shores. As both ecologists and anthropologists have made
clear, coastal environments are among the most productive and beneficial
ecological niches humans can inhabit. They possess several key benefits, including high resource biomass, resource diversity, environmental stability,
and the capability of sustaining high population densities. The ocean demonstrates "the generosity of nature that manifests itself here in all its do-
mains: animal, vegetable, mineral." The modern conception of shorelines
as sites of recreation obscures this deeper truth: that we have always lived,
worked, and thrived in the semi-aquatic and tempestuous spaces where
saltwater meets land.[4]

This should lead us to acknowledge that Europe's long and ragged Atlantic coastline was more populated and important to human survival strategies than it is today. Pre-industrial Europeans hugged the water, living in
communities perched on the ocean and its rivers, their faces to sea. These
are the essential observations made first by Barry Cunliffe in *Facing the Atlantic*, and recently reexplored by David Gange in *The Frayed Atlantic
Edge*. As Gange has put it, "Metropolitan culture tends to take today's geography for granted, despite the fact that the British Isles were turned inside
out by roads and rail. . . . Coasts and islands carry very different meanings

than they once possessed: associations with remoteness and emptiness have replaced links with commerce and communication." In the fifteenth and sixteenth centuries the Atlantic Ocean was central, not peripheral, to how societies organized themselves. It should not be surprising, then, that these communities looked first to the water to solve their food problems.[5]

As Helen Rozwadowski reminds us, while the oceans hold rich and varied biological resources, these are distributed unevenly. Vast stretches of the Atlantic Ocean were unfit for systematic fishing, and "patchiness is a general characteristic of the ocean, as of land." Several of the largest pockets had already been integrated into European food systems by the end of the fourteenth century, including the North Sea, Iceland, the Irish Sea, the Norwegian Sea, and the Baltic. Modern marine biologists often term such concentrations large marine ecosystems (LMEs). The great project of European mariners in the sixteenth century would be to exploit and link these different zones of biodiversity. Almost all of these LMEs had been systematically exploited by local communities long before the fifteenth century. European mariners nonetheless constructed and imposed commercial fisheries on top of these systems, connecting them to the European metropole. In the fifteenth century the coastal LMEs of northwest Africa and the mid-Atlantic islands were added to this network. By 1550 Europeans had added the various pockets of the northwest Atlantic, along with those of the Caribbean and Brazil.[6]

Thus did communities like Bréhat hug the coast of Brittany, adapting themselves to take advantage of the pockets of abundance both close at hand and many leagues away. To harvest the plenty of the sea, coastal communities made use of the most advanced technology of their age. The *navires, naos*, ships, dogger boats, carracks, and caravels of the fifteenth and sixteenth centuries were finely tuned machines that could capture the wind and move with minimal friction through water, the one space in the premodern world that allowed machines, rather than living organisms, to harness nonorganic energy to move over long distances at speed. From Bréhat in northern Brittany it was a one-month voyage to Terra Nova. That same amount of time could take a Breton mariner to the Mediterranean for olive oil and wine, or to Morocco for sardines, or far up the Baltic Sea for fish and wheat. For the starving citizens of Lisbon, the Rio do Ouro or Morocco was potentially closer than the farms of central Iberia. The sea gave both coastal and metropolitan communities access to far-flung maritime food resources in a way that erased distance and cost. For European populations clustered along shorelines and waterways, the Atlantic Ocean was often a closer source of food than fertile farmlands.[7]

Even so, the ways in which northeast Atlantic societies exploited marine resources have changed over time in significant ways. Archaeologists have amassed evidence pointing to a seismic change in fish-consumption patterns around the year AD 1000, cheekily termed the "Fish Event Horizon." This primarily affected northwest Europe, especially around the North Sea, and was marked by a significant increase in the consumption and exchange of sea fish. As populations rose from the tenth century onward across western Eurasia, there was a concurrent increase in freshwater fish consumption. This would be the golden age of aquaculture, as fishponds came to dot the landscape, while rivers and lakes were systematically exploited in a process described at length by the historian Richard Hoffmann. Commercial oceanic fishing was slower to emerge, but once begun picked up pace inexorably. Maryanne Kowaleski has argued that commercial fishing in southwest England, centered on the Irish Sea, intensified as early as the fourteenth century and continued well into the sixteenth. The coastal herring fisheries in eastern England on the North Sea were certainly active before the fifteenth century, but joined the general commercialization of herring that took off after 1450. Various Baltic fisheries, especially for herring, enjoyed a brief moment of intensive activity in the fourteenth and fifteenth centuries before temporarily collapsing, while Norwegian coastal fisheries provided a steady if small stream of dried codfish to European markets. Before the fifteenth century, then, many consumers in northern and western Europe had come to expect access to either fresh or preserved fish, in a process Hoffmann has reconstructed in detail. In turn, the legal and technical groundwork had been established for the exploitation and, in some cases, careful management of marine resources. In the fifteenth century a second major change in seafood consumption would take place, one that brought more of the Atlantic Ocean into European consumers' orbit.[8]

It is undeniably the case that the Atlantic of the fifteenth century had much greater biological resources and biodiversity than it does today. Industrial fishing, climate change, and global pollution had not yet remade sea life. There were localized problems of overfishing, to be sure, even by the fifteenth century. From the turn of the second millennium onward, the North Sea and Baltic Sea were both systematically fished by nearby communities using sophisticated and disruptive methods. The Mediterranean had been scoured for fish and other aquatic resources for centuries, and had reached the limits of sustainable exploitation. Yet in most of the Atlantic Ocean fish were bigger, more numerous, and more varied. Consumers expected their fish to be big; in sixteenth-century Southampton, port officials reckoned any codfish under two feet in length was too small and had to be sold two for one. Marine biologists have attempted to reconstruct fish stocks in the pre-industrial northwest Atlantic. For this period we can use an estimate of 3 million tons of codfish, or 8.2 tons per square kilometer. By contrast, in the 1990s the biomass was under 1 ton per square kilometer. One estimate suggests that, toward the end of the sixteenth century, fishworkers at Terra Nova were catching and processing up to 75,000 tons annually—an impressive catch, but only a fraction (around 2.5 percent) of the total biomass. In the fifteenth century the Mare Oceanum, that boundless sea west of Europe, held the promise of endless exploitation and opportunities for food.[9]

In this light, we can better appreciate the behavior of the mariners of Bréhat. Instead of living at the fringes of the European landmass, we can see them as ideally perched upon the edge of the vast and valuable expanse of the Atlantic Ocean. Their far-ranging fishing voyages targeted select large marine ecosystems, pockets of biomass that were far richer than they appear today. They built upon five centuries of change, but offered a greater scale of intensity and geographic scope.

An Atlantic Energy Crisis

At the heart of fifteenth- and sixteenth-century European expansion was a problem of energy. The multitude of social and economic transformations within Europe required tremendous amounts of work, primarily done by humans. Each ship that departed a European port required dozens if not hundreds of mariners to operate it; urban growth in coastal cities produced thousands of new mouths to feed; agricultural expansion was made possible by human and animal labor; and the ecological transformation that underlay the new colonies required human and animal labor (often coerced) to effect new kinds of terraforming. The energy to fuel this work had to be provided by food, a problem that stretched the very limits of European agricultural systems and the weak states they sustained. This was made considerably harder by increased cycles of political upheaval and violence, and the climate catastrophe of the Spörer Minimum (a short period of falling temperatures and poor weather). Colonization only made things worse: the settlement of the Atlantic islands, the establishment of trade posts in West Africa, the increased southbound trade out of the Tagus-Guadalquivir deltas, and ultimately the dispatching of ships to the Caribbean all required fish to fuel mariners.

The availability of food resources in the Atlantic basin was a pressing concern during Europe's bleak fifteenth century. The preceding century had experienced outright catastrophe in the form of plague and famine, while subsequent generations experienced rapid and remarkable socioeconomic change. But in between the lives of fifteenth-century Europeans were marked by widespread dearth, violence, political instability, and uncertainty—what Emmanuel Le Roy Ladurie has described as the "low-water mark of a Society." Lisbon, for instance, was a city always eager for new sources of food, and a metropole that had considerable difficulty exporting its wheat to far-flung settlements. "In this country [Lisbon] there is but little corn," wrote the English merchant-geographer Roger Barlow, but "[it] is a good city and the greatest that is in Portugal." Food scarcity was a chronic problem in the city; Lisbon's population was highly dependent on imports from across Europe and the Mediterranean. In 1531 the Castilian ambassador in Lisbon noted that the Portuguese were desperately importing wheat from Sicily because they couldn't find it anywhere else, at the same time smugly commenting that this was ("graçias a Dios") not a problem for the Castilians. Imports were nonetheless unreliable, so throughout the fifteenth and early sixteenth centuries Portuguese merchants and authorities looked far and wide for sources of bulk staple foods. Similar strategies would be true of many other Euro-Mediterranean cities.[10]

These issues were shaped by the inherent limits of European agriculture. Historians have long observed that the entire demographic edifice of western Europe was built on a cereal-production system that rarely produced returns of three to five kernels of wheat for every one sowed. In the absence of technical improvements the only way to increase production was to increase the amount of land under cultivation, a time-consuming and difficult process. Peasant agriculture favored intensive regimes of animal husbandry, working the land with plow and fertilizer, and fickle crops like wheat. It did not take much to push farms into crisis. Demographic collapse and war had disrupted the market integration achieved in the late thirteenth century, and shipping food over distances was difficult and expensive. Most cereals and meats, therefore, had to be produced locally, making communities vulnerable to local disruptions to production through war or weather events.[11]

Such structural issues with food production were only part of the problem. From roughly 1450 to 1530 the Northern Hemisphere experienced a climate event known as the Spörer Minimum. Other climate events, especially the Maunder Minimum and Grindelwald Fluctuation, have attracted far more attention from climate historians. Yet according to current climate reconstructions, the Spörer Minimum of the late fifteenth century was marked by an extremely abrupt and precipitous fall in average temperatures. In the long history of the Little Ice Age it was one of the most disruptive periods to weather stability in the Northern Hemisphere. The sudden plunge in temperatures around 1450, and the cold, wet weather caused by a negative North Atlantic Oscillation, would have contributed to lower agricultural yields in lands north and west of the Mediterranean. The speed of this shift is its most notable feature, and the Spörer Minimum would have come as less of a slow decline in conditions than a sudden shock. As M. G. Ogurtsov has put it, "The Spoerer Minimum was not only longer, but also deeper than the [better known] Maunder Minimum." This downturn would have added pressure to an already difficult food-supply system, made worse by the rise in inter-dynastic conflict across Europe from 1490 to 1530. Coastal and freshwater fisheries may have succumbed to the environmental pressures of colder weather, though offshore oceanic fishing grounds would largely have been unaffected. The inherent limitations in European agriculture, compounded by climate fluctuations, created an energy crisis in Europe and the Mediterranean.[12]

It is tempting to draw a neat line between climate change and fishing expansion. The Spörer Minimum chronologically overlaps with the long period of maritime expansion and the formation of new fisheries. Unlike the Fish Event Horizon of the tenth to twelfth centuries that took place during the warm and stable Medieval Climate Anomaly, the growth of commercial fishing in the fifteenth and sixteenth centuries occurred as northern temperatures were steadily cooling. The period of climate instability in the mid-fifteenth century may have made access to certain northern and southern fishing grounds more attractive: the waters around Iceland would have been warmer, as would those around the mid-Atlantic coasts of Africa. Sam White has argued that the 1530s, and again toward the end of the century, were potentially opportune moments for fishing in the northwest Atlantic due to climate fluctuations. Nonetheless, as Dagomar Degroot has painstakingly demonstrated, drawing direct correlation between climate anomalies and the behavior of historical actors is a difficult and often misleading process. Moreover, marine biologists and climate scientists have faced difficulty understanding the relationship between climate and North Atlantic fish stocks. The consequences of temperature change on a particular species or community are often highly localized, and it has proved difficult to correlate predictions with archaeological evidence. As a result, we must be carefully circumspect about drawing a neat line between climate change and the rise of a new fishing regime. It is likely that the Spörer Minimum put pressure on existing food supplies, driving demand for more intensive maritime exploitation, but it does not necessarily follow that this directly opened up or encouraged fishing in the Atlantic Ocean.[13]

The troubles and climate disruption of the fifteenth century, and the limits of European agriculture, became more acute as most of the European continent entered a period of sustained population growth around 1500.

The reasons for such growth were complex, but in many ways the crises of the fifteenth century gave room and impetus for the growth of the following century. There was more land to put under the plow, more room to establish new settlements, and in general a pressure to recover the lost population of the post-plague era. In some regions populations doubled across the century, but in most places 40–60 percent growth was more typical. Cities in particular grew quickly, both generating their own population and absorbing rural families as the century wore on. Rouen, that crucial center of the Terra Nova trade, grew from forty thousand to sixty thousand souls between 1500 and 1600, a 50 percent gain despite several rounds of brutal wars passing through its neighborhood. For our purposes, this population growth only increased the incentives and even the pressure to make use of marine resources. Agricultural techniques and productivity did not improve noticeably even as populations were increasing, leading to more mouths to feed and the same limits on the European capability to feed them.[14]

Against this backdrop of disruption, population growth, harsh weather, and food insecurity, communities like Bréhat colonized the coastal shelves of the eastern Atlantic basin in search of food and fuel. Europeans had always fished, but the fifteenth century saw a turn to much more intensive, systematic, and widespread commercial fishing operations. Many previously existing commercial coastal and oceanic fisheries were fished more intensively by more ships than ever before, and in some cases entirely new fisheries were created. Some historians have begun to call this the "Atlantic Fish Revolution," an apt name for a major shift in how humans produced seafood. I disagree with these scholars only in that I think the revolution was a bit earlier (pre-1500) and more widespread (beyond northern cod and herring) than we often recognize. Although operations off the American coasts have attracted considerable attention, the majority of this expansion took place in the eastern Atlantic. From the edges of the Arctic to the deserts of Africa, the sea became a patchwork of floating fishing stations.[15]

In an age before fossil fuels, human societies still needed oil. Oils from animals and plants were extensively used for industrial purposes in the fifteenth and sixteenth centuries: as lubricants in such machinery as existed and burned in lamps for light. Oil was an essential ingredient in the woolen cloth industry, used to prepare the wool for spinning. Yet Europe in the fifteenth and sixteenth centuries was often at a loss for fuel, much as it was for food. There were few vegetal sources of fuel, and producing them required diverting land and labor away from food. As was the case for calories and protein, Europeans would turn to the sea to solve this shortfall. In both mammals and fish it is the coldness of the water that compels the development of fat, and that fat produces oil in abundance. The oil in fish and mammal fat—that much-reviled source of the "fishy" smell and taste—can be rendered into a yellowish, viscous liquid through heat processing. This liquid was called train oil by sixteenth-century English sources, a blanket term for any oil refined from marine animals, though French and Spanish sources tended to specify the animal of origin: *huile de balleine* (whale oil), *aceite de ballena* (whale oil), *huile de morue* (cod oil), *azeite de taratuga* (sea turtle oil). When fifteenth- and sixteenth-century crews caught fish they did not let this opportunity go to waste, and countless contracts and port records show that they extracted oil and brought it to market along with the salted, preserved flesh of their catch. Fishworkers set aside cod livers when processing their fish, letting them render in vats in the sun to produce train oil. One Basque involved in an English lawsuit in 1597 noted that his ship at Terra Nova caught 120,000 fish, which produced thirty-six hogsheads (a large barrel of 60–120 gallons) of train oil over a summer season. This would suggest one barrel for every three thousand cod caught. At Labrador and in northern Spain Basque whalers built ovens to boil and render whale blubber, a technique likewise applied to walrus and seal fat. Seal oil was probably produced along the coast of northwest Africa from the fifteenth century on, and later at Terra Nova. Oil production was thus integral to fishing, an essential by-product, if not an outright adjacent industrial enterprise. Fishworkers did not merely feed the hungry cities of Europe and the Mediterranean, they kept them warm and running smoothly.[16]

What drove fishworkers to more intensively exploit the Ocean Sea for food and fuel? Some historians, especially Jeffrey Bolster, have argued that this was a response to crisis within European waters. His opening chapter, "Depleted European Seas and the Discovery of America," sets the tone for an argument that "while it is impossible to state with any certainty whether or not most European sea fish stocks were being affected, it is clear that the system as a whole had been significantly degraded by 1500." If that is true, this crisis would set up a simple and satisfying narrative: European food production was faltering, Terra Nova appeared suddenly as a solution, and so transatlantic fishing grew rapidly. Such a crisis-centric argument has developed only since the collapse of the modern Newfoundland fishery in the 1990s. In our present age of fisheries collapse and oceanic turmoil, this view of an Atlantic crisis seems intuitive and familiar, and many historians have followed Bolster's lead.[17]

Yet I do not think that there was a marine crisis that would adequately explain the rise of a new fishing regime. Too much of the surviving evidence comes from coastal and freshwater sites, skewing our perception of crisis. Declines and collapses at one site, especially a coastal one, were often due to localized conditions and rarely indicate a much wider problem. Fish produced in coastal fisheries were often meant for local consumption, being rarely preserved, and were unsuited for mass export. Bolster acknowledges this problem, pointing out that herring fisheries were expanding, but still uses coastal evidence to argue for a more widespread change in fishing. Likewise, historians have focused too much on evidence from northern Europe, especially around the North Sea basin. If we concentrate too much on the British Isles and North Sea, we miss out on the bigger picture of growth. In other words, we must consider both the localness of fishing and the overall scale and scope of European operations. It may indeed be that in some places in the fifteenth century coastal, riverine, and freshwater fisheries hit their limits of usefulness. Yet we don't see strong evidence of fish consumption declining—instead, ocean fisheries picked up the slack. Quantitative work that would illuminate this issue has been the focus of the Norfish project, featuring a team of international fisheries scholars who have tried to quantify and analyze centuries of fishing in the North Atlantic using available data. Their efforts have underlined the unparalleled expansion of cod and herring fishing after 1450. As the project makes clear, growth took place in all oceanic fisheries, not just the northwest Atlantic, from the fifteenth century onward. Herring fishing in the North Sea would not peak until far into the seventeenth century. Likewise, Arnved Nedkvitne has shown that the price of dried codfish plummeted during the last half of the fifteenth century—before ships even reached Terra Nova—at Bergen and London, falling by over half in the former city. Similar evidence from English monasteries at the turn of the sixteenth century shows that monks were eating truly prodigious quantities of seafood, the majority of it preserved fish, all of it from the eastern Atlantic. By the 1490s the Castilians and Portuguese were even fighting over access to lucrative African fisheries, and the English and Danish crowns were locked in an endless debate over who got to fish the bountiful Icelandic waters. Such indication of fish consumption and competition all predate the development of Terra Nova as a source of fish, indicating that the commercial fisheries of the eastern Atlantic were having an impact before 1500.[18]

Because modern scholars take the meaning of Terra Nova (with the stress on *nova*) or New-found-lands at face value, they all too often overemphasize the newness of this maritime space in the minds of European mariners. For decades historians have latched onto the extravagant descriptions of a handful of (mostly English) colonizers, explorers, and promoters who portrayed the novelty and abundance of the new-found-lands. In so doing, they consciously or unconsciously foreground the new—new world, new riches, new opportunities, new-found-lands. Some have gone so far as to suggest that Terra Nova "evoked the mythic origins of a virgin territory, exempted from original sin. . . . The term expressed the hope of attainment of the utopia of the terrestrial paradise." It is a wonderfully poetic image in which the island and waters of Terra Nova rise out of the Atlantic like a gift from heaven, providing opportunity and easy riches to any who crossed the Ocean Sea. In truth, most mariners were less than impressed with Terra Nova. A cold and dangerous place, it was to be briefly visited during the warm months and then left for the rest of the year. The English, who first reported on the abundance of fish and brought back the first catches, were in fact the last community to engage systematically with the sixteenth-century fishery. The English fishing fleet did not grow beyond a few dozen ships to become a serious competitor at Terra Nova until after the 1570s, a source of much complaining from advocates like Anthony Parkhurst. The *gran capitano* who wrote about visiting the fishery in Giovanni Ramusio's famous collection of navigational essays gave a dry, practical description of Terra Nova that offered no image of novelty or abundance. The navigator and author Jean Alfonse compared the region to Spain rather than Eden, commenting only that it had "many fisheries." The waters of the northwest Atlantic held vast stores of fish, it is true. But so did those of Iceland, the North Sea, and countless other corners of the ocean. Off the Rio do Ouro in Saharan Africa, according to one Portuguese mariner, one could catch enough fish to fill a ship in only four hours of handlining. The Venetian merchant Alessandro Magno marveled in his travelogue at how much fish was to be had along the coast of Spain in the 1560s, describing the waters in the glowing terms we normally associate with Terra Nova. The North Sea's herring fishery was known as the "Golden Mountain" to the Dutch by the 1570s. As late as the 1590s, an English military manual was recommending that soldiers be fed "shotland [Shetland] cod" (rated at a "stockfish and a half") to ensure they stayed strong and fit—nearly a century after the rise of the Terra Nova fishery. The northwest Atlantic was not always as *nova* as modern historians assume.[19]

It is therefore hard to reconcile the image of ecological crisis put forward by Bolster and others with the consistent sixteenth-century descriptions of massive fisheries and abundant catches. Well after the founding of a commercial fishery at Terra Nova, thousands of European mariners still preferred the eastern Atlantic. Rather, Terra Nova was part of a more widespread and successful response to a provisioning crisis within Europe. It was not the sole response, as some historians have it, but instead part of a network of enduring and mutually reinforcing fisheries.

Fishing the Eastern Atlantic

On September 20, 1546, the Basque merchant Antón de Alchacoa received good news while waiting in his home port of Fuenterrabía. His ship the *Nicolasa*, which he had chartered out to two other Basques, Juanicot de Sanzu (from Saint Jean-de-Luz) and Juan Pérez, had just returned from a successful voyage to Terra Nova. A local notary dutifully recorded that payment had been rendered to Alchacoa; the deal was closed out. We might take this as yet another merchant-mariner investing in the Terra Nova fishery, if it were not for the fact that barely two weeks later, on October 3, Alchacoa appears in yet another record. Here we find him outfitting a ship for a voyage not to Terra Nova but to the coasts of Galicia. The intention was to onload a cargo of prized Galician sardines at Muros, Curcubión, or Muxía near A Coruña and carry them back to San Sebastián for sale. Antón de Alchacoa reminds us that as much as we wish to focus on the history of fishing at Terra Nova, for many Europeans there were just as many opportunities to find food and energy close to home.[20]

If in the year 1400 a handful of commercial fisheries clustered around the Baltic, the North Sea, and the Irish Sea, by the time of Caboto and Corte Real the eastern Atlantic was covered by large commercial fishing operations stretching from the edge of the Arctic to the coasts of West Africa (see figure 12). Although each fishery followed its own history and served particular slices of the European population, across the board this expansion was marked by similar patterns: more intensive fishing by more ships; a focus on a narrow range of pelagic species; a focus on preserving fish for export over long distances; and the use of increasingly sophisticated financial and organizational techniques. Fisheries tended to be spaces where multiple harvesting strategies overlapped, along with different kinds of occupation and resource-gathering strategies. One ship might be processing fish for export alongside another that was casually catching fish for provisions, while nearby other crews hunted seals or seabirds. These were both places and operations, sites and systems.

Each fishery had its own history, but together they formed a new network of maritime activity. Some, like Iceland, were transformations of older fisheries. Settled by the Norse during their ninth-century expansion, Iceland was surrounded by icy cold waters rich in codfish and ling, two species well suited to preservation. Importantly, it also lay just a few days' sail from northern European ports. Under pressure from foreign fishing ships and given the precarious position of the island in the middle of the North Atlantic, the Danish crown fought a losing battle across the fifteenth century to preserve exclusive right to control access to Iceland's codfish-rich waters. English fishworkers began sailing to Iceland by at least 1415, when their arrival in force prompted formal complaints from the Danes and a new licensing regime. In 1490 the crowns of

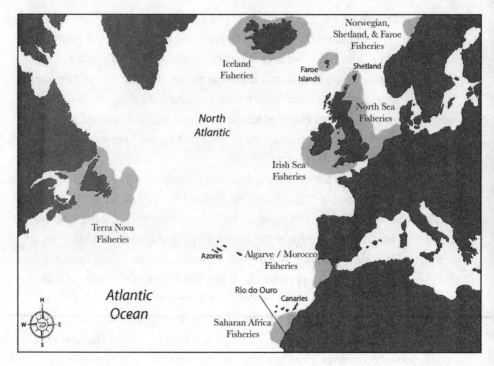

Figure 12. Important European commercial fisheries, mid-sixteenth century. (Prepared by SEH Mapping.)

England and Denmark reached an agreement that permitted English vessels to sail directly to Iceland to fish, so long as they had a license. They were joined by several fleets of ships from Bremen, Lubeck, and Hamburg that sailed with strong Danish backing. By the 1520s almost all the ports of East Anglia were sending ships north to Iceland on a yearly basis. The description by Olaus Magnus in book XXI ("Monstrous Fishes") of his *A Description of the Northern Peoples* offers an engaging picture of the international mid-sixteenth-century Iceland fishery:

> Countless numbers of fish, of a different variety and nature, are caught in Icelandic waters by the inhabitants of that island. . . . The highly-prized fish caught there and known as *marlucz* [cod] by Italians and Spaniards is transported by the Spaniards and Portuguese

even as far as Rome. The season for taking them falls in February, March and April. When these fish are caught they are dried out by the cold winds and in due course arranged in the open fields like piles of firewood. Measured by length in long ells or, as they do in Italy, rods, they are sold in their thousands to German merchants or exchanged for corn, beer, cloth and similar commodities. . . . Its [Iceland's] economy is based on butter and dried fish, an equivalent of richer treasures.[21]

As Magnus's description suggests, by the 1550s Iceland was already viewed by many as a purely extractive colony, one where the food products of butter and fish dominated commerce. It also points to two important features of the Iceland fishery that were paralleled at Terra Nova. First, operations drew mariners from many different ports. Although we tend to associate the fishery with England, there were Hanse German, Danish, Flemish, Dutch, and Scottish fishworkers who visited in large numbers. Second, exchange was part of the fishery, for visiting fishing boats also traded with Icelanders for "corn, beer, cloth and similar commodities." In the sixteenth century, as we will see, the fishery at Terra Nova was marked by sustained exchange with First Nations as an integral part of food production. It is not clear that fishworkers at Terra Nova consciously copied those of Iceland. Rather, Terra Nova fit a similar pattern and mold, building on the more general experience of fishing in the fifteenth century.[22]

The experience at Iceland was repeated in many corners of the eastern Atlantic Ocean. English, Basque, and Breton fishworkers swarmed to the Irish Sea each year to extract all variety of fish. Hake, herring, cod, sardines, and others were carried from the coasts of southern Ireland to cities like Bordeaux, Bilbao, and London. The North Sea was a patchwork of fishing grounds, exploited by Hollander, Zeelander, Flemish, English, Scottish, and German mariners in hundreds of small boats. In some cases mariners ran into legal barriers, like the Anglo-Danish disputes at Iceland. In others, states were powerless to control these far-ranging and multinational operations. There was outright conflict at times, especially during periods of interdynastic warfare, but nothing could stop the surge of European investment in extracting resources from the cold North Sea. The ongoing work of European fisheries historians to quantify the catch of northern fisheries points to rising catches across the sixteenth century.[23]

These fisheries could be quite large, even in comparison to what would take place at Terra Nova. By the 1560s the North Sea herring fleet numbered 700 ships, double the size of the Terra Nova fleet but composed of much smaller craft. Within a century the North Sea would probably be the largest fishing operation on the planet, the "mountain of gold" that underlay Dutch growth. In 1535 an English official reported "600 sail" of fishing ships operated in Ireland and by the 1570s it was reported that 600 "Spanish" fishing ships visited Ireland every year—a fleet again double the size of that at Terra Nova. By the early 1520s English sources reference an "Iceland fleet" that returned each year. In 1528 a count of merchant ships in England was undertaken by the crown, showing that East Anglian towns possessed 150 ships dedicated solely to the Icelandic trade. In the 1590s some 45 ships were still sailing to Iceland each year, constituting a sizable and ongoing English presence. Clearly the commercial fisheries of the fifteenth and sixteenth centuries remained vibrant and productive well to the end of the sixteenth century. For example, analysis of fish bones by archaeologists has shown that when the warship *Mary Rose* sank in the 1540s it had a hold full of codfish from Iceland and Norway, not Terra Nova. Fishing in the eastern Atlantic was robust throughout the long sixteenth century, even as Terra Nova began to take off.[24]

By the late fifteenth century, European mariners were going even farther afield in search of their fish, and many of them were going south. As early as the 1450s observers noted a fishery along the coast of Saharan Africa between Cape Bojador and Arguim Bay. Around that date a Venetian observer wrote, "All along this coast we find a great fishery and no end of diverse and excellent fish." A generation later, a geographer in Lisbon writing around 1507 declared that at the Rio do Ouro (modern-day Dakhla, Western Sahara) there was "a great fishery." He went on to write of the turtle hunts and birds in Arguim Bay, also visited by Portuguese fishworkers. Amerigo Vespucci stopped at the Rio do Ouro en route to the Americas to load up on fish, and Portuguese ships headed to São Tomé took on provisions in the waters where desert met the sea. Of the four great Eastern Boundary Currents, global oceanic systems marked by exceptional fish stocks, two are along the western coast of Africa, including the Canary Current, which gave the Rio do Ouro its wealth of marine life. The coasts here teemed with fish, including small fare such as sardines and bream and larger tuna, which were suitable for preservation and could have been shipped to Iberia. In 1462, for instance, a Portuguese ship under Guomçallo Fernandez encountered what was likely the Azores islands while it was "coming from the fisheries of the Rio de Ouro in the direction north-west of the Canary Islands and the island of Madeira." In the 1550s an English traveler observed that "seven or eight leagues off from the River del Oro or Cape de la Barbas, there come many Spaniards and Portuguese to fish during the month of November." Near Cabo Branco another found "certain Caravels fishing for porgies" in December. This was a long-distance fishery akin to that of Terra Nova or Iceland, with Portuguese vessels sailing as far south as modern Mauritania to catch or purchase fish for market.[25]

Such experiences along the Saharan coast of Africa remind us that the history of fishing in the Atlantic was about much more than northern Europeans in the subarctic. Many sources related to northwest African coasts use the same language that Europeans would employ a century later to discuss the Terra Nova fishery at its height. Perhaps the clearest testament to how the Rio do Ouro fishery operated came from a French observer in the 1580s, who wrote: "In Galicia . . . they have Caravels and sail as far as Cap Blanc in Africa to fish for dogfish and mullet and other fish which they salt and dry in the sun, just as one makes saltcod at Terra Nova." Before there was Terra Nova there was the Rio do Ouro, and before fishworkers went west to find their catch they went south.[26]

New Frontiers

In light of the above, we can see how the seeming leap to Terra Nova around 1505 was only one in a series of moments of maritime expansion by maritime communities in search of food and fuel security. From newfound seas and newly intensified coastal shelves came calories and oil in great abundance.

The sixteenth-century fishing system can be seen in the outfitting of two caravels in Seville in 1563. Part of the *Carrera de Indias*, the *Sancti Spiritus* and *Nuestra Señora de Gracia* were outfitted using the city's ample and sophisticated provisioning infrastructure. The ships were loaded with smoked sardines from Galicia (eight thousand), dry-salted cod (*bacalao*, twenty-four dozen), and porgies (fifteen dozen). The sardines were purchased from Andrés Cotanda, a Valencian merchant; the *bacalao* from the French merchant Martin Sáez; the porgies from the Portuguese resident Vicente Yáñez. Thus each of Iberia's major fish sources was represented on the same ship: sardines from the local fisheries, cod from Bretons or Normans in the North Atlantic (Terra Nova or Ireland), porgies from the Portuguese in northwest Africa. This was typical of how Europeans interacted with the Atlantic Ocean in the sixteenth century, drawing simultaneously on multiple sources of food and resources.[27]

In expanding Europe's energy frontiers, commercial fisheries helped create new colonial frontiers. Many commercial fisheries were associated with sites of colonial activity. This was certainly true at the older Norse colonies of Iceland, the Faroes, Shetland, and Orkneys. It was even true in Ireland, where fishing was often strongest near English coastal settlements. In Morocco and Saharan Africa fishworkers followed in the wake of state-backed navigators and military expeditions to establish an offshore presence. At Terra Nova that process would repeat, as Breton and other mariners filled the vacuum left by Caboto, Corte Real, and other explorers. In time the food and fuel made in these fisheries would drive further expansion. Sardines and saltcod from the eastern Atlantic were used to feed the sailors, settlers, and conquistadors who sailed to the Americas. The fish caught on the Rio do Ouro helped feed crews of slave traders bound for the Guinea Coast or the sugar islands of São Tomé, Madeira, and the Canaries. The new food frontier was made possible by the new colonial frontiers of the early Atlantic, and in turned helped push them outward.

Yet the actions of European mariners from Bréhat and elsewhere set in motion even deeper changes in global food systems. The food historian Christopher Otter has persuasively outlined how Britain sought a "large-planet" solution to its food problems in the nineteenth century. Rather than rely on intensified domestic agrarian production, industrializing Britain expanded its food frontier to incorporate the whole globe, importing wheat, beef, sugar, and other staples from the Americas, South Asia, and beyond. This was an inflection point for human histories of food, environment, and health. Likewise, Kenneth Pomeranz has famously argued for the centrality of these Atlantic (and later global) "ghost acres" to the development of industrial capitalism in nineteenth-century northwest Europe. I am suggesting that a similar process, albeit on a different scale, took place in the fifteenth and sixteenth centuries. In the face of food insecurity, Europeans sought a "large-planet" or a "large-ocean" solution by expanding their maritime food frontiers. Saharan Africa, Iceland, the mid-Atlantic islands, and ultimately Terra Nova became the outer food frontier of Europe by 1550. A narrow range of species dominated the new commercial fisheries: cod, herring, and sardine above all. Other fish and shellfish were still harvested—we will see them appear throughout this book—but the new commercial fisheries themselves focused on maximizing the output of a small number of easily processed and profitable kinds of food. The ghost fathoms created around the turn of the sixteenth century point to a much longer, and more aquatic, history of ecological integration, capitalist production, and food globalization.[28]

The long-term consequences of this maritime food transformation have been profound. Fifteenth-century mariners established a template for harvesting marine life that influenced global operations until the industrialization of the mid-nineteenth century. Until transportation and freezing techniques made fresh fish available in the twentieth century, most consumers in the Atlantic ate fish according to the basic pattern set down in the fifteenth century, which dictated large quantities of a limited variety of preserved sea fish. The new commercial oceanic fisheries proved to be durable and long lasting, in almost all cases surviving for centuries. The fish they produced are still popular and familiar in the twenty-first century, evidence of their culinary influence. Many of us still eat fish caught at the same commercial fisheries that fed European cities five hundred years ago, whether we realize it or not. Few other European colonial ventures have endured so long.

SIX

Circulations

Sometimes we find references to Terra Nova in surprising places. A manuscript currently kept in the Bibliothèque nationale de France, catalogued as Ms.Fr. 24269, shows us how the experience of Terra Nova was remembered and connected to other parts of the Atlantic basin. We believe this manuscript was written by a person living in Normandy in the 1540s, though it is uncertain who he was. It is a long, detailed, often quite mundane guide to the proper techniques for calculating a ship's position at sea. The handwritten guide must have been painstaking to make, and it is little wonder that toward the end the author's attention wanders. Most of the text is unremarkable, but several folios at the conclusion are taken up by a pair of unexpected additions in the same hand: two dual-language vocabularies, word lists compiled to aid mariners and merchants traveling to new colonial outposts in the Atlantic. The first vocabulary is for the *langaige de guynée* (language of Guinea), the second for the *langaige du bresil* (language of Brazil). The former includes a variety of words in Kru (from present-day Liberia) and their French equivalents. The latter likely represents a Tupí language, and Norman traders were known to voyage to the coast of Brazil in the early sixteenth century. Together they represent some of the earliest evidence of Norman interactions with communities in West Africa and South America, and the ethnographic knowledge accumulated in this process.[1]

Whoever wrote this text then did something remarkable. At the bottom of the penultimate page, taking up half of the leaf, are two paragraphs written in a dense and hurried hand. Bearing the title "For Terra Nova," the text constitutes a brief personal note about the fishery. It describes, seemingly as a memory aid, how to recognize when one has arrived off the coast of Terra Nova, and where our anonymous author has stored his fishing boats over the long winter. It includes descriptions of birds, the Grand Banks, Renews harbor, and the kinds of marks used by fishworkers to identify their boats. The note is an invaluable text for modern historians. Brief as it is, it is perhaps the only surviving account of the early sixteenth-century fishery and its environment in the hand of a mariner who worked there.

Yet it is the physical and conceptual position of Terra Nova in the book, relative to the Brazilian and Guinean vocabularies, that is most striking. The note follows directly from, and is almost embedded within, the languages of Brazil and Guinea. As we page through the manuscript we can see the author's thoughts move from Guinea to Brazil to Terra Nova, so that the harbor at Renews forms one point in a maritime network and lived experience that had brought the Norman mariner to the estuaries of West Africa and the dense forests of Brazil. A century later these same places would be bound together in the oceanic trades that drove life and death in the Atlantic, as salt cod from Terra Nova fed enslaved peoples from West Africa who labored in the American tropics. This is an essential triptych of Atlantic history, the great and terrible engine of the eighteenth-century economy, represented here hundreds of years earlier than we would typically expect.

We must see Terra Nova as our Norman mariner-author did, as one place in an emerging constellation of sites for contact, exchange, and exploitation in the Atlantic basin. The tendency to flatten the fishery into a binary relationship between a fishing ground and the metropolitan market does not do justice to how people and commodities moved. It was never a closed system, but a point where different migratory, commercial, and exchange systems came together. Across the sixteenth century, many people came to Terra Nova from outside. They visited, they worked, they left. In short, Terra Nova must be understood as embedded in wider global systems of circulation. Terra Nova was a place where three circuits of circulation converged

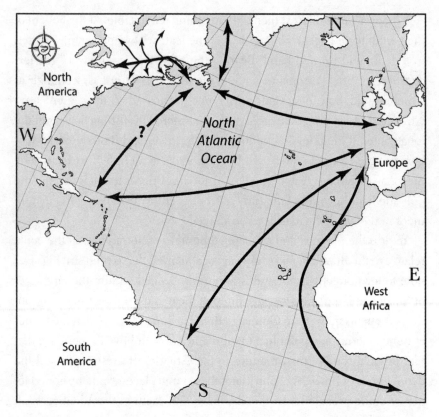

Figure 13. Atlantic circulation routes connected to Terra Nova. (Prepared by SEH Mapping.)

(see figure 13). The first was a North American circuit that linked the Gulf of Canada to the interior via the River of Canada, and down into the Gulf of Maine via various riverine networks. This American circuit would become important to the development of exchange between Europeans and First Nations at Terra Nova. The second was a circumpolar circuit. Inuit communities stretching across the High Arctic linked Terra Nova to high-latitude exchange networks. The third would be a circum-Atlantic network, the emerging European Atlantic system. Terra Nova was embedded in this set of transoceanic routes and commercial ties. Together, the convergence of these three circuits at Terra Nova every summer made the northwest Atlantic an overlooked entrepôt in the sixteenth century.

American Circuits

Several decades ago, the linguist Peter Bakker made a startling observation: there is evidence that many of the "Algonkian" words recorded by early seventeenth-century French Jesuit visitors to Mi'kma'ki were actually Basque words. Indeed, as he argued in a series of studies, there seems to have been a trading pidgin language in place around the coasts of Terra Nova that combined Basque and Algonkian vocabulary. Such a pidgin language could develop only if there was sustained mutual contact between Basque fish-workers and Mi'kmaq communities before 1600. This kind of indirect evidence of exchange between Europeans and Indigenous peoples offers a tantalizing glimpse into what is otherwise an obscured history of sixteenth-century contact. It is also a reminder that one of the major consequences of the sixteenth-century fishery was not just to produce food and fuel, but to connect Europeans with Indigenous North American exchange routes.[2]

Recent archaeological work has confirmed and expanded Bakker's insight. Thanks to the efforts of Brad Loewen and his collaborators, we now understand the connection between Basques and First Nations, especially around La Gran Baya, to have been sustained and marked by extensive material exchange. One telling example Loewen has highlighted is the spread of a signature Basque tool, the *txalupa* boat, to Indigenous communities. By the end of the sixteenth century the *txalupa* had been adapted by Innu, Mi'kmaw, Saint Lawrence Iroquoian, and even Inuit mariners, who employed the sturdy and maneuverable craft for hunting and trading voyages. More remarkably, the *txalupa* appears far to the south in New England by the early 1600s. An English expedition in 1604, sailing by the southern coast of Maine, encountered peoples who sailed out to greet them in "Biscay shallops" and who "with a piece of chalk drew the coast thereabouts, and could name Placentia of the New-found-land." Both the ship technology of the *txalupa* and the geographic knowledge of Terra Nova had traveled down the rivers and coasts of Maine via Indigenous trade routes even before Europeans arrived in force. As with the exchange of words, we have evidence that Indigenous American exchange routes were thriving in the age of Terra Nova.[3]

When the first Portuguese, Breton, and English mariners began to work the waters of Terra Nova around 1505, they found themselves in a world already networked into long-distance exchange routes. Matthew Bahar has reconstructed how the Gulf of Maine was an Indigenous maritime world trading north and south at the moment of European contact, one that endured and expanded into the early eighteenth century. Indigenous communities used rivers, coasts, and overland paths to link communities throughout northeast North America with the waters of the Atlantic. Terra Nova was superimposed upon and connected to this system. European states and the navigators they dispatched to the northwest Atlantic were very interested in these Indigenous populations and their trade. They vacillated between trying to establish commercial relations and more violent attempts to control the flow of goods. Zuan Caboto reported that he had seen people at a distance, but he does not seem to have made contact with any First Nations in his initial voyage. The Corte Real expeditions brought captives back to Lisbon, as did an English expedition around 1503, but we hear nothing of what they told Europeans. As William Gilbert has shown, we can rarely determine which community any of these different individuals came from, but all are identified as living in the vastness of Terra Nova. Even when a fishery supplanted island colonies as the model of European occupation in the northwest Atlantic, contact and possibilities for exchange persisted.[4]

Archaeological research has made clear that the Innu, Mi'kmaq, and potentially the Beothuk were aware of neighboring Indigenous communities both near and far, and were trading with them before, during, and after European arrival. They were exceptionally well positioned to do so, as they occupied one of the major maritime crossroads of the northeast of North America. The Gulf of Canada was the point where two major long-distance exchange routes came together. The first ran down the River of Canada into the heart of the continent. The second were a series of north-south riverine routes that connected the Gulf of Maine with the people living around the Gulf of Canada. There is abundant evidence that the north-south exchange routes were important vectors for the transmission of both European goods and ideas throughout the sixteenth century. It did not take long for people in the Gulf of Maine to gain access to goods and ideas from Terra Nova, thanks to preexisting networks.[5]

The arrival of European mariners every summer made these exchange circuits much more valuable to adjacent communities. Access to European metalware (traded or taken from abandoned fishing camps) and beads gave Innu and Mi'kmaq the opportunity to act as middlemen for the greater northeast woodlands. The Mi'kmaq in particular seem to have taken to this role with increasing enthusiasm as the century wore on, and by the turn of the seventeenth century they were recognized by Europeans as the most active participants in the trade. The connection of European trade to North American circuits attracted the attention of Indigenous communities beyond Terra Nova. Archaeologists have recently suggested that the Saint Lawrence Iroquoians, who typically lived far up the River of Canada near modern Montréal and Québec City, ventured into the Gulf of Canada regularly from the mid-sixteenth century on. They did so to take advantage of the presence of Europeans, bypassing Innu and Mi'kmaq communities that normally controlled exchange. Archaeologists have also been able to trace the exchange and movement of European pottery, beads, and metal kettles from contact zones in Terra Nova across northeast North America.[6]

The historian Matthew McKenzie has argued for the potential to view the Gulf of Saint Lawrence (or the Gulf of Canada, as fishworkers would have known it) as the center point, or the pivot, of the economy of the greater northwest Atlantic in the modern era. This reflects the hydrological and biological reality of the region, which depends on the gyres and movements of the Gulf of Saint Lawrence to create the fishing grounds of Terra Nova and New England. McKenzie's argument relates primarily to nineteenth- and twentieth-century fishwork, but it holds true for the sixteenth century in light of these American circuits. Algonkian-speaking communities acted as the central node that linked different exchange routes, drawing in European goods and pumping them outward along river routes into the interior. Before the 1580s this system was still relatively low scale, as explored below, but the mere existence of such trade networks indicates the importance of First Nations at Terra Nova to the greater history of the American northeast.[7]

The existence of such long-distance exchange networks confirms a few important things about Indigenous communities in the northwest Atlantic. It indicates that describing Algonkian-speaking communities as "hunter-gatherers" does not do justice to the complex economic and social systems that allowed them to live in the ecological rhythms of the northwest Atlantic. Even as they were moving around the coasts and forests in the wake of birds and fish, they were maintaining major trade routes into the heart of the continent. It also indicates that Indigenous communities were much better than Europeans at integrating riverine and coastal spaces to move over the long distances of the northwest Atlantic. The Saint Lawrence Iroquoians used the River of Canada and its tributaries to carry European goods into the heart of the continent. While the Mi'kmaq were sailing the Gulf of Canada, they were sending trade expeditions down the rivers of Maine. Finally, these exchange networks make clear that the watery world of Terra Nova was connected not merely to an Atlantic world but to a continental American world as well. Circulation took place over more than just ocean spaces, and goods and ideas circulated through woods, riverways, and towns far removed from the coastal northwest Atlantic.

Was this exchange or trade? The main goods Europeans offered were metallic objects and tools (knives, hatchets, nails, and so on) and glass beads. These were portable and repurposeable goods ideally suited to the seasonally mobile First Nations at Terra Nova. In exchange, European fish-workers and merchants wanted furs like beaver and marten pelts. The fur for metalware aspect is the most consistently attested to in our written records, while beads and pottery are indicated through archaeological finds. I do not think that, at least before 1580, this constituted a distinct trade. From the European perspective, the exchange of metalware and beads for furs formed an ancillary component of fishing and was conducted by the mariners themselves, rather than by traders or European merchants. In the sixteenth century the trade for pelts provided mariners with a new source of income and a hedge against a poor catch (and must have helped relieve the tedious monotony of the fishery), but it was not a distinct branch of commerce in the Gulf of Canada. It was therefore likely a sustained exchange but probably not one that was crucial to either party in the sixteenth century. Indeed, the mobility of the Innu, Beothuk, and Mi'kmaq gave them a flexibility and capability to avoid contact if they wished. Mi'kmaw and Innu groups could simply avoid fishing harbors during the height of the season if they were uninterested in exchange, while the Beothuk often avoided contact in favor of scavenging for metal left behind by Europeans at the end of the season. Without higher European demand for furs, neither side yet had sufficient leverage over the other. Enough exchange took place that it clearly shows up in our archaeological records, yet we should not overstate how transformative this was prior to the 1580s.[8]

Arctic Circuits

As First Nations made the Gulf of Canada into a hinge of northwest Atlantic exchange during the sixteenth century, they were soon joined to a new set of exchange routes. These routes would make Terra Nova not just a site of contact but an ecological-cultural meeting zone where the High Arctic connected to the Atlantic. In the sixteenth century European mariners rarely ventured northward along the east coast of Labrador toward the Davis Straits and beyond. Indigenous communities that already lived in the High Arctic were well adapted to their environment, and they seem to have aggressively kept out European visitors. Jean Alfonse and other early geographers clearly viewed the region with trepidation and had only a vague sense of what lay beyond Terra Nova. They wrote of people with tails living underground, dressed in furs and eating raw fish. Such descriptions may reflect the reports of early explorers and fishworkers who encountered the southern fringes of this polar world, or who heard secondhand accounts from Innu and Beothuk communities. Nor did groups like the Innu migrate too far north into Labrador during the sixteenth century. But there was no reason that communities couldn't come south out of the High Arctic to create a new form of contact in the northwest Atlantic.[9]

In the sixteenth century most of the eastern Arctic was dominated by Inuit communities, descendants of a mass migration over three centuries earlier that had carried coastal communities clear across the Arctic rim all the way to Greenland. The Inuit Nunangat, stretching from Greenland to Alaska, was but one part of a wider Arctic realm inhabited by a wide variety of communities. These groups maintained exchange networks among themselves and between one another. The result was a circum-Arctic system of exchange, a circle of circulation that was often invisible to outsiders. Even now it is only imperfectly understood by scholars, who have long relegated the polar regions to a kind of isolation, disconnected from Atlantic and Pacific histories. Only with European whaling in the eighteenth and nineteenth centuries does the Arctic assume sizable importance to many historians, despite how long humans have lived in these spaces.[10]

Around 1500 Inuit communities were largely confined to what is today northern Labrador, and rarely had contact with Algonkian-speaking peoples further south. The current evidence strongly suggests that Inuit communities migrated southward across the sixteenth century, and that by the end of the century were more regularly venturing into La Gran Baya. By the seventeenth and eighteenth centuries the presence of Inuit communities in southern Labrador is very clear and consistent. They seem to have been drawn at least in part by the potential for exchange with Europeans. The arrival of Inuit communities at La Gran Baya toward the end of the sixteenth century was a moment of world-historical significance. The consequences for all parties were far-reaching, though most impacts would be felt only in the seventeenth century. The Inuit migrations southward connected Terra Nova with their circum-Arctic exchange networks. Europeans had accessed these Arctic circuits once before, during the period of Norse expansion. Now Inuit expansion drove reintegration, carrying European goods northward in a process we are only beginning to understand. Not all circulation was voluntary. Inuit raids on Innu and European mariners probably led to many goods being seized. In the early seventeenth century this conflict in northern Terra Nova provoked considerable anxiety among the Breton mariners at Saint Malo, who complained to their city council. Eventually they agreed to outfit ships to "make war upon the natives of Terra Nova" who had "murdered the mariners of this city who go to the cod fishery." Yet some of this contact may have been outright exchange rather than raids, something that became more common by the eighteenth century. It is unlikely that Inuit settlements appeared around Terra Nova at this earlier date, though some settled at Sandwich Bay by the end of the century, but instead summer expeditions—yet another migratory cycle—brought them into the contact zone of La Gran Baya.[11]

Our knowledge of this process of exchange is growing rapidly thanks to the work of archaeologists like Lisa Rankin who have carefully searched the east coast of Labrador for evidence of sixteenth- to eighteenth-century Inuit habitation and trade networks. This work has shown the growing presence of European trade goods in Inuit sites from the mid-sixteenth century onward. Here Rankin's phrasing is revealing: "Inuit villages did not house a global population per se, but might be considered cosmopolitan in the sense that the Inuit who occupied them were aware of the world and of the peoples who existed beyond their territories, and they worked diligently to develop relationships (and economies) with those who came from different nations near and far." Inuit communities, in short, were far from isolated Arctic peoples. Archaeological work has also shown that traded goods moved, north up the coast of Labrador and then around the Arctic. A recent archaeological discovery of Venetian beads in Alaska, for instance, has opened the question of whether these arrived in the early fifteenth century from East Asia or whether they were carried westward from Terra Nova in the sixteenth century. Much as goods moved down the River of Canada into the American continent, so too did they move along frozen coasts between Inuit communities.[12]

The study of the Arctic has traditionally been separated from Atlantic studies, existing as a vibrant and specialized field. For that reason, Inuit history has always sat uneasily within the wider narrative of the Atlantic world. In considering the history of Terra Nova, we see that we cannot so easily separate the Arctic from the Atlantic. European colonization created a moment and a space for a connection to form between transoceanic, transcontinental, and circum-Arctic circulation. This was due to Indigenous actions, and the Inuit deserve a place in the Atlantic world. At a location like Terra Nova the distinction between Atlantic and Arctic breaks down, and we must adjust our spatial and chronological framework accordingly.

Atlantic Circuits

In 1560 an English mariner returning from a voyage to West Africa remarked that he had sailed abroad for twenty-eight years. During his long tenure he had served on ships to "the Newe Fownde land, Russia and other places." His view of Terra Nova, then, was shaped by a lifetime of sailing between different corners of the Atlantic and Arctic, linking them with European ships. Certainly, his story would have resonated with the Norman mariners described at the start of this chapter, and it points to a wider experience. Sir Humphrey Gilbert's expedition to Terra Nova in 1583 included a man nicknamed Brasile because of his frequent visits to that land. We may imagine that other ships carried similarly well-traveled Atlantic mariners. Around 1510 an isolated literary reference to the northwest Atlantic sets the region alongside other frequent destinations when a mariner remarks: "Sir, I have been in many a country / As in France, Ireland and Spain . . . Brittany, Biscay and also in Gascony / Naples, Greece, and in the midst of Scotland / At Cape Saint Vincent, and the New Found Island." As such a text suggests, Terra Nova was always embedded in a wider set of Atlantic circulations, driven by growing European colonial and commercial activities.[13]

To get to Terra Nova, European mariners had to set out into the wider Atlantic basin and aim for the northwest (see figure 2). The preferred jumping-off points were Ushant in Brittany, hewing to a westerly course, or northwest Galicia, heading northwest toward the fishery. Some ships cut directly across, despite fierce winds and currents, but many preferred to drop down to the latitude of the Azores archipelago before aiming northwest toward the bank. Jean Alfonse observed that the Azores were "halfway along the route [*la moictie du chemin*] between Portugal and Terra Nova." Whether this referred to an abstract distance or an actual route (*chemin*) is unclear. Between their departure points and Terra Nova there were rarely any places to stop, requiring month-long voyages on the open sea. Still, some of the sailing routes used in the sixteenth century may have brought fishworkers into contact with the wider Atlantic system. Some ships leaving from Galicia would have passed close enough to the Azores for mariners to stop. One of the return routes for fishing ships appears to have involved sailing east from Terra Nova and dropping south into the North Sea, thence home. It is possible that some ships returning from Terra Nova passed close by Greenland and Iceland. In describing Greenland, the Swedish author Olaus Magnus makes vague reference to "Spanish and French ships [that] have also been driven by ferocious winds and . . . landed against their will on these inhospitable shores [southern Greenland]." In the 1540s Spanish ships ambushed a

French fleet off the coast of Flanders; the French ships are described as returning from Terra Nova, a position that makes sense only if they were returning by a very northerly route past Iceland and around the northern British Isles. In the transit to and from Terra Nova, fishworkers were more exposed to wider Atlantic circuits than we often assume.[14]

Earlier in this book we saw how early European interactions with Terra Nova were shaped by experiences on other Atlantic islands, and the expectations that Newfoundland might be another Española. Even as dreams of settlement evaporated, surviving records preserve glimpses of wide-ranging connections. In the introduction we met Martin de Artalecu, a lifelong outfitter of fishing voyages at Terra Nova who died on a trading mission to Puerto Rico. In 1527 an English expedition sailed from Terra Nova to the Caribbean (much to the surprise of Spanish officials). The captain Jon Rut, who wrote an important letter describing Sam Joham/Saint John's harbor, found himself impounded by curious Spanish officials who seemed surprised that anybody had come down from the icy north. In a later reversal of this trend, by the 1580s, as English activity at Terra Nova increased, some English corsairs raided the fishing grounds while returning from more notable targets in the Caribbean. Their attacks appear to be opportunistic, but they point toward more systematic raids on Terra Nova that would become common by the early seventeenth century. Such examples may be scattered across time and space, but they indicate deeper patterns of sustained contact with the wider Atlantic basin.[15]

The nature of commerce at Terra Nova offers an indirect reason to suspect wider Atlantic links. As did voyages to the Caribbean, Brazil, or mid-Atlantic islands, those to Terra Nova drew on the labor and resources of regional port cities in coastal Europe. We know that these port cities were sending ships to each of these regions simultaneously. By the early seventeenth century, after decades of expanding traffic, the residents of Le Havre in Normandy could boast that they had two hundred ships sailing each year to Terra Nova and the West Indies, among other destinations. Small-scale urban merchants and shipowners outfitted voyages to each, sometimes in the same year and sometimes in alternating seasons. The clearest evidence appears only after 1570, primarily in Normandy. These were small ships, often under one hundred tons, outfitted by pooling resources in a city like Rouen or La Rochelle, or an outport like Honfleur, Île de Ré, or Saint Jean-de-Luz. A Norman merchant might dispatch a ship to fish at Terra Nova one summer and to trade in the Caribbean the next. As the century wore on, more and more shipowners added corsairing in Europe and the western Atlantic to this mix. In the spring of 1596 a merchant of Honfleur outfitted his ship *La Perle* to catch cod at Terra Nova. That winter, though, we find the *Perle* refitted to sail to "the coasts of Spain and thereabouts to make war against the enemies of his Majesty [the king of France.]" The ways in which small merchants swapped ships from one venture to another indicates how ships, crews, and captains could find themselves carrying wider Atlantic experiences to Terra Nova and vice versa.[16]

An example illustrates the kinds of mariners who sailed between Terra Nova and other parts of the Atlantic basin. In 1553 a group of captains from the small Basque port town of Saint Jean-de-Luz banded together to launch a pirate raid on the Caribbean. Cruising the coast of Spain, the four Basque captains made for "the island of Peru and the Indies," where they seized and plundered Spanish ships. Their ships had been outfitted for a "voyage to Terra Nova or the Indies," their regular routes, which deceived authorities. The language used in the surviving documentation implies that a voyage to Terra Nova or the Indies was considered similar in terms of outfitting, and either might be undertaken by a merchant-mariner from a small port like Saint Jean-de-Luz. But while fishing at Terra Nova was perfectly acceptable to the French crown, a raid on the Caribbean was not. Despite their perfidy, the group of ship masters was able to extract a royal pardon, carefully deposited in the city archives of Saint Jean-de-Luz, bearing witness to the transatlantic rovings of these Basque captains.[17]

More direct connections between Terra Nova and the rest of the Atlantic basin are generally hard to reconstruct before the 1580s. In the seventeenth century it was common for fishing ships to carry their catch directly from Terra Nova to markets in the western Mediterranean and even the Caribbean. This was a system Peter Pope reconstructed in his revealing *Fish into Wine*, but the evidence for such direct commercial links in the sixteenth century is much more tenuous. The first clear reference to a fishing ship carrying cod directly from the northwest Atlantic to the Caribbean dates only to 1611, though this may have already been a common practice by then. Records of voyages directly from Terra Nova to ports in southern Iberia, southern France, and Italy appear regularly only toward the end of the century. Instead, most fish seem to have been carried back to home ports along Europe's Atlantic littoral. From there, the carrying trade shipped cod to markets elsewhere as needed. But this means that direct connection between the waters of Terra Nova and more southern markets was limited before the turn of the seventeenth century. There is still need for a thorough study of the surviving mercantile records, but those who study Terra Nova have uncovered very little evidence that the Caribbean was a regular destination before the end of the sixteenth century. Only closer to the turn of the seventeenth century would these conditions change.[18]

What may we conclude from this? Clearly there was not a great stream of traffic between the northwest Atlantic and the rest of the Americas, or even yet with the Mediterranean. Terra Nova was never fully integrated into the wider Atlantic system of the mid-sixteenth century, as it would be by the mid-seventeenth century. But for all that fishworkers and mariners who sailed to Terra Nova were familiar with and sometimes had connections to other colonial outposts and contact zones. Merchants were very likely to be investing in Terra Nova's fishery at the same time they were trading in the Caribbean, Brazil, or West Africa. Some fishing ships passed close by other Atlantic islands and ports, or carried men who had sailed to many colonial sites already. And the snapshots that have survived suggest that we have yet to fully appreciate the extent of inter-Atlantic contact in these earliest years. This allowed for the circulation of ideas, people, and goods in ways we are only starting to fathom.

A Seasonal Entrepôt

Every summer after the mid-sixteenth century, three long-distance exchange networks converged on the coasts of the northwest Atlantic. La Gran Baya was the focal point of this process, and the harbors of Brest and Butus were sites where thousands of miles of distance collapsed into the exchange of furs for metal. An Innu family could swap a beaver pelt for some metal hatchets with a Breton fishworker, and then turn around to swap those for other trade goods from an Iroquoian trader, who would carry them downriver to Hochelaga. Or perhaps an Inuit party would arrive to swap walrus ivory from the Arctic for metal, which would then get carried up into the depths of the frozen north. Rankin's contention that Inuit peoples expressed a cosmopolitan thinking tells us how much participants understood themselves as being embedded in these routes of circulation.

As a result, starting in the second half of the sixteenth century, Terra Nova functioned as a kind of floating seasonal entrepôt. It was the clearinghouse for the circulation of goods across the Atlantic, around the Arctic, and into North America. Like so much else, this trade fair was temporary, lasting only a few months each year. Much of this exchange was informal, and certainly nobody had planned to make La Gran Baya a major trading center. Indeed, the floating entrepôt was never the most important part of European activity in Terra Nova, nor would it ever displace fishwork and whaling as the main activities. Informal practices had crafted an entrepôt at Terra Nova, offering alternative ways to procure goods and—for Europeans, at least—make money. It was an entrepôt that sustained low-level exchange, and First Nations and fishworkers could enter or leave as they wished. Nor was this floating entrepôt the most important economic activity for First Nations or Inuit in the sixteenth century. Rather, it was created through and sustained by these other activities of food production and encounter. This is one of the many paradoxes that defined sixteenth-century Terra Nova: the exclusivity of codfish production over time produced a floating entrepôt.

When the Norman mariner penned his note "for Terra Nova" at the end of his sailing guide, he was thinking about his place within the kinds of Atlantic circuits I have outlined above. Like the many urban merchants who were sending ships to the Caribbean, West Africa, and Brazil, he too saw profit and potential in fishing and trading in the northwest Atlantic. What our writer did not see but no doubt indirectly benefited from was the fact that his was only one of the circulation systems that converged on the little harbor of Renews each summer. Our historical subjects were more cognizant of Terra Nova's place within a wider Atlantic world than modern historians often are, and yet they were also caught up in even bigger systems of migration and exchange that they could only partly see. At last modern scholars are able to get a fuller picture of what this dynamic entrepôt may have looked like, and we can better place Terra Nova in its Atlantic, Arctic, and American contexts.

PART III

Work

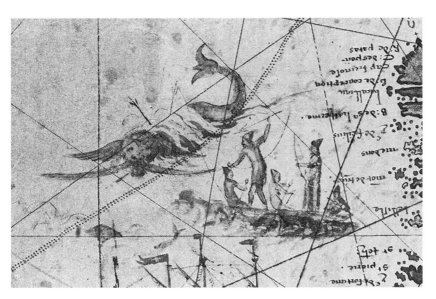

Figure 14. Basque whalers harpooning a whale off the coast of Terra Nova. Detail, 1546 world map by Pierre Desceliers. (Image provided by The John Rylands Research Institute and Library, The University of Manchester.)

Laud to the Lord who gives to this, to that denies his wishes
And dooms one toil and catch the prey and other eat the fishes.
—The Thousand Nights and a Night *(translated by Richard Burton)*

The things that nature made (birds, fish, trees, herbs, and flowers)
perish in order to maintain our miserable life, so violent and difficult
is it to be able to sustain it.
—*Giovanni Maria Bonardo,* Della miseria et eccellenza della
vita humana, 1586

SEVEN

Fishwork

Thomas Honner and his son were fishworkers. In early 1545 Thomas signed up with the good ship *James*, out of Dunwich in East Anglia, for a summer fishing and trading voyage to Iceland. Thomas became too ill to travel, but was paid 40 shillings despite not undertaking the voyage. Yet when the ship returned that fall the accounts note a sum of 16 shillings paid out to "Thomas Honner for his boy's wages in the ship." His son had served in his stead, helping the *James* to catch and dry 3,300 codfish and 3,650 ling (a fish closely related to cod favored by the English) along the coast of Iceland.[1]

Doña Maria Nicolas de la Herreria was not a fishworker, but she helped fishworkers. On February 2, 1562, she lent 12½ ducats to Martin de Areyçaga to buy "sea clothes" for his voyage to the Terra Nova fishery. She demanded to be repaid in full, with an additional "¼ of a normal share," promptly upon his return. This was one of many transactions Doña Maria made related to the fishery that year, including lending money to another ship for ropes, and even receiving a portion of *bacalao* brought from a returning ship in the fall of 1562. Doña Maria never went to sea, but her work was crucial to the functioning of the fishery. Her loan on February 2 allowed a mariner to buy the necessary gear to catch and process fish half a world away, and her contribution shows the blurry line between fishwork and other forms of labor that made a venture like Terra Nova possible.[2]

Marguerite Menault was likewise not a fishworker, but she was an expert at networking fishwork. She was a *bourgeoise* (civic citizen) of the city of Paris and the widow of the merchant Jacques le Bosse. Menault spent part of the 1530s working the fish trade all along the Seine River valley. On October 15, 1532, Menault was granted permission to store around four thousand codfish in the city of Rouen before selling them either locally or upriver in Paris. Cities like Rouen were careful about letting outsiders conduct business in their city, and someone from Paris like Menault had to receive a special dispensation (called a *gagé*). A local man, Jehan de Loraine, represented her before the city council of Rouen, but it was the *bourgeoise* who was responsible for moving and storing the fish. Rouen was already becoming the key fish market in northern France, and Menault was one of the merchants who made the flow of food and energy possible.[3]

Esteban Rodrigues, Juan Devilles, and Pedro Tilleyro were all fishworkers. All three signed up with the crew of a small *pinança* in the Galician port of Pontevedra in September 1517. The ship was outfitted to sail south to the Canary Islands, where it was meant "to fish for all the fish which God is pleased to grant us." The contract they signed makes one important distinction about Esteban, Juan, and Pedro that set them apart from the rest of the crew. All three were listed as *o moço*, "the boy," indicating that they were young apprentices like the *grumetes* who had served with Robert Lefant at Caprouge. Perhaps this was their first fishing voyage, and it was hoped that a season at the Canaries would teach the three young men the proper methods of fishwork that would serve them for years to come.[4]

Honner, Doña Maria, Menault, and the Pontevedran *moços* were all living through a time of transformation in the nature of work in premodern Europe. In the great commercial fisheries that sprouted up and down the Atlantic basin during the fifteenth and sixteenth centuries, increasingly one no longer fished, one did *fishwork* to produce the required quantities of salable, preserved, and consumer-pleasing fish. The growing commercial oceanic fisheries such as Terra Nova or Iceland required European communities to adopt complex systems for sharing information, financing voyages, organizing labor, and moving food commodities over water and land. We ought to distinguish the kind of labor that allowed these commercial fisheries to function from other forms of maritime food production. The Irish Sea or Algarvian fisheries were as different from a coastal fishery near Southampton or a riverine eel fishery in Holland as my backyard garden is from the vast maize fields of Nebraska. The oceanic fisheries of the fifteenth and sixteenth centuries existed to produce vast quantities of processed, preserved fish for export. The amount of labor required to run a fishery grew steadily, so that Terra Nova or the North Sea absorbed thousands of mariners every year. This new labor would be defined by several important features. Mariners focused on harvesting a narrow range of species using teams of coordinated labor. Fishing took place in short, intensive windows of seasonal labor. One could serve in a commercial fishery temporarily or commit one's life to it or move between different kinds of work over time, making fishing flexible. Where we can see them in the records, workers were skilled and hired for their labor, though the forms of payment varied: cash, shares, in kind. Different kinds of work and skills were networked in a process described below, embedding laborers in wider chains of production.

To describe this new kind of work, I follow anthropologist Jennifer Lee Johnson's use of the terms *fishwork* and *fishworkers*. In her studies of lakeside communities and food in southern Uganda she has stressed the complexity and significance of the work women do to make fish into food, at both the local and global level. The use of *fishworker* and *fishwork* is as apt for fifteenth-century Iceland as it is for twenty-first-century Uganda. But I think we must go further in understanding how varied fishwork had to be. In many ways what defined fishwork was its ability to connect to other networks of labor. Although some of this might be subsumed under the general activity of "merchants," the auxiliary forces that supported fishing were more complex. Doña Maria and Menault did not sail to Terra Nova or handle fish themselves, and so could not themselves be fishworkers per se. But their labor, investment, and knowledge made the fisheries possible. Fishwork is about networked labor and collaboration, not just the efforts of the individual. It would be fishworkers and their collaborators, not fishermen or fishers or fisherfolk, who created Terra Nova and turned it into one of the largest commercial food operations in the Atlantic basin.[5]

Thinking with Fishwork

The harvesting, killing, processing, and consuming of fish is a ubiquitous process in human history—we are ichthyophagous creatures. It is one of the first ways our species learned to find food, and it remains an essential source of global nutrition. As John Gillis, Brian Fagan, Helen Rozwadowski, and others have diligently shown us, the archaeological, anthropological, and historical evidence for fishing indicates it was one of the first and most consistent ways in which humans procured food. "Fishing is as old as humanity," Fagan has declared, and evidence of deliberate fish harvesting has been found at the earliest archaeological sites in Africa. Thousands of generations later this was still true, and for coastal communities in places like Norway, Ireland, the Algarve, and Holland marine life was more easily accessible than any livestock or farmland. In the broad swaths of Europe that adhered to Catholicism fish was an essential part not merely of the diet but of an individual's spiritual journey through life. Eating fish on key days of the year, including every Friday, was an obligation of the faithful and an act that demonstrated self-control and devotion. Killing and eating fish was not merely an option for peoples living around the North Atlantic, it was essential.[6]

Yet there are so many ways to do this, at so many scales and for so many different reasons. Social scientists have long run up against the problem of language in describing such work. In English, terms like *fish*, *fishery*, *fisherman*, and *fishing* all encompass broad and varied kinds of food production and economic operations. I have sometimes found that when I tell people I study fishing, they assume I am interested in angling or sportfishing—an entirely different and (to me, at least) unrelated kind of activity from the industrialized food work that is at the heart of this book. It has likewise been frustrating to look up studies of *fishers* and *fisherfolk* only to find them focused on peasant-fishers and coastal harvesters. Further, our vocabulary surrounding marine food production is often determined more by what cultures think that work should be rather than what it is. Hence the ubiquity of the gendered term *fisherman/men* in English to describe all kinds of fishing-related activities. It reinforces the idea that fishing is an activity for men, and that it is also a kind of identity. As Matthew McKenzie has noted of modern New England, the idea of the *fisherman* has been repeatedly deployed as a

weapon by mariners, politicians, and artists for political, economic, and social advancement. It is a term that obscures more than it describes, blunting
our understanding of maritime labor and those who practice it.[7]

Even if we set aside the problem of language, the truth is that it has been
hard to get scholars to pay attention to fishing as an important element in
premodern history. In the case of the sixteenth century, this reflects modern
assumptions about oceanic space. Most historians follow the pathbreaking
work of Lauren Benton, who has shown how European cartographers, navigators, and state actors thought of the Atlantic Ocean itself in terms of routes,
passages, and itineraries that crisscrossed a flat and barren surface. These
were modes of thinking grounded in movement, in using the ocean as a
means to an end by connecting points of land. But Benton and others have
overlooked the degree to which water, ocean water especially, was also something valuable in and of itself for many Europeans. To fish required one to
work with and in water, to know what lay beneath the surface. It encouraged
the development of deep and closely guarded knowledge by generations of
fishworkers and mariners. Those who practiced the "wet" fishery at places
like Iceland and Terra Nova, catching and salting fish in barrels onboard a
ship, might never even set foot on distant shores during their summers
of food production. The ocean stopped being a highway, a flat surface to be
traversed, and became a place that could be manipulated and exploited.[8]

Yet turning the sea itself into a site of continual labor required new forms
of work. Of particular importance was a shift in scale and diversity toward
large multinational crews, and in the interfacing of fishing with new financial instruments and port infrastructure. Only this kind of networked system
could sustain operations on the scale necessary to feed starving European cities. Hundreds of ships worked the Irish Sea, Iceland, Rio do Ouro, and Terra
Nova each year. Each required tremendous inputs of human energy and resources to function—there is a reason they were called fishing "fleets," after
all—and outfitting a fleet takes time, resources, and work. Often it would be
simple, mundane things that called up auxiliary forms of labor, like carrying
fish from ship to shore or carting extra ship biscuit to a waiting crew. It is also
the case that networked labor allowed mariners and merchants to overcome
the more basic problem that threatened fishwork: the sea itself.

The sea gave, and the sea took away. "The perils of the sea" (or often "the perils of the sea and war") was a ubiquitous phrase in Norman and Biscayan loans contracts, used to justify sky-high interest rates. For there were many risks indeed, both natural and man-made. For those fishing near shorelines, the ever-present danger of rocks, shoals, and sandbars was a constant source of anxiety. Fire was a serious threat (mariners did, after all, have to cook their food each day over open flames), and lightning might strike a ship at sea. In the subarctic Atlantic icebergs and fog were notoriously pervasive, appearing unexpectedly to blind or capsize ships. At Terra Nova visitors complained that in some parts the sun was too hot in the summer and burned drying fish, or that in others there was scarcely a day without rain. In other cases mariners faced a slow and torturous end, as when the wind became becalmed and a ship sat listlessly in the midst of the ocean while stores ran out. Corsairs, pirates, and privateers abounded in the seas of the sixteenth century—and they knew fishing ships to be slow moving and valuable targets. They themselves rarely sailed to Terra Nova, instead lying in wait for returning vessels in European waters at the end of the fishing season. In late 1560 the French ship *Francois*, returning from Terra Nova, was taken by an English corsair off the coast of Brittany, within sight of home. The master and nineteen of his men were dumped in "two little small boats a hundred and sixty miles or thereabouts from land," left to die while their ship was taken to Dundee to be sold as a prize. Iceland was even more dangerous, for English ships had to run the gauntlet past their Scottish foes during much of the sixteenth century.[9]

Such natural and human-made obstacles and threats were only part of the problem. Maritime labor was difficult work, one in which just staying alive required constant effort. Mariners were constantly exposed to the elements, even in the best conditions, their skin burned by the sun and encrusted with salt spray. The poor diet encouraged malnutrition and dehydration. Discipline was far less violent and rigorous than it would be in the seventeenth- and eighteenth-century Atlantic, but punishments like keelhauling or the lash were widely practiced. Even the smallest fishing smack was a complex machine requiring steady rowing and attention, while the large *naos* and *caravels* that served the major commercial fisheries required constant maintenance, sail adjustment, rope hauling, and other work. Fishing was not yet mechanized. The human body had to do all the work of catching and pulling live fish from the sea. Leaning over a rocking shallop, hauling up a struggling and angry fifty-pound cod, it was easy for something to go wrong. Mariners fell overboard, sometimes by accident and sometimes pushed by their supposed brothers. In an age when few Europeans could swim, almost all died a painful death. Maiming and disfigurement were always possibilities, to say nothing of the potential for illness like scurvy onboard a small, tightly packed ship. In recognition of such harsh realities, in 1597 the city council of Aberdeen made an exception to new regulations on overseas trade that mandated the importation of bullion, noting that "herring and *keeling*[dry cod]" were "hazardous wares and subject to many misadventures and not stable wares" and therefore absolved the fishing trade from most of the new duties. Working aboard a sailing vessel was not necessarily more backbreaking than the labor of a farmer or servant, but in turning to the sea many coastal communities committed their members to a demanding, dangerous, and physically degrading life.[10]

What exactly was fishwork? We may understand it as a labor of transformation—the work that one does to turn marine life into a processed commodity. Most often this is a processed foodstuff, but it may also be oil, ivory, baleen, and the like. Fishworkers labored to harvest fish, often to the exclusion of other living things, and transform them into pickled herring, dried stockfish, salty *bacalao*, brined sardines, and other exportable goods. Yet to do so meant more than just catching, killing, and drying fish. It meant navigating a three-masted sailing ship across the Atlantic Ocean for a month straight before even reaching Terra Nova, Iceland, or the Rio do Ouro. It meant using carpentry skills to set up a beachside base camp, and employing foraging skills to find wood, water, and food to sustain the crew while they worked. It meant knowing how to haggle when buying salt from the merchants of Brouage, or when selling your *bacalao* to the merchants of Bordeaux. All of these were steps in the transformation of fish into food, and all are subsumed within fishwork.

Thinking in terms of fishwork reminds us of an important aspect of fish-food production in the sixteenth century, which was that it could often be a temporary role. The term *fisherman/men* denotes both an occupation and an identity. Fishwork was more fluid, and only sometimes became an identity. Some people spent years working at fisheries, developing reputations as old fishworkers. Others might participate for a single season, making some cash and never returning. Workers like Thomas Honner, whom we met at the start of the chapter, participated in fishwork only for brief moments. Even over the course of a year, fishwork was rarely sustained. Fishing took place in seasonal cycles, short periods of intense harvesting contrasting with periods when the movement of marine life and weather meant fishwork was not possible. Some mariners spent a summer doing fishwork and then sailed off over the winter on a trading voyage to the Mediterranean. *Fishwork* as a term allows us to embrace the flexibility that was so important to sixteenth-century experiences of maritime labor and food production.

Later generations of maritime labor, especially by the eighteenth century, were marked by more "motley" heterogenous crews and labor pools. Transatlantic shipping and fishing often relied on floating pools of wage workers that could be hired, or rounded up, in many ports and urban centers. Yet this was not the case in the sixteenth century, and crews at Terra Nova were strongly marked by regional or communal differences in the trade. English crews may have had different expectations than Portuguese mariners, and perhaps Norman ship masters could ask more (or less) of their men than a Breton counterpart. Sixteenth-century mariners were very conscious of regional differences, and often carefully distinguish the identity of crews in our sources. To the sixteenth-century mind, Saintongeois were different from French Basques, who were different from Spanish Basques, who were different from Portuguese, and so on. These distinctions certainly reflect language, clothing, and cultural differences, but also that different crews were seen as having different characters. All, however, regardless of their distinct community, faced the challenges of work, survival, and commerce at sea.[11]

Networks of Fishwork

To overcome the difficulties of ocean spaces and to maximize the harvest, fishwork evolved in two important ways across the fifteenth and sixteenth centuries. The first was that fishing, especially in big commercial fisheries, was organized around complex teams of mariners. The fishing crew sup-planted the lone fisher or small coastal boat at Iceland, Ireland, Galicia, and elsewhere. Basque fishing and whaling crews in particular were notorious for their communal approach to work, including the practice of multiple crews coming together to bring down the same whale rather than compete with one another. Fishing crews were large, packing twenty to fifty adults onboard a single small ship. At sea, while catching and processing fish, fish-ing crews worked communally, dividing labor according to skill and experi-ence. They became assembly lines of food production, resembling later maritime wage labor and early industrial production. All of this meant that it was communal work, not individuals, that mattered most.[12]

The success of premodern commercial fisheries was based on the inte-grated networking of different kinds of labor and organization, which could take many forms and faces. (See figure 15 for an artistic representation of networked fishwork.) Men and women shipowners provided vessels for fish-ing; men and women acting as financiers provided capital through loan and outfitting contracts; men and women worked as bakers, sailmakers, rope makers, tailors, coopers, wine merchants, salt merchants, and in other roles to provide the provisions, clothing, equipment, and supplies necessary for the voyage; men hired for the voyage sailed the ship and caught and pro-cessed the fish; men and women acting as porters and fish merchants were hired to offload the catch, to take it to market, and to negotiate prices; women sold the catch in the marketplace to women who cooked it at home. An entire salt industry and international salt trade developed to sustain the new fisheries, enriching salt farmers and merchants alike. For a fishing crew of twenty or so fishworkers, dozens of others labored to make their voyage possible. It quite literally took a village to make a fishing voyage.

Was everyone who contributed to a commercial fishery a fishworker? Not quite. Fishwork was the act of transforming sea organisms into processed food, something that only those on the boats actually did. This is how Jen-nifer Lee Johnson defines fishworker in the modern context as well. The many other kinds of labor noted above contributed to and sustained fish-work, but these contributors were not themselves fishworkers. And yet here we must stress an important point: just because these additional workers

Figure 15. Networked labor in action in the Low Countries: fishworkers, fishmongers, and merchants work together to catch, process, and sell fish in Claes Jansz. Visscher, *Een haven met vismarkt,* 1600. (Courtesy of the Rijksmuseum, Amsterdam.)

were not themselves fishworkers does not mean we should separate their labor from the rest of the fishery or that we should ignore their contributions. The reason I stress networked labor is because even if someone like Doña Maria or Marguerite Menault did not themselves do fishwork, their actions were inseparable from the fishwork of those who did. No one role was possible without the other, and it was the integration of these different social and economic roles into a single web that made the scale of fifteenth- and sixteenth-century fisheries possible.

The voyage of the ship the *James,* the fishing vessel from eastern England that sailed with Thomas Honner's son to Iceland in 1545, is emblematic of how labor and capital were organized in the new fishery regime. Based in Dunwich, the *James* was nominally owned locally by Sir Thomas Darcy. In the summer of 1545 Darcy sought investors for a fishing voyage to Iceland, and a one-quarter share was purchased by a second nobleman, Sir Thomas Cawarden, who lived in London. Cawarden may never have seen the *James* in person, but he had invested some £58 in its success along with other, anonymous investors. The ship carried both a captain, Sander "of Dunwich," and a supercargo (a merchant in charge of trade goods), Geoffrey Smith, as well as around thirty-four crew members. Many mariners appear to have been recruited within families, for there are numerous repeated last names. Although most of the crewmen were generic mariners, a few were valuable specialists: Edmond Albright the soldier, William Cortes the carpenter, John West the cook, even George Smith the ship's boy. Such specialists were paid two to three times as much as the regular crew members, and Thomas Honner's boy earned only one-tenth of what the captain was paid. According to the records, the crewmen were paid wages for their work, not shares, with part of it before departing Dunwich and the rest upon return.

The voyage was a success, and the *James* returned laden with codfish from Iceland, and Cawarden made a tidy profit of £32. All these wages and profits, and every item of cargo and provisions purchased throughout the year, were scrupulously recorded so that all accounts could be settled and nobody brought to court. Even a pound of black pepper for the captain's table made it onto the list. Yet these fishworkers were only part of the labor pool that contributed to the success of the *James*'s voyage. Detailed financial records show all the different people who were pulled in the *James*'s orbit before and after the voyage: two men were paid for milling the wheat for the ship's provisions; a man was hired to ride to London with the news of the ship's return; two men were hired to replace sick crew members; many men had to be hired to offload the ship in Dunwich harbor. Dozens of people were hired for part-time work or to supplement fallen mariners, and the ample provisions (beer had to be purchased at least five separate times to keep the crew happy!) were bought from local Dunwich sources who profited by the voyage. None of these were fishworkers (not a single one actually caught or processed a fish), but without them no fishwork could have taken place. In the pages of the *James*'s accounts we can see the networking connections of fishworkers' labor to the financing of the metropole and to the work of locals who contributed directly and indirectly to the success of the fishing voyage.[13]

Within these new networks of labor and capital were numerous spaces for women at different social levels to contribute to and profit from fishwork. This represents a departure from how we often write and think about premodern fishing. Lisa Norling has recently suggested that a major part of the fisheries revolution was a more strict bifurcation of gender roles in fishing—men became fishers, women were consigned to supporting roles. It is true that fishing ships at Terra Nova, as far as we can tell, carried only men in the sixteenth century. Indeed, Peter Pope has argued for reading the Terra Nova fishery itself, especially regarding shore operations, as a distinctly masculine space of fisher*men*. The five months a fishworker spent at sea would have been an unusual experience for European men in the almost total absence of women. Anthony Parkhurst was thrilled to declare, "These men [fishworkers] . . . are honest, for that they find not in this country [Terra Nova] wine nor women." We may doubt that many of the fishworkers felt the same gratitude about five months in a world without the women and drink that were such familiar and important parts of European household life.[14]

Yet reading the fishery as a markedly masculine social space makes sense only if we collapse the fishery as a whole into the simple act of catching a fish. Instead, as I have tried to make clear, it was the networked nature of fishwork that deserves our attention. The work sixteenth-century women did in support of commercial fisheries was not ancillary, it was essential. If women had not funded voyages, sewed clothes, sold fish and cooked it, then the fishery could not have worked. In this light, women's work was everywhere woven into the new commercial fisheries. Women owned fishing ships, purchased shares, lent money, and provided supplies to outbound vessels. Darlene Abreu-Ferreira has meticulously documented the numerous ways in which Portuguese women in the sixteenth century were involved with the Terra Nova fishery, including their widespread activities as wholesalers and retailers of codfish, and Annette de Wit has done similar work for Holland in the seventeenth century. As numerous historians have noted, women were especially active in selling and preparing fish—one couldn't eat fish without the work of women in many parts of Europe. The bifurcation of labor that Norling notes, then, was matched by more intensive work within the new spaces of networked fishwork.[15]

Knowing Fishwork

The second change brought about by the fishwork revolution was the increasing importance of knowledge circulation within fishworking communities. Fishing crews were not merely work teams but microcommunities that developed and refined information—how to best catch and process fish, where to find different marine life, how to sail over long distances, where and how to sell the catch in Europe. Particularly important was the transmission between generations, from old hands to young *grumetes*. Because of the importance of knowledge transmission, certain communities often became associated with fishwork. It was easier to keep practical knowledge circulating within a tight-knit community than to diffuse it outward. In port towns like Bréhat, Saint Jean-de-Luz, or Dunwich, the large number of fishworkers shared knowledge within the community and created deep pools of expertise. This is the reason that the same coastal communities keep showing up again and again in the history of fishwork in the fifteenth and sixteenth centuries, and why the same coastal communities often engaged with several fisheries simultaneously. This was a prime example of the knowledge and systems of transition that underlay vernacular industries, as Peter Pope has explained at length. As he noted of the fishery, "The ability of early modern communities to transmit skills from one generation to another, irrespective of literacy, through informal apprenticeship systems was crucial to the reproduction of these vernacular industries." Vernacular knowledge also promoted stability and adaptability, allowing workers to move in and out of fishwork or to shift from one fishery to another without losing crucial expertise. This became essential as the number and scale of commercial fisheries expanded in the fifteenth and early sixteenth centuries, allowing mariners to adapt experiences from one place to exploit another. It is highly unlikely that Terra Nova could have existed without the vernacular cultures of the late fifteenth-century fisheries.[16]

Many generations after the fishworkers described in this book, the English diarist Samuel Pepys recorded an observation about fishwork. Writing of mariners who went to Terra Nova, he noted: "Mr Sheres tells me . . . how it comes to pass that our Newfoundland men of the west country, who are wholly illiterate, do make shift to keep their ships' way and do their business as well for aught appears, as those who have more art. He tells me their masters, though they have not much science, yet they can all subtract, multiply and divide and have somebody or other [who] can take an observation, and by practice can tell of the ships by 'flinging a chip' and looking overboard, and by then walking on the deck, near as well as others do by the log." Pepys's seventeenth-century comments would have been true in the sixteenth century as well. Many fishworkers, even ship masters, were illiterate. We know that because many of them signed contracts with as simple mark, often a crude drawing or X. Yet their work required them to know difficult and complex tasks. They had to be able to interpret natural and man-made signs quickly and efficiently, to navigate over vast distances, and to track fish in familiar harbors. Ignorance was a liability, both for investors and for a crew that needed to work together to survive.[17]

As such, fishwork was not unskilled labor. Although mariners might move in and out of fishwork over the course of their lifetime, it was a type of labor that benefited from long-term commitment and the accumulation of knowledge and skill. Practical information about work at sea, from how to sail a ship to how to bait a line for cod, was transferred between generations through word of mouth. But practical information can itself be exceedingly complex. Charles O. Frake has made clear that medieval European seafarers were capable of holding multiple complex maps of time and space in their minds as they moved over the water. As he showed, they had to superimpose tidal (that is, lunar) calendars, solar calendars, spatial maps, and mental maps of marine life onto one another to navigate. This behavior was essential for navigation and survival at sea, even if it was rarely written down. It is also an indication that mariners were capable of crafting and articulating quite complex mental maps of oceanic space, which they revealed only when compelled to by adverse circumstances. "Old hands" who knew their way about a given fishing ground could be worth their weight in gold, and skilled pilots who could guide a fishing crew to the best locations safely commanded high prices in the sixteenth century.[18]

Because it was rooted in practice, fishwork and all it entailed was made by movement. As Gísli Pálsson has explained, skill and knowledge are embodied processes of movement that must be lived and experienced. None more so than fishwork, which must be learned through practice and through literal voyages through time and space. As Pálsson explains of Icelandic fishworkers, "Icelanders . . . sometimes apply the metaphor of the journey, the fishing trip, to the issue of personal enskilment. This is to suggest that learning is not a purely cognitive or cerebral process, a mental reflection *on* differences in time and space, but is rather grounded in the contexts of practice, involvement and personal engagement. Enskilment is not only *likened* to the physical experience of seasickness, it is indeed a bodily exercise. To become skilled at something like catching fish is to progress from nausea to well-being, to feel at home in both one's body and the company of others." So too did mariners at Terra Nova and elsewhere become skilled and knowledgeable through voyages and the act of fishing. They learned about Terra Nova by being in Terra Nova; they learned about fishing by fishing. Nobody was born a fishworker, nor was it a vocation that could be taught. To become a fishworker you had to move—to get on the boat and go to Terra Nova and learn how to live and work and survive in the northwest Atlantic.[19]

Terra Nova does not make sense without an understanding of fishwork. The concept of Terra Nova was developed through fishwork, as we have seen, and indeed was inextricable from such labor; the seasonal migratory rhythms were built upon the experience of fishwork and its flexibility; and the success of the northwest Atlantic fishery was predicated upon a century of successful fishwork in the eastern Atlantic basin. It was the development and perpetuation of vernacular knowledge through fishwork in the eastern Atlantic that allowed Terra Nova to be rapidly created by mariners. As with other sites of fishwork, Terra Nova would not have functioned without a supporting network of merchants, artisans, laborers, and others who made voyages possible. Fishwork indicates how the history of Terra Nova may simultaneously be as small as the repetitive line-throwing of a first-time fishworker, and as vast as the long chains of labor and finance that brought fishworkers to a fishing ground and transported their catch back to market.

EIGHT

Killing

"Piscium Inexhausta Copia"—An inexhaustible supply of fish. The line was embedded in a letter sent in the summer of 1583 to readers in England by the Hungarian poet Stephen Parmenius. Writing from Sam Joham/Saint John's in Terra Nova, he used the phrase to describe the potential for fishwork in the northwest Atlantic. It is the kind of phrasing that reveals a world of thought about the human relationship to nature in the context of aggressive European overseas expansion. The line echoes a famous description attributed to Zuan Caboto in the 1490s, when he described seas so filled with fish that "they are caught not merely with nets but with baskets" dropped into the water. In the northwest Atlantic, Europeans saw an unlimited supply of energy and opportunity, and in the sixteenth century they committed themselves to taking as much as possible.[1]

Each fish in that inexhaustible supply would have to be killed. This was not the thrilling, sumptuous killing of the aristocratic hunt; nor the ritualistic, carefully planned slaughter of European livestock each spring and autumn; nor even the exhausting, dangerous killing of the all-too-intelligent whale-fish that troubled generations of whalers. Rather, it was the banal, rote butchery of the skilled professional: dispassionate, repetitive, methodical, and rapid. Pull the line—kill the fish—pull the line—kill the fish. Sometimes the cod fought back, sometimes they did not, but each was added to the growing pile of lifeless fish flesh at the bottom of the boat. The supply was limitless, or so it appeared, so fishworkers did what they could to catch as many as possible. Each fish killed meant one fewer hungry stomach back home—and a bigger wage for the crew. To the fishworker, a living codfish was worthless; in death it had the power to grant life.

Every year Europeans arrived in the northwest Atlantic to extract as much energy—both calories for food and combustible energy from oil—as they possibly could. Stored in an easily transported form, like stacks of dried codfish and barrels of brined cod, the nutrition and energy thus harvested could be distributed across the ports of western Europe. Many centuries later, we are living in the shadow of fishwork and *piscium inexhausta copia*, a mindset of harvesting overabundance. Mariarosa Dalla Costa and Monica Chilese have borrowed the language of Jules Verne to cast the ocean as a "vast reservoir of nature." This, as they see it, is a historical framework for understanding the place of marine biological resources in human societies, and "how men behave as predators" when faced with such vastness. So long as we see the sea as a "great reserve of food," an inexhaustible supply of fish, it is exposed to the process of acquiring "a capitalist value in which the most valuable species are appropriated without any scruples for the dominant alimentary system." The groundwork for this transformation was laid in the sixteenth century, at a moment when the supply of fish at Terra Nova was indeed inexhaustible because the technical capacity of European mariners to catch fish, given the numbers and techniques, was insufficient to overfish the sheer abundance of marine biomass available. Also a single ship could carry only so much, hardly enough to feed a single small outport. But as more and more ships joined in, the total energy harvest of the fishery grew exponentially each year. This would change, much sooner than we would expect, but even at the height of the fishery after 1560 the three hundred to five hundred ships visiting every year were still making barely a dent in a sea of fish. It would be in the very long run that changing technical capacities proved capable of seriously impacting fish stocks. By the twentieth century this had brought about disaster. From the earliest days of Terra Nova to the death throes of the Newfoundland fishery in the 1990s, Parmenius's belief persisted.[2]

Colonial Natures

What did this killing-for-energy look like? The daily routine of cod fishing at Terra Nova is known to us in broad strokes. Once arrived at a fishing harbor of their choice, the crew anchored the ship offshore and set up a camp on the beach. Anthony Parkhurst indicated that the first, time-consuming task was always "making our boats and stages. In getting our boats. In making flakes and other drying places." Once the boats were assembled and the drying spots (flakes) were prepared, the real work began. Every morning, crews of fishworkers broke into smaller groups. Some stayed onshore to tend to the drying fish, adding salt and turning them over (this had to be done regularly), as well as managing the camp and foraging for food and water. Most of the crew members were tasked with fishing, which required breaking down further into smaller teams. A few fishworkers would set out from the beach, rowing or sailing onto the ocean. Fishworkers then took long ropes with iron hooks, baited them (often with chunks of fish or bird taken locally), and dropped them in the water. After a time, they drew in the ropes, killed the fish, and stored them in the bottom of the boat until they could be returned to shore and offloaded at camp (see figure 16). Then the cod had to be headed, gutted, split, and salted—organs and face removed, body reshaped, and flesh desiccated. The exact curing process depended on how much salt the crew had as well as the weather conditions. Sometimes fish were soaked in brine first to absorb salt, sometimes rough salt was rubbed directly into the flesh, and sometimes these processes alternated. All were set out in the sun (often tied in bundles) to dry, laid on flat stones or drying racks constructed from local wood. For several days the fish were carefully and repeatedly turned over until they were ready to go into the ship's hold.[3]

Such at least was the routine for the majority of fishworkers who practiced what is often called "shore fishery" or "dry fishery." There would have been important differences for those who undertook the "wet fishery" or "bank fishery," which was focused on producing brined barreled codfish. In such cases the crew stayed onboard the main ship, which would remain offshore on the Grand Banks or similar fishing grounds. Here crews would catch fish and then dismember, heavily salt, and pack them into barrels onboard without having to set them out to dry in the sun. The result was that these crews could rapidly harvest large quantities of cod and return to home ports without ever needing to set foot on shore for extended periods of time. The resulting brined fish did not last as long as those that were dry salted, but they could be eaten quickly in Europe or given a longer dry cure later on. As competition increased toward the turn of the seventeenth century, this wet fishery became increasingly popular as it allowed for more rapid shipments back to Europe. Over time a distinct "green fishery," dominated by Normans and others from the kingdom of France, developed on the Grand Banks. By the end of the century, sometimes a ship would come from Europe to pick up the wet catch mid-season and bring it back to home ports, where the fish were given a finishing drying session in the sunny conditions of Spain or France. Even so, across the sixteenth century many crews mixed the two approaches, onshore drying and offshore brining, to produce a mix of food through a combination of labor.[4]

What shall we call this system of killing, processing, and storing marine life? This European activity in the northwest Atlantic fulfilled the basic purpose of a colony: to place a region's resources (in this case mainly biological resources) at the disposal of the metropole through long-term occupation and extraction. It was a colony without settlement and without empire, but a colony nonetheless. Continual cyclical, seasonal fishing operations constituted a permanent presence, a coastal occupation, in the northwest Atlantic by European mariners from the early sixteenth century onward. How, then, do we describe such a kind of colonization, one that put killing and energy at the center of operations?

The historian Nancy Shoemaker has offered us a provocative typology of colonialisms to help explain the variability in colonial practices across time and space. She defines extractive colonialism according to a simple logic, and it was this that drove European occupation at Terra Nova. "All the colonizers want is a raw material found in a particular locale." It is telling, however, that Shoemaker's description seems modeled on seventeenth- and eighteenth-century colonial projects. "A slash-and-burn operation, extractive colonialism does not necessarily entail permanent occupation, but it often seems to follow. Extractive colonizers might destroy or push away indigenous

Figure 16. Fishworkers in small boats catch cod by hand near Cape Breton. Note the seabirds and plentiful marine life. Detail, map of Terra Nova by Giacolmo Gastaldi, 1606 edition of 1556 map. (Courtesy of the John Carter Brown Library, Creative Commons license CC by 4.0, https://creativecommons.org/licenses/by/4.0/.)

inhabitants to access resources but more typically depend upon native diplomatic mediation, environmental knowledge, and labor. Consequently, marriage 'in the custom of the country' is more common with extractive colonialism than with settler and planter colonialism." Her emphasis on Indigenous intermediaries and exchange as a basis for resource extraction seems to come out of New France. But at Terra Nova there were no Indigenous intermediaries, nothing between fishworkers and their catch. Terra Nova was an extractive colony in the purest sense. Energy extraction was the sole focus of the European presence in the northwest Atlantic, and everything was shaped around it. We can see this in the way that fur was treated as an ancillary product rather than a focus of exchange, while whale hunting attracted considerable investment. We can see this in the way Europeans eschewed year-round settlements but returned each spring like clockwork. Most important, we can see this in the way that Terra Nova was never formally integrated into empire. It was so extractive, so simple, that it resisted control from the top. Fishworkers floated offshore for brief periods of time and harvested marine life without recourse to permanent settlement or even trade.[5]

Let me suggest that Terra Nova represents a particular twist on Shoemaker's typology. Perhaps we can call this a "floating extractive colonialism." In the literal sense the colony of Terra Nova floated, for it was built of wooden ships rather than settlements. But it floated figuratively as well. Terra Nova was unfixed and mobile, a feature we have seen was essential to its nature. Europeans floated from one fishing ground to another, or between different kinds of marine life (birds, whales, seals, and so on) that could be killed. Above all, fishworkers were aliens who floated above and beyond the ecologies they extracted. They were untethered, uninvested in the ecologies of the northwest Atlantic. Floating extractive colonies left a light human footprint on the landscape but could deeply impact biomass over the long run. There is something about aquatic resources and maritime spaces that allows for and encourages these floating extractive forms of colonization. The fifteenth-century Portuguese fishery along the coast of Saharan Africa or the English fishing-trade experience at Iceland are early models. Even today the world struggles to deal with massive long-distance fisheries like those off the coast of West Africa or around the Indian Ocean and South China Sea. As such examples indicate, even if they lacked permanent physical settlements, floating extractive colonies functioned as forms of occupation. Although seasonal, because they were continual across many years such colonies became de facto permanent in the sixteenth century. Moreover, these floating extractive colonies could be quite large. Because there is a direct relationship between labor inputs and extractive outputs in the premodern world (the more workers, the more gets harvested), Europeans were incentivized to concentrate fishworkers at places like Terra Nova during the viable fishing seasons. Freed from the difficulty of supplying a settlement year-round, these floating colonies could rapidly expand. The question is, by how much?

Scale

In the fall of 1573, John Parsons made a terrible mistake. Hired to guide a ship called the *John* into the harbor of Exmouth in England, by his "craft, fault, ignorance, rashness, and negligence" he caused the ship to run aground (such, at least, was the finding of the High Court of the Admiralty). The *John* had just returned from Terra Nova, and its cargo hold was stuffed with 70,000 salted codfish. Thanks to Parsons's error, 18,000 of the fish fell into the river and were lost. The merchants who had organized the voyage, understandably upset by this foul-up, brought suit against Parsons to get back the profits lost when piles of dead, salty fish tumbled into the brackish waters of the River Exe. The owners of the *John* believed the 18,000 fish they lost were worth £260, or a bit over £14 per thousand fish. Interestingly, the "breaking up and loss of the ship" was reckoned at only £66, showing how much more valuable the fish were to these merchants. The cargo as a whole may have been worth up to £980—a princely sum in the sixteenth century, though most of that was tied down in paying outfitters, creditors, and fishworkers. To put it one way, the crew of the ship *John* in 1573 must have been catching, killing, and processing something like 750 codfish a day to fill the hold with 70,000 saltfish. The 18,000 fish lost at sea represented three weeks' work—no wonder the owners were so irate.[6]

Far more precious were the calories and protein lost when the fish fell overboard. It only took a small amount of codfish to make a big difference in provisioning human populations. In 1522 on the warship *Mary Rose* it took eighteen thousand dried cod, the same number as fell from the *John*, to feed three thousand mariners for eight weeks (the cod being consumed primarily on fish days). A dry-salted cod could have been worth 1,250–1,750 kilocalories apiece, a battery that could power a human for a day. The full cargo of seventy thousand codfish the *John* carried in 1573 may well have contained around 100 million kilocalories of energy. And that was on just one small ship—there would be a hundred just like it arriving in European ports every autumn. The case of the *John* gives us a glimpse into the quantities and values of food extracted from the northwest Atlantic in the mid-sixteenth century. At the time the *John* sailed in 1573, it is likely that upwards of three hundred vessels were making that same voyage every summer, perhaps as many as five hundred. Any discussion of harvesting must acknowledge that the Terra Nova fishery was a major operation relative to other harvesting and commercial European endeavors in the sixteenth-century Atlantic.[7]

The scale of the fishery between 1500 and 1600 is a matter of a debate that will likely never be settled given the paucity of our sources. The surviving records are simply too scattered and limited to provide the necessary quantitative data. The entirety of the notarial records of Lower Normandy, for instance, have been lost (blown to pieces during World War II), yet we know that numerous ships sailed from ports like Granville, Cherbourg, and Avranches. Because it lacks a tradition of notarial contract record-keeping, southwest England doesn't have reliable sources of ship counts until close to the seventeenth century. Even when we have records, a key question remains unanswerable: what percentage of voyages required contracts versus those that were arranged solely by oral agreements? Not every voyage made it into the notarial records, but the latter are the only kinds we can see and count. It would matter if half of all voyages required a formally written loan, or if two-thirds did, or only a quarter, for each gives us a different estimate. Unfortunately there is no way to be certain, and most scholars (myself included) can only assume that after 1540 recorded contracts represent a high proportion of overall voyages leaving Europe. What we must do, then, is estimate for certain points in time based on the bits of data that have survived. Laurier Turgeon has set the baseline for these attempts with a detailed study of notarial records in Bordeaux, La Rochelle, and Rouen. Using his study as a starting point, we may hazard some conclusions.[8]

Scholars have variously estimated that after the mid-sixteenth century, somewhere between three hundred and five hundred ships sailed annually for the fishery at Terra Nova. The highest estimates are at least five hundred ships carrying twenty thousand or more mariners to Terra Nova in the second half of the sixteenth century. This is a liberal but nonetheless plausible estimate. At least one observer in the 1580s thought that five hundred ships sailed from French ports alone. My own reading of the evidence suggests that in the mid-1560s around three hundred ships annually sailed for Terra Nova from European ports. About half of these were a mixture of Norman, Saintongeois, and Basque ships outfitted in the three ports of Rouen, La Rochelle, and Bordeaux. The remainder were small contingents of Breton, Spanish Basque, West Country, and Portuguese vessels. The average size of a ship was probably around eighty to one hundred tons, carrying some twenty to thirty fishworkers. This means that in the 1560s the fishery constituted some seventy-five hundred to nine thousand mariners in twenty-seven thousand to thirty thousand tons of shipping. My count of three hundred ships is lower than the highest estimates and suggests that the fishing fleet was about double the number of recorded voyages. It is intended less as a firm estimate than as a baseline: I think it highly unlikely that fewer than three hundred ships sailed, but the number could easily have been higher.[9]

It is harder to determine how the fishery fluctuated in scale over time. The number of ships headed to Terra Nova before 1520 was likely low; one observer around that date reports only 100 or so ships. From the 1520s the rate of traffic began to grow, rising in erratic ways as more and more coastal ports joined in. Then suddenly in the early 1540s the scale of operations increased significantly across the board, perhaps doubling to 150–200 ships a year. Thereafter growth was relatively steady, until in the 1560s–70s some 300 or more ships sailed every season. Peter Pope, Brad Loewen, and others note that after 1580 the size of the fleet probably increased again as more English ships joined the fishery and competition intensified. By the year 1600 an estimate of 500 ships seems a reasonable baseline. Within these general patterns are numerous peaks and troughs. Surviving records suggest that some years saw great hosts departing Europe for Terra Nova, bursts of activity that stand out. At other points we have almost no evidence, an indication that interest occasionally waned. Such was the nature of fishwork, an industry bound to natural rhythms, cycles of war, and changing consumer demand.[10]

All these estimates, regardless of which ones we accept, point to a single and inescapable conclusion: the scale of operations at Terra Nova was vast, especially relative to other European ventures in the Atlantic basin. The number of documented fishing voyages in the year 1565, a total of 153, is far greater than the number of ships departing Seville for the Americas that same year (sixty-six ships, plus another thirty-four from La Palma). Terra Nova ships were smaller than those that sailed to the Caribbean, it is true, but there were many more of them. It was very likely more than the number of ships regularly sailing to West Africa or Brazil in the same century. Three hundred ships and at least ten thousand men represented a substantial fraction of Europe's total maritime resources, and this concentration of European men rivaled the European population of many early colonies in the Americas.[11]

The numbers of ships and mariners tell only part of the story. Each crew was capable of harvesting and processing a large quantity of fish, so as the number of vessels grew so did the intensity of extraction. Small ships (in the range of sixty tons) could hold ten thousand to twenty thousand fish; larger ones could hold one hundred thousand or more. These were large catches for the time, though they are tiny by modern standards. Fishwork was itself an energy-intensive activity, yet the economic logic of a long-distance fishery held true. A team of scholars has recently investigated sixteenth-century naval diets, and using their data we may estimate the daily caloric intake of a mariner at around four thousand kilocalories. This was consumed in the form of bread and preserved foods from Europe mixed with fresh protein and plants from Terra Nova. A fishing ship of twenty fishworkers would therefore require eighty thousand kilocalories a day, or 12 million over the course of a five-month voyage. They would have to catch and process just under ten thousand fish to cover their own energy costs. Since most crews returned with several tens of thousands of salted cod, such as the seventy thousand carried by the *John*, we may see that in terms of energy flows transoceanic harvesting easily operated as a net gain.[12]

The relatively small size of fishing ships, however, complicates how we think of harvesting and points to another one of those ironies that defined Terra Nova. Sixteenth-century European fishworkers did not put limits on their harvest. Even so, the actual scale of the catch was far less than what later generations of fishworker were capable of. The seventy thousand codfish carried by the *John* was impressive to its crew and remarkable by sixteenth-century European standards, but was less than a drop in the bucket of the biomass of the northwest Atlantic. Given their small ships, most crews could not have overfished even if they had wanted to, for there would have been no way to ship the catch home. We must thread this needle between an uninhibited desire to harvest biomass and firm limits on the capacity to do so.

Importantly, even if sixteenth-century fishworkers were technically incapable of draining the *piscium inexhausta copia*, we should not underestimate the broader potential for premodern fishworkers to do so. A recent series of investigations by the Norfish project has reached a striking conclusion: premodern handline fishing was indeed capable of extracting cod from the northwest Atlantic at levels comparable to modern industrialized fishing. Their painstaking analysis has shown that it was merely a matter of scale, not technology or technique, that made the difference to catch rates. As the fishery grew in the seventeenth and eighteenth centuries, so too did annual catches. "[Premodern] levels . . . are fairly similar to those existing in the 20th century at the time of depletion of cod stocks. This effectively extends and expands the baseline for the debate about the overexploitation of Newfoundland cod resources by a matter of centuries." Fishing peaked in 1788, with over six hundred thousand metric tonnes of cod captured, all of it by handline. This comes with an important qualification. The intensity of fishing reached its peak only in the mid- to late eighteenth century; sixteenth-century rates were far lower (one-fourth to one-half the cumulative catch) than those achieved two hundred years later. The three hundred to five hundred ships of the late sixteenth century could not achieve the vast industrial operations that were normal only a few generations later. Even so, the Norfish study indicates that we must take the capabilities of premodern fishworkers seriously. Despite lacking trawlers and steamships, fishworkers had the potential to extract tremendous amounts of marine life from the waters of the northwest Atlantic, so long as they achieved a certain scale of operations.[13]

This is why I and other scholars of premodern fisheries take places like Terra Nova so seriously, and why we are so frustrated when environmental and Atlantic historians treat the northwest Atlantic as a blind spot. Even with the limits of the source base, the reality screams at us from notarial entries and court cases and geographic treatises: a lot of Europeans worked at Terra Nova from an early date, and they were on the path to pulling a shocking amount of marine life out of its waters. The fishery was a vast and growing floating colony that allowed thousands of mariners to work simultaneously on an effort to exhaust an inexhaustible supply of food and fuel.

Beyond Cod

Not everything that Europeans killed in the sixteenth century was cod. Among the earliest creatures brought back from the northwest Atlantic were "hawks from the new found Island" which appeared in London in 1503. Early European visitors were interested in pursuing a variety of commercial options before focusing exclusively on fish. To that end, one of the first living organisms harvested by Europeans at Terra Nova were other human beings. In London in 1502 a trio of men "were brought unto the king . . . taken in the New Found Island. . . . These were clothed in beasts' skins and eat raw flesh and speak such speech that no man would understand them." Yet the tale takes a turn when the same observer noted, "Two years later I saw two of them appareled after English men in Westminster Palace, which at that time I could not discern them from Englishmen until I was told who they were." What became of these visitors is unknown, but clearly their appearance made a lasting impression. Gaspar Corte Real was reported to have taken fifty men and women back from Terra Nova to Lisbon in 1500. It was one of the largest mass abductions of the early sixteenth century Atlantic. Jacques Cartier abducted at least two people from the "Land of Canada" who were brought back to Saint Malo and baptized in 1539. On occasion humans from Terra Nova appear in Europe without full explanation. Two accounts written in northern France around 1509 attest to the presence of up to seven men in the city of Rouen. One describes them as "from Terra Nova," the other as having been picked up by a French ship off the coast of England. For a few decades in the early sixteenth century, then, Indigenous Americans from Terra Nova could be found in many European cities. The repeated abductions of human beings in the northwest Atlantic were not haphazard but part of a wider European strategy of commerce and colonization in the Atlantic basin. Some abducted individuals were no doubt meant to serve as translators and go-betweens, key tools Europeans could employ to expand their control over trade and power in the western Atlantic. Other individuals were likely meant to be sold as slaves. References to such kidnappings become rarer after the 1530s before picking up again toward the end of the century with the resurgence of exploration and settlement. Yet we may wonder if the practice was ever entirely abandoned, or if it was merely unrecorded.[14]

More enduring and visible in our sources are the other-than-human animals that Europeans coveted. Here we must draw an important distinction between those other-than-human creatures killed for commercial reasons (to be sold back in Europe), and those killed to sustain the fishery through immediate consumption. As regards the former, it is noteworthy that beyond cod a surprisingly narrow range of other-than-human creatures were killed for commercial reasons in the sixteenth century. Not that some didn't see riches beyond cod. English promoters from the late sixteenth century carefully listed and extolled all of the potential victims: from foxes to herring to bears to finches. We know that salmon and herring were beloved foods in much of Europe, and seals and walruses were much-sought sources of oil and hides. Writing with hindsight in 1618, at a moment when Terra Nova was being supplanted by new colonial regimes, France's premier navigator-cum-settler-cum-imperial propagandist Samuel de Champlain surveyed the potential biological resources of the northwest Atlantic. Dispatching a letter to an anonymous French *chambre de commerce*, Champlain laid out what he saw as the financial value of life at Terra Nova. Cod fishing alone was estimated to be worth 1 million *livres* each year. Whales, prized for both their oils and baleen, could bring in (along with walruses and seals) another 700,000 *livres*. To this he added salmon, sturgeon, eel, herring, and sardines, worth some 300,000 *livres*. This was a major untapped source of revenue, and Champlain's tallies were not hypotheses but estimates based on contemporary fishing and whaling activities. Yet before 1618 little attempt was made to develop sustained and organized exploitation of these marine resources. Sixteenth-century Europeans were in fact unusual in focusing so much on a single species, the Atlantic cod, in their efforts.[15]

One glaring exception complicates this narrative. We know that some Europeans invested quite a lot of effort and capital into hunting, killing, and processing whales. A great deal of scholarship has been devoted to the development of an intense whaling industry by Basque mariners around La Gran Baya. There are two reasons for this interest. First, unlike cod fishing, whaling generated far more paperwork and evidence, since it was a much more complex and expensive enterprise. We also have the benefit of underwater archaeology as well as documentary sources, and the investigation of the Red Bay site has given us unparalleled detail on a sixteenth-century voyage. The second reason is that the Basque whaling enterprise was a genuinely novel achievement that had a major long-term impact. The first long-distance whaling industry in the Atlantic basin, it set the template for all subsequent iterations. We can trace the killing fields of Spitsbergen, Greenland, Berengia, and the Pacific back to La Gran Baya.[16]

We must be careful not to overemphasize the impact and importance of whaling in the sixteenth century. The whaling fleet was always many times smaller than the cod fishing fleet, fluctuating between perhaps fifteen to thirty vessels instead of hundreds. These ships were much larger and had bigger crews, however, and required much more money and equipment. Unlike the multinational fishery, whaling seems to have been the exclusive concern of Basques from Gipúzcoa and Labourd, and was concentrated largely along La Gran Baya until the end of the century. Individual whaling voyages could generate considerable profits, again attracting much attention in our sources and from scholars. The oil they brought back to Europe was extremely valuable and welcome in a continent starved for fuel. So we would do well to understand the whaling industry as a small, concentrated subset of European operations within Terra Nova itself, albeit one that had an outsized impact and legacy.

In general, whaling crews had a different experience at Terra Nova than did fishing crews. Whales were the hardest sea creatures to kill at Terra Nova, and the process was often described as hunting (*chasse à la baleine* in French, *caza de ballenas* in Spanish) in reference to its intensive and specialized nature. One could not catch a whale, which was too big and too intelligent. "This whale," wrote André Thevet, "is very dangerous on the sea if you meet one, as those of Bayonne well know from experience." Instead, you had to track, chase, attack, weaken, pursue, gather, and finally butcher the whale. Basques perfected the hunting of whales on the open sea and were much renowned for their skill and expert knowledge. They turned the *txalupa* into a swift, sturdy vessel for chasing down and inflicting trauma upon whales. The goal was to inflict sufficient pain and exhaustion to kill the animal. When a whale was sighted, a harpooner, standing at the prow of the *txalupa*, hurled his barb at the animal. Sometimes many *txalupas*, often from different crews, converged on the same whale when it was sighted, adding their own weapons (see figure 14). The harpoon caused painful, bloody wounds, slowing down the whale. After a time the exhausted animal would cease to resist and could be dragged to shore for processing.[17]

Whaling also had a different impact upon the environment of Terra Nova than fishing did. Whales had to be butchered and carved up into constituent elements, a process that took place in the water near the shoreline. Whale blubber was steadily boiled in large ovens built onshore and rendered into train oil, which was brought back to Europe. Basques brought tiles, kettles, nails, and even soil with them to Terra Nova to build their sturdy ovens at places like Butus harbor. Whaling required infrastructure in a way that fishing did not, making it more expensive and intensive, and thus less often practiced. Basques further had significant impacts on marine life through hunting whales. The whale population in the northwest Atlantic was smaller than that of other marine life, and therefore more susceptible to disruption. Basque whalers do seem to have diminished and disrupted the size of whale populations in La Gran Baya. Loewen has estimated that between 1530 and 1600, Basque whalers killed some thirteen thousand individual whales. This was a substantial death toll, largely concentrated along the southern coast of Labrador. By the early seventeenth century we see Basque whalers shifting toward the River of Canada, possibly chasing whale populations as they became depleted farther north. Although a small industry, whaling quickly shaped aquatic environments.[18]

Whaling at least was related to cod fishing in that it was a maritime activity. Yet when later generations of Europeans, in the seventeenth and eighteenth centuries, thought of harvesting the northwest Atlantic, they would not have thought of cod or whale oil but of furs. The processed pelts of beavers were among the most important organic commodities extracted from North America in the premodern period. Even today they receive a great deal of scholarly attention. This is common in the historiography of early Canada, which emphasizes the fur trade as the true genesis of colonialism and Canadian nationhood. The political, economic, social, demographic, and environmental impact of the post-1600 fur trade would overshadow Terra Nova in many eyes.[19]

For all that, the extraction of animal fur from Terra Nova before 1600 was less important to European activity than we would suspect. Indeed, a distinct fur trade took much longer to develop than a fishing or whaling industry. Though furs, including beaver, were regularly brought back by mariners across the century, the overall quantities—and thus the impact—seem to have been much lower than they would be after 1600. This may not have been intentional; as Laurier Turgeon has pointed out, from a very early date French merchants evinced a desire to construct a hegemonic, sustained fur trade in the northwest Atlantic. As he notes, mid-sixteenth century texts used the word *conquête* to describe their ambitions, suggesting that merchants wanted to conquer commerce and seize control from Indigenous hands. That same language was markedly absent from the fishery. Yet it was the fishery that rapidly grew in scale while the fur trade struggled to grow. Though a handful of ships were outfitted in French ports to specifically purchase furs in bulk as early as the 1560s, such voyages are quite uncommon until after the 1580s. Only after this date do we see a distinct and sustained fur trade developed by European merchants. This might be symbolized by the establishment of a regular trade outpost by Basques at Tadoussac, the site where the Saguenay and River of Canada converge. This outpost marked a turning point toward a clear fur trade, quickly becoming the crucial node for yearly exchange, yet it was founded only in 1579–80. Instead, before 1580 furs seem to have been acquired by fishworkers haphazardly as part of their regular visits. Furs were exchanged for European goods in an ad hoc manner, and brought back alongside fish and oil in small quantities.[20]

In practice fur was of ancillary importance to European interactions with the region until much later in the century. It was largely a by-product of the fishery rather than a distinct and transformative trade in its own right. As Turgeon notes, many notarial contracts simply lumped furs into the "other goods and merchandise" clause appended to a description of fishing. In 1596 a Hollander ship sailed to Plymouth to pick up "pelts and fish" from "Terra Neuf" for resale in Spain, indicating that the two trades were still intermixed. This means that the impact on animal populations around Terra Nova must have been limited before the 1580s. It also means that the impact on Indigenous communities would have been—again compared to later generations—moderated as well. As with whaling, we can see the groundwork being laid by mariners for industries that, at later times and places, would have transformative and disruptive impacts. Yet the killing of codfish remained the overriding commercial focus for most Europeans in the sixteenth century.[21]

Not all killing was for commercial reasons, and may other-than-human lives were lost in service to the cod fishery. Fishworkers needed to be fed; food begets food. We know that Europeans brought food with them during their summer voyages, as the bulk of their provisions (especially ship's biscuit and alcohol) were bought and onloaded at outfitting ports just before the ship left for its voyage to Terra Nova. Yet that European food had to include ingredients local to the northwest Atlantic. Codfish, the very thing that brought them to Terra Nova, was also a key element in fishworkers' diets along with other seafood like capelin, salmon, and mackerel. Berries, seaweed, shellfish, and small game were easy to find near beaches. For an experienced forager, the subarctic could enliven even the most boring ship's rations.[22]

The most important source of food for fishworkers and for many Indigenous communities at Terra Nova was not fish but birds. The northwest Atlantic is home to a wide variety of land- and seabirds, but the latter were more important to coastal fishworkers. Some of these seabirds breed in massive offshore colonies, while others pass through Terra Nova during the summer as part of yearly migratory cycles. Once fishworkers realized the scale of bird populations, seabirds played an important role in European

provisioning. Seabirds were already eaten in some parts of Europe, and David Gange has drawn attention to the importance of seasonal seabird hunts
in places like Shetland and the Orkney isles. Seabirds offered the prospect
of fresh meat and salted protein, as well as eggs. After a month of living on
hardtack and dried meat, the first bite of auk or guillemot after arriving at
Terra Nova must have been heavenly.[23]

Every autumn Europeans left behind beaches strewn with crushed egg-
shells and rotting bird bones. Cod was precious and had to be carried to Europe; birds were to be eaten and discarded. Many fishworkers were delighted
to find such a useful and easily harvested food source so close to their seasonal camps. While visiting the Isle des Ouaiseulx (Isle of Birds) in 1534,
Jacques Cartier wrote: "And there are very fat birds which are a truly marve-
lous thing. We named these birds *Apponatz* and we loaded up two of our
barques with them in less than half an hour, like stones, of which each of
our ships salted four or five *pipes* [a small barrel], without which we would
have been unable to eat."[24]

As Cartier's description suggests, French ships preferred their birds pickled. In this they came to resemble cod, an avian analogue to *morue verte*
(green gannet?). Many crews dispatched hunting parties to offshore breeding islands, where they used firearms and nets to gather up parents and eggs
alike. The English under Richard Hore in 1536 "drove a great number of the
fowls into their boats upon their sails, and took up many of their eggs; the
fowl they flayed and their skins were like honeycombs full of holes being
flayed off." Poor auks, flayed alive by birdshot until their Swiss-cheese bodies were put into the communal dinner pot. But without such provisions on
the wing, there may never have been a sustained fishery.[25]

Elizabeth Kolbert has famously drawn a direct causal line between this
early slaughter to provision fishworkers and the extinction of the great auk,
the "original penguin," in the nineteenth century. By 1800 the great auk had
been effectively exterminated from the northwest Atlantic. In between it became hunted not just for food but for its feathers, as bait, for oil, and other
uses. As Kolbert has noted, this provided an early and shocking example of
the possibilities of extinction to Europeans, who had thought such rapid biological upheaval impossible. A similar causal line—thin at first, then growing

over time—might likewise be drawn between the early killing of birds and the collapse of cod fishery in the late twentieth century. The sixteenth-century fishery was possible only because of local food sources like seabirds. Many crews specifically guided their boats to harbors near offshore bird breeding grounds in order to have easier access to provisions. This practice became embedded in the fishery as it grew over the centuries. Fueled by bird flesh, fishworkers would so destabilize the aquatic ecosystem of the northwest Atlantic by the mid-twentieth century that the fishery as a whole would go the way of the great auk.[26]

There also had to be a way to cook the different animals turned into food-stuffs. An often overlooked provision that was critical to fishworkers was firewood. Each meal required fuel to make, and it was bulky and expensive to bring firewood from Europe. Wood would also have been important to the construction of drying racks, campsites, and the other flimsy edifices of a seasonal work camp. So fishworkers foraged for fuel as well as food, gathering materials to cook their stews and porridges each day. This is the kind of activity rarely mentioned in our sources, but it must have been essential. We can surmise that fishing sites were chosen by virtue of their proximity to trees and scrub that could be used as firewood and drying racks. In the stew pots in their seaside encampments, European biscuits were mixed with local meats and cooked over American trees to fortify fishworker stomachs.[27]

Sometimes European mariners did more than just forage. In at least one case they transplanted other-than-human animals to be killed for food. The Isle de Sable is a long, curved sandbar lying off the southeast coast of what is today Nova Scotia. We know that at some point in the early sixteenth century Portuguese fishworkers deposited European cattle on the island. An account of Gilbert's 1583 voyage notes that the English met a Portuguese mariner "who was himself present when the Portuguese, about thirty years ago, landed on this island and put there both cattle and swine to breed, which have exceedingly multiplied. This seemed like happy tidings to us, to have an island so near the mainland where we intended to settle, whereby we might at all times conveniently take victuals and animals to breed." Samuel de Champlain, visiting in 1604, repeated the story and timeline, emphasizing that the Portuguese had left "fine cattle" sometime around the 1540s.

The initial arrival of European animals seems to have been deliberate, and the English clearly thought it a good idea. By the mid- to late sixteenth century this initial planting had grown into a herd of wild cattle. It is not clear to what extent fishworkers actually relied on this provisioning station, or if it was treated as a kind of curiosity. The Isle de Sable was distant from most of the fishing sites and most seabird colonies in the sixteenth century. The introduction of cattle may have been an attempt to make up for this shortfall in flying life and help crews interested in the nearby Banquereau sand bank. If so, it is one of the few instances in which adaptation broke down in favor of direct intervention, and European mariners deliberately introduced Afro-Eurasian fauna to the coasts of the northwest Atlantic before the first permanent settlements were ever constructed.[28]

Legacies

The sixteenth-century floating extractive colony at Terra Nova was the starting point for the systematic exploitation of Arctic and subarctic biomes by European merchants, mariners, and hunters over the past five centuries. On the south coast of Labrador, Basque whalers pioneered techniques for industrial, commercial killing and processing of whales. Many of these techniques were then spread, often deliberately, across the Atlantic basin and eventually to the Pacific. A key part of the new European approach to the Arctic and subarctic, pioneered at Terra Nova, was maintaining alienated harvesting as a core mechanic. Europeans arrived from the outside, established temporary extractive camps, and departed. They had no stake in the ecosystems or localities they plundered for food and fuel (and eventually furs). This is perhaps why it has been so easy for later generations and scholars to ignore these frigid killing grounds. What is nonetheless striking about Terra Nova is the degree to which this extractive regime arose organically from within a decentralized and multinational maritime world. It was not planned, but it proved enduring.

The advent of an extractive regime in the subarctic—and eventually the Arctic itself—represented a long-term threat to Indigenous communities and ultimately the world. Food and fuel are not truly *inexhausta copia* in the northern latitudes. They are finite, and therefore every ounce harvested by Europeans deprived Indigenous communities of the same. The effects of this process would begin to manifest in the northwest Atlantic around the turn of the seventeenth century, affecting Beothuk and Mi'kmaq and soon other communities beyond Terra Nova. We can now see, in the even longer term, that this extractive regime also represents an existential threat to us all. All the animals first harvested in the sixteenth century at Terra Nova—cod, whales, beaver, walrus, seal—have subsequently seen population collapse and near annihilation. In turn their deaths fueled growth in the metropole. The Europeans who were fed *bacalao* would go on to develop the tools to overheat our planet, melt the Arctic, and threaten us all.

And yet, none of this was apparent from the vantage point of the sixteenth century. That is the problem: the tension between intention and outcome that environmental historians struggle with. I do not want to suggest that Breton or Portuguese fishworkers, standing on the shores of Terra Nova catching cod, had any intention of collapsing the global ecology and killing every living thing north of the 40th parallel. They seem to have genuinely believed that marine resources were inexhaustible, and it's true that even with their overwhelming concentration of ships and fishworkers in the northwest Atlantic they were unable to make much of a difference. The road to our present climate-ecological crisis was paved with good intentions; the earnest desire of sixteenth-century European fishworkers to feed and fuel their communities by harvesting a seemingly unlimited biomass was a reasonable and understandable set of choices. Only in subsequent generations, as the number of ships continued to rise and the belief in inexhaustible supplies never wavered, did this become the path to catastrophe.

NINE

Commons

On August 3 in the year 1583, Sir Humphrey Gilbert, English aristocrat and adventurer, sailed into Sam Joham/Saint John's with three small ships. Bearing a royal decree from the queen of England, a minor northwest European state attempting to punch well above its weight, Gilbert had arrived partway through the fishing season to lay claim to the entirety of what he viewed as the New-found-lands. Gathering together members of the thirty-odd fishing crews already working in the harbor, he read out his writ, declared himself master of the coasts and fishery, and demanded that crews turn over much-needed supplies. The assembled fishworkers immediately agreed (or so we are told by English sources), and Gilbert enjoyed his brief time as Lord of the Fishery before sailing home a few weeks later. It was the kind of theatrical moment that later generations would celebrate as a bold, ambitious act announcing England's arrival on the Atlantic stage. Gilbert had even dragged along his favorite poet, Stephen Parmenius, to write a paean (in proper Latin) to his glorious achievements, but the Hungarian would die before this could be accomplished. Gilbert died too, drowned along with his crew when he foolishly guided his ship homeward through a storm against the advice of more seasoned mariners.[1]

There are many ways we could interpret this story: from a noble quest gone awry to a slapdash misadventure to a cynical power play that failed. Let me suggest that we borrow a page from literature and read it as a farce. Gilbert's declaration of ownership was ludicrous and invalid from the second he uttered it. Terra Nova was not the queen's to give away, and Sir Humphrey had no practical way to enforce his claims beyond localized brute force. Gilbert showed up in a busy harbor two-thirds of the way through a fishing season and tried to convince a polyglot (and likely well-armed) assortment of crews that he was somehow in charge. That they gave him supplies may have been an act of sympathy rather than submission, for it was patently clear that Gilbert and his crew were ill prepared to survive long in the northwest Atlantic. Even his own promoters noted that many members of Gilbert's crew ran away to hide in the woods or join other ships as soon as they arrived in Sam Joham/Saint John's, desperate to escape his service, forcing the would-be master of Terra Nova to abandon one of his ships and return home early. It did not make for a particularly impressive scene. We may imagine the fishworkers in Sam Joham/Saint John's harbor chuckling as they humored this pompous aristocrat, nodding along in the hope that Gilbert might be willing to exchange some goods for fish. When Gilbert managed to get himself killed on the voyage home, that was the end of it.

On a fundamental level, Gilbert's adventures reveal a misunderstanding about what the Terra Nova fishery was. Gilbert entered a harbor filled with self-regulating fishworkers operating according to a social-property system that was now several decades old, and tried to tell them that the world was about to be turned upside down. His actions rested on an assumption that the water and fish of the northwest Atlantic now belonged to a single distant monarch, and that all the old customs that apportioned access to fishworkers were now invalid. To explain Gilbert's folly, I believe that we should consider Terra Nova as a space outside of empire—as a commons. Codfish were treated by fishworkers as a commonly held resource and individual fishing grounds as a commons. The Terra Nova fishery was not embedded within wider legal and political systems that we call empires, and it lay beyond the practical and conceptual limits of European states.

The study of empire has long dominated Atlantic history. Indeed, the most frequent and stinging critique of the field remains that it is little more than imperial history with a new name. Even so, it is hard to avoid the fact that the formation of new imperial systems across the Atlantic basin, centered on European metropoles, was one of the defining features of the fifteenth through eighteenth centuries. For all the messiness of imperial formation in practice, the coercive and information-gathering structures developed by states like Spain and France did have real and powerful impacts on populations around the Atlantic basin. Yet inter- and extra-imperial spaces abounded, including zones that functioned like commons. Although more attention has been paid to borderlands, frontiers, and contact zones at the margins of empire, we here must consider places that are both outside imperial limits and were organized along European lines not as a borderland but as a commonly held resource. Examining Terra Nova as a commons outside empire allows us to address a fundamental problem: the northwest Atlantic was marked by tension between political chaos and social coherence. From the top, there was no single legal or political framework that embraced the whole northwest Atlantic, no empire within which it can be studied and classified. Yet from the bottom, there is remarkable coherence in how mariners from different communities behaved, harvested, and cooperated in the sixteenth century. Unity of purpose without unity of politics sits awkwardly in a historiography that continues to emphasize the role of state-backed settlements and interstate warfare in the formation of a new Atlantic world.

Authority

Pierre de Bocal could not catch a break. A French-speaking mariner who plied the Terra Nova trade, he kept finding himself locked up in Spanish ports under suspicion of piracy. In 1551 the city of Castro or Laredo in Cantabria (nobody could recall which) had captured Bocal as he came back from Terra Nova with a ship loaded with whale oil. He was released when a group of merchants from the commercial hub of Bilbao threw their weight into an appeal to free the captain. In 1552 the captain general of Gipúzcoa in Fuenterrabía locked Bocal up yet again, asking around town if he was a French corsair. Once more a group of local merchants and fishworkers came forward to attest that this was not the case. Instead, in response to an official inquiry they described Pierre de Bocal as a "quiet man" who regularly took his ship to Terra Nova to fish for *bacalao* and whales, and at other times worked the wine and wheat trade between La Rochelle and Bordeaux. What exactly Bocal had done to convince everyone he was a pirate is unclear, but the fact that fellow merchants kept jumping to his defense means that reports may have been greatly exaggerated. For our purposes, the case of Bocal points to the confusing and limited ways in which state authority was felt by fishworkers at Terra Nova. As Bocal kept learning, such authority was arbitrary, disruptive, easily challenged—and also confined to the beginning and especially the end of a long summer's voyage.[2]

Most fishwork activities within Europe itself were subject to overlapping, and at times contradictory, state and quasi-state authorities. I am here using "state" in an extremely broad sense, for the weak and heterodox political assemblages that dominated western Europe in the sixteenth century were anything but modern states. In many cases it would be cities—chartered municipalities like Rouen and Bordeaux—that acted as the state, regulating and attempting to control the behavior of fishworkers, merchants, and mariners. Many ports in sixteenth-century Europe functioned as semi-independent communes enjoying considerable local authority. For this reason it was often the town councils that acted as "the state" from the viewpoint of fishworkers. Sometimes these activities contrasted with royal intentions, sometimes they synergized, and sometimes the crown was compelled to follow the lead of their cities. It was further the case for much of the sixteenth century that fishworkers tended to come from regions that were already at the legal, social, and cultural margins of European states. Normandy enjoyed considerable historical and legal autonomy, while the marsh-dwelling Saintongeois were seen as barely French by Parisian authorities. The West Country of England had a reputation as a kind of lawless pirate nest. The major outfitting port of La Rochelle was not just semi-autonomous but also a haven for recalcitrant Huguenots. The relationship between fishery, community, and kingdom produced problems for many fishworkers.[3]

Overlapping and competing authorities at home also offered opportunities. It was possible for a mariner or merchant to appeal to the crown to override a city council, or to go to Parlement to challenge the local church officials. In other instances, merchants who were citizens of a particular city could persuade local authorities to bend the law in favorable ways. Mariners were quick to exploit these overlapping authorities and regional differences, working the edges of different legal regimes to their benefit. In the year 1559 the residents of Saint Jean-de-Luz begged the French king for legal protection against fellow subjects. Addressing the crown, the luziens asked for intercession to protect them from the merchants of many neighboring cities, stating that they "have need of the voyages which they make to Terra Nova for the fishery, and returning from there they come into our ports and harbours of Rouen, Bordeaux, La Rochelle and Nantes in which places they wish to sell their catch and other goods." Yet the *bourgeois* (civic citizens) of these towns were preventing the returning ships from selling their catch, and thus competing with local mariners. The towns listed, three in the Bay of Biscay and one in Normandy, were all major outfitting centers whose notarial records attest to the number of Basque fishworkers who took out loans from local merchants. For many luzien fishworkers being barred from these ports would be a threat to the entire system of credit and distribution that made their operations possible. Here subjects of the French crown from one province were appealing to their sovereign to protect them against the city communes in other provinces that were subject to the same monarch. It is an indication of the ways in which mariners could exploit overlapping levels of authority, but also a reminder that these opportunities were limited to European ports.[4]

These spheres of authority vanished as one passed beyond Europe's waters and sailed for Terra Nova. At Terra Nova itself, in the absence of top-down authorities, power functioned in different ways. For most mariners, authority was centered on the ship, and lay with the ship master. Below the master, the ship hierarchy was likely rather flat. Disputes onboard were quickly resolved by the master, though it is likely that they were guided and limited by prevailing customary laws, which could often empower regular sailors. Disputes between ships, however, had no third party to mediate or adjudicate in the absence of a recognized state authority. Not that some mariners would not try to use state authority to legitimize their actions at Terra Nova, especially acts of violence. The English pirate Hugh Oughtred claimed he was acting as a privateer for the English crown when he raided

Renews harbor in 1582, just before Humphrey Gilbert brandished his royal writ in Sam Joham/Saint John's harbor. Most of these attempts failed, either ignored or ending in lawsuits. Instead, for a few months each year migratory mariners were free of the confines of the state. But this moment of legal vacuum was bracketed by time in port at the start and end of the voyage when one was very much exposed to the power of the law. Improper sale of fish, insufficient taxes to the church, breach of contract, piracy and corsairing, unpaid wages: all of these were charges that might be levied against fishworkers at home, if not at sea. If one wished to invoke an authority, it had to be done at the end of the voyage, in the ports and courts of coastal Europe. It would be a gamble, an attempt to resolve past actions that had taken place on the other side of the ocean, but many plaintiffs tried their luck. In 1524 a lawsuit was brought against the residents of the small Norman port town of Saint Waast (modern Saint Vaast-la-Hogue). Local authorities were irked that the fishworkers of Saint Waast were not paying the proper taxes, the *dix-iesme*, on "the codfish which the said subjects can fish for at Terra Nova or other overseas regions." Presumably the fishworkers felt that their catch, taken from such distant waters, was not subject to the same regulations as something caught nearby. Like many records related to the early fishery, the suit is retroactive and reflexive, an attempt to understand and control what was already in motion. After all, by the time the fishworkers of Saint Waast were made to testify before the Parlement, the fishery was already two decades old.[5]

In the examples above, we can see the overlapping and often contradictory lines of authority that mariners had to navigate over the course of their voyages to and from Terra Nova. Depending on their physical position — in a home port, in European waters, at Terra Nova — they might be subject to authority as distant as a royal court or as close as their ship's captain. There were two potential ways for the divergence between Terra Nova and European waters to be remedied. One was for a European state authority to be projected across the sea, in a process we now recognize as the formation of imperial structures and new colonial legal regimes. The other would be to substitute an entirely new system of authority that functioned outside of a state apparatus.[6]

Control

Empires need nodes of control—points of coercive power and information gathering through which authority can be exercised. "Empire is, at its root, a territorial project," as Ashley Carse has put it. "Its architects establish outposts far from home from which to project power. . . . The imperial state then establishes and extends its authority through governmental techniques aimed at both large human populations and more intimate spaces and the territorial politics of landscape transformation." As James Scott has similarly argued, it is through these nodes of control that may be created "State Space," fluctuating zones of authority over human subjects. These nodes must be, in most cases, *lugar* in the sixteenth-century sense: they must be fixed points of settlement, and in the sixteenth century chartered cities and settlements were the key mechanisms by which imperial authority was constructed and spread. The ability of permanent settlements to gather, synthesize, and transmit information was crucial. Spanish power in the Caribbean and continental Americas rested on the empire's capacity to move information, human beings, and commodities through the ports, which acted as nodes in its imperial network. On occasion, a European state may create a mobile, temporary node that can impose a kind of temporary, localized control. These are the armies and navies that project force into, and thus control, the colonies. A royal galleon or state-sponsored corsair cruising the coast acts as a kind of imperial node. Gilbert himself tried to act as a mobile node of imperial control, but his failures show how transitory and localized such control could be.[7]

Oceans have always resisted nodal-imperial formation, and Terra Nova was at its heart a maritime enterprise. Historians' obsession with the writings of Hugo Grotius have largely warped these kinds of discussions, encouraging us to see freedom of the seas as a sort of uniquely European invention. As Renisa Mawani has discussed, Grotius's writings were never meant to be authoritative, nor were they widely accepted at the time. They also have no place in the sixteenth-century world of Breton and Basque fishworkers. If Terra Nova was a *mare liberum*, it was not because of some grand legal principle embraced by mariners but rather for much more practical reasons.[8]

The only potential for imperial formation at Terra Nova lay in the creation of coastal nodes through permanent settlements, as would be the case in later centuries. The repeated failure of early settlement attempts, discussed in earlier chapters, made this impossible. Without permanent settlements, European states or quasi-state actors lacked the coercive tools to exclude anyone from a fishery on the other side of the Atlantic Ocean. They were unable to project force into the northwest Atlantic, to employ coercive means to control space. It is a remarkable fact that across the sixteenth century no European state pursued a sustained claim to Terra Nova. If on occasion some freebooter with a royal warrant showed up and claimed ownership in the name of a far-off monarch (like Gilbert), such moments tended to pass quickly and quietly. Some mid-century Spanish sources describe "Our Province of Terranova," but this seems to refer more to the preponderance of Spanish subjects working there than any specific claims to ownership. The northwest Atlantic was not formally, or even informally, integrated into any European imperial system. Portugal, Spain, and England might all advance various claims to possess Terra Nova, but they lacked nodes to radiate authority and solidify these aspirations. They soon gave up serious efforts to claim or control the region until a revival at the turn of the seventeenth century.[9]

As a consequence, Terra Nova was outside empire. In the parlance of piracy, it was "beyond the line," a legal gray zone that lay apart from the clearer lines of authority within European empires. This is the problem that lies at the heart of the region's history in this earliest era, and what sets it apart from so much of the wider Atlantic basin. Yet this raises the question: if Terra Nova was outside of empire, then what was it? It was far from a lawless or chaotic zone; surviving evidence makes clear that fishwork in the northwest Atlantic was remarkably coherent, peaceful, and organized. To explain that, we must consider the role of the commons in maritime history.

Commons

The European fishery in the northwest Atlantic functioned according to a system of property rights and social norms that, borrowing an English term for meadowlands, generations of scholars and activists have called the commons. It was both legally a commonly held space and set of resources (principally codfish) and a social system that encouraged co-management among fishworkers. At its core, a commons is defined by property rights and the ways in which they control access to a resource as opposed to a scheme of private property. Yet in the premodern world, the commons was also often a human system. It was an elaborate system of hierarchies, rules, taboos, rituals, and beliefs that governed how those property rights functioned in practice.[10]

One way to understand Terra Nova as a commons is to consider the role of property rights and control. The northwest Atlantic comprised a set of key resources (fish and other marine life) and a physical space that contained those resources (Terra Nova), both of which might be treated as property by European mariners. Harold Demsetz's classic formulation holds that property is defined by a bundle of rights, chief among them rights of access. It is possible that all or part of Terra Nova might be treated as belonging to a given European entity (say, the Portuguese Empire); that all or some of the fish might be considered the exclusive property of the same; or that the space might be assigned to one entity (the empire itself) and the resources to another (specific noble families, guilds, and so on).[11]

The absence of imperial nodes in the northwest Atlantic made it impossible for European states to control space and impose access restrictions during the sixteenth century. Fishworkers did not need to get permission before sailing to Terra Nova, or to sell their catch at home. Toward the end of the sixteenth century we see references to safe-passage documents and passports, but these seem to have been deployed to protect against pirates on homebound voyages, not as permission to work at Terra Nova. Nobody could own Terra Nova inasmuch as nobody could prevent anyone else from sailing there, obviating the potential for the space itself to be held as property. Particular sites—a harbor, a fishing bank—might be rendered exclusive by fishworkers themselves. There are scattered instances of this occurring, though it is much more common by the seventeenth century. For Terra Nova as a whole, one would be greeted by birds and fish rather than patrolling warships and imperial administrators.

What of the fish themselves? Most European societies granted property rights to some specific marine resources, such as an oyster bed, an eel run, or an estuary. Some states also reserved particular marine life—notably whales—as property of the crown if they were caught or found on the shore. These were exclusively coastal and freshwater resources, however. Pelagic fish were not treated as a resource that could be restricted to a narrow right of access. In 1577 the English author John Dee tried to argue otherwise, launching a full-throated defense of exclusive English possession of any fish within the country's coastlines. "So, here, the British Seas are common and free for all ships of all nations to pass in and upon; But, as concerning the fish under the water of those seas (which fish, God and nature bring favour-ably within the peculiar bounds and jurisdiction of our Royal Precinct), no foreign subject ought, customably or otherwise, therein (presumptuously) to cast net for the same." The tone of his argument, and its relative obscu-rity, suggests that this was a substantial departure from the norm. It also ap-pears to have been unconvincing, as fish continued to be treated as an open resource for many decades.[12]

In the sixteenth century, the community that held common rights to Terra Nova and its fish seems to have been quite broad indeed. It is not clear that fishworkers at Terra Nova organized themselves in ways that would be recognizable today. Modern studies of aquatic commons have typically identified cases in which commons are organized within a single commu-nity and divided up between members. This was the case with the twenti-eth-century lobster fishery described by James Acheson. If the Maine fishery as a whole was a commons, fishing crews and communities tended to divide up space among themselves: "From the legal view, anyone who has a li-cense can go lobster fishing anywhere. In reality, far more is required. To go lobster fishing, one must be accepted by the men fishing out of a harbor. Once a new fisherman has gained admission to a 'harbor gang,' he is ordi-narily allowed to go fishing only in the traditional territory of that harbor. . . . The system is entirely the result of political competition among groups of lobstermen. It contains no 'legal' elements." Such patterns hold true else-where, including the fact that members of the community often live near or even on the body of water they are managing.[13]

At Terra Nova, four key problems meant that this was not how things operated. First, multiple fishing communities visited the northwest Atlantic in the sixteenth century. There was no one overarching bond between the Basques, Bretons, Galicians, Hollanders, and Normans who might all be working the same harbor in a given season. Second, fishing crews did not always commit to the same port either year after year, or even within the same year. European mariners needed a system that was flexible, accommodating both the complex mix of communities and the shifting fishing grounds. Third, the commons itself, as we have seen, was embedded within a bigger system of cyclical, seasonal migration. Fishing by Europeans took place during a few months only, and was bracketed by the migration of thousands of mariners. Fourth, Terra Nova itself was far removed from Europe. Any resource-sharing system had to be projected thousands of miles across the Atlantic Ocean from the home ports of Europe.

How, then, did fishing crews organize their commons in the sixteenth century? A division of space seemed to have existed at the heart of the fishery. On one level, Terra Nova as a whole was an open, common space. Anyone with a ship could visit and fish, taking as much as they wanted or could carry. Yet within this, individual sites were more carefully managed and fishworkers' behavior more controlled. A particular harbor, cove, river, shoal, or bank would be subject to localized co-management between fishing crews. The result was that fishworkers experienced Terra Nova as two overlapping kinds of commons—one a vast expanse of open opportunity, the other a daily experience of working within a shared system of rules and customs. Within this multilayered commons was the balance of access and management that allowed for a multinational, long-distance, seasonal fishery.

Much of this system is, and will remain, invisible to us. We can see in the records the upper level, the open and common access to the northwest Atlantic as a whole. How fishworkers explained this concept to one another, or how they welcomed newcomers, is unknown. Anthropologists studying contemporary fisheries and fishworkers have shown the myriad approaches fishworkers use to regulate a commons. These include not just customary practices but complex sets of taboos, rules, and spiritual ideas. Yet such practices are rarely written down, and fishworkers at Terra Nova were rarely asked about what they were doing. We may suspect that a variety of religious practices and beliefs, especially Catholic, played an important role in socializing sixteenth-century mariners to the floating commons. It is only at the localized level of the commons that we can see such things operating in practice.[14]

Governing the Commons

The one important customary practice used to regulate the localized commons of which we know any details is the admiralty system, sometimes called the fishing admirals. Within a given harbor that served as a fishing base, one ship captain was appointed "admiral" for a set period of time. Sometimes this was the entire season, but at Sam Joham/Saint John's harbor in 1583, one of Gilbert's lackeys noted that admirals rotated on a weekly basis. In some cases the first ship to arrive got to declare its captain as admiral, in other cases the admiral was selected by all the ships in the harbor. Practice probably varied from harbor to harbor, and a major site like Sam Joham/Saint John's likely had different rules from a smaller port like Caprouge or Renews. The fishing admiral was then responsible for adjudicating disputes and maintaining order in the harbor, acting as supreme local authority. These little harbor lords allocated space on beaches to newly arriving ships, adjudicated disputes among fishing crews, and enforced mariner customs across the season. Their ships probably served as informal local social hubs, and some admirals held dinners and traded with others in the harbor. Exactly what they did or how much power the admiral wielded is unclear— it is not as though they left written records of their decisions—but everyone seems to have been happy with this approach. The system was simple, flexible, and decisive, affording fishworkers clear lines of decision and authority within a given space.[15]

Two points are worth making here. First, the admiralty system appears in records by the late sixteenth century, the 1570s–80s, but likely developed much earlier. In 1578 Anthony Parkhurst refers to the system, commenting that English crews "commonly are lords of the harbors where they fish." (This was a refrain the English often repeated.) He notes that this was "ac-

cording to an old custom of the country," suggesting it was already well established in the northwest Atlantic. There is no evidence in the 1542
testimonies that Robert Lefant or any other Basques had heard of the admiralty system, so it likely emerged in the later 1540s–50s as the fishery expanded quickly. Perhaps it was a reaction to this rapid growth, a way to
manage the increasing pressure of competition before things got out of
hand. Second, the admiralty system appears to have been developed by fishworkers themselves. It did not grow out of any formal legislation in any European state, and it does not seem to have been transferred from European
practices. Historians have treated the admiralty system as unique to the
northwest Atlantic, and its creation in the mid-sixteenth century is testament to the ability of fishworkers to pioneer novel solutions to resource
management. It was an organic, bottom-up solution to the problem of fisheries management.[16]

The fishing admiral system neatly resolved the four problems noted
above by offering a commons-management framework that was intended to
be temporary and flexible. Fishing admirals were appointed on a seasonal,
and sometimes weekly, basis. Each year a returning fishworker might find
an entirely different admiral or arrangement in the same port, or he could
switch between different ports and encounter different admirals. In treating
each season as a clean slate, the admiralty system reconciled the need to
manage access to particular locations with the decentralized, cyclical nature of a migratory fishery. The irony is that fishworkers borrowed the term
admiralty, an emblem of state power, to describe this system. Appropriating
the name of state-sanctioned authority at sea, common fishworkers applied
it to a temporary and localized kind of rule that existed beyond state control
or even knowledge. Every captain of a fishing ship, no matter how small or
from where, had the potential to spend a summer as an admiral on the other
side of the ocean.

The designation "admiral" also points to something worth emphasizing:
fishworkers did expect some kind of powerful authority to manage the commons. The fallacy of the "Tragedy of the Commons" is the idea that communal resource-management is a free-for-all. In reality, most commons have
been marked by coercive authorities and strict rules. The admiralty was a

rejection of simple egalitarianism, instead vesting legal and economic power over fish access in a single individual for an entire season. Nor could it be anyone, as the admiral had to be a ship's captain, indicating that power remained centered on the top of the ship's social hierarchy. In later centuries the harbor admiral even got first pick of shoreline to set up his fishing booths, a significant advantage. Yet in concentrating all local authority in a single figure, fishworkers were able to avoid inter-communal disputes and provide organized access to a common fishing ground. For co-management to work, there had to be someone in charge. In general, there is a relationship in most times and places between migratory harvesting and coercive authority. There are, for instance, strong parallels between the admiralty system and modern Cree "hunting bosses" in northern Québec. In both cases individuals are empowered to manage food production within carefully delineated zones. The admiral's authority seems to have been consensual and limited, extending no further than a single harbor and no longer than a single season (or occasionally a single week). Their power was also directly tied to food production and the concentration of labor this necessitated. The admiralty system gives evidence of the kinds of social transformations taking place within migratory fishing communities, and how they sought to adapt to transatlantic migration by organizing themselves in similar ways to Indigenous communities and other hunter-gathering societies.[17]

Yet if it was a successful framework for managing a multinational fishery in its earliest century, the creation of a fishing commons on the northwest Atlantic was also an act of exclusion, for it imposed a system of access on a space that was simultaneously being used by Indigenous communities. The fishing commons at Terra Nova allowed broad access to codfish, but only for Europeans. No member of the Mi'kmaq or Innu communities would ever be an admiral. In the sixteenth century this may have had little practical impact, for as we've seen competition and contact between fishworkers and Indigenous communities was relatively limited. In the long run, however, it established a basis for outright dispossessing Indigenous peoples of coastal spaces as the scale and intensity ratcheted up across the seventeenth century. As Allan Greer has observed, "Common property was a central feature of both native and settler forms of land tenure in the early colonial period and that dispossession came about largely through the clash of indigenous commons and a colonial commons." A vast decentralized commons like Terra Nova was as effective as a fence-lined farmstead in seizing control of space for European extraction. What is truly remarkable about this arrangement is that European mariners created an exclusionary commons within a space on the opposite side of the Atlantic from their homes, and within which Indigenous groups were already living. This is a necessary corrective to our assumption that it was English-style enclosure that drove dispossession. It was, relative to other colonial regimes, modeled on a radically different kind of social organization that, if not egalitarian, at least allowed for cooperation and broad consensus across different maritime communities. Yet it was still an act of colonization, a system designed to favor European extraction of natural resources over Indigenous subsistence.[18]

We may use this history of the commons to read certain events in a new light. When Humphrey Gilbert demanded that ships in Sam Joham/Saint John's harbor hand over supplies and food, his hagiographers believed that this power was given by right of his authority as lord of Newfoundland. It is equally possible, however, that it was already regular practice for fishing crews to share supplies. Yet at the same time he was demanding the right to be fishing admiral not of just one harbor but all harbors. This was both a serious violation of custom and an impractical goal. He wanted to collapse both layers of the fishing commons into one, limiting access to Terra Nova as a whole while simultaneously regulating each locality. Such a wholesale rewriting of the right of access, of control and authority, of the nature of space itself in the northwest Atlantic, pointed the way forward toward the expanding ambition of empire as the sixteenth century closed out. That Gilbert failed so utterly indicates the durability, practicality, and collective investment in a commons framework by fishworkers across the century.

A Bloody Commons

As the coercive structures of the admiralty system show, the aquatic commons at Terra Nova was not always a peaceful space. The commons, here as elsewhere, served to channel and contain rather than eliminate violence.

For all that, our surviving sources are remarkably unclear for much of the sixteenth century when it comes to violence between fishworkers, which is much more visible in our sources from 1580 on. In part this reflects the increased role of English mariners, and the particular focus of English sources on admiralty disputes and piracy. Earlier generations may have been less inclined to record or dispute their actions. We cannot say for certain whether this seemingly more peaceful sixteenth century reflects lived reality or, once again, is shaped by the kind of evidence that has survived.

Violence against Indigenous communities is particularly murky in our sources. We have already noted the persistence of abductions, but there would also have been violence between mariners and Indigenous communities over access to fishing grounds, food, and water. Once again, more direct descriptions of violence against Beothuk and Mi'kmaq peoples appear only when English participation accelerates at the end of the sixteenth century. Yet how many fishworkers stole from Innu fishing camps or killed a Beothuk party that came too close to their ship? In 1593 the crew of the *Marigold*, hunting walrus on the Isles de la Madaleine, stole water from a Mi'kmaw fishing camp. When the owners returned and protested, there erupted an altercation in which the English "bestowed half a dozen musket shots upon them," causing the Mi'kmaq to flee. The inverse violence is murky as well. In his 1542 testimony, Martin de Artalecu recounted that he had heard that Indigenous people up the River of Canada were "fierce and valiant" and had killed carpenters brought by Cartier and Roberval, a clear act of violence. But when pressed, he stated, "In the port of La Gran Baya and several leagues farther on they found a more kindly people." We have already seen that the Portuguese settlement of 1520 was lost potentially due to the intervention of Mi'kmaq communities. So we know that relations between Indigenous and European mariners on the aquatic commons of Terra Nova were not always peaceable, even as they were exchanging goods and working side by side in many cases.[19]

There are two reasons why mariners may have used violence against one another or against Indigenous peoples at Terra Nova. The first is piracy, predatory maritime violence. We know that fishing ships were very often targets of pirates. Their bulk cargoes were just valuable enough to be worthwhile targets, and the fact that most ships returned fully laden at the same time (late summer) made them easy marks. In 1584 an assembly of merchants in Rouen went so far as to draft a public complaint that corsairs sailing under the Spanish flag were so numerous as to "interrupt the trade with Barbary and the Terra Nova fishery," seriously impeding local commerce. We know that across the century returning ships had to run the gauntlet of roving pirates as soon as they entered coastal waters. In 1560, just as the last of the Habsburg-Valois Wars wound down, a suit between two non-Scottish subjects worked its way through the admiralty court of Scotland. The dispute was between a Biscayan fishing crew ("of the town of Saint Martin in the Ile de Ré") and an English corsair ("Johnne Quhitheid [Whitehead] captain of an English ship"). The former had been returning from Terra Nova with fish when it was captured off the cost of Brittany by Whitehead, who took the ship to Dundee in Scotland to sell as a prize. This normal practice was interrupted when suddenly the Breton counter-master of the vessel suddenly appeared and appealed to the Scottish admiralty to restore the ship. At dispute were whether or not the attack took place after a peace treaty between France and England had been signed, and whether or not the Scottish crown was obligated to turn over property of one foreign subject that had been seized by another. After a contentious deliberation, the ultimate verdict was a positive one on both counts, and the French subjects received their ship back. The case indicates the vulnerability of fishworkers to violence during times of war, and the degree to which that vulnerability increased when they reentered Europeans waters. It also indicates the international dimensions of violence, which could drag mariners from the waters of one kingdom into the courtrooms of another in pursuit of justice.[20]

A second reason for violence was competition. There was a finite number of good fishing harbors in Terra Nova, and a few well-known fishing grounds. Food, fuel, and water resources were necessary to sustain the fishery, and these could be flashpoints of competition. These same resources were also used by Indigenous groups like the Innu and Mi'kmaq, potentially pitting fishworkers against First Nations. This kind of killing is much harder to establish from our sources, though in the early seventeenth century it would not be uncommon for fishworkers to raid and disrupt each other's camps. Our best evidence for competitive violence at Terra Nova is indirect: many sixteenth-century fishing ships left port carrying artillery and small arms, clear indications that they expected to either defend themselves or to harm others. In 1552 the large *Saint Esprit* of Saint Jean-de-Luz and its crew of forty fishworkers sailed from Bordeaux with an assortment of arquebuses, crossbows, large and half pikes, ammunition, and twenty pieces of artillery. The armaments were carefully laid out in the ship's charter party contract, indicating that defense was carefully thought out and planned by financial stakeholders. The record makes clear that the crew of the *Saint Esprit* headed to Terra Nova prepared for violence.[21]

On at least one occasion we catch glimpses of violence between fish-workers that looks like outright warfare. In 1555, a number of Spanish Basque mariners were interrogated about recent acts of violence at Terra Nova. In previous years enterprising Spanish Basques had outfitted ships to raid fellow fishworkers, including French Basques and Bretons, along the shores of the northwest Atlantic. Within these records are the words of Martin Perez de Hoa, a pilot of San Sebastián who in 1553 had served under the raider Juan de Erauso. In his testimony of October 15, 1555, he notes that during one raid the ship he served on "went to another port in the northern parts of Terra Nova, and there found eight large French ships loaded with *bacalao*, all arranged for combat, and which were guarded by a large and well-armed ship, which was called the *Great Francis* of Saint Malo, and in the entrance to the harbour they had made their bastions and forts, and had placed much artillery, with which they began to fire and prevented the said captain Juan de Erauso from entering the said harbour." Despite their preparations, the end came swiftly. Hoa reports that Erauso "landed the majority of his men [close by], and with their banners and ordinance, in formation, marched through the night until they were close by the bastions and fortification of the enemy, and gave them battle and made an assault and took them; and with the same artillery which had been in them, he brought his ships to the harbour, and fought with all eight of their ships, but they were all tied together, and he forced them to surrender." The Spanish claimed to have killed seventy-two Bretons and seized their fishing ships and cargo[22]

This incident raises more questions than it answers. We don't know where this event took place, but the description makes clear that in a harbor of Terra Nova Breton crews had brought cannon on their ships, and some of these were taken onshore and placed in fieldworks. Why were the Bretons so well armed and prepared? Was this a new fortification, or had this harbor always been so well guarded? Was this unusual fighting, or did fishing crews raid each other regularly? We could read Hoa's account as describing an act of war by Spanish Basques against French foes, taking place in a harbor that had been permanently fortified as part of the rising rates of violence in Terra Nova. Alternatively, we could read it as describing a one-off raid against a hastily entrenched fishing harbor. Perhaps it was sparked by competition, perhaps by greed and piracy. The truth is we do not have enough information to contextualize a moment like this 1553 assault, but it does open the possibility that violence was more systematic than we have surmised, and that Europeans were shaping the landscape more than we have guessed. The fishing commons at Terra Nova was more transformative than historians typically recognize.

An Atlantic Commons

On some underlying level, our master narrative about Atlantic history is one of enclosure rather than commons. European empires claim land (and sometimes seas), closing off access to create new terraformed, productive spaces for resource extractions. Islands and continents and shores get carved up by states and later companies. The creation of a multilayered commons in the northwest Atlantic, then, gave the European presence an unusual character. In Terra Nova, Europeans would fail to transplant the kind of hierarchies and property regimes that marked settlement-based colonial projects elsewhere in the early Americas.

In the half century after 1580 the commons would largely be destroyed. Competition between mariners increased. Violence became more common at Terra Nova itself. The first permanent settlements were (fitfully, admittedly) planted. On Newfoundland island, in Acadie, and along the banks of the River of Canada, year-round European outposts formed nodes of exclusion and control. Mariners increasingly clustered together with mariners from the same community, or even the same kingdom. The southeast became the English shore, the Grand Banks a Norman zone, the north coast of Newfoundland the *petit nord* for Breton and other French fishworkers. In the very long run the northwest Atlantic would be decisively enclosed by European, and later North American, states. Today it is divided up between three different nations (Canada, the United States, and France) and six different provinces and states (Newfoundland and Labrador, Québec, Nova Scotia, New Brunswick, Prince Edward Island, and Maine). If fishing commons may still exist within these boundaries, Terra Nova as a whole has been irreparably divided into property.

But this lay in the future. From the perspective of 1583 and a burgeoning fishery, the middle of the Atlantic Ocean was a vast commons, a space open to mariners from many different communities that offered (as they saw it) limitless and easily accessible commercial fishing. Terra Nova was not the only fishery that divided the Atlantic into common spaces. In 1547 one English mariner boldly declared that Iceland "was and is a place entirely free and public, and that the right of fishing there was and is common to all men [*omnibus commune fuisse*]." This would have been quite surprising to the Danish authorities who thought of Iceland as their own fiefdom. Even a fishery like Iceland, however, could not compare to the scale of the floating commons at Terra Nova. It was an aquatic meadow unlike anything else in the Atlantic basin.[23]

The history of Terra Nova as commons is easy to frame as a declension narrative. I could end this chapter by bemoaning the loss of Terra Nova, the end of a free fishworkers' world, and the triumph of an alien empire over a mariners' commons. Instead, what I have tried to suggest throughout is that the mariners' world of Terra Nova was remarkable in many ways, but not necessarily a good thing. It was a bottom-up creation of fishwork, but it denied Indigenous access and concepts of space. It was an aquatic commons in an age of empire, but one that was used to extract huge amounts of biomass for European consumers. Fishing crews were relatively egalitarian and multinational, but they still embraced despotic fishing admirals and outright violence when it suited them. Even when things changed, on some level it was still all about extracting biological resources for Europe's insatiable world-ecology. So things changed, but let us hesitate before we say that things were lost.

PART IV

Food

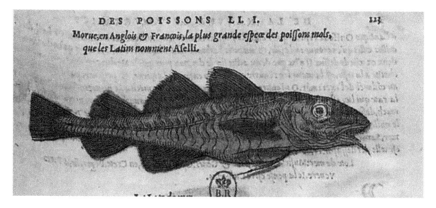

Figure 17. *La morue* (cod) in Pierre Belon, *La nature et diversité des poissons*, 1555. (Courtesy of the Bibliothèque nationale de France, gallica.bnf.fr/.)

For suppose a man were eating rotten stockfish, the very smell of which
would choke another, and yet believed it a dish for the gods, what
difference is there as to his happiness?
—*Desiderius Erasmus*, The Praise of Folly, *1509*

Sods and rinds to cover your flake,
Cake and tea for supper,
Codfish in the spring of the year,
Fried in maggoty butter.
—*"I'se the B'ye," Newfoundland folk song*

If some food arrived in front of my face without context, I would
not eat it. And that is how I know I am better than a fish.
—*Guy Montgomery, comedian, 2020*

TEN

Bourgeois

O n the twenty-third day of February in the year 1544 (though it was still written out in the old style as late 1543), Clemente de Conihout, called Huppé, stood before a pair of notaries in the city of Rouen to finalize a contract. Huppé was a fishworker born into a family from the small Norman port of Jumièges, which had been outfitting and sailing ships to Terra Nova for a decade (in 1544 alone three members of the Conihout clan served on or invested in five separate ships). This February a ship of which Huppé was part owner ("bourgeois" in the original), holding an eighth share, the *Margueritte*, was waiting at the quay to leave for Terra Nova. Earlier in February the ship's master (the captain in charge of daily operations) Guillaume Boutard had already taken out a loan of 120 *livres* from two different merchants in the city to outfit the vessel. But now a further sum of 40 *livres* was required to finish preparations, so Huppé had made the trip down the river from Jumièges to negotiate the second loan on behalf of his fellow investors. In the urban parish by the riverside in Rouen he found Michel de la Rue, a citizen ("bourgeois" in the original) and merchant living in Rouen, who agreed to lend him the sum.

Across the table from Huppé and de la Rue were two men, Jehan Godes and Jacques Prioret, royal notaries for the city of Rouen. They were the two scribes who took down the contract dictated by Huppé and Michel de la Rue on that day in February, covering both sides of a large blank sheaf in their three-hundred-page record book. The shipowner and creditor had come to them that day, probably in a room near the riverside port, and paid Godes and Prioret to make their agreement official in the eyes of the legal entity that was the City of Rouen. We don't know exactly which one wrote out the contract, as neither signed and both attested to having witnessed the deed, but the handwriting suggests it was Prioret. As was often the case with these minor business contracts, whoever did the work used a rushed and messy hand, hastily scribbling shorthand phrasings of important legal terms and not even bothering to get signatures. It was a rush job, but expressed in the wonderfully economic and formulaic language that notaries like Godes and Prioret had perfected, the text contained all the necessary information: "The 23rd day of February One thousand five hundred forty three, before Jehan Godes and Jacques Prioret royal notaries: Made for Clement de Conihout called Huppé resident of Jumièges owner [bourgeois] for a half-quarter of a ship named the Margueritte in port of sixty tons or thereabouts of which is Master after God Guillaume Boutard called Cordoemyde . . . to go make a voyage this spring to Terra Nova . . . [to whom] Michel de la Rue bourgeois living in Rouen loans the sum of forty livres tournois." The details having been agreed, the contract went into the yearly records of Rouen. Huppé gave the money thus raised to Boutard, who finished outfitting the Margueritte; Huppé himself soon boarded another ship of which he was master, the Saulver, and after taking out a second loan for this vessel from the merchant Michel de la Rue set sail for Terra Nova. The merchant de la Rue stayed behind, waiting for the fishing fleet to return in the fall, when his investment would bear fruit. Godes and Prioret moved on to the next contract, continuing their endless task of recording the daily lives and business dreams of Rouen's residents.[1]

This is how we most often see Terra Nova in the sixteenth century: through the eyes of notaries sitting in port towns. The case of the Margueritte and its outfitting offers insight into how sixteenth-century fishing voyages were organized, who organized them, and what it took to make an expedition successful. For historians working with such incomplete records, the organization of fishing voyages is the one thing we know quite a bit about. Many voyages left paper trails in the communal archives of Europe, as the litigious merchants of various port cities insisted that contracts and agreements be made in writing. We can use these surviving records to help us understand the voyage of the *Margueritte* as a business enterprise, as a long-term process of labor organization, as an urban phenomenon, and as an ecological relationship between different European microecologies. This chapter does just that to show how a typical voyage began, ended, and shaped urban life in the sixteenth century.[2]

The Discreet Charm of the *Bourgeois(e)*

It is a curious artifact of sixteenth-century French that the word *bourgeois* had two meanings. The first, more common one denoted someone who was a member of a city's civic body, a citizen of the *bourg*. Michel de la Rue was a *bourgeois* of the city of Rouen. The second, less common meaning denoted the owner of a ship, either in whole or in part. Huppé was a *bourgeois* of the *Margueritte*, inasmuch as he owned a share of the ship and its outfitting. This distinction between city *bourgeois* and ship *bourgeois* is uniquely French, but somehow captures a relationship that was universal in the sixteenth-century fishery. Fishing voyages began by pairing the interests and power of the two *bourgeois*. Shipowners, many of whom came from small outports, put together the money and resources to procure a ship for a seasonal voyage. They then made use of the financial resources of urban *bourgeois* merchants to procure loans, supplies, and market access. Huppé provided the ship, but Michel de la Rue provided the cash necessary to complete the initial outfitting. A ship like the *Margueritte* needed both, a ship *bourgeois* and an urban *bourgeois*, to function.[3]

It is hard to generalize about either category of *bourgeois*, for in many ways it was the variety of backgrounds and statuses that defined them. To begin with, many *bourgeois* of either kind were really *bourgeoise*. Women served regularly as shipowners as well as financiers. This has been carefully detailed in the Portuguese case by Darlene Abreu-Ferreira, but appears to hold true as well for ports in the kingdom of France and probably Spanish Basque Country. Consider Marie de Sugarette, a Basque woman and widow who in 1590 outfitted a ship she herself owned, the aptly named *La Marie*.

To serve as master she selected her son, Johannes de Balda, who took out a loan in La Rochelle before sailing to Terra Nova. Or consider Francoise Chemeur, a resident of La Rochelle who in 1565 loaned 100 *livres* to the Basque master Johannes de Gabere for his voyage to Terra Nova in a different *Marie*. Thanks to her loan the *Marie* made a successful trip to and from the fishery. Likewise we find Marie Charon, an "honest woman" and *bourgeoise* of La Rochelle, who in April 1562 collected a large loan on behalf of her husband the financier Yves Terterly a year after it had been lent to the crew of the *Marie* of Saint Jean-de-Luz. Marie signed her name big and bold in the notarial register to close out the account. Three years later in 1565 the couple Marie and Yves jointly loaned a small sum to a Spanish Basque bound to Terra Nova. All of these women represented a different kind of *bourgeoise*, shipowner and urban, and each represents the regular appearance of women in our records.[4]

The ship *bourgeois* and *bourgeoise* were a mixed lot. Some were from small outport villages like Jumièges, others from mid-level cities like La Rochelle or Bayonne. A few appear to have lived in major cities like Paris, Orléans, London, or Bilbao. Sometimes an aristocrat in a major city might buy a share in a small ship; at other times local lords led voyages themselves. Ship *bourgeois* were just as likely to be titleless mariners who invested in the fishery because that was their livelihood. We have already met many of this kind, merchant-mariners who outfitted ships as part of their "most usual trade." Urban *bourgeois* were more consistent in that they were all embedded in the civic life of sixteenth-century European cities. Most appear in notarial records preceded by a string of titles and qualifiers. Some urban *bourgeois* were titled, often *sieur* or *pair*, local lords and city peers who held major positions in civic life. They were, above all, honorable and honest. One had to be an *honorable homme* or *honneste femme* to act as a reliable financier in this age of verbal oaths and sworn statements. Michel de la Rue was described as *honorable* in the notarial records, someone Huppé could trust to carry out his end of the deal. In the urban *bourgeois*, we find civic and mercantile interests fused, so that in the wonderfully revealing language of a 1573 city notary we are asked to observe "the *bourgeois*, mariners and habitants of Saint Malo congregated in their city hall in body politic [*en corps politique*]." This body politic was the group that provided the financial resources and the credibility to underwrite short-term, high-interest loans to ship *bourgeois*.[5]

The Ship and Crew

All fishing voyages start with a ship *bourgeois* deciding to outfit a ship for Terra Nova. That singular decision was repeated hundreds of times across Europe's littoral every year, and thousands of times across the century. Throughout this study we have already encountered a variety of explanations that we can infer from the surviving sources: the quest for food security, the desire for money, a hope to avoid violence, commitment to a family business. But why a particular ship *bourgeois*, or more often a group of them, arrived at their decision is rarely known. Our sources take the logic of fishwork for granted, just as they take it for granted that the fishery as a whole was ad hoc and unsystematic. To put it one way, Clement de Conihout of Jumièges was entirely unaware that fishworkers in Basque Country or Brittany were planning voyages at the same time, yet they all ended up in the same place together on a regular basis. Despite the total lack of central planning, state control, or coordination between different ports, every year several hundred ships left Europe and arrived at the same time in Terra Nova. This contrast between the decentralized, ad hoc nature of the fishery's organization and its incredible scale is one of the hallmarks of the sixteenth-century fishery.

Many of the ships that left Europe for Terra Nova departed from what we may call outports, villages or small cities of various sizes along coasts and rivers that had simple port facilities but could sustain remarkable fishing fleets. The twin ports of Saint Jean-de-Luz and Ciboure (sitting on different sides of the same harbor) in French Basque Country contained only a few thousand residents in the late sixteenth century and were little more than a pair of villages on a beachy harbor. Yet between them in the 1580s they outfitted around fifty fishing and whaling ships annually. The prevalence of fishworkers from these two sites in surviving notarial records in Bordeaux and La Rochelle demonstrates that they were among the most active ports in the second half of the sixteenth century. Huppé and the *Margueritte* hailed from the abbey town of Jumièges, a small village hugging the north shore of the Seine River, some twelve miles or so from the major mercantile hub of Rouen. The village had no port infrastructure to speak of, only a rudimentary slip of sandy beach along the riverbank where a ship could be offloaded. Despite this, we know that the residents of Jumièges dispatched dozens of ships to sail to Terra Nova in the middle of the sixteenth century. Terra Nova was not their only enterprise, but it was certainly one of their most regular and important.[6]

A fishing voyage took time to prepare, far more than just a few summer months, and the decision to go to Terra Nova might be taken far in advance of the trip itself. Taken as a whole, outfitting, undertaking, and concluding a single fishing voyage might stretch from December to October the following year. Many trips to Terra Nova began in the early winter when a group of ship *bourgeois* decided they wanted to send out a ship the following spring. This gave them time to find the ship and crew needed before preparing the actual outfitting in the late winter and early spring. Ships left between late March and early May, depending on their port of origin and destination. Once the voyage returned in late summer, another month or two was needed to offload the cod at market and to settle accounts. Over the course of this ten months, then, only about half the time was actually spent at sea and at work on the fishery. This process became continuous, so that even as a ship was being offloaded in Rouen its owners were considering the next season. For a fishery that only operated for a small time in the northwest Atlantic, the industry was a year-round endeavor.

At the center of the voyage was a ship—a powerful machine but also a risky investment. As a result, at the core of the sixteenth-century outfitting system was an emphasis on risk aversion. Merchants organized voyages to spread risk as much as possible, even at the expense of profit. Many ships were co-owned by multiple parties, insulating individual investors. Loans tended to be small and taken out from multiple parties, rather than one large sum from a single financier. Supplies were often procured from an outfitter (*avitailleur* in French sources) who was separate from the creditor, their services secured under a separate contract. Fishworkers were sometimes paid by shares, so that owners did not have to guarantee wages. By mid-century some shipowners were taking advantage of the growing availability of maritime insurance, though most of this was used primarily for whaling vessels. In lieu of formal insurance contracts most resorted to ensuring multiple and overlapping lines of responsibility and investment. The result was that a failed voyage would not ruin anyone completely.[7]

Following this risk-aversion strategy, ships were owned and operated under complex financial arrangements that made voyages practical, safe, and profitable. Some ships were chartered by merchants (a charter party), who might then hire a separate captain to manage the ship. Most ships were owned by multiple parties, each of whom purchased a part share in the vessel. Typical was the *Marye*, a Norman vessel that met an unfortunate end when a storm hit it after the return voyage in 1559, which was co-owned by three men from Dieppedalle, a small hamlet near Rouen. The three each signed an attestation of the disaster (recorded by a Rouen notary) together, three marks scrawled side by side to show their equal ownership of the vessel. Sometimes shipping arrangements were kept within the family. A generation after the Clement de Conihout we have been following, his descendants Robert and Jehan owned the *Saulver*, a seventy-ton fishing vessel from Jumièges. The pair owned majority shares, and Jehan served as captain. We know this because in late 1572 Robert had his sons Jehan and Denis go together to Rouen to sell his share of the *Saulver* to Jacques Duhamel, sieur de Gouy (another small Seine town), though Jehan was left as master. The notarial records of Rouen or La Rochelle are filled with accounts of such share-trading and master-hiring arrangements. All in all, the typical sixteenth-century fishing ship could be subject to claims of financial liability and authority from five parties: the shipowner(s), the charter party, the captain, the outfitter(s), and the creditor(s). Since each of these parties was often composed of multiple individuals, the physical body of a ship might be subjected to claims of ownership by a dozen or more men and women at once.[8]

We do know what a fishing ship at Terra Nova looked like. The anonymous Norman mariner who penned his note *"pour* La Terre Neufve" in the

1540s described at the start of an earlier chapter, left one more surprise in the manuscript Ms.Fr. 24269. On the last page, one apparently used to make notes and test pens, an image was made of a ship (see figure 18). The image is of a modern (for the 1540s) and intricate design, the kind of ship that could make the voyage to Terra Nova, Brazil, Guinea, or the Caribbean. Such vessels were described in written sources using generic terms for multi-masted sailing ships like *navire, nef, nao.* For the ship *bourgeois* interested in organizing a voyage to Terra Nova, the ship represented the height of technological achievement, capital accumulation, and sophisticated financial practices.[9]

A ship machine was useless without humans to operate it. Recruitment fell to the ship *bourgeois,* who would typically find mariners within their home community or nearby villages to man the vessel. Ship masters and owners spent the late winter searching for and convincing men to work the fishery. Few recruitment or wage records survive, but even so, a few patterns stand out. In the sixteenth century mariners were paid in a combination of wages and shares for their labor, though shares were more common. A share represented a claim to a percentage of the catch, and therefore the value when that percentage was sold. The most common practice was to accord the crew as a whole one-third of the total catch as payment, with each mariner taking a proportional cut depending on how many served on the voyage. For instance, in 1523 the Breton ship *Marguerite* returned from Terra Nova to La Rochelle. In a contract filed in that city, the master Jehan Tredian accepted a third of the catch on behalf of himself and the crew. Thus one-third of the total value of cod brought back would be divided between Tredian and his fellow mariners. This seems to have been a widespread custom, and in 1562 an English ship stipulated that "her lading [catch] shall be equally divided into three parts, between the owners, victuallers and master and company." Toward the end of the century, a ship from Havre in Normandy sailed with "one third part of the ship's lading to be distributed among the crew for their labours and service in the voyage." This pattern was identified by historians of the fishery long ago, though the degree to which the share system broke down over time remains hotly debated. As Peter Pope has noted, the transition from shares to wage payments

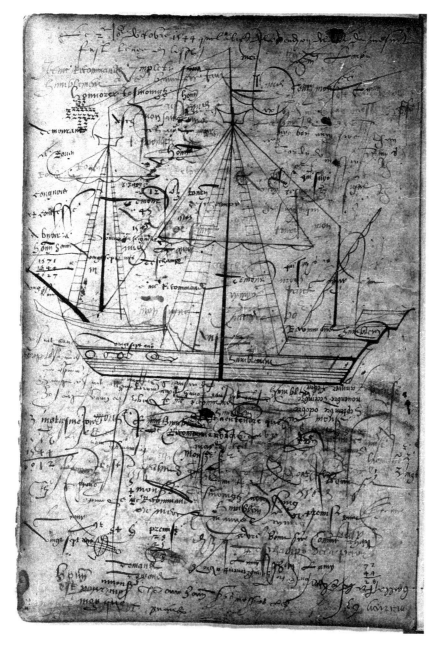

Figure 18. Anonymous sketch of a sailing ship, potentially a fishing ship, from the 1540s. (Courtesy of the Bibliothèque nationale de France, gallica.bnf.fr/.)

was not completed even in the English fishery until the mid-seventeenth century.[10]

As individuals, fishworkers at Terra Nova seem to have conformed to broad patterns. Thanks to surviving court records and official testimonies, we know that most mariners were between twenty-five and forty-five years of age. Few fishworkers were young, as experience was highly valued, though some ships carried *grumetes*, ship's boys, as part of the crew. Given their age, many crew members were likely married men, though not enough legal records survive to establish this with certainty. These were unlikely to be the motley crews of the seventeenth- and eighteenth-century North Atlantic. Fishing crews were recruited from communities in northwest Europe. Although the Indigenous communities that lived in Terra Nova, especially the Innu and Mi'kmaq, had deep pools of experienced fishworkers upon which Europeans might have been able to draw, there is insufficient evidence from the sixteenth century to indicate that Indigenous mariners were employed by Europeans. Instead, the localized recruitment of crews in coastal European towns encouraged ethnically homogenous ships that avoided drawing on the extended labor resources of the far North Atlantic.[11]

Most mariners served voluntarily for wages, and often returned to Terra Nova year after year. There is no evidence for the use of enslaved or coerced labor in the northwest Atlantic fishery in the sixteenth century. For some the work provided steady and appealing pay, and one English observer believed "they are wealthy, for their share is worth three times the wages they would get for voyages to France, Spain or Denmark." Wage data is nonetheless sparse, with one important exception. In 1559 an anonymous shipowner from northern Brittany recorded a short personal note regarding an upcoming voyage to Terra Nova. The ship was based in Plouër, a small port near Saint Malo. Comprising a single page in a notebook otherwise devoted to parish accounts, the text records "the names of my mariners for my ship for Terra Nova" and how much they were to be paid (see box 1). This, the best surviving record related to labor in the sixteenth century fishery, can tell us much about recruitment and payment.[12]

Box 1. *Transcription of the 1559 Crew List*

These are the names of the mariners for my ship for Terra Nova for the year 1559.

First, Pierres André, master after God . . . Must have 40 *livres tounois*, half before the departure and half after the return of the ship
Jacques Briend . . . 7 *escus sol*
Rolland Guihommatz . . . 18 *livres tournois*
Pierre Rozé Ville Agan . . . 8 *livres* 10 *sols*
Amaury Eon . . . 3 *pistoles*
Jacques Jullien . . . 4 *livres*
Jehan Guérin . . . 60 *sols* and he will be given a *myne* of wheat as payment upon return at whatever price it is at that time
Jacques Beletbon . . . 2 *pistoles*
Roullet Hulaut . . . 3 *livres* 10 *sols*
Geffroy Briend . . . 3 *livres* 10 *sols*
Pierres le Déan . . . 30 *sols*
Jehan Pépin de Sainct-Briac . . . 20 *sols*
Fanczois le Couainte . . . 6 *livres tournois*
Pierres Fleury, Franczois Fleury, Jacques Boys, Thomas Rozé, Jehan Rouault le Jeune . . . nothing
Samson Bertre . . . Must pay me 10 *livres* [in margin: "Received 10 *sols*"]
Mathurin de Lechat . . . Owes me 13 *livres* 10 *sols* [in margin: "Received 6 *livres*"]

Note: Livres tournois and *sols* are units of account. *Escus sol* and *pistoles* are hard currencies. A *mine* was a unit of grain, approximately 79 liters.

Source: Archives départmentales de Côtes-d'Armor (Saint Brieuc), 1E 2783, fol. 35.

The text shows that crew recruitment took place locally. Two mariners are identified with geographic markers: Pierre Rozé hails from Agon, a Norman fishing port, and Jehan Pépin comes from the major Breton port of Saint Brieuc, both within a day's sail from the home port of Plouër. Mariners expected to spend their time in Terra Nova in familiar company, even as part of kinship groups serving onboard ships. In 1559 three pairs of mariners (Pierre and Thomas Rozé, Jacques and Geoffroy Briend, Pierre and François Fleury) share the same last name, indicating family bonds. This is perhaps the most perplexing aspect of the transatlantic fishery. Despite the scale and longevity of the sixteenth-century fishery, it was built on an extremely narrow foundation of family ties and personal networks.

The 1559 crew list also points to the complex ways that crew were paid in the mid-sixteenth century. The ship master commands the highest wages by far and expects half in advance and half after his successful return. There is no mention of shares, only precise wages owed to each individual. Most crew members are paid in units of account like *livres* and *sols*, denominations that were used by merchants to record debts but that did not circulate as currencies. By contrast, several crew members were specifically paid in hard cash: *escus sol* or *pistoles*. One is even expecting payment in goods, in the form of a large measure of wheat. Why some and not others? These forms of payment must have reflected personal negotiations and experiences of the kind that were rarely written down. Most remarkably, a number of crew members are listed as being in debt to our anonymous shipowner. The *bourgeois* must have advanced wages to some of his crew, or they owed him from previous voyages. Pierre Rozé was credited his wages, while Thomas Rozé broke even with his debts and was owed nothing at all. One mariner had gone over 13 *livres* into debt before the voyage even began. What all these forms of payment indicate is that there were no clear rules or expectations at the height of the fishery, and payment could take many forms even within the same crew or family.

Assuming that all of these outfitting problems had been overcome—a ship was found, ownership arranged, loans and outfitting costs procured, crew hired—the ship *bourgeois* had now done their part. Yet many found themselves stuck. Once a ship and crew had been found, there were sundry provisions necessary for a voyage. Many outports couldn't furnish these. A small village like Jumièges or Saint Waast lacked the resources to provide food, fishing equipment, and salt for a multi-month voyage. Instead, the ship *bourgeois* had to now reach out to their urban equivalents in search of credit and provisions, and for that they had to visit a port city.

An Urban Fishery

A port city could take many forms, from a seaside haven like San Sebastián or Saint Malo to a river city like Rouen or Bilbao to a purpose-built port like Le Havre. (For a selection of important outfitting cities, see figure 4.) Even a city like Rouen had little in the way of formal port facilities, and sixteenth-century images make clear that most ships simply beached along the riverside outside the city walls. In this they mirrored the beaches and rocky shores that made up the fishing grounds at Terra Nova, so that mariners moved from one beach to another in pursuit of fish and market. All these port cities nonetheless had a place to land safely and to load or offload goods. More important than the port itself was the state of being a city—of being a *lugar*. Sixteenth-century cities were not merely concentrations of humans and animals, they were often legal bodies with important political, economic, and social powers. Civic citizens—the *bourgeois*—enjoyed rights and access within their city. These city ports often served as formal and sometimes informal regional centers of business, state activity, exchange, and political representation. Rouen did this for the Seine River valley, and mariners from many small outports came to the big city to fill out contracts. Bordeaux and La Rochelle were centers for Biscayan France, Saint Malo for upper Brittany, San Sebastián for Guipúzcoa, Bayonne for Labourd. In an outfitting port like Rouen or Bordeaux the fishing trade would always be just one part of the larger mercantile activity that consumed urban merchants. Rouenais merchants were dispatching ships to Brazil, the West Indies, West Africa, and all corners of Europe and the Mediterranean. Yet we should not underestimate the importance of the fish trade in many of these cities. In La Rochelle between 1540 and 1558, of the 228 ships leaving port for which records survive, 71 were bound for Terra Nova. The other ventures were more wide ranging, including voyages to northern Europe, Iberian ports, the Americas, and Africa, as well as privateer expeditions. Thus nearly a third of La Rochelle's commercial traffic was dedicated to the fishery in the mid-sixteenth century. In Saint Malo the city council complained in 1573 that "the better part of their ships, men and munitions are now on voyages on the sea, some to Terra Nova, others in Spain, and others to different places so that today there are fearfully few men in Saint Malo." Fishwork was big business, and in port cities it could have serious social consequences.[13]

Why did Huppé bother sailing upriver to Rouen in 1543? What made port cities so crucial to an expanding fishery? Port cities served as concentration centers for food, supplies, capital, and information. They were the economic-ecological complement to the small outports, providing resources the latter lacked. For this reason, almost all fishing voyages of which we have records began and ended in a port. Along the way, a ship and its crew might pass through many more ports, cities, and harbors. The transatlantic fishery served to link European urban centers with the biology of the subarctic, and in the process helped to foster commercial connections between different cities. Urban centers provided the raw demand and market infrastructure to drive fishing. We should therefore understand the Terra Nova fishery as an urban phenomenon.

Sixteenth-century ships needed large amounts of food and equipment to function. Even a small ship like the twenty-six-ton *Juliane*, a Scottish barque outfitted in Honfleur in 1513, had to buy a wealth of provisions including "seventeen-hundred-dozens" (or around twenty thousand) of ship's biscuit, twenty dozen loaves of fresh bread, two sheep, three barrels of mackerel, a half barrel of verjuice, and of course 120 "large codfish." All fishing ships needed a similar combination of biscuit, salted protein, dried vegetables, and alcohol. Making something like ship's biscuit required gathering wheat, baking the biscuits in huge ovens around the clock, loading them into ready-made barrels, and packing them quickly into the ship's hold. We can see that sometimes this work was done in small outports, but for the larger ships it was likely the numerous bakeries of a place like Bordeaux or Rouen that had the capacity to outfit so many ships at once. Rouen served as a focal point for agricultural produce in Upper Normandy, and boats moved up and down the Seine carrying bulk staples and luxury foods alike to and from the metropolis. Merchants in La Rochelle bought up wine, wheat, cider, beef, and fish from all over the marshy coast of the Bay of Biscay, gathering it on the harborside where it could be loaded onto ships.[14]

Beyond food, fishing crews needed all manner of equipment to make their ship machines function as effective fish harvesters. This included wood and metal devices like barrels and boats, two essential pieces of equipment for a fishing crew. Barrels and boats might be purchased in pieces or fully as-sembled, but were always obtained in considerable quantities. The Terra Nova fishery must have been a business boon to city coopers. Many crews sailed to Terra Nova carrying weapons, especially small arms like pikes and arquebuses, which were purchased from city armorers. Some even had pieces of artillery, which had to be sourced from a major city. By the turn of the seventeenth century, for instance, Plymouth in England earned a good trade by selling artillery to Hollander ships headed for Terra Nova.[15]

Cities also were able to concentrate salt, that essential ingredient in the fishery. Salt was bulky, expensive, and invaluable for many different indus-tries, fishing chief among them. The main salt-producing regions accessible to fishworkers included the many marshy districts around the Bay of Biscay and the Portuguese town of Setúbal south of Lisbon. For mariners living far from these salt-producing regions, only big port cities had the commercial power to buy, ship, and store adequate salt. Rouen is once again instructive. Regular fleets of ships departed the Norman port for the marshy Bay of Bis-cay every winter, where they bought salt from places like La Rochelle and Brouage in bulk. This was brought back to the city of Rouen, typically in January, in time for the Norman fishing fleet to load up before departing for Terra Nova in the spring. The city council took interest in this, carefully reg-ulating and protecting the annual salt fleets against pirates and competitors. Without these regular salt runs, many small outports in Normandy would have been required either to make the long and expensive run to Biscay on their own or to abandon the fishery altogether.[16]

Provisions such as biscuit and salt were useless without the money to buy them. It was not just that cities had the food and equipment; it was only in urban centers that you could scratch together credit quickly and efficiently to get your hands on what you needed. It was the necessity of finding credit and provisions that brought Huppé to Rouen in February 1543, and that found him negotiating with an urban *bourgeois* like Michel de la Rue. Ship *bourgeois* needed cash and credit to buy supplies, and urban *bourgeois* were more than willing to extend credit during the busy outfitting season. This came in the form of short-term, high-interest loans like the one enshrined in the 1544 contract. As part of the deal, Huppé agreed to pay Michel de la Rue back not just the 40 *livres* he owed, but an additional 16 *livres* in interest "because of the perils of the sea as well as of war." That 40 percent interest was quite an incentive for urban merchants like de la Rue.

We know of ships like the *Margueritte* and men like Clement de Conihout only because of the prevalence of loan contracts in sixteenth-century Europe. Short-term loans emerged as the backbone of the fishery in the 1540s, when they became central to the yearly fishery as part of a general concentration of outfitting efforts in a handful of urban ports that allowed for the subsequent growth of the fishery as a whole. Until well into the seventeenth century the extensive use of small-scale credit was a crucial part of the smooth functioning of the Terra Nova fishery. As credit became a basis for the fishery it encouraged more and more participants to join in, increasing the volume of cash that flowed into the system each year. In many notarial registers the months of February and March are filled with page upon page of fishing-related contracts, often two or three in the same day. A given year could therefore generate several hundred short-term loans across Europe, all of which were to be repaid at the end of the fishing season. Within this mass of records there is remarkable consistency in how credit functioned. Loans tended to be for relatively small sums, have high interest rates, and were due at the end of the voyage. In Normandy and Biscay most loans were for 50–100 *livres*, though they could be as small as 20 *livres* or as large as 300. Loans were often taken out right before a ship departed, and many records note that the vessels were already in the port waiting to sail for Terra Nova. Ships were often financed through multiple small loans rather than one big one. Where multiple loans were required, shipowners often took them out from multiple parties rather than a single creditor. Most loans stipulated when and where the loan was to be repaid, making clear that fishworkers were to return to the same port. These patterns emerged in the 1540s and remained the norm through the end of the sixteenth century.

An example of how loans could finance a voyage can be illustrative. On March 4, 1567, the captain Jehan Duboys stood before the notary Tharazon in the city of La Rochelle. Duboys's ship, the *Catherine* out of the small Basque port of Capbreton, was preparing to leave for Terra Nova but had to procure enough supplies for the long voyage. The ship was large, some two hundred tons, making for a costly but potentially lucrative fishing expedition. Duboys took out three loans, each from a different merchant or groups of merchants. They are written on consecutive pages, so it is likely that Duboys had arranged all three loans beforehand and the parties involved arrived at the notary on the morning of the 4th. The total amount was for 4,500 *livres*, with a combined interest owed of 900 *livres*. These were unusually large sums for the mid-sixteenth century fishery, some of the largest recorded in any surviving documents, and all the more remarkable because the entire amount was raised in a single day. The individual loans were nonetheless manageable and were arranged as follows:

> From Sr. [First name lost] Gembarts, merchant and *bourgeois* of
> La Rochelle: 500 *livres* at 20% interest
> From Sr. [First name lost] Gibert, merchant, *pair* and *bourgeois*
> of La Rochelle: 400 *livres* at 20% interest
> From the *honourable hommes* Jehan Manigault and Aubert
> Gibert of La Rochelle, 1350 *livres* at unknown rate of interest
> (but likely 20%).[17]

Of the creditors who provided the cash for Jehan Duboys and the *Catherine,* all were *bourgeois* of La Rochelle. The terms of the loan contracts bound Jehan Duboys to the merchants in La Rochelle for the 1567 fishing season. He was required to return to the city after a successful voyage, and loans had to be repaid within a few days of his arrival at the port. The credit system used by the Basque Jehan Duboys in 1567 is not at all different from the actions of the Norman Huppé in 1544, except that the scale of the loans is much larger. The basic patterns seen here in Biscayan and Norman documents were the norm across the Atlantic littoral in the sixteenth century. Indeed, a description from England at the end of the century could apply to any port from Portugal to Holland: "In England in the West Country . . . the fishermen confer with the money man, who furnishes them with money to provide victuals, salt and all other necessary things. He is to be paid twenty five pounds at the ship's return for every hundred lent." This widespread uniformity in the practice of credit contributed to the long-term stability of the fishery and allowed mariners from one region to outfit their ships in another.[18]

Finally, cities had the one thing that made all these other necessities viable: paper. Urban notaries were essential to the fishery, and the contract was an indispensable tool for would-be fishworkers. Notarized contracts shielded participants against lawsuits, defaults, or disputed business outcomes. As such, legal contracts were the ultimate weapon in the arsenal against risk. Even mariners who didn't purchase their supplies in a port city felt compelled to register their activities with the city. On December 3, 1554, Cardin Guevremont, master of the good ship *Genevyefve*, signed a contract with the baker Ouldin Dubosc. Guevremont was effectively placing an order well in advance, and wanted things committed to paper. He had requested eleven hundred pieces of biscuit, hardtack, to be cooked by Dubosc in exchange for the value of 12 *livres tournois*. This would help feed the twenty-eight mariners the *Genevyefve* would carry the next spring to Terra Nova for cod fishing. The biscuit was to be ready eight days before the ship departed, and when the voyage was over would be paid for in fish. Both the baker Dubosc and the master Guevremont hailed from Trait, a small port downriver from Jumièges on the Seine, but they had come to Rouen to formalize this agreement. Rouen remained the center of gravity for a small outport like Trait, the place where contracts were signed and stored. As they became essential concentration points for food, equipment, finance, and paperwork, urban centers pulled ships toward themselves, redirecting sailing routes and traffic flows over time. In so doing, they made the fishery more and more an urban concern.[19]

Reflecting on the role of paper in shaping how modern historians have studied the fishery, let me suggest that we should understand Terra Nova as an urban phenomenon above all because we are forced to see it through urban eyes. Very few surviving pieces of evidence were made at Terra Nova, or even in the outports that many mariners called homes. Almost all of our surviving documentary records describing the fishery were produced in European cities—or, more precisely, in the offices of notaries located near the docks. In the sixteenth century, many cities had one or several notaries (sometimes assigned parish by parish) who handled this crucial task. If notaries did not record the initial contract, then an urban court might adjucate a subsequent lawsuit. Even something like the story of Robert Lefant comes to us because it was written down by a scribe in the city of Fuenterrabía. As such, our view of the northwest Atlantic is almost always refracted through the notaries and court scribes working in densely packed cities across coastal Europe. We are compelled to gaze at the northwest Atlantic from the docks of European cities.[20]

Return

In the fall of 1543, the town council of Plymouth made note of special payments to "the watchman at Rame when the beacons were burned" and "for his coming here by night when the Newfoundland men came in." Some anonymous watchman had been paid by the town to stand watch at Rame, a peninsula near the harbor mouth, to keep an eye out for the homebound fishing fleet. Everyone was eager to know of their return, and the news must have been met with much celebration and not a little relief that fall. Once they had returned, the process of spending money, eating codfish, and carrying food to the rest of the kingdom began. This is useful evidence to remind us of how important the return of fishing ships was to port cities like Plymouth, and how much the community could be invested in their success.[21]

The pairing of outport and urban *bourgeois* did not end with the signing of a loan contract and departure of the ship. Debtors were often obligated to return directly to port at the end of the season to repay their loan, and sometimes were expected to repay the debt in the form of fish. Huppé agreed to sail to "Rouen or another port or harbour in this land of Normandy . . . upon Return from the said voyage." Even if they repaid in cash, most took the opportunity to sell their catch to local merchants in the same cities. As more fishing voyages became dependent on short-term loans in a handful of port cities, these urban centers in turn became the main distribution centers for codfish. This was the key to a *bourgeois* like Michel de la Rue investing in the fishery, for his contract guaranteed that Huppé and the *Margueritte* would return to Rouen to offload its catch at the end of the season.[22]

Why were urban centers the primary markets for cod from Terra Nova? A fishing ship might arrive in September carrying tens of thousands of codfish. This was far more than a small outport could buy or consume at once, but more than welcome in a city of many thousand souls. Cities had the storage facilities to handle large volumes of cod, and the market infrastructure to sell it. The city council of Rouen frequently granted merchants the right to store small quantities of codfish (literally, "put under cover" in the legal parlance) in city warehouses during the 1530s–40s. The presumption was that these goods were being held temporarily until they could be shipped elsewhere for resale. In addition, cities often contained, or were close to, religious institutions, which were major buyers of fish. Urban centers were also where many armies and naval flotillas assembled, making them useful for military contractors.[23]

One reason for urban dependence on the fishery was outside of the control of city administrators: conflict. The outbreak of hostilities between two states typically unleashed waves of state-sanctioned violence against commercial shipping. This pushed more mariners across the Atlantic by the need to avoid the worst of the summer raids. In the early sixteenth century the number of ships operating in the northwest Atlantic fishery appears to increase during and just after wartime, as more and more mariners were interested in fleeing beyond the reach of states and their hired pirates. There is, for instance, a cluster of records pointing to Norman and Biscayan towns becoming involved in the Terra Nova fishery during the years 1520–26, in the middle of one of the sharpest periods of war between the Habsburg and Valois. Such crises were common, and Europe's coasts were a dangerous place during wartime.[24]

At the same time, conflict opened up important opportunities for the Terra Nova fishery. In urban centers like Rouen, La Rochelle, or San Sebastián, naval conflict could produce an acute need to find new sources of food. Sometimes we can see these moments of urban anxiety in action. On

October 22, 1521, the city council of Rouen passed a lengthy decree in which they called upon the "the salted fish merchants of this city" to "buy cod, herring and other goods" for the city. To achieve this goal, the merchants were authorized to go out and "visit the ports and harbours of this land of Normandy" to find and purchase fish. The council likewise alluded to merchants from Orléans, Paris, and "other cities in the kingdom" that were competing for the same provisions, suggesting a widespread problem in northern France. We also know, though it is not explicitly mentioned in the text, that in 1521 Normandy was suffering from an extended war with England and the Habsburg crown. The Flemish herring fishery had already been ravaged by pirates, and with the autumn fishing season fast approaching, Rouen merchants seem to have been scrambling to find a way to cope with the prospect of a serious shortfall. Later, in 1542, desperate Norman merchants in the port of Dieppe had to turn to Dutch herring to alleviate the serious food shortages during wartime. The man who engineered the deal, which brought fish from the north, was Jean Ango, a member of a family that earlier in the century had turned away from Terra Nova. During such times of crises, the autumn return of the Terra Nova fishing fleets was a godsend. Military contractors meanwhile were on their own quest to buy preservable foodstuffs in bulk. Saltfish like *bacalao* was an ideal commodity for contractors, and was purchased in vast quantities every year to feed naval forces and land armies. For *bourgeois* interested in outfitting fishing ships, this offered lucrative opportunities to sell fish from Terra Nova to starving burghers and contractors each fall.[25]

Early in the sixteenth century, many urban merchants realized that there was more value in reselling codfish from Terra Nova than there was in consuming it locally. A number of outfitting ports rapidly became clearing-houses for the continental fish trade. Small ships flitted between the cities of Europe, carrying barrels of salted cod up and down the rivers and coasts. In 1550 a ferryman from Rouen joined with a merchant from Nogent outside of Paris to carry barrels of cod to the capital, along with herrings, figs, whale oil, and other comestibles. In a city like Rouen, merchants came from Paris, Orléans, and Poitou to buy the fish from ships returning from Terra Nova. One Basque source from the early seventeenth century (drawing on experience over several decades) states that all Basque ships brought their catch to San Sebastián first, whence it was carried across Spain. Not all codfish was eaten, in the end, by urban residents. Much of it ended up in outlying towns and villages. But almost all of the codfish started its journey in a port city, and rural or coastal populations relied on cities to distribute cod through regional exchange networks.[26]

The urban impact of the Terra Nova fishery was much deeper than mercantile records suggest. The yearly return of fish could touch many lives far beyond the wharf. Writing in the 1570s, the English author Anthony Parkhurst noted:

> So that the poor together with the clergy do pray for the prosperous success of these fishermen. And I am well assured so do the gentry, for they all have some profit. . . . This is especially true of the poor hospitals and the poor folk in those shires and ports from whence these ships originate. For there is given out of every fisherman's share, and out of the ship's share, and also the victualer's share, at the least 12 d. from every single share, which on a big ship may amount to the value of £10. Besides there are the broken fish (which is no small quantity, at least two or three thousand), which may be worth £20 or £30, if they are worth selling, and yet as good to eat as if they were whole.

This remarkable glimpse into the local effects of the urban fishery tells us two important things. First, fishworkers were contributing parts of their shares to public charity. Second, fishing ships returned with large amounts of "broken fish" (low-quality discard fish) that could be resold or donated to feed hungry mouths. In some English port cities, then, fishing ships provided cheap sources of food for impoverished households and contributed to the charity work of many religious institutions.[27]

As Parkhurst's letter tells us, when fishing ships did return, the money flowed. That risk aversion that motivated both *bourgeois* had produced a cascading effect on the distribution of profits. Over forty individuals might have claim to a share of the catch and profits after a voyage: two to six shipowners, one to three charterers, a captain, twenty-five or more crew members, one to three creditors, one to three outfitters. But along the way many more parties were paid for their contributions. A contract from 1567, preserved in the notarial archives of northern Spain, gives a rare glimpse of what happened at the end of the voyage. The *Maria*, a Basque ship from Ciboure, returned from Terra Nova to the small port of Castro in Vizcaya. The crew had been successful, bringing back twenty-three thousand *bacalao*, which earned the handsome sum of 3,741 *reales* when sold. To redeem this valuable cargo, the master Juan de Ybayeta ordered the fish shipped in two small pinnaces to the nearby city of Bilbao, where it could fetch a high price. This required him to pay 230 *reales* to hire the small boats, plus another 8 *reales* to hire a group of girls to carry the fish from the boats to a storehouse. But that was not the end of things. A further 48 *reales* had to be paid for a group of men to pile the fish for storage, and then straw had to be bought to cover the fish (for another 12 *reales*). At some point 7 *reales* were used to hire another group of girls to carry the fish to a public scale for assessment, where a further 7 *reales* had to be paid to the man who ran the scales. The whole time the cargo was being sold the master had to pay for room and board. As if this was not enough, the sum of 260 *reales* was paid out to buy colored cloth for Ybayeta and members of the crew to fashion new clothes. When all was done, Ybayeta had just 2,520 *reales* left. The case of the *Maria* and its master Juan de Ybayeta tells us both how complex it was to redeem the value of a successful voyage to Terra Nova and how much overhead the investors might face. Of the 3,741 *reales*, a third had been spent just offloading the codfish at market. The remainder still had to be divided between the crew, Juan de Ybayeta, and the actual owners of the ship, not to mention repay any loans that had underwritten the voyage. From groups of girls to the master of scales, many people otherwise uninvolved with Terra Nova made money when a fishing season ended. The evidence in the case of the *Maria* points to the ways in which secondary parties could profit from the Terra Nova fishery. No wonder, then, that towns outfitted watchmen and took care to await the return of the Terra Nova fleet each autumn.[28]

Urban Ecologies

On May 3, 1539, the merchant John Smyth, a resident of the port city of Bristol whose ledger from the 1530s has survived, agreed to sell some provisions on credit to "Master Ris Moris Abowen of Kermerdine, Gentleman."

The goods were placed in the care of one John Enyon, the "Purser of his ship the Mary Grace." Smythe provided beer, firewood, and "1 qr. [a quarter of a hundred] Newland Fische" worth 3s. 9d. Though we don't know where the *Mary Grace* was headed (the late date suggests somewhere other than Terra Nova), we know that it carried a part of the northwest Atlantic with it. More important, this small sale shows how an urban merchant like Smythe could marshal the biological resources of a city to fuel expansion: beer made from local grains, wood harvested in regional forests, and fish imported from across the sea.[29]

The behavior of a merchant like Smythe, as well as notaries like Godes and Prioret, allows us to understand something important about the ways cities functioned in the Terra Nova fishery. Sixteenth-century Europeans tended to think of cities, as we have seen, as social-legal systems. A city was a human community embodied in its citizens and in the legal charters that protected them. Historians of many stripes have viewed cities as economic, political, religious, cultural, and geographic centers and nodes. Some historians, myself included, believe that there is another way to understand cities, and this is the best way to make sense of what we have seen in this chapter. Cities were, first and foremost, an ecological system. Cities created artificial and distinct spatial and biological arrangements. They also reordered the ecology around them, drawing in the resources of their hinterlands and altering webs of labor, exchange, environmental exploitation, and movement for miles and miles around. This was why cities were so important to the fishery, and why they were useful as sites of concentration and consumption. The urban port acted as a linking node, connecting the regional ecologies of coastal Europe to the northwest Atlantic. Each item carried out from an urban port had been embedded into the regional ecology from which the city drew its resources. The biscuit that went into the ship's hold came from wheat grown on Norman farms, fertilized by local animals. The salt pork was made with pigs that had roamed the common lands and forests nearby before being slaughtered. The pork had been mixed with salt pulled out of marshland many miles away. Cider came from well-tended orchards, wine from vineyards along the major riverways. Rope was made from fibers grown in local fields, hooks from iron imported and then hammered in local forges burning local trees. A ship like the *Margueritte* and its owner like Huppé depended on this ability of urban centers to concentrate and make available for purchase mineral resources in a way that would have been impossible in a small outport.[30]

Consider the problem of ship's biscuit. These dense, hard, bland pieces of dried bread were the basis of the European diet on the high seas, and we know that they were carried on every fishing voyage. Each fishworker needed 250–300 pieces of biscuit for the 150-day (five-month) voyage. For example, in 1552 the fishing ship *Le Saint-Esprit* departed Bordeaux for Terra Nova carrying forty men. To feed them the outfitters purchased 120 quintals of ship's biscuit, approximately 12,000 pieces of hardtack, enough for two pieces per day for each mariner. If we assume that a single mariner required at least 300 pounds of biscuit for a five-month fishing voyage, so that a twenty-person crew required 6,000 pounds, we can translate this into its corresponding value in wheat: around 7,800 pounds, or approximately 120 bushels. The productivity of farmland varied wildly, but I will assume that an acre of sixteenth-century farmland in northwest Europe could pro-duce 8–12 bushels of wheat. Thus, one fishing ship required about 10–15 acres of farmland just to supply its yearly allotment of biscuit. This does not count the land needed to raise pigs, cows, wine grapes, apples, peas, or other food products brought along with biscuit. Most ships were outfitted during the dangerous late-winter lull when stored food grew scarce and new crops were not available, yet *bourgeois* directed that biscuits had to be provided for the voyage. A three-hundred-strong Terra Nova fishing fleet would have consumed the product of 3,000–4,500 acres of farmland just for bread each year. It was cities that allowed this agricultural surplus to be transferred to the food-producing fishery.[31]

In turn, these same cities funneled the marine ecology of the northwest Atlantic into Europe. Dead cod and whales passed through the harbor gates of La Rochelle or Exeter in order to reach European markets. Cities were the distribution centers and first sites of consumption. They were also the clearinghouses and conduits by which preserved fish and oil entered the continent along rivers and roads. Energy flowed from the waters of Terra Nova through the conduits of city ports, fueling human activity across the continent. Urban resources had made the outbound voyages possible, and now urban residents would be responsible for storing, distributing, and often eating the fish from Terra Nova. In that they were repaid for the upfront investment: a small but dear amount of energy in the form of food, loaded onto ships just as the late-winter and early-spring period of dearth was setting in, was now recouped manyfold as cities were flush with cod.

To return to the moment at the start of this chapter, when two notaries take down yet another contract for yet another fishing voyage, we may consider what was actually being agreed to. The dry language of the notary suggests that the transaction was little more than an agreement to lend money with the expectation of more money being returned later. What the contract really represents is an agreement to give a ship *bourgeois* access to the biological, mineralogical, and labor resources of the city of Rouen, and by extension the greater Norman hinterland. In exchange, the ship *bourgeois* agrees that, come September, the people of Rouen will temporarily have access to the biology of the northwest Atlantic. Some Norman wheat today will be repaid with Terra Nova codfish tomorrow. When the contract is signed, a link is forged—in principle at first but soon in very real ways that allow the flow of different forms of life and energy between European cities and the northwest Atlantic.

ELEVEN

Eating

On Sunday, December 22, 1560, the minor Norman nobleman the sieur de Gouberville had to miss Mass. Gouberville was a devout Catholic, and missing the service was upsetting enough to make its way into his carefully maintained diary. He had awoken to find himself feeling "very unwell," a problem that persisted all morning, and though we do not know exactly what was wrong it involved his stomach and some difficulty with urination. Gouberville had no doubt about the source of his illness, and the culprit points to the troubling relationship he and countless others had with the processed food they were eating from the Atlantic Ocean: he had taken ill "due to the codfish which was too salty which I ate yesterday for my supper."[1]

Across the sixteenth century, Europeans consumed millions upon millions of codfish, almost all of it in salted and dried form. You could buy it lightly brined by the piece, dry-salted by the whole fish, or completely dried by the hundred. Monks ate it plain on abstinence days, merchants ate it with mustard and garlic at their Friday table, soldiers and sailors mixed it into their porridge twice a week. A family could eat half a dry-salted codfish in October and expect to eat the second half the following April. Celebrity chef Bartolomeu Scappi declared cod fit for the pope himself, while by the end of the century "Poor John" saltcod was sold to impoverished English households. All of these groups were, through the consumption of preserved codfish, eating the Atlantic Ocean, drawing on the biological bounty of its watery depths and the new routes and techniques European mariners had developed to exploit it.

This chapter explores how Europeans consumed codfish, both before and after the rise of the Terra Nova fishery. I take the time to explore these issues because we must understand how cod was consumed to understand how and why it was produced. The main point I wish to make is that most Europeans ate cod only after it had been physically transformed through salt and sun. This made it one of the earliest and most successful mass-produced processed foodstuffs. This in turn shaped how it was placed in a cultural un-derstanding of health and dietary practices. Unlike some previous studies, I propose to view cod through a pan-European and comparative approach, considering how it was thought about beyond the fishing ports that pro-duced it. Cod was consumed in the context of a wider fish-eating culture that encouraged Europeans to eat many different kinds of marine life simul-taneously. Examined in this broad perspective, we will see that cod was often viewed ambivalently by many Europeans despite its commercial success, sometimes seen as bland and even unhealthy, especially by nutritional writ-ers. In most European households many different pressures converged—the processed nature of cod, the ambivalence about its effect on health, the taste for salty foods, the pressures of faith, the economic logic of mass-produced seafood—to produce a complex food culture in the sixteenth century.[2]

Fish Eaters

Fifteenth- and sixteenth-century Europeans were fish eaters. In a world of precarious food security there was little incentive to avoid fish, and the ma-jority of Europeans lived under a religious compulsion to regularly eat ma-rine foods in lieu of meat. Even so, Europeans certainly had complex feelings about seafood. Some marine animals were highly esteemed, such as salmon, eel, lamprey, dolphin, and sturgeon. At the top of the social or-der, royal households consumed prodigious quantities of fresh fish, even when far from the sea. For Easter in 1554, the French court at Fontaine-bleau demanded a feast of salmon, lamprey, cod, carp, herring, and a dozen other fish, laying out over 30 *livres tournois* to purchase the highly esteemed seafood in very precise quantities. Yet in the humoral concepts of health that prevailed in Europe, fish were held to be excessively cold and wet. They could represent a serious health threat if consumed in excess. The historian Renée Girard has observed that many French Jesuit missionaries in New France were shocked by the amount of fish Innu and Mi'kmaq peoples consumed—according to Galenic theories they should have been dead from such an imbalanced diet. Thus fish could be royal and reviled, a plentiful source of food and a threat to one's bodily integrity.[3]

In fifteenth- and-sixteenth century Europe, fish were not just food, they were salvation. A good Christian had to eat fish according to a steady yearly rhythm of fish days and Lenten cycles. This religious compulsion, this sacralization of fish, hangs over any discussion of sixteenth-century fishing. Few foods were subject to such rigid demand, especially for those who were sworn to religious vows. As Barbara Harvey has shown, in the 1490s–1510s the monks of Westminster Abbey (who were especially stringent in following such rules) were served fish for some 570 meals a year, about half of it preserved. In the priory at Worcester, far from the coast, during the first week of Advent 1521, there was herring, conger eel, ling, codfish, eel, unspecified fresh fish, and stockfish served in various combinations across the three fish days. During Lent fish was eaten daily, including both fresh and salt salmon, hake, and lamprey along with the ubiquitous herring and stockfish. In 1515 at Saint Swithun's Priory in Winchester the monks enjoyed on the Feast of the Epiphany (Friday, January 6) dried ling, fresh cod (referred to as "millwell"), an appetizer of minnows, and a special pittance of imported rice, with mustard on the side for flavor. These religious institutions were major markets for the new generation of commercial fisheries.[4]

But if religious abstinence was one driver of fish consumption, then the earthly concern of warfare was another. The near-ceaseless wars of the sixteenth century relied on state-organized armies and navies across northwest Europe. Soldiers and sailors had to be fed, and their provisions were often arranged by military contractors. In the wars of Henry VIII and Edward VI the English crown paid £2,607 for 116,378 saltfish. A further £2,800 was paid for 700 tons of red and white herring from local fisheries, indicating the scale of demand. Sailing ships and military organizations were the only two social spaces besides religious institutions that could enforce fish days. In 1569 the city council of Saint Malo specified the daily food allowance of fifty soldiers stationed in the city, including "one small codfish or four herring" served with peas on "fish days." Similar provisions exist for various English expeditions across Europe later in the century. So long as both religious institutions and military contractors demanded codfish, albeit for very different reasons, fishworkers would have reason to visit the northwest Atlantic.[5]

Beyond the walls of the monastery and garrison, good Christians did their best to eat fish. In most households Friday was fish day, and usually Saturday as well. The sieur de Gouberville, wandering around Normandy in the 1540s, often recorded in his diary that he purchased fish on Thursdays and Fridays in preparation for the weekend. Wednesday was often a fish day as well, depending on where one lived. During the forty days of Lent one abandoned meat for fish, and even some Protestant sects continued the practice of fish days across the sixteenth century. In mid-century England at least one author advocated keeping Wednesday as a fish day in order to relieve pressure on the beef industry, not merely for religious reasons. In sum, a European household could easily find itself required by religious (and sometimes secular) rules to eat fish for a third of the year. In practice, religious compulsions affected people unevenly. Nonconformism was widespread, especially for a practice like fish consumption, which was costly, depended on access to fish, and was of unclear value. Whether an average household actually adhered to Lenten and abstinence day requirements was highly variable and difficult for historians to see in the surviving records.[6]

Not all Europeans ate seafood in the same ways, and distinct regional foodways formed the basic way through which communities accessed food. There were not yet national cuisines as we now understand them, but rather localized ways of cooking and thinking about taste, shaped by local ecologies and traditions. Basque methods of cooking cod probably differed from those of Bretons in ways that sixteenth-century Europeans would have understood intuitively. Unfortunately, these regional foodways and differences are very difficult to see in our sources. Recipes and cooking guides, either manuscript or printed, typically reflect a kind of cosmopolitan, aspirational haute cuisine rather than quotidian practice (as indeed they continue to do today). I use them here because they let us see pan-European trends in food thinking, but we should realize that most people ate fish according to traditions produced by a multiplicity of food cultures. In the long run, Terra Nova would influence many of these traditions, as seen in modern differences in *bacalao*'s popularity between northern and southern Europe, or differences between Basque, Portuguese, and Italian ways of cooking saltcod.

Of course, Europeans were not the only fish eaters in the Atlantic, or indeed at Terra Nova. Marine foods often constituted a much higher proportion of Indigenous Americans' diets than Europeans' over the course of the year. It certainly appears that European mariners viewed the people they encountered at Terra Nova as ichthyophagists. The anonymous *gran capitano* who wrote about Terra Nova in 1539 described the Beothuk as fishing "for seals, porpoises and certain sea birds, called *Margaux*, which they take on the islands to dry. They make oil out of the fat of these fish." A decade later Jean Alfonse found Beothuk and Mi'kmaq on Newfoundland island who "live on fish, flesh, and the fruits of the tree." An English crew at the Isles de la Madaleine in 1593 found "certain round ponds artificially made by the Savages to keep fish in," suggesting the Mi'kmaq practiced aquaculture. André Thevet similarly claimed in his *Grand Insulaire* that on some islands the Mi'kmaq maintained reservoirs filled with fish that they sometimes sold to passing European crews. Nonetheless, the consumption of cod by Indigenous communities differed from European practice in two crucial ways. First, it was not processed and eaten in a dry-salted or wet-salted form as it typically was in Europe. The use of salt-intensive cures to preserve fish, especially cod, seems to have been uncommon and possibly unknown among First Nations in Terra Nova. Although they may have smoked and dried fish, there is no archaeological evidence that cod was traded over distances, as it would be in Europe. The *gran capitano* even believed that cod was caught only by Bretons and Normans at Terra Nova, not by Indigenous peoples at all, perhaps reflecting a difference in scale and use. Second, cod was only one tiny part of a wide variety of marine protein sources consumed by Indigenous communities. Whereas European fishworkers at Terra Nova tended to treat cod as a kind of living monocrop, Algonkian-speaking communities harvested all manner of fish and shellfish. Seals, for instance, were a crucial food source for many pre-sixteenth-century Indigenous groups, whereas they were far less important in European diets. What a community consumed must have changed depending on the part of the season and the location of summer camps. Herring and salmon might sustain one community, while next door it was mussels and capelin that went into the communal pot. The collision of European mariners and Algonkian-speaking communities in the northwest Atlantic was therefore an encounter between two fish-eating societies, but they treated marine foodstuffs in different ways.[7]

Cod and Its Discontents

When you bit into a piece of codfish in sixteenth-century Europe, you tasted cold water and salty marshland. The fish itself was born out of the frigid, shallow waters of the northwest Atlantic. Cod flesh is flaky, white, and firm, and it offers a fresh, oil-free taste that can border on bland. That clean and mild taste was a virtue, but more so was the nutrition packed into the meat of this large and active fish. But the key to unlocking the cold-water flavor was the salt that had seeped into the fish, drying the flesh and curing it. That salt came not from the northwest Atlantic but from the low-lying marshland around the Bay of Biscay. Here brackish water was put out in vast troughs to evaporate by the marsh-dwelling workers who tended the saltpans until all that was left were piles of gray, rough, intensely flavored salt. This was Bay Salt, and ships came from across Europe to buy this precious mineral, making fortunes for merchants in towns like Bourgeneuf, La Rochelle, and Brouage. It was the gray salt of Biscay that turned codfish into something that could be stored and transported across the Atlantic basin. Each bite was a reminder of that pairing of marsh and ocean, of Europe and the Atlantic.

To hungry Europeans, the value of cod lay in its ability to be preserved. It could take a salt cure or drying without losing too much nutrition, texture, and flavor. Three types of preserved codfish dominated European markets in the sixteenth century, produced by a series of trade-offs between time, salt, and sun. The first and oldest variety was stockfish, the air-dried codfish originating in northern Norway. Left to hang without salting for a long period of time in a dry, cold climate the fish became entirely desiccated and rock-hard. Norwegian air-dried stockfish circulated across northern Europe from the eleventh century, and within a few centuries would be joined by more dried cod from Iceland, the Faroes, Shetland, and elsewhere. At the other end of the spectrum was green cod, *morue verte*, whole or parts of codfish pickled in a salt-heavy brine. Most green cod were packed in wooden barrels with ample salt and left to cure in a process close to the production of pickled herring. Sometimes a lighter brine was used to minimize the pickling process, though the fish would not last as long. In between these two extremes was dry-salted cod, *bacalao*, which balanced salt and time. Whole or parts of fish were rubbed with salt and left out in the sun to dry. Salt was used to speed up the drying process, drawing moisture out of fish flesh, but the sun did most of the work. Saltcod was easier to rehydrate and use than stockfish, and it lasted longer than green cod. Stockfish, which only used sun, was popular but difficult to produce at scale. Primarily salt-cured *morue verte* and *bacalao* were made at Terra Nova.[8]

In salting and drying cod, Europeans were processing their food. Fish that has been salted and dried is physically different from fresh fish, bearing a different texture and ultimately a different taste. In the late seventeenth century the English author Thomas Willis believed that salt "bestows a Compaction and Solidity on things, and also weight and duration." This was a fair summation of what salt did to cod. A dried codfish might lose upward of 75 percent of its original mass, and one modern study shows that 4.7 pounds of live cod produced 1 pound of dried fish. Dried or dry-salted codfish is nutritionally dense, up to 80 percent protein by weight and perhaps five times as dense as fresh fish. Live cod might be 15–130 kilograms and over two meters long, though in processed form they varied considerably in size and weight. The dense concentration of protein and calories meant that a little bit went a long way. Half a salted cod might feed one worker for a day, or at other times a whole one was split four ways. It was an efficient source of energy for hungry Europeans, a transportable battery that could sustain a human being more effectively than many other fish or meats. Even resuscitated saltcod would never be quite like fresh fish, always remaining firmer, more fibrous, and denser. After a time it could even develop a slightly funky, fermented smell that lingered on the palate. Each bite was an inescapable reminder of a food that had been processed and remade by humans.[9]

Codfish (salted or otherwise) was fairly boring fare. Compared to fattier, richer fish like eel, salmon, or sturgeon, it was underwhelming, even undesirable. Consequently, cod appears relatively rarely in fifteenth- and sixteenth-century cookbooks and recipe collections. Cooks lavished much attention on how to prepare dishes from tastier and more interesting seafoods, and more chefs aspired to use conger eel or porpoise than stockfish. There is a distinct impression, though a hard one to quantify, that Europeans were not terribly excited about their *bacalao* and *morue verte*, even if they increasingly imported it from far afield. It is surprising, and more than a little bit funny, how much space the great thinker Erasmus of Rotterdam devoted to trashing cod and other saltfish, including an entire dialogue between a butcher and a saltfish monger in which the latter inevitably came across as the worse party. To that end Thomas Moffet wrote many years later, "Erasmus thinks it is called Stockfish because it nourishes no more than a dried stock [of wood]; wherefore however it be soaked, buttered, fried, or baked, and made both tastier and delectable by good cookery, yet a stone will be a stone, and an ape an ape, however the one be set up like a Saint, and the other dressed like a judge." Erasmus and Moffet were drawing on European thought that equated flavor and aroma with nutrition. The blandness of cod, especially dried stockfish, was viewed as robbing the fish of its healthful qualities.[10]

Yet that blandness proved to be a virtue in one important respect: the large amount of meat and low oil/fat content of Atlantic cod allowed salt to impart the gift of longevity. The active processing that humans imparted through salt and sun had produced something entirely unlike the fragile, natural fish from the Atlantic Ocean. This was living flesh that resisted decomposition, remaining stable long after it was supposed to rot. Willis described how salt "retards the dissolution of Bodies, and promotes Congelations and Coagulations, and very much resists Putrefaction, Corruption, and Inflammation." Dry-salted cod lasted a long time—months or even years if treated right. "Spend herring first, save saltfish last, / for saltfish is good, when Lent is past," advised Thomas Tusser in his 1573 book *Five Hundred Points of Good Husbandry*. The implication was that salted cod bought in the autumn would be good the following April, whereas the herring would have gone bad. Stockfish could make the trip from northern Norway or Iceland all the way to Rome, Munich, or Budapest without spoiling, while *bacalao* carried from the northwest Atlantic to southern Iberia, Italy, or the Caribbean would remain fresh for months. Because it resisted decomposition, preserved cod was one of the few ocean fishes to have an impact on diets beyond the coast. The French naturalist Pierre Belon described cod as "one of the most common in our lands," where it was eaten as far inland as Orléans and Lyon. Dried stockfish was a notable ingredient in a late-century Hungarian cookbook, as well as several German cookbooks and recipe manuscripts, a sure sign that it was being exported into the depths of the continent. One did not need to live near the coast to eat codfish, but in turn one would only ever eat codfish that had been preserved and thus altered in important ways.[11]

For consumers, the presence of salt in food was a matter not merely of preservation and flavor but of health. According to prevailing Galenic medical theories, salt was considered hot and dry. As "all fish are generally cold and moist," salt was a natural corrective. Writing in 1599 Henry Butts offered a balanced view of salt and its consequences for health: it was used "in almost all meats, to season or preserve; by drying, resists poison; consumes all corrupt humours." But one had to be careful to "eat little of it, and that in or with moist meats," for too much "makes you soon look old; dries the body; wastes seed; engenders sharp and biting humours; causes itch and scabs." Salt had to be eaten in moderation or else it could harm the body. The nutritional text *La singolare dottrina* by Domenico Romoli equivocated on the matter of salt's healthiness, urging moderation in some cases and heavily salted foods in others. It did, however, make one pronouncement clear: "Salted fish is more healthful than fresh fish, because it is dried of the humidity and coldness by the salt." For these reasons, to separate the salt entirely from the fish before cooking was frowned upon.[12]

Sometimes consumers even chose to buy fresh or brined cod and then turn it into a salted, dried provision. In 1517 Coventry, some fishmongers were accused of buying fresh cod and salting it at home for resale. The city council had to intervene and lay out public laws to prevent such practices. Thomas Tusser, in his guide to proper household management, offers a note of advice about storing one's fish. As part of December's husbandry, he advises households that: "Both salt fish and ling fish (if any ye have) / Through shifting and drying, from rotting go save; / Lest winter with moistness do make it relent, / And put it in hazard, before it be spent." The advice assumes that most fish is bought in the autumn, but the wet winter weather could cause rot. Moving the fish around was one solution to prevent buildup of moisture. The other was to dry out the fish further, in essence turning saltcod into stockfish to make it last longer. Tusser even offers a useful guide to this practice: "Broom faggot is best to dry *haberden* [saltcod] on, / Lay board upon ladder, if faggots be gone: / For breaking (in turning) have very good eye, / And blame not the wind, so the weather be dry." As these descriptions suggest, households carefully managed their cod through drying and careful storage to maximize longevity.[13]

Buying Fish

Given its nutritional efficiency, codfish was found in marketplaces across Atlantic Europe. Our sources hint that some codfish was bought in bulk at fairs rather than in local markets. In England several major fairs were associated with the purchasing of fish, Scarborough in the north being the most popular. In East Anglia alone there was Saint Gregory's fair at Sudbury as well as major fish fairs at Saint Ives, Sturbridge, and Ely. In the 1580s an English report from Normandy stated that over two hundred Flemish and Dutch merchants came to Rouen in the winter to purchase fish from a fair. It appears that by this date Rouen was more than a Norman entrepôt; it had become a major hub for buying fish. These fairs served as massive clearinghouses for the distribution of fish to the interior, or as centers for the purchase of fish in bulk by elite households, religious orders, and military contractors. Thomas Tusser explicitly advocates this in his advice to thrifty households: "When harvest is ended, take shipping or ride / Ling, Saltfish and Herring, for Lent to provide." In other words, come the harvest season, it was worth taking a trip to a major fish fair to buy preserved fish. Whatever you purchased could then be "stack[ed] up dry" at home to be eaten months later during Lent. But the expense of travel and storage would not be a problem: "To buy at first, as it cometh to rode / shall pay for thy charges thou spendest abroad." Buying in bulk when the fish was plentiful saved households in the long run.[14]

Such fairs served the largest, wealthiest consumers, but most codfish were likely purchased by households at small, dedicated market stalls that specialized in fish. In his journal, the sieur de Gouberville makes repeated references to a "*poysçonnerye*" (fish vendor) in the town of Bayeux in Normandy who sold both fresh and preserved marine products. In many English towns there were informal fish markets, though most were carefully regulated by the local town councils. At Coventry, the fishmongers set out simple boards on which to sell their fish, along with basins of water to soak their stockfish and saltcod. Fish were supposed to be laid out for sale by 7 in the morning, and had to be sold by 2 in the afternoon. As soon as the fish was sold the fishmongers were supposed to take their boards and leave, indicating how flimsy and transient these markets could be. At times these municipal fishmongers were subject to scrutinous city and provincial regulation, although kings were far less interested and rarely interfered. The various kinds of processed cod that circulated in sixteenth-century Europe passed through the hands of these small-time, locally regulated vendors.[15]

As noted earlier, by the mid-sixteenth century many people bought their codfish in cities. In some cases, preserved fish were sold by generalized merchants, mixed in with other provisions. The Bristol merchant John Smythe occasionally sold small amounts of "Newland fish" (sometimes just one or two pieces) to locals along with beer and other fish like hake. Yet alongside such generalists a group of dedicated, professional fish merchants had appeared across northwest Europe. London's preserved fish trade was dominated by Hanse merchants and the Worshipful Company of Fishmongers, which operated from its famous guildhall on the River Thames. In Rouen and Nantes there were the *vendeurs des poissons sallée* (sellers of salted fish) who are described in city records during the first three decades of the sixteenth century—those who had been granted "the right to trade in green, dry, and salted fish." By the late sixteenth century the French crown would begin to regulate the fish trade through these merchants, using them as a vector to manage the quality and quantity of fish eaten in the kingdom. In Coventry, the city council distinguished between regular fishmongers and "saltfishmen [and] their wives," who were prohibited from interfering in the sale of fresh fish. It would be this broad group of professionals who moved preserved cod from boat to market.[16]

By the late sixteenth century distinct, permanent fish markets began to appear in the cities of northwest Europe. These are seen in Dutch and Flemish artwork around the turn of the seventeenth century, but they were likely known earlier. An illustrated guide to London from the 1590s, Hugh Alley's *A Caveatt for the Citty of London*, clearly shows a fish market in the city. "Newe Fishe Streete" reveals a row of market stalls selling fish of all kinds, whole and in baskets (see figure 19). As this illustration shows, in the marketplace it was very often women who controlled the resale of fish. Late sixteenth- and early seventeenth-century Dutch artworks likewise show women running fish stalls in the Low Countries, and early seventeenth-century court records from La Rochelle show that women were the primary sellers of fish in the city *halles*. Darlene Abreu-Ferreira has argued, "In northern Portugal, merchandising fish was a woman's prerogative at both the retail and wholesale levels . . . men were fishers, but women were fish vendors, and often women were also responsible for transporting fish from port to inland markets." As we have already seen, women in Portugal, Basque Country, Normandy, and elsewhere were also at the forefront of organizing, financing, and outfitting voyages to and from Terra Nova. This meant that women played significant, and in some cases central, roles at the beginning and end of the transoceanic fish trade.[17]

In selecting their preserved fish, consumers had a great many options. A family might purchase a whole codfish to take home, or an individual could purchase it by the piece. We know that codfish were graded in the marketplace by the mid-sixteenth century, organized and valued according to size and quality. Records from Bristol in the mid-sixteenth century rate codfish according to a three-tiered scale of quality, and according to their size within these categories. Buyers had to be careful, and Tusser again cautions his reader, "Choose skillfully Saltfish, not burnt at the stone" — that is, fish that

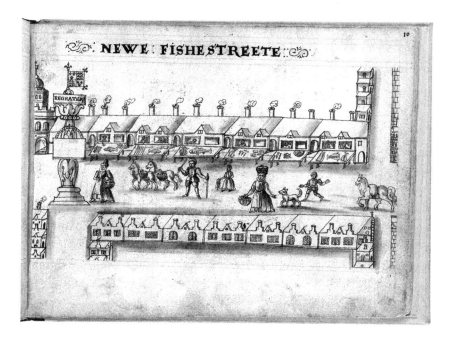

Figure 19. "Newe Fishe Streete" in London, 1598, in Hugh Alley, *A Caveatt for the Citty of London*. (Courtesy of the Folger Shakespeare Library, Folger call number V.a.318.)

had not been burned by being left in the sun too long while drying. We have already seen that "broken fish" was sold to feed the poor, even if the fish was in a sorry state. In Coventry in 1512, the town affirmed that only eight people, besides the fishworkers themselves, were allowed to cut up sea fish for sale, thereby indicating that the parceling out of fish parts was both expected and carefully managed. As Laurier Turgeon has noted, sixteenth-century Europeans ate and esteemed more than just the fillets and flesh of the cod. Tongues, cheeks, and tails were all much prized (even today cod tongues are a well-known delicacy in the fishing communities of Newfoundland). Thomas Moffet explained to his readers, "Cods have a bladder in them that is full of eggs or sperm, which the Northmen call the *kelk*, and they believe it is a very dainty meat; they have also a thick and gluey substance at the end of their stomach called a *sowne*, more pleasant to eat than good for you; for the toughest fish-glue is made from that. Of all the parts of the fresh cod, the head, lips, and tongue are preferred, being a very light though slimy meat."

The sieur de Gouberville describes buying cod in all manner of forms, from whole to piece to morsel, from fresh to salted to dried, even spending five *sous* on salted cod entrails (*noös de morue*) as a treat. No part went to waste, and every part of the cod had value.[18]

Making a Meal

Cod was a processed food, and to eat it for dinner one had to unprocess it. This was an intensive affair. "One must beat stockfish," declared Balthasar Staindl in a lengthy entry on cooking stockfish in his 1544 *Kochbuch*. Cooks learned that beating, soaking, and burning the freeze-dried cod produced a softer, moister fish that could be boiled, roasted, mashed, or fried. Special stockfish hammers were sold to make this easier, and some communities built wind and water mills to run stockfish pounders. The mid-century German cookbook of Sabina Welseren called for soaking the stockfish with a mixture of water and lye, a chemical solution that was a south-German variant of Scandinavian *lutefisk*. Preparing salted cod required basins of water, which were swapped out every few hours. The papal chef Bartolomeu Scappi advised, "Get dried *merluccia* and soak them in warm water for eight hours more or less, depending on their size[,] for, even though some people pound them with a rod to make them tender, nevertheless I do not advise that, it being better to let them soften by themselves, as experience has shown me." Much of this work was likely done by women, both fishmongers in the marketplace and cooks in the household, who took time and energy to soak, beat, burn, debone, and ultimately cook the fish.[19]

Though much of the water processing was done at home, we do know that some merchants soaked their codfish before offering it for sale. In London, an entire part of town was devoted to unprocessing stockfish. Passing through London in 1562, the Venetian Alessandro Magno noted, "There is a street which has many shops on both sides where they do nothing for three days of the week but tie this fish [dried cod] into bundles and batter it continuously. This makes the fish very white, tough and flavourless; they send quantities of it to Flanders and to Germany." Thomas Moffet later observed of the same place that "the Stilliard Merchants lay it twenty four hours in strong lye, and then as long again in warm waters; afterwards they boil it in abundance of butter, and so serve it in with pepper, and salt, which way (if any way) it is most nourishing, because it is made not onely tender, but also more moist and warm." It is evidence that on the Thames waterfront the Hanse merchant community (which occupied the Steelyard Wharf) was selling stockfish that had not merely been soaked but also cooked and seasoned. The reference to butter and pepper even suggests that one could buy cooked stockfish ready to eat, a kind of sixteenth-century takeout.[20]

Whether beating, soaking, dressing, or boiling, working and cooking with cod was a multisensory experience. Whole preserved cod had to be carefully boned by hand, for it was often shipped with the spine and bones intact. Stockfish skin was legendarily messy, sticking to the cook's hands and clothes. "Daughter," says Christ to Margery Kempe in her fifteenth-century spiritual biography, "for you are so obedient to my will and stick as fervently to me as the skin of stockfish sticks to a man's hands when it is boiled." The Son of God himself spoke of the banal experience of eating messy codfish. Elsewhere, he invokes another unpleasant image that must have been common in many households: "Thou shalt be eaten and gnawed of the people of the world as a rat gnaws the stockfish." Improperly stored saltcod might get wet and rot, producing a revolting odor. Even when properly handled the fish could smell, especially as it sat for hours or days soaking in a basin. The city council of Coventry mandated in 1511 that "no man cast out any fish-water that fish have been watered in after 3 o'clock in the morning and before 9 o'clock at night," while in Southampton the city officials admonished fishmongers who allowed their soaking cod to befoul the air. The streets of cities like Rouen must have reeked with the telltale smell of cod every Friday in the long winters of the mid-sixteenth century.[21]

Once processed, the fish had to be cooked, and it was here that one could hide the blandness of saltcod or stockfish under sauces and herbs. The English author Thomas Cogan claimed to quote Erasmus when he wrote, "I have eaten of a pie made only with stockfish, which hath been very good, but the goodness was not so much in the fish as in the cookery, which may make that savoury which of itself is unsavoury." Preserved codfish appears haphazardly in published and manuscript cookbooks from the fourteenth through the seventeenth centuries. When they do appear in circulation, most recipes give instructions for the preparation of stockfish rather than saltcod, with detailed instructions for soaking and beating the dried fish. The fish was then typically boiled or, more rarely, fried, before a sauce is applied. The sauce was an important part of codfish consumption, and indeed sauces were generally important to elite European cookery. Most recipes prescribe either a mustard sauce or a garlic-based sauce, something strong and sharp. As early as 1400 the *Libro de arte coquinaria* recommended a simple but strong sauce of white mustard. Scappi advised his readers that one could serve *merluccie secche* (dried cod) "parboiled, and when that's done you can make a potage of them with beaten onions. Otherwise you can cook them in a broth made of oil and spices. They are served dressed with a garlic sauce or some other sauce." Should you wish to fry the fish instead, then serve it "with orange juice and pepper over them and with mustard in dishes." The early sixteenth-century Catalan *Libre del coch* recommended a sweet-sour sauce, combining vinegar-soaked bread with honey and spices. The Dutch even had their own name (*Mocloock*) for a sauce made of minced garlic and sage that was specially concocted to be served "with *aberdan* [saltcod]" that appears in the 1510 *Een notabel boecxken van coekeryn*. The preference for strongly seasoned sauces reflects the relative blandness of desalinated or rehydrated codfish. It helped balance the weakness of the fish and guard against ill-health effects. Only in the seventeenth century would tastes begin to change.[22]

These were the recipes intended for well-to-do tables. How the *bourgeois* of Rouen or the monks outside London or the sailors onboard Galician ships ate their codfish is not clearly known. Mariners likely mixed their saltcod or *morue verte* in with their daily porridge. Preserved cod added protein, texture, calories, and strong flavor (of both fish and salt) to their starch-heavy stews. Ship's biscuits were soaked, mixed with pulses and chunks of *bacalao*, and perhaps enlivened with a dash of vinegar. Most consumers must have had their own little preferences and touches—a dash more salt, a pinch of herb, a dollop of mustard—that enlivened their cod stews and made the bland fish palatable. Whether it was offered in a small urban home or a major monastery, most cod was eaten communally. Diners tore chunks of cooked fish from the bone, ladled spoonfuls of stew into their bowls, or grabbed handfuls of shredded and seasoned flesh. All knew it as a filling and satisfying food, a welcome respite in an age of food insecurity.

Tastes

One of the great insights of food studies in the past several decades has been that taste matters. Not everything is subject to the dry calculus of calories-per-work-hour. In this light, Donald Holly Jr. has recently made the valuable point that even among hunter-gathering societies in places like the subarctic, societies anthropologists have long treated as following purely rational food-gathering strategies, matters of taste, preference, identity, and culture all shaped which foods were eaten and often excluded major sources of energy. He has called for a more rigorous "social archaeology" of food in such hunter-gathering societies that takes ethnography and culture into account. Likewise, urban and rural Europeans chose what to eat based on personal preferences, cultural norms, and changing ideas of the "good." In so doing, they chose what got made, sold, and bought. This point attempts to bridge the gap between those who see food studies as being about energy flows, and those who see it as being about cultural understanding of food and health. All of us, as in the past, experience this in the middle, somewhere between cold caloric rationality and personal preferences.[23]

The harvesting of preserved codfish at Terra Nova seems to be the epitome of industrial logic: one fish was mass-produced to meet the energy demands of a continent. We have just seen that the practical benefits of dry-salted or dried cod often outweighed the ambivalence about its bland unhealthy nature. Yet matters of taste run through our records and were clearly a concern of sixteenth-century Europeans. European tastes in the sixteenth century were different than ours today, but those tastes could also change. Over time, economic logic became taste and this in turn drove new economic choices. Importantly, the interplay between taste and practicality helps explain what kinds of cod Europeans made at Terra Nova across the sixteenth century. To see this, we will consider three examples of the relationship between production and taste: short term, medium term, and long term.

In the short term we can see a change in who could eat cod from Terra Nova. Between the beginning and the end of the sixteenth century, the accessibility of preserved codfish underwent a significant shift. For the first half of the century salted cod, especially from Terra Nova, was relatively expensive. Darlene Abreu-Fereira has argued it was not much cheaper than beef in Portugal, and Daniel Vicker's price series suggests that cod became markedly more expensive at mid-century before stabilizing at a lower cost. Nor was saltcod from Terra Nova available in very large quantities outside of coastal western Europe until after the 1580s (unlike stockfish or North Sea cod). Contemporary observations suggest that the price had fallen by around 1600, although hard evidence is lacking. In 1599 English households were still paying 6d. per piece of *haberdine* (dry-salted cod) at Stourbridge, a price the working poor could hardly afford. Even so, by the turn of the seventeenth century, English sources cast saltcod and *haberdine* as food for the poor, even calling it *Poor John*. There appears to have been a shift over the course of several decades toward salted cod being identified increasingly as a lower-class and common foodstuff. This was a change in the subjective, social place of cod that shaped tastes in advance of tangible economic changes.[24]

In the medium term we see the expansion of a now-forgotten form of codfish at Terra Nova. This was green cod, *morue verte*, codfish that was salted but not dried. It appears in some of the earliest records associated with the fishery, showing up in Bordeaux in 1517 and La Rochelle in 1523. Laurier Turgeon has convincingly argued that real production did not gear up until later in the century, when the Grand Banks became a major site of the "wet fishery" in the last third of the century. This is surprising inasmuch as green cod has so thoroughly fallen from grace today. You would be hard-pressed to find a recipe for pickled codfish in any modern cookbook, or a market that still sells barrels of brined cod. Indeed, it is even difficult to determine exactly what sixteenth-century *morue verte* looked, felt, and tasted like. We cannot always be certain if it was heavily salted and pickled, like herring on the North Sea, or lightly brined instead. Yet we know that it was widely consumed and absorbed a growing number of expeditions in the last decades of the century.[25]

The answer to *morue verte*'s rising popularity may ultimately reside in the question of taste, not economics. *Morue verte* was consumed mainly in northwest Europe, especially within the kingdom of France. The wet-style preparation had two virtues to northwest European consumers: it was salty, and it felt fresh. The saltiness of fish may have been more desirable in the sixteenth century, likely appealing to a palate that has since been lost. As Alison Locker has argued, northwest European foodways saw a long-term decline in the taste for salty foods from the fifteenth through the twentieth centuries. She points to the fact that premodern diets involved the heavy consumption of salted foods, normalizing saltiness as an expected part of good food and good health. If too much salt was taken out, the result was a bland and unappetizing slab of meat. "[Codfish that has been] soaked too much is no good," advises the fourteenth-century author of the *Menagier de Paris*, "and for this, whomever buys it, must test it by taste and eat a little bit [before buying]." Likewise, when properly prepared, *morue verte* is closer in texture to fresh cod than *bacalao* or stockfish. Because it was not dried in the sun, the flesh remained moist. If properly soaked a piece could pass for a slightly salty version of fresh fish. An eighteenth-century description indicates that *morue verte* was often soaked by merchants before sale in a process called *enroquer*, and then presented as fillets of fresh cod. In the sixteenth century, most codfish from Terra Nova (in any form) was eaten by the communities that produced it. For this reason the codfish had to appeal to the tastes of consumers in this narrow arc. Pickled fish was very popular across coastal Europe, from herring in the north to anchovies and sardines in the south. *Morue verte* fit this pattern of salty, perhaps slightly sour, but fresh-tasting flesh in a way that dried fish did not. They liked the brined taste of *morue verte* more than the blandness of dried stockfish or sun-cured *bacalao*.[26]

This taste for salty, fresher fish ultimately drove changes to production at Terra Nova. As Olaf Janzen has argued, which kind of preserved cod fishworkers made was determined by "the preference of the particular market they planned to supply" rather than production costs. The manufacture of *morue verte* increased markedly in the second half of the sixteenth century as certain regions developed a taste for brined cod. In these later decades we see more and more references to ships working "the banks," indicating that they were staying offshore on the Grand Banks for long periods of time. Though never the dominant form of preserved cod, *morue verte* was attracting more and more attention from fishworkers as consumers sought out brined fish. This shift in production to match taste had real impacts on the experiences of mariners at Terra Nova. Some crews spent their summers onshore at work, others afloat for months on end. The Grand Banks became more and more important to the fishery in turn. Across the sixteenth century, then, we see an interplay between a European taste for salty, fresh-feeling fish and the structure of transatlantic fishwork.[27]

In the long-run beyond 1600 we see an important shift in what kind of codfish circulated out of Terra Nova. By 1700 Terra Nova was largely identified with dry-salted codfish, often called *bacalao*. *Bacalao* is a word that today often signifies a particular kind of processed food—dry-salted cod—and it was used this way in the sixteenth century. But it also functioned as a signifier for both a processed end product (the dry-salted cod) and the living codfish itself. The fact that the term *bacalao/bacalhau/bacallà* only dates in written form to the sixteenth century may suggest that it was explicitly associated with Terra Nova and the rise of a major fishing industry there. Indeed, as we have seen, *bacalao* was a term sometimes used to describe space in the northwest Atlantic: certain mapmakers and geographers (especially from Italy and Iberia) used a variation of *Bacalaos/Terra de bacalao* to describe Terra Nova. *Bacalao* thus could mean, in the sixteenth century, a living creature, a processed foodstuff, and a physical space.

Bacalao is a baffling word of uncertain origin, despite its global popularity. The apparent relation to the Germanic *cabilaud* seems to be more than coincidental, and many etymologists believe that one is an inversion of the other: *cab-* became *bac-* or vice versa. As the weight of historical research has swung toward the Basques, some have argued that Basque *bakala* is the original form of the word, which then spread outward. The Spanish linguist Joan Coromines has argued for a Gascon origin, spreading south and north to Basque and German. I prefer a much simpler explanation. It makes sense that the name originates where the fish lives, and here it appears first in the historical record. The Germanic *cabilaud/kabbeljauw/cabeljau* is attested to consistently in written form from the twelfth century, but *bacalao* only from the sixteenth. Codfish is native to the waters that touch the shores of German-speaking communities, such as the North Sea, whereas it is a foreign fish that must be imported into Iberia. Linguistics cannot ignore historical context, and supporters of a southern origin would have to explain these discrepancies by postulating an expansive Iberian-centered cod trade centuries before Terra Nova (and why German speakers would adopt a distant name for a local fish), which would run counter to what we see in the surviving evidence. Given the timing and location, it makes sense that *bacalao* was a Germanic loanword, and a reminder that the history of cod consumption in Europe long predates the ascent of Iberian fishworkers at Terra Nova.[28]

Yet it is *bacalao*, not *cabilaud*, that has gone global. If *morue verte* was appealing to northwest European consumers, dry-salted cod was preferred in more southern communities. Starting in the late sixteenth century, English and Dutch merchants mass-exported dry-salted codfish to southern Iberia, southern France, and parts of Italy. From there it spread outward across the Atlantic. By the turn of the eighteenth century *bacalao* was a staple source of protein for enslaved peoples in the Caribbean and Brazil, nutritious and cheap to buy in bulk, fueling the sugar plantation complex. Dry-salted cod fueled population growth in Europe, Atlantic slave-labor camps, and transoceanic shipping well into the nineteenth century. Even as the economic logic of saltcod has fallen away, the taste for it has remained across the Atlantic basin. *Bacalao* is today a key ingredient in Iberian, Italian, and Afro-Caribbean cuisine. It is, arguably, the national dish of Portugal. Even in the modern Netherlands, on the shores of the North Sea, one is more likely to find Surinamese *bakkeljauw* than Dutch *kabeljauw* sold in markets and restaurants. What seems to have happened is that over time the Mediterranean and Iberian taste for *bacalao*, born of the early seventeenth-century turn toward exporting by English and Dutch merchants, swamped everything else. Mediterranean-Iberian demand for *bacalao* was so great as to drive production and shipping not just to Europe but to the rest of the Americas as well. As they changed commercial patterns they changed Atlantic tastes in codfish. The ubiquity of *bacalao* from the eighteenth century onward reflects this combined mixture of economics and taste.[29]

These three shifts in taste—a short-term change in accessibility, a medium-term taste for brined cod, a long-term triumph of *bacalao*—confirm two points I have tried to make in this chapter. First, the ways in which Europeans across the continent ate codfish were neither static nor simple. It was constantly being compared to other fish, or to other versions of itself, so that tastes could change over time. In turn, so too did production shift across the sixteenth century and beyond. Second, what defined codfish in the sixteenth century was its processed nature. It became cheap because it was mass-produced; *morue verte* grew in popularity because it had the benefits of processing without a loss of taste; and *bacalao* eventually triumphed due to its remarkable processed qualities. These two trends speak to how people actually experienced Terra Nova in the sixteenth century—through their stomachs, one bite of salty cod at a time.

TWELVE

Commodities

W e can sometimes catch glimpses of how Europeans thought about codfish in the earliest decades of the sixteenth century by searching through brittle registers for brief mentions scribbled in a neat hand. At Fécamp in Normandy in 1520, a scribe tracking the import of goods made note of the arrival of cod in the monastic port. The entries are wedged between dozens of similar goods that were offloaded in the port, bland descriptions of loads of salt and bolts of cloth, and above all barrels and barrels of herring in the fall. Then suddenly: "The 15th day of the said month [September 1520] Jehan Pailherbe master of a ship of Fécamp requests permission to discharge a thousand of codfish which is worth 3 *sol* 4 *denier*. . . . The 24th day [of September 1520] a master of a ship from Honfleur requests permission to discharge eleven hundred of codfish and pays for each hundred 4 *deniers*." These were small quantities of codfish, but they stand out among all the cloth and herring. To the south in the port of La Rochelle, a notary known as Hémon made a similar record just a few years later. On October 1, 1523, he recorded a contract between a merchant from La Rochelle and one from Bordeaux for the sale of "eleven thousand and nine hundred *morues vertes*" and "fifteen thousand five hundred dried cod." A complex business deal had to be hashed out, but in the end many thousands of codfish from an unknown origin flowed through the city gates of La Rochelle.[1]

Both of these entries are found in the records of port cities engaged in the early Terra Nova fisheries. The two entries for cod are rarities, but they indicate that codfish was already being traded and consumed in Normandy and southwest France by the early 1520s. In neither case do we know where the cod was coming from (Terra Nova? Iceland? Shetland?) or how it was used. Even the names used are unusual, reflecting regional differences already emerging in the early sixteenth century. At Fécamp, our monk uses the northern French *morue-* root but adds the popular *-lx* plural ending (as in *Bordeaulx, deulx*) to write *morruelx* for *morrues*. At La Rochelle, by contrast, the notary prefers the southern French *moullue* spelling, so that we see the arrival of *moullues vertes* and *moullues sèches*. Cod was appearing in many names, but it was also appearing as yet another good to be imported, taxed, stored, and recorded. Its origin was immaterial, its history irrelevant. It was a food, not a fish, brought to be consumed by hungry friars and eager *bourgeois*.

At some point between being pulled out of the cold waters of the North Atlantic and being offloaded onto a dock at Fécamp or La Rochelle, the living organism codfish had been transformed into a commodity (see figure 17). This commodity took on many names, from *haberdine* to *forillion* to *abadejo* to *merluccia*. All these names indicated a form of processed food, a salty, dried slab of white fish that Europeans were vaguely aware had come from somewhere to the west. That transformation, and renaming, was essential to how the codfish trade from Terra Nova functioned. It determined how consumers would interact with cod and, by extension, the North Atlantic itself. The scholars Stefano Longo, Rebecca Clausen, and Brett Clark have insightfully argued that we must understand "the tragedy of the commodity" as the essential framework for fisheries history and management. It is not the mismanagement of common resources or insufficient policy oversight that degrades and destroys fish stocks, but rather the human act of turning living marine organisms into marketable, consumable commodities. In the long term this commodification is certainly what took place in the northwest Atlantic, as nearly every fish and crustacean has been subjected to the production regime of commercial capitalism. Yet when does a fish become a commodity, a tragedy-in-waiting, and what does that look like? This takes place in the mind as well as the marketplace, through processes historians have difficulty reconstructing. If indeed this shift took place before 1600, then this would tell us two important things. First, that the impact of fishing in the northwest Atlantic was more significant and rapid than we might otherwise assume. And second, that commodification can take place even with salvage accumulation and the preindustrial harvesting practices of sixteenth-century fishwork.[2]

In this chapter I explore how codfish functioned in its commodity form across the sixteenth century, and what that might tell us about how European consumers thought about Terra Nova. I want to stress the confusion Europeans felt at what exactly cod was, and what the living organism's relationship was to the food on their plate. We can do this by considering the role of names, of scientific learning, and of the marketplace in shaping the movement of this cod commodity. We will first look at sixteenth-century scientific thinking about cod as a species of ocean life. We will then turn to what happened when cod appeared in the marketplace, and the many names Europeans assigned to it. A selection of these names can be found in appendix A. In the end, we will see the confusion that these practices created, and how in the sixteenth century many Europeans did not mentally connect the food on their plates and in their markets with its origins as a living fish in the waters of the northwest Atlantic. Instead, they understood codfish as a commodity—as a processed foodstuff produced somewhere abroad under uncertain labor practices. Indeed, even this sentence is problematic—in modern English "codfish" indicates a living animal in a way that many sixteenth-century languages would not have been able to convey. Instead, Europeans described preserved fish in ways that obscured not just its origins but even the species of fish.

The Largest Type of Soft Fish

We should begin by considering what sixteenth-century Europeans knew about cod the fish. Or rather, what they did not know and what they thought they knew. It is wrong to assume that sixteenth-century consumers, mariners, intellectuals, and others thought of codfish, or indeed fish in general, as we do. Instead, Europeans (especially those farther from the Atlantic coast) had complex and at times very confused ideas about what cod was, its relation to classical learning, and its place in the web of life.

In his remarkable *Visboek* (Fish Book), the Dutch author Adriaen Coenen offers the clearest and most striking visual reproduction of a codfish from the sixteenth century. Created in the 1570s–80s by Coenen, this one-of-a-kind manuscript was a handwritten and illustrated guide to fish and sea life from the perspective of the Low Countries. Compiling mid-sixteenth-century natural histories, local history, and a personal knowledge of the fishing industry, the work contains several pages devoted to describing different kinds of fish. In a brief note written in French, Coenen describes *den kabbeljau* (the cod) as "the largest type of soft fish [*poisson mol*] which the Latins called *Aselli.*" Accompanying the description is a large hand-made drawing of the fish, colored gray and set against a blue background. Coenen's image of the codfish would probably have been startling to many sixteenth-century readers (see figure 20). Most had likely never seen a whole, live cod, although many surely had eaten its salted and dried forms.[3]

Long before it was dinner, cod was a fish in the sea, a living organism swimming in the cold and deep waters of the northern Atlantic Ocean. The cod's natural range is quite vast, extending in an arc from the North Sea zone to the coasts of New England. The fish could be found in the Arctic waters of northern Norway, in the English Channel and around the coasts of Ireland, or as far off as Labrador and the Gulf of Maine. It was therefore both a familiar local creature for coastal European communities, and one that was imported from the other side of the ocean. It was this tension between familiar and foreign that confused European natural philosophers in the sixteenth century and made it difficult to identify what kind of a fish cod was. Today, we understand cod as being a distinct species in a global hierarchy of ocean fish. The scientific name of the Atlantic cod, *Gadus morhua*, derives from the Greek word for fish (*gados*) and a Latin name for codfish (*morhua*). It was bestowed by Linneaus in 1758, many centuries after codfish became a popular foodstuff. In addition, a number of species of sea fish are closely related to cod and inhabit the same stretches of the North Atlantic, including haddock, pollock, hake, and whiting. These fish are grouped together in the family Gadidae, the "true cods," and are often called *gadids* because of their similarity. The Integrated Taxonomic Information System lists eighty-one separate species in the Gadidae family, attesting to the varied

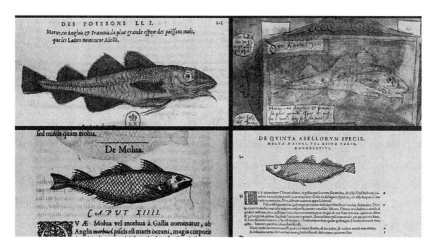

Figure 20. Four representations of codfish. *Clockwise from top left*: detail from Pierre Belon, *La nature et diversité des poissons*, 1550; detail of "Den kabbeljau" (codfish) in Adriaen Coenen, *Visboek*, 1570s; detail of cod in Conrad Gessner, *De Piscium & Aquatilium Animantium*, 1558; detail, Guillaume Rondelet, *De Piscibus Marinus*, 1554. (Courtesy of the Bibliothèque nationale de France, gallica.bnf.fr/; World Digital Library; and Biodiversity Heritage Library.)

and vast number of fish closely related to and associated with cod. This is, however, a modern, post-Linnaean conception of fish.[4]

In the 1550s three natural historians, writing in a mixture of French and Latin, attempted to explain the world of fish. In 1554 Guillaume Rondelet of Lyon published a Latin history of fish, *De Piscibus Marinus*. The next year, in his *La nature et diversité des poissons*, the Parisian writer Pierre Belon catalogued and described all the known sea creatures of his day, including their culinary value. Finally, in 1558 Conrad Gessner, a German-Swiss polymath, published volume 4 (*De Piscium & Aquatilium Animantium*) of his *Historiae Animalium* in Zurich. In all three works fish were categorized by type, what we would today understand as species, and include brief descriptions, lavish illustrations, history, defining characteristics, and often the fish's uses in cookery. These three studies represented a very particular view of the natural world, one that drew heavily on classical training and the most recent work being done in European cities by the learned and wealthy.[5]

Rondelet, Belon, and Gessner all described cod in nearly the same manner. They chose to group cod with other, similar fish, those which we would
today recognize as Gadidae. But in all three works the group is labeled not
as Gadidae but as *Aselli*, those related to *Asellus*. The name *Asellus* was not
a noble one, for it is the diminutive of the word for ass, the pack animal,
making any *Aselli* "small ass-fish." This classification derived not from observation or experience but from a (mis)reading of Pliny the Elder's *Natural
Histories*. Alfred Andrews has made the convincing case that originally *Asellus* probably referred to hake. Hake is a *gadid* easily conflated with codfish
(even today it is hard to tell them apart in the supermarket), but unlike cod
can be found in the Mediterranean. Sixteenth-century authors were nonetheless keen to connect their humble cod to the renowned Pliny. Indeed,
many cod enthusiasts were bothered by the absence of this wonderful food
in classical writing. Belon declared that since cod were *Aselli*, then they
must have been known to the Romans—after all, he said, "If the ancients
had ignored it, or had not mentioned it, this would have been a wonder."
Even he had to admit, though, that "the English take many kinds of salted
fish, of the type known as *Aselli*, which the ancients did not know of, and of
which the French do not speak." The repeated use of *Asellus* reinforced this
widespread desire to Romanize the Atlantic cod and to therefore make it a
legitimate topic of study and veneration. Despite such confusions, Rondelet, Belon, and Gessner would prove to be very influential, and the *Aselli*
model survived into the early seventeenth century.[6]

Vulgar, marketplace names of codfish repeatedly work their way into the
classical-inflected texts of these three natural historians. As the words in appendix A attest, there was no shortage of terms that might describe the living
fish or a preserved piece of meat. These were the words that competed with
Asellus and proved far more popular and durable. The three natural historians were themselves embedded in cultures that had developed names and
ideas about fish independently of Roman authors. Rondelet's Latin text
gave French and English names for cod, and the author could not resist
mentioning a French proverb. "[A codfish] has large eyes, which cannot see
clearly, from which comes the French proverb '*Occuli morhuae/Yeux de
Morhue* [Eyes of a Codfish],' which is to say one who cannot see well." A

common saying heard on the streets here intruded into a dry encyclopedia. In his Latin text Gessner had to admit that his *Asellus Magnus* was Italian *merluccia*, and he described it as a fish that was caught in England, Scotland, and elsewhere, then "from there sent across Europe in a salted and dried condition." By contrast, *molua* was "throughout England and Germany salted and dried and called '*Stockfisch*,' " here dropping into his native German. When the English author Thomas Moffet tried to borrow the *Aselli* framework for a treatise on food, he ended up incorporating his own experience at the English marketplace. He assigned new names based on common culinary practices: *Asellus Islandicus* was "nothing but an Island Cod," saltfish from Iceland. *Asellus aridus* was stockfish, air-dried (arid) *Aselli*. Haddock, as a smaller fish than cod, became the diminutive *aselluli*. Like the continental authorities he tried to emulate, Moffet was refracting classical learning through his lived experience as a consumer of codfish.[7]

There was, in short, more than a little confusion in the sixteenth century about what kind of a fish cod was. Some thought it a noble Roman fish, others the largest soft fish in the Atlantic, still others were sure it was called *stokfisch* and came only from Norway. The intervention of learned writers hardly clarified matters, instead fueling the fires by adding a layer of neoclassicist artificiality to the debate. Since few consumers ever actually interacted with a live, whole cod, these were largely academic disputes. But they do point to the contested ways in which Europeans categorized and described marine life in the sixteenth century. Thinkers like Belon and Gessner were working forward from unclear Roman sources and backward from the slabs of dried white fish they found at their local market. Their real-world experiences appear in otherwise dense, backward-looking texts, and we see local names for fish like *cod* appear alongside venerable *Asellus*.

Names and the Marketplace

The truth was that the overwhelming majority of Europeans did not encounter cod as a living organism in the sea. They encountered it as a processed food in the marketplace of their hometown. The act of salting, drying, and processing codfish did not merely change its physical composition. It changed what Europeans called the fish, and how they thought about it. Between the fishworker and the consumer stood legions of merchants who did not just move and sell the codfish but also changed its name. These names classified codfish parts in ways that allowed consumers to understand their properties as foodstuffs, and allowed merchants to understand their value as marketable commodities.

Only a few pages into his masterpiece *Don Quijote de la Mancha*, Miguel de Cervantes recounts an episode in which the titular hero finds himself in a small inn ordering supper: "As it happened, this particular day was a Friday, and in all the inn there was nothing save a few pieces of a fish which in Castile is called *abadejo*, and in Andalucia *bacalao*, and in other parts *curadillo*, and elsewhere *truchuela*." Cervantes has given us a brief glimpse of how residents in different parts of Spain talked about codfish in the early seventeenth century. Each region was known to have its own name for the same kind of preserved fish, and apparently this was so taken for granted that it could be used as a joke in Spain. Around the same time the English author Thomas Dekker, in *The Famous History of Sir Thomas Wyat*, made a jest based on this common practice:

> *Bret*: Philip is a Spaniard, and what is a Spaniard?
> *Clown*: A Spaniard is no Englishman that I know.
> *Bre*: Right, a Spaniard is a Camocho, a Callimanco, nay which
> worse, a Dondego, and what is a Dondego?
> *Clo*: A Dondego is a kind of Spanish Stockfish, or poore Iohn.
> *Bre*: No, a Dondego is a desperate Viliago, a very Castilian, God
> blesse us.

The punchline was based on the idea that the Spanish had too many funny-sounding (to the English ear) words for cod, and the Clown has mixed up "Dondego" for a word like *bacalao* or *curadillo*. It is noteworthy, though, that Dekker's own joke betrays the fact that the same complexity was found in English. The Clown does not know whether to describe *Dondego* as stockfish, a very old German-derived term for dried cod from the north, or Poor John, a new colloquial term for saltcod. No matter where one went in Europe, the ways to describe codfish were varied and local.[8]

A vast vocabulary existed in fifteenth- and sixteenth-century Europe to describe codfish and its many processed variations. Almost all of this has been lost, but around 1540, the discerning consumer looking for dried cod on New Fish Street in London would be able to tell their *coarsefish* from *wokedfish*, their *titling* from *cropling*, and might ask if the merchant was selling *Islandfish* from Iceland or *Newland fish* from Terra Nova. Perhaps instead they would opt for *milwell*, fresh cod, or dried *keeling* from Scotland, or the ever-popular salted *haberdine*. Pierre Belon, who tried more than most to incorporate contemporary practices into his natural histories, was given to exasperation when addressing how the English talked about their salted fish:

> [The English] take salted fish in great quantities . . . but they know much diversity under two names: know that the one is called Milwell, and the other Ling. They sometimes call various fish Stockfish: for dried fish, which have been salted in another manner, and which must be beaten before being cooked, several fish are called stockfish; but they give particular names: Ling fish, Shetland fish, Bremen fish, "Out of the West Country Fish" [literally, "Ex uuest contre fisch"], Newport Fish, Heligoland Fish, Merlandfish, Rodfish, Milwell, Scarborough Fish, which is all one with the big Neulzod, Iceland Fish, Haddock. They call another species Richtholland Fish which is thought to be the most delicate.

And this was just England, for which the most detailed vocabulary evidence survives. In all these names and descriptors we can see one throughline: the names described aspects of cod as a consumable commodity, not as a part of nature. The food product was assigned a name based on its origin, state of preservation, and relative quality, not what kind of a fish it had once been. An important consequence of this practice is that many of the ways of describing "cod" could, and did, apply to different species of fish. Something like *Islandfish* or *Bergefish* merely indicated a salted or dried white fish from Iceland or the Bergen trading houses—whether it was cod, haddock, ling, or pollock was irrelevant. *Haberdine* might be any number of closely related fish, much as *bacalao* today sometimes embraces more than just cod. In the marketplace they all looked similar. This was the confusion of names which scholars like Belon and Gessner were trying to reconcile with their neat *Asellus* classification.[9]

Of particular importance to European thinking was the entrenched dominance of air-dried cod, known as stockfish, in late fifteenth-century Europe. So widespread was the consumption of Norwegian stockfish that as of 1500, many Europeans seem to have thought that stockfish *was* codfish. A German translation of Gessner's fish book went so far as to group all *Aselli* together as "Stockfisch," treating the preserved food as a distinct genre of fish. John Maplet, in his natural history and catalogue of animals A *Greene Forest*, included stockfish as an entry unto itself in between the stork and the badger. It is telling that the earliest report to survive of fish in Terra Nova, written in Italian, describes waters filled with "stochfissi," not cod—before Terra de Bacalao, there were Stockfish Seas. Indeed, over time similar things seem to have happened to the words *bacalao* and *morue*, which often signified processed dry-salted cod rather than the living animal. Living things became conflated with their processed forms, and consumers thought the Atlantic Ocean was filled with stockfish, or *bacalao*, or *merluccia*. This is rather like saying a farmyard is filled with chicken nuggets and hamhocks.[10]

Stockfish was used to signify cod because well before the rise of a fishery at Terra Nova around 1500, it had become a common part of daily culture in many parts of Europe. It was common enough to pass into popular naming conventions: in 1537 in London there was a foreign merchant named Robert Stockfish who, ironically, traded in glass. For many, the familiar need to beat stockfish before cooking meant that it became a watchword for physical violence and control. A popular English ballad that circulated from the fifteenth through the early eighteenth centuries jauntily listed things that, by their nature, had to be beaten. In most variations this includes the trio of a mill, a stockfish, and a woman. According to the English author Maplet, the German taste for stockfish had led to a popular association with physical violence against women. "Among the Germans it has raised a proverb," which was "More foolish or wanton than a stockfish: applied to such as have their minds set upon wantonness." The German solution, according to Maplet, took the form of a ditty: "As muddy as a stockfish am I / which never will be sod [washed] / Unless she has good store of stripes / and be beaten with a rod." Such snippets of popular culture indicate that stockfish was familiar enough to have become part of everyday speech in some parts of Europe by the early sixteenth century. Over time saltcod would displace air-dried fish (centuries later, for instance, words for cod became slang for prostitution in many parts of France), but during the earliest years of engagement with Terra Nova it was this cultural power of stockfish that shaped European attitudes toward the sea.[11]

Through these names we can see an important moment in the transition toward fish as commodity in the sixteenth century. For many Europeans, names increasingly reflected consumption. They were determined by origin, grade, and type of processed fish, not what the fish itself was. In this shift there was a subtle rupture, a breaking of the link between the living fish and its processed derivatives.

Confusion

Looking backward, we may wish to reconcile the two strands of thought outlined above. One was a top-down scientific thinking about cod as a living animal. The other was a bottom-up classification of processed cod through an elaborate list of very precise market names. The point I wish to make is that we cannot reconcile these any more than Europeans in the sixteenth century could. The primary consequence was confusion, a bewildering uncertainty in our sources about what exactly cod was, how it related to its processed forms, where it came from, and what it should be called. These can be seen in the term *merluccia*.

In Italy, the culinary and economic heart of the western Mediterranean, one did not eat *bacalao* (though eventually one would eat *baccalà*). In his *Opera*, potentially the first celebrity-chef cookbook in premodern Europe, the papal chef Bartolomeu Scappi devoted a lengthy discussion to a kind of fish he called *merluccia*. This "is a fish of a green-grey colour, with a big, flat head and big, sharp teeth in its mouth; it is long in the body with very small scales. It is not much esteemed fresh around here. They are dried on Spanish shores and brought to Italy cut apart, those being much bigger and better than the ones from Rome's shores. Their proper season goes from August to the end of March." What was *merluccia?* The description certainly sounds like cod. But the references to sun-drying in Spain sounds more like the fish we know as hake, which was often dried and sometimes salted in southern Iberia, or even Italy, then shipped across the Mediterranean. Earlier in the century, the Roman author Paolo Giovio had described *merluccia* as a fish with a large, flat head and many large teeth, much like Scappi. He likewise gave conflicting geographic origins: he describes it as local but further noted, "They also bring from Gotland and from Norway *merluccie* a cubit long, as hard as iron, like a pair of sticks; which are considered a great delicacy of the Germans, who reside in Rome." This was a clear reference to stockfish from Norway. His *merluccia* could, once again, be cod or hake, and Giovio explicitly compares it to local fish and animals, suggesting it was caught in the Mediterranean. This one term *merluccia* was alternately described as a local fish, a regional import from Spain, and a preserved fish imported from the Baltic by German merchants.[12]

Indeed, the truth is that many European authorities were not entirely sure where codfish came from. Laurier Turgeon has argued that sixteenth-century Europeans identified Terra Nova with cod because so many notarial and court records specify that this is where fishing took place. But these records were meant for merchants and mariners, not for the consumer at the market stall. When we look more widely, we see confusion among those who only knew of salty whitefish from far away. The Lyonnais writer Jean Baptiste Bruyerin was fairly certain that "the Mediterranean Sea does not sustain them [codfish]," but that "there are islands which sea-faring sailors and fishworkers call *Molluas* [cod], in which I hear a great many of these fish can be caught." What islands this could mean is unclear (Newfoundland? Iceland? Shetland?), and likely reflects Bruyerin's own confusion. The Venetian merchant-traveler Alessandro Magno believed that there was found in England "a certain dried fish which comes from the Indies," which in the 1560s was called both stockfish and *bacalla.* We have just seen the Roman confusion about *merluccia,* and whether it came from Spain, Norway, or the coasts of Italy. Fishworkers at Terra Nova certainly knew where their cod lived, but clearly consumers were far from sure.[13]

In the case of *merluccia*, it is likely that Scappi and Giovio did not mean to distinguish between cod and hake. Both of these fish, from their perspective in Rome, were dried white fish with a similar taste and texture that came from far away. Even today it is difficult to tell cod and hake apart in the marketplace, and both are often cooked in similar ways. The word *merluccia*, in other words, was meant to signify cod and hake at the same time. But in another sense it was neither: *merluccia* was its own entity, a dried and salted white ocean fish, and what animal it originally came from was immaterial to how it would be treated by chefs and households. The name *merluccia* tells us about how Europeans thought of fish and food in the sixteenth century: as outputs and outcomes, not as living organisms from specific parts of the world.

Erasing Atlantic Labor

In terms like *merluccia* we can see the confusion that prevailed among consumers in sixteenth-century Europe. Confusion is interesting, but why is it important? This confusion indicates that across the sixteenth century cod was undergoing a transformation into a consumable commodity. The market names bestowed on processed cod allowed it to be reborn as a new thing. In light of all this, the entries in the annals of Fécamp and La Rochelle with which we started the chapter make more sense. The creation of a commodity as a distinct entity—the normalization of *morruelx* or *haberdine* or *morue verte* as distinct from codfish—is the essential step in the alienation of production from consumption that underlies industrial capitalism.

Did Europeans truly eat the Atlantic in the sixteenth century? Not as we might expect them to, and not in ways that would always have been apparent to them. European fishworkers were clearly harvesting and exploiting the bountiful Ocean Sea, from Terra Nova to Iceland to Ireland and beyond. A cod imported from Terra Nova traveled several thousand miles to reach a table in Europe, and if it was caught in late May it was unlikely to be eaten before October. Along the way the fish changed names several times. These transformations broke mental connections and created new ones—turning cod into *haberdine* or *dogrdrawe*, or into *morue verte* and *forillon*. It had also been physically transformed. As the head was removed (keeping the tongue as a delicacy), the guts eviscerated (salting the intestines as a treat), the tail lopped off (sold later for soup stock), the body split at the spine (to create the familiar triangle shape), the flesh salted (giving it a fiery spirit), the fish left in the sun (removing any last trace of moisture), the whole bundled up in barrels and shipped across the sea, the final result was a food that bore little to no resemblance to the animal it had once been.

As the food was turned into a commodity, the fishwork fell away. The anthropologist Anna Tsing has described similar processes taking place in the modern capitalist global economy. Tsing's mushroom pickers in Oregon harvest high-value fungi using relatively simple techniques that form a kind of vernacular industry, including an emphasis on experience-derived expertise. They have no control over how and why the mushrooms grow, no more than a fishworker can control his cod. By the time the mushrooms arrive in the markets of Tokyo or New York, they have been transformed into a commodity ready to be consumed by wealthy elites who have no idea of their origins in the Pacific Northwest. Tsing describes the process as "salvage accumulation." Her work draws on twenty-first-century mushroom pickers, but we can see the same system at work in the sixteenth-century northwest Atlantic. Men like Robert Lefant, working in the summer of 1542 at Terra Nova, might have been amused to know that their catch would someday appear in marketplaces as *curadillo* and *truchuela*, eaten by European and Mediterranean households that might never have known where it came from. The process of transferring cod from ship to shore, of integrating it with prevalent European foodways, had broken an essential mental link between the act of harvesting and the act of consumption. From small beginnings in the northwest Atlantic, where fish were still caught by hand by small teams of fishworkers, cod had become something much bigger, pointing toward a future of a consumable, de-contextualized ocean.[14]

Conclusion

Writing in 1620 and openly advocating the replacement of Terra Nova with a colonial English Newfoundland, the fishworker-turned-settler Richard Whitbourne could not help but look back wistfully on the history of the northwest Atlantic. Having himself served on several fishing voyages in the 1580s–90s, the Englishman advocated for new island settlements but still wanted the fishworkers' world to get its due. His epitaph for Newfoundland island resonates today: "Among my undertakings and employment in seafaring, the most part have been to an island, called New-found-land, in part heretofore outwardly discovered, but never looked into by those discoverers as it deserved."[1]

This book has been an attempt to look into the story of Terra Nova as it deserved. The previous pages have shown that we can tell a story of the northwest Atlantic in the sixteenth century treating it as a distinct and fully fleshed-out subject. We have seen the same space through twelve different thematic lenses, each illuminating a different part of a vibrant world. There is plenty that can be recovered from the years before 1600, or even 1580, a period that is usually hardest to describe. Often this has meant showing how terms or ideas competed in the minds of Europeans, making our story more confusing but richer. Not all Europeans thought there should be only a fishery in the northwest Atlantic in the earliest decades after encounter; many tried to found colonies or explore alternative commercial prospects. The taste for mass-imported saltcod from Terra Nova was something that had to be created in the sixteenth century, not something already present. Even the road to collapse and ruin at the end of the twentieth century looks very different from the start of the sixteenth, when the will to exploit was there but the tools were not.

A final irony, then, about Terra Nova is that while it was defined and shaped by the unifying act of mass fishwork, the region looks different depending on whose perspective we take. Everyone knew about the fishery, but even so Europeans could not help seeing different things in the waters of the northwest Atlantic. Robert Lefant saw some harbors and beaches beside the sea. Jacques Cartier, João Fagundes, Juan de Agramonte, and Richard Hore all saw island worlds ready for settlement. The poet Stephen Parmenius could only lament after visiting the shores of Newfoundland island: "What am I to say, my dear Hakluyt, when I see nothing but desolation?" The navigator Jean Alfonse looked at the same coast and saw "the best ports and harbours in all the sea, and big rivers, numerous fisheries." For the *bourgeois* of towns like Saint Jean-de-Luz, Rouen, Fuenterrabía, or Pontevedra, Terra Nova was one of the bedrocks of the local economy and a source of prosperity. For someone like Sir Humphrey Gilbert or Samuel de Champlain, it was a commons waiting to be enclosed and captured by empire. Countless European consumers saw only dried stacks of *bacalao* or *haberdine* in their local fish markets, with little sense of where they had come from or who had made this food for their families.[2]

The view was very different for residents of the northwest Atlantic who were excluded from Terra Nova. Beothuk and Innu families saw the same coasts they had been visiting every summer but now populated with floating interlopers cutting down trees and eating all the fish. Sometimes they saw their friends abducted, and at other times they saw their friends visit Basque or Breton ships to swap goods, stories, and food. Inuit traders and raiders saw opportunity to the south of their Arctic homes, and found a way to extend their polar communities into La Gran Baya. The Mi'kmaq saw their world of migration and exchange suddenly expand into the heart of the Atlantic through new trade routes, even as French merchants pushed them toward a devastating fur trade. All these groups heard visiting fishworkers use the term *Terra Nova*, but it would have meant little to people who had their own conceptions of geography and place-names. What about the other residents? To the codfish, Terra Nova looked like cold waters, plentiful food, and the chance to breed. Only occasionally did an individual fish from their inexhaustible numbers end up on the end of a fishhook, hauled gasping out of home waters into the bottom of a *txalupa*. The gannet or shearwater knew the northwest Atlantic as only one stop on their yearly migrations, but increasingly they saw it as a place where their young were killed and cooked by fishworkers.

These differing visions do not mean there was no Terra Nova. All of these actors were, after all, talking about the same things in the same place. And all eventually would have to deal with the driving logic of fishwork and occupation. What they show us is that the first century of European occupation at Terra Nova was complex, dynamic, and contested. I wrote this book to push back on the tendency of historians to "flatten" the history of the northwest Atlantic by focusing on the seventeenth century, using modern geographies, and isolating the fishery in the wider Atlantic. Such approaches do not do justice to the multiplicity of experiences and mentalities that came out of the creation of Terra Nova.

Of course, there is more to this book than unflattening, and "It was complicated" is hardly an argument. Instead, the many experiences of Terra Nova are precisely what allow us to make sense of how the fishery was structured, but also why it was so important in the sixteenth century. Our sources present a view of Terra Nova across the sixteenth century that seemingly juxtaposes the thrilling and the mundane. Even the most routine fishing voyage had an element of adventure: the small wooden ship, fighting fog and swells in equal measure as it traverses the tempestuous North Atlantic, guided by a redoubtable pilot and worked by a close-knit crew. A bird is sighted—the Grand Banks are near!—and all breathe a sigh of relief as they realize that soon they will be catching cod, swapping stories with other crews, and enjoying fresh bird eggs. Meanwhile, some elite Europeans were drawn by dreams of insular settlements, rich forests and fields, the potential for exchange, and a conquering fur trade to fund risky ambitious schemes. These are the stories and dreams that draw us to Terra Nova now, even as they kept the northwest Atlantic alive in the imaginations of sixteenth-century Europeans.

Yet the essence of Terra Nova was always fishwork, the mass-production of bulk calories. Terra Nova was built on the killing and processing of codfish, a species that most Europeans frankly associated with blandness in the sixteenth century. Bulk caloric production lacks the disruption, novelty, excitement of what took place in many other corners of the Atlantic. Lefant's story of fishwork may not entice us (or his Spanish interrogators) as much as that of a Spanish conquistador, French corsair, Mexica warrior, or Tupí go-between. But to countless fishworkers and merchants it was their "most usual trade," a reliable and repeatable opportunity for work and investment. Terra Nova attracted vast stores of labor and shipping in an age when those things were scarce, and for good reason: people were hungry, and the floating colony in the northwest Atlantic was a way to solve these fundamental problems of food security. This was the point of Lefant's interrogation, when officials looking for stories about bold settlement in Canada instead uncovered information about a fishing beach beside the sea. The seemingly mundane process of fishwork mattered a great deal, and when seen through the eyes of those who worked there, it takes on a thrilling quality all its own.

Though the space mariners knew as Terra Nova would eventually change and be supplanted, the history of what happened in the sixteenth century is still with us today. Many people still eat food made by commercial fisheries and processed using techniques that were developed during the fifteenth and sixteenth centuries. I can go to the store and buy *bacalao* that is nearly identical to what Robert Lefant made in the summer of 1542. Many European languages still preserve the term *Terra Nova*, even if they use it in different ways. If you visit the coast of eastern Canada, you drive or sail past sites first named in the sixteenth century: Cape Breton, Bonnavista, Saint John's, Cape Race, and many more. On a more troubling level, we are living in the shadow of overfishing, ocean degradation, and overextraction, all of which can trace at least part of their genesis to Terra Nova. The alienated harvesting of marine life, the slaughter of birds and whales, the nascent development of a fur trade, the occupation-through-extraction: all of these defined sixteenth-century fishwork in the northwest Atlantic, and all underlie our present ecological-climate crisis.

From what's on our dinner plates to the oceans we swim in, we are living in a world made by fishworkers at Terra Nova. That is a novel idea to many of us today, but one that would have been obvious to Europeans in the sixteenth century when Terra Nova was one of the centers of their emerging Atlantic world. For this reason, Terra Nova deserves to be treated by scholars and teachers as a part of Atlantic history, and a key moment in global environmental history. Lives may be saved or lost, fortunes can be made, ecosystems shattered, tastes subtly altered, histories created and forgotten, and global foodways forever changed by what happens on some beaches and harbors alongside the sea.

APPENDIX A

Cod Names

Latin

Morhua — Cod.

Asellus/Aselli — Scientific name for cod and related fish. See chapter 12.

English

Cod/Codfish — Standard English name for the fish and often the food. Etymology uncertain, unique to English.

Saltfish — Not exclusively salted codfish, but most commonly applied to salt-cod.

Stockfish — Dried cod, primarily air-dried cod from Norway, Iceland, and the North Sea islands. Occasionally used to signify the fish itself, not just the food.

Millwell — Fresh codfish, distinguished from preserved varieties.

Haberdine — Common term for dry-salted white fish, primarily cod. Name origin is unclear (the OED belief that it comes from *Labourd* is untenable chronologically). It is probably a derivation of Aberdeen (in Scotland), though Pierre Belon suggests it comes from Iceland.[1]

Poor John — Nickname for *haberdine*, appears late in the sixteenth century, but more popular in the seventeenth.

Keeling/Kelling — Dried codfish, used primarily in Scotland and northern England.

Green fish — Brined cod or other white fish, equivalent of *morue verte*.

Cropling/Titling/Coarsefish/Racklefish — Grades of stockfish used in fifteenth- to sixteenth-century London.[2]

Wokedfish/Weakfish—Stockfish or saltcod that has been soaked ("weakened") in water.

Islandfish—Common term for preserved cod and other fish imported from Iceland.

Dole fish—Cod given to fishworkers as compensation.[3]

Dogdrawe—Alternative name for haberdine or kelling.[4]

Newland fish—Cod from Terra Nova.

French

Morue—Most common term in French languages for cod and cod products. Around 1600 sometimes written as *moruë*, suggesting it was pronounced as three syllables. Very often spelled *mollue/moullue* in southwest ports like La Rochelle and Bordeaux.

Cabillaud—Alternative, German-derived name for cod. It is possible that some French speakers made a distinction between *morue* and *cabillaud*, the former for preserved cod and the latter for fresh.[5]

Morue sallée—Saltcod.

Morue sèche/parée—Dried cod.

Morue verte—Green cod, fish that has been brined by packing with salt in barrels.

Forillon—Name refers to Ferryland (*Forillon* in French) on the Avalon Peninsula of Newfoundland.[6]

Spanish

Bacalao—Widely used term for codfish and codfish products in the sixteenth century. Sometimes used to signify the fish itself, sometimes to signify saltcod.

Abadejo—Given by Cervantes as an alternative name for *bacalao*. Today used for pollock.

Curadillo—Given by Cervantes as an alternative name for *bacalao* in Castile.

Truchuela—Given by Cervantes as an alternative name for *bacalao*. Literally, "small trout."[7]

Portuguese

Bacalhau—Portuguese variant of *bacalao*, used in the same way.

Bacalhau de pasta—Green cod, similar to *morue verte*.

Italian

Merluccia—Common word for codfish in Italy. Meaning confused; see chapter 12.

Stoccafisso—Stockfish.

Baccalà—Italian variant of *bacalao*.

Battuto—Stockfish. Name refers to the practice of beating stockfish to soften it.[8]

Scarmo—Alternative to *merluccia*.[9]

Dutch

Kabbeljauw—Dutch word for codfish, used as in English.

Aberdaan/Laberdaan—Dutch version of *haberdine*, saltcod.

Stockvis—Stockfish.

German

Kabeljau/Cabelau—Codfish.

Dorsch—Alternative name for cod.

Stockfisch/Stockvisch—Stockfish.

Sources

Recovering Terra Nova means coming to terms with the limits of historical inquiry. Much has been lost, but even more was never recorded in the first place. What has survived is irrevocably fractured, spread across dozens of archives in several different countries. There is no archive for Terra Nova—there is a document here in this city, a partial notarial series in that one, and a lone map held somewhere else. Piecing together the necessary sources from scattered sites is a first step in any research project on the northwest Atlantic. For those interested in researching Terra Nova this presents a series of major practical and conceptual challenges. Happily, you do not have to go it alone, thanks to decades of work by historians, archaeologists, and archivists.

Most of the written evidence for Terra Nova is held in government archives in Europe. The most important for my study are regional ones, like the French *archives départmentales,* which hold records for an entire administrative region like Seine-Maritime or Calvados, including notarial documents. One step below regional archives are city-level archives like the *archives municipales* of Saint Malo, which include city council deliberations and ordinances. I have made only limited use of national-level archives like the Bibliothèque nationale de France or the British Library, whose holdings related to Terra Nova are more haphazard. One other important kind of archive consists of independent research libraries, and I have made extensive use of the excellent map collection of the John Carter Brown Library as well as the surprising and varied holdings of the Folger Shakespeare Library.

The bulk of documentary sources on sixteenth-century Terra Nova share certain important features. They were typically produced in a handful of coastal cities in the kingdoms of France, Spain, Portugal, and England; they were typically handwritten manuscripts; they were typically directly related to business practices and legal agreements; they were typically produced right at the start or end of a voyage; and they were typically written by a formal scribe recording the words of mariners and merchants. Such are the features shared by notarial contracts and city-council deliberations preserved in city archives and court cases conserved in regional and national archives. It is tempting to take such sources at face value, but they are notoriously tricky and subject to the biases and opaque practices of notaries. If used judiciously, however, they provide the one thing other sources do not: breadth of information across time, space, and social status. I have used these notarial records and related documents to make a database of around 350 voyages between Europe and Terra Nova in the sixteenth century—not an exhaustive list but a representative one, with enough quantitative information to draw important conclusions. A list of the archives (including notarial series) used for this study can be found in the "Short Titles and Abbreviations" section before the notes.

In my approach, the urban business records are supplemented by four broad groups of sources. The first are sixteenth-century maps, predominantly produced in Portugal, Spain, Italy, and northern France. The second are archaeological reports by modern scholars working in eastern Canada. The third are the printed writings of European navigators, geographers, colonial promoters, and natural scientists. These include well-known authors and editors like André Thevet, Jacques Cartier, Stephen Parmenius, Richard Hakluyt, and Giovanni Ramusio. The fourth are what might be termed miscellaneous textual references—handwritten notes, drawings, letters, and the like that are scattered around European archives and that offer unique glimpses into the sixteenth century. It is through a broad, comparative approach that we can tease out patterns of sixteenth-century thought and experience.

I am fortunate in that many original documents from European archives have been transcribed and published since the mid-nineteenth century. Two collections of edited archival material are particularly important to this book, and the reader will find them cited throughout. The first are a pair of collections of transcribed and translated documents gathered by the Canadian archivist H. P. Biggar in 1911 and 1930. These include documents in both the original languages and English translation from England, France, Spain, and Portugal. Though only covering up to 1545 or so, they offer an invaluable catalogue of the earliest documents related to European voyages in the northwest Atlantic. The second is the underappreciated collection edited by David Quinn, Alison Quinn, and Susan Hillier entitled *New American World*. In five volumes, these authors collected translations of hundreds upon hundreds of texts related to the colonization of the Americas. Volume 1 covers early exploration and contact, and volume 4 is specifically devoted to the northwest Atlantic. Neither source offers much commentary, instead providing extensive transcripts and translations.

This project has benefited significantly from the increased digitization of pre-twentieth-century material, both archival documents and printed books. To be blunt, it is unlikely that my work would have taken the form it has without the existence of GoogleBooks, which has allowed me to rapidly find and access a wide variety of printed material. Nor would much of this have been possible without the digitization of holdings in institutions such as the Bibliothèque nationale de France, or the map collection at the John Carter Brown Library. I have been afforded breakthroughs and insights thanks to digitized artifacts, like BnF Ms.Fr.24269 or Hercules O'Doria's map, that I have never seen in person. The notarial records used in this study have rarely been fully digitized, though the Archives départmentales de Seine-Maritime and the Archivos historico provincial de Guipúzcoa have made almost all of the notarial records for the sixteenth century available online, a massive resource for those interested in the fishery.

NOTES

Short Titles and Abbreviations

Printed Collections

Biggar, *Cartier and Roberval*: Biggar, Henry Percival. *A Collection of Documents relating to Jacques Cartier and the Sieur de Roberval*. Ottawa: Public Archives of Canada, 1930.

Biggar, *Precursors*: Biggar, Henry Percival. *The Precursors of Jacques Cartier, 1497–1534: A Collection of Documents relating to the Early History of the Dominion of Canada*. Ottawa: Government Printing Bureau, 1911.

NAW: *New American World: A Documentary History of North America to 1612*. Edited by David B. Quinn, Alison M. Quinn, and Susan Hillier. 5 vols. New York: Arno, 1978.

Archives

France

ADC	Archives départmentales Calvados (Caen)
	Série 8 E Fonds notaires de Honfleur
ADCA	Archives départmentales Côtes-d'Armor (Saint Brieuc)
	1 E 2783 Seigneurie de St Paul en Plouër
	H 69 Fonds de l'abbaye de Beauport
ADCM	Archives départmentales Charente-Maritime (La Rochelle)
	3 E Notaires
ADG	Archives départmentales Gironde (Bordeaux)
	3 E Notaires
ADLA	Archives départmentales Loire Atlantique (Nantes)
	B Cours et jurisdictions, B 21

ADSM	Archives départmentales Seine-Maritime (Rouen)
	1 B Parlement de Normandie: nos. 324 (1508), 388 (1524)
	201 BP Table de marbre de Rouen: no. 694
	204 BP Table de marbre de Rouen: no. 80, "Amirauté d'etretat"
	216 BP Amirauté du Havre
	2 E 1 Notaires de Rouen
	2 E 70 Notaires du Havre
	3 E 1 Archives communales de Rouen
	A and B Déliberations du conseil municipale
	7 H 294 Registre de la recèpte des droits de la Vicomt de Fécamp, nos. 2–4
AM Bayonne	Archives municipales de Bayonne
	BB Déliberations du conseil municipal
AM Capbreton	Archives municipales de Capbreton
	CC 5
AM du Havre	Archives municipales du Havre (Le Havre)
	BB 116 Vendeurs du poisson
	CC 36 Affaires de Lardinière
	EE 78 Armements navales
AM La Rochelle	Archives municipales de La Rochelle
	HH 14 328 Corporations, no. 107, "Marchands au poisson"
AM Saint Jean-de-Luz	Archives municipales de Saint Jean-de-Luz
	1 AA 3, no. 33
	3 EE 1 Piraterie, corsairs
AM Saint Malo	Archives municipales de Saint Malo
	BB Déliberations du conseil municipal
ANF	Archives nationales de France (Paris)
	Notaire Michel de Felin
BnF	Bibliothèque nationale de France (Paris)
	Ms.Fr. 24269

Ms.Fr. 20008, "Extraict des observations de
Nicolay d'Arfeville . . ."
Ms.Fr. 1382, "Description de tous les portz de mer
de l'univers," par Jehan Mallart

Spain

AHPG-GPAH   Archivos histórico provincial de Guipúzcoa–
                   Gipuzkoako probintziako artxibo historikoa
                   Series 1 Notarial registers of Motrico
                   Series 3 Notarial registers of Hondarabbia

Netherlands

Koninklijk Bibliotheek (The Hague)
                   Adriaen Coenen, *Visboek*, KW 78 E 54
Stadsarchief Amsterdam
                   Notarial archief, 75, 157
Zeeuws Archief (Middelburg)
                   243 Admiraliteit te Veere, 1460–1562, no. 7

United Kingdom

BL   British Library
                   Cotton MS Nero B III, no. 29
                   Add. Ms. 34729
                   Add. Ms. 61823
                   West Papers, vol. III, Add. Ms. 34729
National Archives
HCA   High Court of the Admiralty (England)

Germany

BSB   Bayerische Staatsbibliothek
                   Codices Hispanici 2, "Descriptio Africae"
                   Codices Iconographici, 132, "Portulan (Atlantik)"

United States

FSL   Folger Shakespeare Library

L.b. 340 "Darcy, Sir Thomas. The Cargis of a Good Schype Callyed the Jayms . . ."

V.a. 259 "Account of Alessandro Magno's Journeys to Cyprus, Egypt, Spain, England, Flanders, Germany and Brescia, 1557–1565"

Z.e. 2 "Selection of Accounts of the Households of Various French Sovereigns, 1554–1594"

V.b. 303, no. 1. "Touching the Great Expense of Fleshe"

V.a. 318 "A Caveatt for the Citty of London; or, A Forewarninge of Offences against Penall Lawes, 1598"

JCBL   John Carter Brown Library

Map Collection

Introduction

1. Biggar, *Cartier and Roberval*, doc. CCXII, 447–67. For context: Richard Fiset and Gilles Samson, "Charlesbourg-Royal and France-Roy (1541–43): France's First Colonization Attempt in the Americas," *Post-Medieval Archaeology* 43, no. 1 (2009). For Spanish concerns over the Caribbean, see Biggar, *Cartier and Roberval*, 426.
2. Biggar, *Cartier and Roberval*, 450–51.
3. In the original, the spelling is "sy ay lugar." *Lugar* appears as the third word in Miguel de Cervantes' *Don Quijote*, where it carries the meaning of "una pequeña población rural." Miguel de Cervantes, *Don Quijote de la Mancha*, ed. Francisco Rico (Madrid: Real Academia Española: Asociacion de Academias de la Lengua Española, 2015), 27, n.3. Tellingly, an early seventeenth-century French dictionary gives *lugar* as equivalent to *ville*, but also to *ciudade* and *villa*. Jean Pallet, *Diccionario muy copioso de la lengua espanola y francesa* (Paris: Matthieu Guillemet 1604), n.p.
4. For some foundational overviews of the long-term history of the fishery: Harold Innis, *The Cod Fisheries: The History of an International Economy* (Toronto: Ryerson, 1940); George A. Rose, *Cod: The Ecological History of the North Atlantic Fisheries* (Saint John's, NL: Breakwater Books, 2007); W. Jeffrey Bolster, *The Mortal Sea: Fishing the Atlantic in the Age of Sail* (Cambridge: Harvard University Press, 2014); Mark Kurlansky, *Cod: A Biography of the Fish That Changed the World* (New York: Walker,

1997); D. W. Prowse, *A History of Newfoundland from the English, Colonial, and Foreign Records with Numerous Illustrations and Maps* (London: Eyre & Spottiswoode, 1896); Charles de la Morandière, *Histoire de la pêche francaise de la morue dans l'Amerique septentrinale des origines à 1789* (Paris: Maisonneuve et Larose, 1962). On European interactions with the northwest Atlantic more broadly, including settlement, see David B. Quinn, *North America from Earliest Discovery to First Settlements: The Norse Voyages to 1612* (New York: Harper & Row, 1977).

5. In this geographic thinking I am following the pioneering work of D. W. Meinig, *The Shaping of America: A Geographical Perspective on 500 Years of History*, vol. 1: *Atlantic America, 1492–1800* (New Haven: Yale University Press, 1986). See also *Historical Atlas of Canada: From the Beginning to 1800*, ed. R. Cole Harris and Geoffrey J. Matthew (Toronto: University of Toronto Press, 1987). On recent human geographies: Bathsheba Demuth, *Floating Coast: An Environmental History of the Bering Strait* (New York: Norton, 2019); Joshua L. Reid, *The Sea Is My Country: The Maritime World of the Makahs* (New Haven: Yale University Press, 2015); Ernesto Bassi, *An Aqueous Territory: Sailor Geographies and New Granada's Transimperial Greater Caribbean World* (Durham: Duke University Press, 2016); Sharika Crawford, *The Last Turtlemen of the Caribbean: Waterscapes of Labor, Conservation, and Boundary Making* (Chapel Hill: University of North Carolina Press, 2020).

6. The topic of colonies and empire will be explored later in this book, but my thinking is influenced by Nancy Shoemaker, "A Typology of Colonialism," *Perspectives on History* 53, no. 7 (2015); Jason W. Moore, "The Capitalocene, Part I: On the Nature and Origins of Our Ecological Crisis," *Journal of Peasant Studies* 44, no. 3 (2017); James C. Scott, *Seeing Like a State: How Certain Schemes to Improve the Human Condition Have Failed* (New Haven: Yale University Press, 1998); Allan Greer, *Property and Dispossession: Natives, Empires and Land in Early Modern North America*, Studies in North American Indian History (Cambridge: Cambridge University Press, 2018).

7. On Indigenous concepts of space and place in northeast North America/northwest Atlantic, see: Anja Kanngieser and Zoe Todd, "From Environmental Case Study to Environmental Kin Study," *History and Theory* 59, no. 3 (2020); Zoe Todd, "Fish Pluralities: Human-Animal Relations and Sites of Engagement in Paulatuuq, Arctic Canada," *Études/Inuit/Studies* 38, nos. 1–2 (2014); Susan M. Manning, "Contrasting Colonisations: (Re)storying Newfoundland/Ktaqmkuk as Place," *Settler Colonial Studies* 8, no. 3 (2018).

8. For some of this literature, see Peter E. Pope, *Fish into Wine: The Newfoundland Plantation in the Seventeenth Century* (Chapel Hill: University of North Carolina Press, 2004); Peter E. Pope, "Transformation of the Maritime Cultural Landscape of Atlantic Canada by Migratory European Fishermen, 1500–1800," in *Beyond the Catch: Fisheries of the North Atlantic, the North Sea and the Baltic, 900–1850*, ed. Louis Sicking and Darlene Abreu-Ferreira (Leiden: Brill, 2009); *Los vascos en el marco Atlántico Norte: Siglos XVI y XVII*, ed. Selma Huxley Barkham (San Sebastián, Spain: Etor,

1987); Selma Huxley Barkham, "A Note on the Strait of Belle Isle during the Period of Basque Contact with Indians and Inuit," *Études/Inuit/Studies* 4, nos. 1–2 (1980); Selma Huxley Barkham, "The Basque Whaling Establishments in Labrador, 1536–1632—A Summary," *Arctic* 37, no. 4 (December 1984); Michael Barkham, "La industria pesquera en el País Vasco peninsular al principio de la Edad Moderna: Una edad de oro," *Itsas memoria: Revista de estúdios marítmos del País Vasco* 3 (2000); *Contact in the 16th Century: Networks among Fishers, Foragers, and Farmers*, ed. Brad Loewen and Claude Chapdelaine, Mercury Series (Ottawa: University of Ottawa Press); Laurier Turgeon, "Pour redécouvrir notre 16 siècle: Les pêches à Terre-Neuve d'après les archives notariales de Bordeaux," *Revue d'histoire de l'Amérique française* 39, no. 4 (1986); Laurier Turgeon, "French Fishers, Fur Traders, and Amerindians during the Sixteenth Century: History and Archaeology," *William and Mary Quarterly* 55, no. 4 (1998); Laurier Turgeon, *Une histoire de la Nouvelle France: Français et amérindiens au XVI siècle* (Paris: Belin, 2019); Brad Loewen and Vincent Delmas, "Les occupations basques dans le golfe du Saint-Laurent, 1530–1760: Périodisation, répartition géographique et culture matérielle," *Archéologiques* 24 (2011); Miren Egaña Goya, "Basque Toponomy in Canada," *Onomastic Canada* 74, no. 2 (December 1992): 53–74; Jacques Bernard, *Navires et gens de mer à Bordeaux (vers 1400–vers 1550)* (Paris: S.E.V.P.E.N., 1968); de la Morandière, *Histoire de la pêche francaise de la morue dans l'Amerique septentrinale des origines à 1789;* Darlene Abreu-Ferreira, "The Cod Trade in Early-Modern Portugal: Deregulation, English Domination, and the Decline of Female Cod Merchants" (PhD diss., Memorial University Newfoundland, 1995); Darlene Abreu-Ferreira, "Terra Nova through the Iberian Looking Glass: The Portuguese-Newfoundland Cod Fishery in the Sixteenth Century," *Canadian Historical Review* 79, no. 1 (March 1998).

9. Jon Coleman, *Vicious: Wolves and Men in America* (New Haven: Yale University Press, 2004), 196.

10. *La cuisine de la République: Cuisinez avec vos deputes!* ed. Françoise Branget (Paris: Cherche-Midi, 2011). Normandy: "Le grand métier—La pêche à Terre Neuve, un patrimoine disparu," *Patrimoine normand*, no. 8 (April–May) 1996: 50–53. The term *terre-neuvas* is a modern French term for fishing ships that operate at Terra Nova, as is the term *morutier*. Portugal: *Público* (Lisbon edition), July 10, 2017. "Um engano" can carry the implication of "deception" as well, though in this case the emphasis is on the mistakes of centuries of fishing.

11. Jakobina K. Arch, *Bringing Whales Ashore: Oceans and the Environment of Early Modern Japan* (Seattle: University of Washington Press, 2018); Richard C. Hoffmann, *The Catch: An Environmental History of Medieval European Fisheries* (New York: Cambridge University Press, 2023).

12. The unit "ton" (*tonneaux, tonelada*) was used in the sixteenth century as a unit of volume for the carrying capacity of merchant vessels. A sixty-ton vessel could, in theory, carry sixty ton-sized (about 252 gallons) barrels of cargo. The unit varied wildly

from place to place, and one ship might be recorded as having different sizes at different stops along its trade route. Accordingly I treat these records as vague estimates by port officials rather than precise measurements of ship sizes.

13. With thanks to Bryn Tapper for sharing these photographs.

14. The name is spelled Actalecu in the 1542 testimony, but appears as Artalecu in most notarial records. 1541: AHPG-GPAH 3/0327,D:6r–7v. A translation also found in NAW, 4:91–92. 1549: AHPG-GPAH 1/2575, A:14r–14v. 1555: AHPG-GPAH 3/0341, A:144r–150v.

15. Renisa Mawani, *Across Oceans of Law: The Komagata Maru and Jurisdiction in the Time of Empire*, Global and Insurgent Legalities (Durham: Duke University Press, 2018), 8–10. Quote: Renisa Mawani, "Oceans as Method: Law, Violence, and Climate Catastrophe." *Funambulist*, no. 39 (December 2021): 16.

16. On Atlantic history: W. Jeffrey Bolster, "Putting the Ocean in Atlantic History: Maritime Communities and Marine Ecology in the Northwest Atlantic, 1500–1800," *American Historical Review* 113, no. 1 (February 2008); Jack P. Greene and Philip D. Morgan, *Atlantic History: A Critical Appraisal* (Oxford: Oxford University Press, 2011); *Soundings in Atlantic History: Latent Structures and Intellectual Currents, 1500–1830*, ed. Bernard Bailyn and Patricia L. Denault (Cambridge: Harvard University Press 2011); John K. Thornton, *A Cultural History of the Atlantic World, 1250–1820* (Cambridge: Cambridge University Press, 2012); Peter A. Coclanis, "Atlantic World or Atlantic/World?" *William and Mary Quarterly* 63, no. 4 (2006); Paul Cohen, "Was There an Amerindian Atlantic? Reflections on the Limits of a Historiographical Concept," *History of European Ideas* 34, no. 4 (2012).

17. Matthew Restall, *Seven Myths of the Spanish Conquest* (New York: Oxford University Press, 2004); Matthew Restall, "The New Conquest History," *History Compass* 10, no. 2 (2012); Bassi, *An Aqueous Territory*; Crawford, *The Last Turtlemen of the Caribbean*; Tessa Murphy, *The Creole Archipelago: Race and Borders in the Colonial Caribbean* (Philadelphia: University of Pennsylvania Press, 2021); Ida Altman and David Wheat, *The Spanish Caribbean and the Atlantic World in the Long Sixteenth Century* (Lincoln: University of Nebraska Press, 2019); David Wheat, *Atlantic Africa and the Spanish Caribbean, 1570–1640* (Chapel Hill: University of North Carolina Press, 2016); Ida Altman, "Key to the Indies: Port Towns in the Spanish Caribbean: 1493–1550," *The Americas* 74, no. 1 (January 2017); Pablo F. Gómez, *The Experiential Caribbean: Creating Knowledge and Healing in the Early Modern Atlantic* (Chapel Hill: University of North Carolina Press, 2017); Anthony M. Stevens-Arroyo, "The Inter-Atlantic Paradigm: The Failure of Spanish Medieval Colonization of the Canary and Caribbean Islands," *Comparative Studies in Society and History* 35, no. 3 (1993); Molly A. Warsh, "A Political Ecology in the Early Spanish Caribbean," *William & Mary Quarterly* 71, no. 4 (2014). A recent collected volume has attempted to take a new perspective on early Canadian history which, while not explicitly following the Caribbean model, achieves similar goals: *Before Canada: Northern North*

America in a Connected World, ed. Allan Greer (Montréal: McGill-Queen's University Press, 2024). For environmental histories of Canada, see Cole Harris, *The Reluctant Land: Society, Space, and Environment in Canada Before Confederation* (Vancouver: University of British Columbia Press, 2009); Graeme Wynn, *Canada and Arctic North America: An Environmental History* (Santa Barbara, CA: ABC-CLIO, 2007); James Murton, *Canadians and Their Natural Environment: A History* (Toronto: Oxford University Press, 2021).

18. Roger Schlesinger and Arthur Stabler, *André Thevet's North America: A Sixteenth-Century View* (Montréal: McGill-Queen's University Press, 2014), 22; Brian M. Fagan, *Fishing: How the Sea Fed Civilization* (New Haven: Yale University Press, 2017), ix–x. On maritime history from below, see Marcus Rediker, *Between the Devil and the Deep Blue Sea: Merchant Seamen, Pirates, and the Anglo-American Maritime World, 1700–1750* (New York: Cambridge University Press, 1987); Pablo Emilio Pérez-Malláina, *Spain's Men of the Sea: Daily Life on the Indies Fleets in the Sixteenth Century*, trans. Carla Rahn Phillips (Baltimore: Johns Hopkins University Press, 1998).

19. Liam Campling and Alejandro Colás, *Capitalism and the Sea: The Maritime Factor in the Making of the Modern World* (London: Verso Books, 2021).

20. Anna Lowenhaupt Tsing, *The Mushroom at the End of the World: On the Possibility of Life in Capitalist Ruins* (Princeton: Princeton University Press, 2015), 63.

Part 1. Terra Nova

Epigraph: Paul Carter, *The Road to Botany Bay: An Exploration of Landscape and History* (St. Paul: University of Minnesota Press, 2010), xiii. Copyright 1987 by Paul Carter. Used by permission.

1. Stories

1. AM Bayonne BB 36, fols. 294–95; see too BB 38, fol. 85.
2. On Caboto, see Peter E. Pope, *The Many Landfalls of John Cabot* (Toronto: University of Toronto Press, 1997), 3–42, 69–90. Quote: John Gimlette, *Theatre of Fish: Travels through Newfoundland and Labrador* (New York: Knopf, 2005), xvii.
3. Harry Thurston, *The Atlantic Coast: A Natural History* (Vancouver: Greystone Books, 2012), 39–75; *The Natural Environment of Newfoundland, Past and Present*, ed. Alan G. Macpherson and Joyce Brown (Saint John's, NL: Dept. of Geography, Memorial University of Newfoundland, 1981).
4. Matthew W. Betts and M. Gabriel Hrynick, *The Archaeology of the Atlantic Northeast* (Toronto: University of Toronto Press, 2021); James A. Tuck, *Maritime Provinces Prehistory*, Canadian Prehistory (Ottawa: National Museum of Man, 1984).

5. Birgitta Wallace, "The Norse in Newfoundland: L'Anse aux Meadows and Vinland," *Newfoundland Studies* 19, no. 1 (2003); Stephanie Pettigrew and Elizabeth Mancke, "European Expansion and the Contested North Atlantic," *Terrae Incognitae* 50, no. 1 (2018). On Norse in historical memory: Annette Kolodny, *In Search of First Contact: The Vikings of Vinland, the Peoples of the Dawnland, and the Anglo-American Anxiety of Discovery* (Durham: Duke University Press, 2012).

6. On the early Atlantic in general, see *Studies in the Medieval Atlantic*, ed. Benjamin T. Hudson, The New Middle Ages (New York: Palgrave Macmillan, 2012). On Portuguese expansion, see *Portuguese Oceanic Expansion, 1400–1800*, ed. Francisco Bethencourt and Diogo Ramada Curto (New York: Cambridge University Press, 2007); A. R. Disney, A *History of Portugal and the Portuguese Empire: From Beginnings to 1807*, 2 vols. (New York: Cambridge University Press, 2009); Vitorino Magalhães Godinho, *Os descobrimentos e a economia mundial* (Lisbon: Editorial Presença, 1981). On Iceland: "A Privy Seal, for Orders to Prohibit English Ships from Sailing towards Iceland (Lat.) Nov. 28, 1415," BL, Cotton MS Nero B III No. 29. For some context, see the discussion of English fishing in Iceland in Prowse, A *History of Newfoundland from the English, Colonial, and Foreign Records*, 24–29; Evan T. Jones, "England's Icelandic fishery in the Early Modern Period," in *England's Sea Fisheries: The Commercial Sea Fisheries of England and Wales since 1300* (London: Chatham, 2003), 105–10.

7. For a long-term view of ecological exchange across the far north, see Christopher Parsons, "Maple, Beaver, and New Roots for a Global Early Canada," in Greer, *Before Canada*.

8. Quote: Biggar, *Cartier and Roberval*, 462. Sara Spike, " 'A Salubrious, Saline Exhalation': Fog and Health in Colonial Newfoundland and Nova Scotia," NiCHE: The Network in Canadian History & Environment, 2020, https://niche-canada.org/2020/08/27/a-salubrious-saline-exhalation-fog-and-health-in-colonial-newfoundland-and-nova-scotia/.

9. For bird names, see Jacques Cartier, *Relation originale du voyage de Jacques Cartier au Canada en 1534*, ed. H. Michelant and A. Ramé (Paris: Librarie Tross, 1867), 12.

10. The name Corte Real can be written many ways. I use this variation as it is closest to that in the oldest documents. In thinking about a multitude of voyages, I am following chapter 1 in Restall, *Seven Myths of the Spanish Conquest*. For some overviews of these early voyages, see Samuel Eliot Morison, *The European Discovery of America: The Northern Voyages* (New York: Oxford University Press, 1971); Quinn, *North America from Earliest Discovery to First Settlements*; John L. Allen, "From Cabot to Cartier: The Early Exploration of Eastern North America, 1497–1543," *Annals of the Association of American Geographers* 82, no. 3 (1992). For the Norman case, see Michael Wintroub, *The Voyage of Thought: Navigating Knowledge across the Sixteenth-Century World* (Cambridge: Cambridge University Press, 2017).

11. Early English fishing: NAW, 1:110 (no. 75), 117–18 (no. 84). Early Bretons and Normans: Giovanni Battista Ramusio, *Terzo volume delle nauigationi et viaggi*, 3 vols., vol. 3 (Venice: Luca Antonio Giunti, 1556), 423–34. 1506: Biggar, *Precursors*, 96–97. 1508: ADSM 1 B, no. 324, October 21, 1508. 1515: ADSM Fonds communales de Rouen, A 10, December 24, no folio. 1517 cargo: Jacques Bernard, "Les debuts de la peche a Terre-neuve, vus de Bordeaux (1517–1550): Bilan et perspectives," Bordeaux, Université de Bordaux III, 1984), 12–13. "Fleet" quote: Biggar, *Precursors*, 142–43. Estimate "French" fleet: NAW, 1:168–71.

12. Rut letter: Biggar, *Precursors*, 165–68.

13. Biggar, *Cartier and Roberval*, 43–44. On La Gran Baya and names: Barkham, "The Basque Whaling Establishments in Labrador," 516.

14. Ship counts are discussed more below, but for an overview see Turgeon, "French Fishers, Fur Traders, and Amerindians."

15. For an example, see ADSM 2 E 1, 440, February 17, 1564. The *Marye* of Caudebec departed Rouen for Terra Nova, planning to stop at La Baye or Brouage for salt before heading to Terra Nova to fish for cod. On salt fleets: ADSM Fonds communales de Rouen A 19, July 18, 1575. See also ADC 8 E 6198, fol. 469 for an example of a salt run from Honfleur in the 1570s.

16. The first whaling ships attested to in the archives arrived in 1543, but the industry seriously took off only after the 1550s. Whaling is discussed more below, but a good overview is found in volume 1 of *The Underwater Archaeology of Red Bay: Basque Shipbuilding and Whaling in the 16th Century*, ed. Robert Grenier, Willis Stevens, and Marc A. Bernier (Ottawa: Parks Canada, 2007).

17. Keith Matthews, "A History of the West of England–Newfoundland Fishery" (PhD diss., University of Oxford, 1968); Gillian T. Cell, *English Enterprise in Newfoundland, 1577–1660* (Toronto: University of Toronto Press, 1969); Maarten Heerlien, "Van Holland naar Cupidos Koe: Hollandse Newfoundlandhandel in de context van de internationale kabeljauwvisserij bij Newfoundland in de zestiende en de zeventiende eeuw" (PhD diss., Rijksuniversiteit Groningen, 2005).

18. On seventeenth-century colonial attempts, see Raymonde Litalien and Denis Vaugeois, *Champlain: La naissance de l'Amérique française* (Paris: Septentrion; Nouveau Monde, 2004); David Hackett Fischer, *Champlain's Dream: The European Founding of North America* (New York: Simon & Schuster, 2008); Éric Thierry, *La France de Henri IV en Amérique du Nord: De la création de l'Acadie à la fondation de Québec* (Paris: H. Champion, 2008); Cell, *English Enterprise in Newfoundland*; Pope, *Fish into Wine*.

19. Samuel de Champlain, "Les voyages du sieur de Champlain Xaintongeois, Capitaine ordinaire pour le Roy" (1613), in *Ouevres de Champlain*, ed. C.h. Laverdiére (Laval: Université de Laval, 1870), 3:156;. Charles Bréard and Paul Bréard, *Documents relatifs à la marine normande et à ses armements aux XVIe et XVIIe siècles pour le Canada, l'Afrique, les Antilles, le Brésil et les Indes* (Rouen: A. Lestringant, 1889), 102.

2. Names

1. Bruneau de Rivedoux, *Histoire veritable de certains voiages perilleux & hazardeux sur la mer, ausquels reluit la justice de Dieu sur les uns, & sa misericorde sur les autres: Tres-digne d'estre leu, pour les choses rares & admirables qui y sont contenues* (Paris, 1599), 108–9.

2. The use of *Terra Nova* as a substitute for *Newfoundland*, typically as *Terranova*, has increased in some parts of the scholarship, particularly those who work on the participation of Spanish Basques in the fishery. For examples, see Selma Huxley Barkham, "The Spanish Province of Terranova," *Canadian Archivist* 2, no. 5 (1974); Grenier, Stevens, and Bernier, *The Underwater Archaeology of Red Bay*; Miren Egaña Goya, "Basque Toponomy in Canada," *Onomastic Canada* 74, no. 2 (December 1992). It is briefly noted in Harris and Matthew, *Historical Atlas of Canada: From the Beginning to 1800*.

3. Consider examples from the Pacific that show how mental maps worked: Judith Binney, "Tuki's Universe," *New Zealand Journal of History* 38, no. 2 (2004); Margaret Jolly, "Imagining Oceania: Indigenous and Foreign Representations of a Sea of Islands," *Contemporary Pacific* (2007).

4. Paul Carter, *The Road to Botany Bay: An Exploration of Landscape and History* (New York: Knopf, 1988); Yi-Fu Tuan, "Language and the Making of Place: A Narrative-Descriptive Approach," *Annals of the Association of American Geographers* 81, no. 4 (1991); Tim Ingold, *The Perception of the Environment: Essays on Livelihood, Dwelling and Skill* (London: Routledge, 2002), 219.

5. Biggar, *Precursors*, doc. XXXV, 116–18. Original: ADLA B 21, fols. 15–16.

6. See ADCM 3 E 203, notaire Bibeard, fol. 89r; ADCM 3 E 221, notaire Cousseau, fol. 66v.

7. Plurals: In January 1576 the notary duo Gonnyer and Champaigne in the Norman port of Honfleur recorded a contract for the ship *Le Jehan*, which that spring made a "Terras Novas voyage/*des* Terres Neufves." In the next entry, on the bottom of the same page, they recorded that the ship *L'esperance* was going on a "Terra Nova voyage/*de* Terre Neuve." ADC 8 E 6500, fol. 22.

8. Nova Terre appears in an English document of 1501, but otherwise is not commonly found in written sources. The fact that it is in Latin and the word order (Terra Nova is always written noun-adjective) do distinguish it from the Portuguese phrase that became popular after 1501, and we should be hesitant to treat it as more than an isolate. Margaret M. Condon and Evan T. Jones, "William Weston: Early Voyager to the New World," *Historical Research* 91 (2018): 631.

9. Laurier Turgeon, "Codfish, Consumption and Colonization: The Creation of the French Atlantic World during the Sixteenth Century," in *Bridging the Early Modern Atlantic World: People, Products, and Practices on the Move*, ed. C. A. Williams (Burlington: Ashgate, 2009), 46–49. 1502: Biggar, *Precursors*, doc. XXIV, 67–70. 1506: Biggar, *Precursors*, doc. XXVIII, 96–97.

10. 1508 record: ADSM 1 B, no. 324, October 21, n.p. 1507–8 map: Johannes Ruysch, *Universalior Cogniti Orbis Tabula Ex Recentibus Confecta Observationibus* (Rome, 1508), Map Collection, JCBL. Nantes: ADLA B 21, fols. 15–16. Beauport: ADCA H 69. Capbreton: AM Capbreton CC 5. Galicia: Caroline Ménard, "La pesca gallega en Terranova, siglos XVI–XVIII" (PhD diss., Universidad de Sevilla: Consejo Superior de Investigaciones Científicas; Diputacion de Sevilla, Area de Cultura e Identidad, 2008), 417. "Newland fish": In 1520, while outfitting two ships for a voyage to Ireland, a state document makes reference to purchasing "200 Newlond fishe." Public Record Office, *Letters and Papers, Foreign and Domestic, of the Reign of Henry VIII*, 21 vols., ed. J. S. Brewer (London: H.M. Stationery Office, 1920), vol. 3, part I: 1519–21, no.800, 279. For a later reference: In 1582 a prize cargo was described as *"piscium vocatorum Newland fishe"* — "Fish Called Newland fish." National Archives, HCA, file 52, no. 120. Bristol: On October 1, 1516 the *Frances* of Saint Brieuc and on September 10, 1517 the *Kateryn* of Honfleur each offloaded fish, both coming from what was written as *Terra Nova*. On the freely available database the two entries are rows 13–14 and 3515–16. Susan Flavin and E. T. Jones, "Bristol 'Particular' Customs Account, 1516/17" (April 3, 2009), accessed via https://www.bristol.ac.uk/Depts/History/Ireland/datasets.htm. For context of this data, see Susan Flavin and Evan T. Jones, *Bristol's Trade with Ireland and the Continent, 1503–1601: The Evidence of the Exchequer Customs Accounts* (Dublin: Four Courts, 2009).
11. Pettigrew and Mancke, "European Expansion and the Contested North Atlantic."
12. 1508: ADSM 1 B, no. 324, October 21, 1508. Later language: ADCM 3 E 203, notaire Bibeard, 1592; ADC 8 E 6510, notaires Barne et Robinet, 1598. Amsterdam: Stadsarchief Amsterdam, Notarial archief, 75/99–101, October 10, 1596. Ship *de Zeeridder* bound for "Terra Neuf" to buy fish.
13. Note: BnF Ms.Fr. 24269, fol. 55r. Crew list: ADCA 1 E 2783, fol. 35.
14. Schlesinger and Stabler, *André Thevet's North America*, 54; NAW, 4:7.
15. Chet Van Duzer and Lauren Beck, *Canada Before Confederation: Maps at the Exhibition* (Wilmington: Vernon, 2017); Kirsten A. Seaver, "Norumbega and Harmonia Mundi in Sixteenth-Century Cartography," *Imago Mundi* 50, no. 1 (1998).
16. Visconte de Maggiolo, *[World Map]* (Naples, 1511), Map Collection, JCBL.
17. For a good discussion of Bacalao as place–name, see Egaña Goya, "Basque Toponomy in Canada," 55–57. For other examples, see Van Duzer and Beck, *Canada Before Confederation* 36, 68–69. See too the example of how Champlain uses Bacalao in the early seventeenth century to denote a small island. Miren Egaña Goya, "Presencia de los pescadores vascos en Canadá s. XVII: Testimonio de las obras de Samuel de Champlain (1603–1633)," *Zainak, cuadernos de antropología-ethnografía* 33 (2010): 384. For a Portuguese map: BSB Codices Iconographici, 132. On Ruysch: Gregory McIntosh, *The Johannes Ruysch and Martin Waldseemüller World Maps: The Interplay and Merging of Early Sixteenth-Century New World Cartographies* (Long Beach, CA: Plus Ultra, 2012), 115–16.

18. Birds: BnF Ms.Fr. 24269, fol. 55r. Parmenius: *The New Found Land of Stephen Par-menius: The Life and Writings of a Hungarian Poet, Drowned on a Voyage from New-foundland, 1583*, ed. and trans. David B. Quinn and Neil M. Cheshire (Toronto: University of Toronto Press, 1972), 173; Moyne: NAW, docs. 148–52, 1:206–14.

19. Ingold, *The Perception of the Environment*, 229–30 (italics in original); Ricardo Pa-drón, "Mapping Plus Ultra: Cartography, Space, and Hispanic Modernity," *Repre-sentations* 79, no. 1 (Summer 2002).

20. María Nieves Zedeño, "On What People Make of Places: A Behavioral Cartogra-phy," in *Social Theory in Archaeology*, ed. Michael B Schiffer (Salt Lake City: Uni-versity of Utah Press, 2000), 107; Christer Westerdahl, "The Maritime Cultural Landscape," *International Journal of Nautical Archaeology* 21, no. 1 (1992), 5.

21. For Pope's approach, see "Transformation of the Maritime Cultural Landscape of At-lantic Canada by Migratory European Fishermen, 1500–1800."

22. Fikret Berkes, *Sacred Ecology: Traditional Ecological Knowledge and Resource Man-agement* (Philadelphia: Taylor & Francis, 1999). Renews: BnF Ms.Fr. 24269, fol. 55r. See discussion in chapter 6.

23. 1521 prospects: Biggar, *Precursors*, 136. Gilbert: NAW, docs. 148–52, 1:206–14; *The New Found Land of Stephen Parmenius*, 169.

24. Martin de Hoyarsabal, *Les voyages avantureux du Capitaine Martin de Hoyarsabal, habitant de Cubiburu* (Bordeaux: Jean Chouin 1579); Michael M. Barkham, "New Documents concerning the French Basque Pilot, Martin de Hoyarsabal, Author of the First Detailed Rutter for the 'New Found Land' (1579)," *Newfoundland and Lab-rador Studies* 19, no. 1 (2005).

25. Charles Travis et al., "Inventing the Grand Banks: A Deep Chart: Humanities GIS, Cartesian, and Literary Perceptions of the North-west Atlantic Fishery ca 1500–1800," *Geo: Geography and Environment* 7, no. 1 (2020); Craig E. Colten, "Currents of Influence: Indigenous River Names in the American South," in *Mapping Nature across the Americas*, ed. Kathleen A. Brosnan and James R. Akerman (Chicago: Uni-versity of Chicago Press, 2021). Cape Breton: William Francis Ganong and Theo-dore E. Layng, *Crucial Maps in the Early Cartography and Place-Nomenclature of the Atlantic Coast of Canada* (Toronto: University of Toronto Press, 1964), 35–38. Basque names: Miren Egaña Goya has traced many place-names that were taken from towns and harbors in Basque Country. Selma Huxley Barkham has tried to chart the presence of Basque names down the west coast of Newfoundland island. Egaña Goya, "Basque Toponomy in Canada"; Miren Egaña Goya, "Los puertos vas-cos del Golfo de Bizkaia. Reutilización de sus nombres en las pesquerías del Atlán-tico Norte. S. XVI y XVII," *Oihenart* 18 (2000). Selma Huxley Barkham, *The Basque Coast of Newfoundland* (Plum Point, Nfld.: Great Northern Peninsula Development Corporation, 1989).

26. Brian M. Fagan, *Fish on Friday: Feasting, Fasting, and the Discovery of the New World* (New York: Basic Books, 2006). For Caboto: Evan T. Jones, "Alwyn Ruddock:

'John Cabot and the Discovery of America,' " *Historical Research* 81, no. 212 (2008): 245–49. On Saint John's harbor, see the 1519 Miller Atlas, where Saint John's appears as "R: de sam joham." Pedro Reinel, António de Holanda, Jorge Reinel, and Lopo Homem, *Nautical Atlas of the World*, Folio 6 Recto, North Atlantic Ocean, 1519, Library of Congress, https://www.loc.gov/item/2021668715/. Fagundes: Biggar, *Precursors*, 130. Burials: Lori M. White, "The Saddle Island Cemetery: A Study of Whalers at a Sixteenth-Century Basque Whaling Station in Red Bay, Labrador" (PhD diss., Memorial University of Newfoundland, 2015); Miren Egaña Goya, "A Permanent Place in Newfoundland: Seventeenth-Century Basque Tombstones in Placentia," *Newfoundland and Labrador Studies* 33, no. 1 (2018); Barkham, "The Spanish Province of Terranova," 76, n.10, 78–79.

27. Kanngieser and Todd, "From Environmental Case Study to Environmental Kin Study," 386. See too Todd, "Fish Pluralities: Human-Animal Relations and Sites of Engagement in Paulatuuq, Arctic Canada"; Manning, "Contrasting Colonisations: (Re)storying Newfoundland/Ktaqmkuk as Place." On Algonkian place-names: Bernard G. Hoffman, *Cabot to Cartier: Sources for a Historical Ethnography of Northeastern North America, 1497–1550* (Toronto: University of Toronto Press, 1968), 197–212.

28. Quote: E. Ducéré, *Histoire maritime de Bayonne. Les corsaires sous lancien régime* (Bayonne: E. Hourquet, 1895), 333–44. Secrecy: Bror Olsen and Trond Thuen, "Secret Places: On the Management of Knowledge and Information about Landscape and Yields in Northern Norway," *Human Ecology* 41, no. 2 (2012); Trevor A. Branch et al., "Fleet Dynamics and Fishermen Behavior: Lessons for Fisheries Managers," *Canadian Journal of Fisheries and Aquatic Sciences* 63, no. 7 (2006); Thorolfur Thorlindsson and Thorlindsson Thor, "Skipper Science: A Note on the Epistemology of Practice and the Nature of Expertise," *Sociological Quarterly* 35, no. 2 (1994).

3. Rhythms

1. AM Bayonne BB 6, fols. 91r/v. Biran had organized a Terra Nova voyage the previous year with a different partner, and similarly had to ask special permission from the city of Bayonne. AM Bayonne BB 6, fol. 189.

2. Rachel Carson, *The Sea around Us* (New York: Oxford University Press, 2018), 29.

3. NAW, 4:31. I have translated "fruition" in the original as "run of" to give the sense of having full access to the abundance of the region.

4. Adrian Howkins, *The Polar Regions: An Environmental History* (Cambridge: Polity, 2016), 44; Todd J. Kristensen, "Seasonal Bird Exploitation by Recent Indian and Beothuk Hunter-Gatherers of Newfoundland," *Canadian Journal of Archaeology* 35, no. 2 (2011); T. J. Kristensen and J. E. Curtis, "Late Holocene Hunter-Gatherers at L'Anse aux Meadows and the Dynamics of Bird and Mammal Hunting in Newfoundland," *Arctic Anthropology* 49, no. 1 (2012); Todd J. Kristensen and Donald H.

Holly Jr., "Birds, Burials and Sacred Cosmology of the Indigenous Beothuk of New-foundland, Canada," *Cambridge Archaeological Journal* 23, no. 1 (2013); Donald H. Holly Jr., "The Place of 'Others' in Hunter-Gatherer Intensification," *American Anthropologist* 107, no. 2 (2005), 208.

5. *The Jesuit Relations and Allied Documents: Travels and Explorations of the Jesuit Missionaries in New France, 1610–1791*, 73 vols., ed. Reuben Gold Thwaites (Cleveland: Burrows Bros., 1896–1901), 40: 216–17.

6. On the currents and hydrology of the northwest Atlantic, see Rose, *Cod*, 43–45.

7. Samuel de Champlain, *Ouevres de Champlain*, 2nd ed., 5 vols., vol. 1, ed. C. H. Laverdiere (Laval: l'Universite de Laval, 1870), 355.

8. For the relationship between the subarctic environment of the northwest Atlantic and human adaptation, see Donald H. Holly Jr., *History in the Making: The Archaeology of the Eastern Subarctic* (Lanham: AltaMira, 2013).

9. NAW, doc. 590, 4:103–4; AM Bayonne BB 6, fol. 91r.

10. *Les Micmacs et la mer*, ed. Charles A. Martijn (Montréal: Recherches amérindiennes au Québec, 1986); Jack D. Forbes, *The American Discovery of Europe* (Urbana: University of Illinois Press, 2007); Andrew Lipman, *The Saltwater Frontier: Indians and the Contest for the American Coast* (New Haven: Yale University Press, 2015); Jace Weaver, *The Red Atlantic: American Indigenes and the Making of the Modern World, 1000–1927* (Chapel Hill: University of North Carolina Press, 2014); Nancy Shoemaker, *Native American Whalemen and the World: Indigenous Encounters and the Contingency of Race* (Chapel Hill: University of North Carolina Press, 2017).

11. Matthew R. Bahar, *Storm of the Sea: Indians and Empires in the Atlantic's Age of Sail* (New York: Oxford University Press, 2019). On seafaring: Charles A. Martijn, "Early Mikmaq Presence in Southern Newfoundland: An Ethnohistorical Perspective, c. 1500–1763," *Newfoundland and Labrador Studies* 19, no. 1 (2005). See the example of seal hunting at Port au Choix in a much older but telling context. This includes a breakdown of winter and spring hunts and migrations. *The Cultural Landscapes of Port-au-Choix: Precontact Hunter-Gatherers of Northwestern Newfoundland*, ed. M.A.P. Renouf, Interdisciplinary Contributions to Archaeology (New York: Springer, 2011), 131–60.

12. A good summary of the Mi'kmaw case can be found in Martijn, "Early Mikmaq Presence in Southern Newfoundland: An Ethnohistorical Perspective, c. 1500–1763," 49–55. See too William Craig Wicken, "Encounters with Tall Sails and Tall Tales: Mi'kmaq Society, 1500–1760" (PhD diss., McGill University, 1994); Betts and Hrynick, *The Archaeology of the Atlantic Northeast*, chaps. 10–11 in general for discussion of settlements. See too Peter Rowley-Conwy, "Settlement Patterns of the Beothuk Indians of Newfoundland: A View from Away," *Canadian Journal of Archaeology/Journal canadien d'archéologie* (1990). Quote: *The Cultural Landscapes of Port-au-Choix*, 275.

13. William Gilbert, "Beothuk-European Contact in the 16th Century: A Re-evaluation of the Documentary Evidence," *Acadiensis* 40, no. 1 (2011), 36 (translation of original Italian); Betts and Hrynick, *The Archaeology of the Atlantic Northeast,* 270.

14. *The Jesuit Relations and Allied Documents,* vol. 3 (Cleveland: Burrows Brothers, 1898), 77, 79; Carla Cevasco, *Violent Appetites: Hunger in the Early Northeast* (New Haven: Yale University Press, 2022), 22–53.

15. Gilbert, "Beothuk-European Contact in the 16th Century"; Donald H. Holly Jr., Christopher Wolff, and John Erwin, "The Ties That Bind and Divide: Encounters with the Beothuk in Southeastern Newfoundland," *Journal of the North Atlantic* 3 (2010); Ralph Pastore, "The Collapse of the Beothuk World," *Acadiensis* 19, no. 1 (1989); Rowley-Conwy, "Settlement Patterns of the Beothuk Indians of Newfoundland."

16. For a modern take on this problem and study of migratory fishwork, see Marie-Christine Cormier-Salem, "Pêcheurs migrants et paysans-pêcheurs: Deux modèles de gestion de l'espace irréductibles?" in *La recherche scientifique face a la peche artisanale* (Paris: ORSTOM, 1991).

17. Biggar, *Cartier and Roberval,* doc. CCXII, 462–63.

18. Biggar, *Cartier and Roberval,* doc. CCXII, 453–54. Lefant is likely speaking of the Innu as well. The Gascon language was still being used in official records into the 1530s in Bayonne, but *gascona* may be a garbled transliteration of *vascona,* Basque.

19. Ken Coates and William Morrison, "Winter and the Shaping of Northern History: Reflections from the Canadian North," *Northern Visions: New Perspectives on the North in Canadian History* (2001): 9. For a good recent summary of long-term environmental change, see Amitav Ghosh, *The Nutmeg's Curse: Parables for a Planet in Crisis* (Chicago: University of Chicago Press, 2021), 49–62.

20. Jason W. Moore, *Capitalism in the Web of Life: Ecology and the Accumulation of Capital* (New York: Verso, 2015), 3.

Part 2. Water

Epigraphs: John Heywood, *Two Hundred Epigrammes, vpon Two Hundred Prouerbs with a Thyrde Hundred Newely Added and Made by Iohn Heywood* (London: T. Berthelet 1555), n.p.; Biggar, *Precursors,* doc. VIII, 15–16.

4. Islands

1. Biggar, *Precursors,* doc. XXXII, 102–11, quote 104. Spread of news: "The John Day Letter," https://www.heritage.nf.ca/articles/exploration/john-day.php.

2. Biggar, *Precursors,* doc. XVI, 31–32, 127–31.

3. Hercules O'Doria, [*Map of Newfoundland South to the Caribbean,* 1592], JCBL Map Collection, 67-485-2, Courtesy of the John Carter Brown Library at Brown University, https://jcb.lunaimaging.com/luna/servlet/s/gm351v.

4. Little is known about Agramonte or his voyage. See Gustave Lanctot, "Agramonte, Juan de," in *Dictionary of Canadian Biography*, vol. 1, University of Toronto/Université Laval, 2003–, http://www.biographi.ca/en/bio/agramonte_juan_de_1E.html.

5. Documents from Biggar, *Precursors*, docs. VI–VII, 12–13, doc. XVII, 32.

6. See in particular the discussion of islands in the French mind, including Newfoundland island, in F. Lestringant, *Le livre des îles: Atlas et récits insulaires de la Genèse à Jules Verne*, Cahiers d'humanisme et Renaissance—Les seuils de la modernité (Geneva: Librairie Droz, 2002).

7. Christina Gillis, *Where Edges Don't Hold: A Small Island Miscellany* (CreateSpace Independent Publishing Platform, 2017), 9, 11. On the earlier history of islands as provisioning centers in the Atlantic, see Jack Bouchard, "Shetland Sheep and Azorean Wheat: Atlantic Islands as Provisioning Centers, 1400–1550," *Global Food History* (2020). Quote: Gary Y. Okihiro, *Island World: A History of Hawai'i and the United States* (Berkeley: University of California Press, 2008), 211.

8. John R. Gillis, *Islands of the Mind: How the Human Imagination Created the Atlantic World* (New York: Palgrave Macmillan, 2004). For some of the literature on islands, see Stefan Halikowski Smith, "The Mid-Atlantic Islands: A Theatre of Early Modern Ecocide?" *International Review of Social History* 55, no. Supplement (2010); William D. Phillips, Jr., "Africa and the Atlantic Islands Meet the Garden of Eden: Christopher Columbus's View of America," *Journal of World History* (1992); Thomas H. McGovern et al., "Northern Islands, Human Error, and Environmental Degradation: A View of Social and Ecological Change in the Medieval North Atlantic," *Human Ecology* 16, no. 3 (1988); Stevens-Arroyo, "The Inter-Atlantic Paradigm"; David Abulafia, *The Discovery of Mankind: Atlantic Encounters in the Age of Columbus* (New Haven: Yale University Press, 2008). *Isolario*: George Tolias, "The Politics of the Isolario: Maritime Cosmography and Overseas Expansion during the Renaissance," *Historical Review/La revue historique* 9 (2012). Anastasia Stouraiti, "Talk, Script and Print: The Making of Island Books in Early Modern Venice," *Historical Research* 86, no. 232 (May 2013).

9. Nicolo di Caverio, Nautical Planisphere, Library of Congress, circa 1504 https://www.loc.gov/item/2021668721/. Day Letter: "The John Day Letter." Trees and Caboto: Biggar, *Precursors*, 20. Trees and Corte Real: Biggar, *Precursors*, 66–67.

10. Note, for instance, the division in Samuel Eliot Morison's dated but popular and influential studies of early American settlement and exploration by Europeans. Samuel Eliot Morison, *The European Discovery of America* (New York: Oxford University Press, 1971) covers "northern" voyages, while Samuel Eliot Morison, *The European Discovery of America: The Southern Voyages, A.D. 1492–1616* (New York: Oxford University Press, 1993) covers the Spanish Americas. This division is preserved in the massive collection of translated documents in *New American World: A Documentary History of North America to 1612*, 4 vols., ed. David B. Quinn, Alison M. Quinn, and Susan Hillier (New York: Arno, 1978). Quinn et al. separate their collection geographically, including an entire separate volume on the northwest Atlantic.

11. Ernesto Bassi, "Beyond Compartmentalized Atlantics: A Case for Embracing the Atlantic from Spanish American Shores," *History Compass* 12, no. 9 (2014). Portugal: Abreu-Ferreira, "The Cod Trade in Early-Modern Portugal." France: Céline Carayon, *Eloquence Embodied: Nonverbal Communication among French and Indigenous Peoples in the Americas* (Chapel Hill: UNC Press for the Omohundro Institute of Early American Studies, 2019).

12. Little information survives that would allow us to reconstruct the lives of the Corte Real brothers. For surviving documents, see Biggar, *Precursors*, 32–37, 59–70, 92–97. For these early voyages, see also Hoffman, *Cabot to Cartier: Sources for a Historical Ethnography of Northeastern North America, 1497–1550*; Richard Goertz, "João Alvares Fagundes, capitão de Terra Nova, 1521," *Canadian Ethnic Studies/Etudes ethniques au Canada* 23, no. 2 (1991).

13. Biggar, *Precursors*, 31–32, 67.

14. In the first two decades after Caboto's expedition, it is likely that at least two major efforts were made to settle in the northwest Atlantic, though others may have been attempted. The first was part of Caboto's last expedition. The second was the ill-fated voyage by John Rastell in 1517 that ended before it began. Jones, "Alwyn Ruddock"; Morison, *The European Discovery of America*. On climate: Nicolás Wey Gómez, *The Tropics of Empire: Why Columbus Sailed South to the Indies* (Cambridge: MIT Press, 2008). Quote: John Mason, *A Briefe Discourse of the Nevv-Found-Land with the Situation, Temperature, and Commodities Thereof, Inciting Our Nation to Goe Forward in That Hopefull Plantation Begunne* (Edinburgh: Andro Hart, 1620), n.p.

15. Biggar, *Precursors*, 127.

16. A description of the Portuguese settlement can be found in the 1570 text *Tratado das Ilhas Novas e descrobimento dellas outras couzas*. Excerpts and translation printed in Biggar, *Precursors*, 197. For the textual evidence on Fagundes's expedition: Biggar, *Precursors*, doc. XXXIX, 127–31. Jean Alfonse, *Les voyages auantureux dv capitaine Ian Alfonce, Sainctongeois auec priuilege du roy* (Poitou: Mellin de Saint-Gelais, 1559), fol. 28. "Terre qui est la plus basse" seems to imply a coast surrounded by rocky shoals. Jehan Mallart, "La description de tous les portz de mer de l'univers, avecques summaire mention des conditions différentes des peuples et adresse pour le rung des ventz propres à naviguer" (sixteenth century.), BnF Ms.Fr. 1382, fol. 40r.

17. On the French shift to Saint Lawrence: Meinig, *The Shaping of America*, vol. 1: *Atlantic America, 1492–1800*, 25–26. Allen, "From Cabot to Cartier," 516–17.

18. Ribeiro: Planisphere by Diogo Ribeiro, Madrid, Royal Academy of History, Section of Cartography and Graphic Arts, C-018-014, accessed via *Google Arts&Culture*. Lopo Homem: Lopo Homem, *Planisphere*, c. 1554, Museo Galileo, facsimile, https://catalogue.museogalileo.it/gallery/PlanisphereInv946.html. Santa Cruz: Santa Cruz, Alonso De, cartographer, *General Atlas of All the Islands in the World*, 1539, map, fol. 298, https://www.loc.gov/item/2021668468/. For context, see *Cartography in the European Renaissance*, 6 vols., vol. 3: *The History of Cartography*, ed. David Woodward (Chicago: University of Chicago Press, 2007), nos. 38, 40.

5. Frontiers

1. Most records related to Terra Nova use money of account to record transactions. These were standardized, theoretical units of money that merchants used to keep track of debts and investments. Actual payments might then be made in many forms of hard cash. Most regions followed the old three-part Roman model of currency, *l./s./d.* at a 1:20:12 ratio. One *livre* or pound sterling was equal to 20 *sous* or shillings, which was in turn equal to 12 *deniers* or pennies (abbreviated *d.*), so that 240 *deniers* equaled 1 *livre*. *Livres tournois* were the most common unit of account used in France. From the late sixteenth century, the gold coin *écus sol* replaces the *livre tournois* in some records. In Spain, records were recorded in *reales* and *maravedis*, at the ratio of 1 *real* to 34 *maravedis*.

2. Beauport Monks: ADCA H 69. Transcript in Biggar, *Precursors*, 118–23. On Breton context: Alain Croix, *La Bretagne aux 16e et 17e siècles: La vie, la mort, la foi*, 2 vols., vol. 1 (Paris: Maloine, 1981), especially T.1 graphique 87. Harbor of Bréhat: ADSM 1 B, no. 324. The document is briefly discussed in Michel Mollat, *Le commerce maritime normand a la fin du Moyen Age: Étude d'histoire économique et sociale* (Paris: Plon, 1952), 262–63.

3. Moore, *Capitalism in the Web of Life*. Quote: Jason W. Moore, " 'Amsterdam Is Standing on Norway,' Part II: The Global North Atlantic in the Ecological Revolution of the Long Seventeenth Century," *Journal of Agrarian Change* 10, no. 2 (2010): 191.

4. On the opportunities of marine coastal ecosystems: David R. Yesner et al., "Maritime Hunter-Gatherers: Ecology and Prehistory [and Comments and Reply]," *Current Anthropology* 21, no. 6 (1980). Quote: Mariaros Dalla Costa and Monica Chilese, *Our Mother Ocean: Enclosure, Commons, and the Global Fishermen's Movement*, trans. Silvia Frederici (New York: Common Notions, 2014), 13.

5. Barry W. Cunliffe, *Facing the Ocean: The Atlantic and Its Peoples, 8000 BC–AD 1500* (New York: Oxford University Press, 2001); David Gange, *The Frayed Atlantic Edge: A Historian's Journey from Shetland to the Channel* (Glasgow: William Collins, 2019), 5–6.

6. Helen M. Rozwadowski, *Vast Expanses: A History of the Oceans* (Chicago: Reaktion Books, 2018), 23; Kenneth Sherman, "The Large Marine Ecosystem Concept: Research and Management Strategy for Living Marine Resources," *Ecological Applications* 1, no. 4 (1991).

7. An excellent introduction to this history before the sixteenth century can be found in Hoffmann, *The Catch*. It should be noted that Hoffmann's work was published after most of this present book was written, but it now fills a gap in our scholarship with a thorough synthesis of the research on medieval fishwork.

8. For an overview: Hoffmann, *The Catch*, chaps. 7–8; James H. Barrett, Alison M. Locker, and Callum M. Roberts, "The Origins of Intensive Marine Fishing in Medieval Europe: the English Evidence," *Proceedings of the Royal Society of London B:*

Biological Sciences 271, no. 1556 (December 2004); Sophia Perdikaris et al., "Across the Fish Event Horizon: A Comparative Approach," in *The Role of Fish in Ancient Time*, ed. H. H. Plogmann (Rahden, Westphalia: Verlag Marie Leidorf, 2007); Richard C. Hoffmann, "Economic Development and Aquatic Ecosystems in Medieval Europe," *American Historical Review* 101, no. 3 (1996); Maryanne Kowaleski, "The Expansion of the South-western Fisheries in Late Medieval England," *Economic History Review* 53, no. 3 (2000); *Cod and Herring: The Archaeology and History of Medieval Sea Fishing*, ed. James H. Barrett and David C. Orton (Oxford: Oxbow Books, 2016); Poul Holm et al., "Accelerated Extractions of North Atlantic Cod and Herring, 1520–1790," *Fish and Fisheries* 23 (August 2021). See essays in *Beyond the Catch: Fisheries of the North Atlantic, the North Sea and the Baltic, 900–1850*, ed. Louis Sicking and Darlene Abreu-Ferreira (Leiden: Brill, 2009).

9. For an overview, see Johanna J. Heymans and Tony J. Pitcher, "A Picasso-esque View of the Marine Ecosystem of Newfoundland and Southern Labrador: Models for the Time Periods 1450 and 1900," *Fisheries Centre Research Reports* 10, no. 5 (1995). For a nuanced view of this in the Newfoundland context, see Matthew W. Betts et al., "Zooarchaeology of the Historic Cod Fishery in Newfoundland and Labrador, Canada," *Journal of the North Atlantic* 9, no. 24 (2014). Size: A. L. Merson, ed., *The Third Book of Remembrance of Southampton, 1514–1602: Volume III (1573–1589)*, Southampton Records Series, vol. 8 (Southampton: Southampton University Press, 1965), 23. Biomass: Johanna J. Heymans and Tony J. Pitcher, "A Model of the Marine Ecosystem of Newfoundland and Southern Labrador (2J3KLNO) in the Time Periods 1985–1987 and 1995–1997," *Fisheries Centre Research Reports* 10, no. 5 (2002): 48–19. Pope gives seventy-five thousand metric tons live catch as the potential take around 1580, assuming the 350 ships cited in Parkhurst. He notes that the actual number of ships might have been much higher, and therefore gives two hundred thousand metric tons as a potential upper limit for the catch in 1580. Pope, *Fish into Wine*, 19.

10. Emmanuel Le Roy Ladurie, *The Peasants of Languedoc*, trans. John Day (Urbana: University of Illinois Press, 1974), 11; Roger Barlow, *A Brief Summe of Geographie*, vol. 69, ed. E.G.R. Taylor, The Hakluyt Society Publications (London, 1932), 35. Quote: Lope Hurtado de Mendoza et al., *Correspondance d'un ambassadeur castillan au Portugal dans les années 1530, Lope Hurtado de Mendoza* (Paris and Lisbon: Centre culturel Calouste Gulbenkian/ Commission nationale pour les commémorations des découvertes portugaises, 2001), 480.

11. A good summary of agricultural practices is in Brian Donahue, *The Great Meadow: Farmers and the Land in Colonial Concord* (New Haven: Yale University Press, 2004), chap 3. For a comparison to Indigenous and colonial agriculture in the Americas, see John C. Super, *Food, Conquest, and Colonization in Sixteenth-Century Spanish America* (Albuquerque: University of New Mexico Press, 1988), 20–23. Geoffrey Parker, *Global Crisis: War, Climate Change and Catastrophe in the Seventeenth Century* (New Haven: Yale University Press, 2014), 55–76.

12. On climate in general: Wolfgang Behringer, *A Cultural History of Climate* (Cambridge: Polity, 2010); Dagomar Degroot et al., "Towards a Rigorous Understanding of Societal Responses to Climate Change," *Nature* 591, no. 7851 (2021); Bruce Campbell, *The Great Transition: Climate, Disease and Society in the Late-Medieval World* (Cambridge: Cambridge University Press, 2016). Longer, deeper Spörer Minimum: Chantal Camenisch et al., "The 1430s: A Cold Period of Extraordinary Internal Climate Variability during the Early Spörer Minimum with Social and Economic Impacts in North-western and Central Europe," *Climate of the Past* 12, no. 11 (December 2016): 2116. M. G. Ogurtsov suggests up to 150 years in "The Spörer Minimum Was Deep," *Advances in Space Research* 64, no. 5 (2019).

13. Sam White, *A Cold Welcome: The Little Ice Age and Europe's Encounter with North America* (Cambridge, MA: Harvard University Press, 2017), 202–3; Dagomar Degroot, *The Frigid Golden Age: Climate Change, the Little Ice Age, and the Dutch Republic, 1560–1720* (New York: Cambridge University Press, 2018); Astrid E. J. Ogilvie, "Fisheries, Climate and Sea Ice in Iceland: An Historical Perspective," *Marine Resources and Human Societies in the North Atlantic since 1500* (1997); Charles H. Greene et al., "Arctic Climate Change and Its Impacts on the Ecology of the North Atlantic," *Ecology* 89, no. 11 (2008; George A. Rose, "Reconciling Overfishing and Climate Change with Stock Dynamics of Atlantic Cod (Gadus morhua) over 500 Years," *Canadian Journal of Fisheries and Aquatic Sciences* 61, no. 9 (2004).

14. *Cities and Social Change in Early Modern France*, trans. Sian Reynolds, ed. Philip Benedict (London: Routledge, 1992), 7–66. See especially table 1.2 for urban population estimates. For a regional explanation of this long-term demographic trend, Le Roy Ladurie, *The Peasants of Languedoc*.

15. Poul Holm et al., "The North Atlantic Fish Revolution (ca. AD 1500)," *Quaternary Research* 98 (April 2019); Holm et al., "Accelerated Extractions of North Atlantic Cod and Herring, 1520–1790"; Poul Holm et al., "New Challenges for the Human Oceans Past Agenda," *Open Research Europe* 2, no. 114 (2022).

16. 1597 train oil: NAW, 4:78. On whales, oil, and industry, see Demuth, *Floating Coast: An Environmental History of the Bering Strait*; Huxley Barkham, *Los vascos en el marco Atlántico Norte*; Huxley, "La industria pesquera en el País Vasco peninsular al principio de la Edad Moderna"; Louwrens Hacquebord and Dag Avango, "Settlements in an Arctic Resource Frontier Region," *Arctic Anthropology* 46, nos. 1–2 (2009). Seals: Godinho, *Os descobrimentos e a economia mundial*, 4:132.

17. White cites and reinforces Bolster: White, *A Cold Welcome*, 203; Bolster, *The Mortal Sea*, 34.

18. Holm et al., "The North Atlantic Fish Revolution (ca. AD 1500)"; Holm et al., "Accelerated Extractions of North Atlantic Cod and Herring, 1520–1790"; Arnved Nedkvitne, "*Mens Bønderne seilte og Jægterne for*": *Nordnorsk og vestnorsk kystøkonomi 1500–1730* (Bergen: Universitetsforlaget, 1988), 25, 42. Also found in Poul Holm, "The Decline in Fishery and Fish Trade from West Jutland, c. 1550–1860," in *Facing*

the North Sea: West Jutland and the World, ed. Mette Guldberg, Poul Holm, and Per Kristian Mades, Proceedings of the Ribe Conference, April 6–8, 1992 (Esbjerg: Fiskeri-og Søgartmuseet, 1993), table 3; Barbara Harvey, *Living and Dying in England, 1100–1540: The Monastic Experience* (Oxford: Clarendon, 1993), 47. Harvey notes that at least half of all the fish was preserved, and "nearly the whole was sea-fish."

19. See a summary of this pro-novelty position in Bolster, *The Mortal Sea,* 34–48. Quote: Turgeon, "Codfish, Consumption and Colonization,"49. Parkhurst: NAW, 4:7. Gran Capitano: Giovanni Battista Ramusio, *Delle nauigationi et viaggi,* 3 vols. (Venice: Luca Antonio Giunti, 1550–59), vol. 3; Alfonse, *Les voyages auantureux,* 27–28. Shetland cod: William Garrard, *The Arte of VVarre Beeing the Onely Rare Booke of Myllitarie Profession* (London: Roger VVarde, 1591), 362. Sahara fisheries: Ramusio, *Delle nauigationi et viaggi,* 1:301. Spain: Alessandro Magno, "Account of Alessandro Magno's Journeys to Cyprus, Egypt, Spain, England, Flanders, Germany and Brescia, 1557–65," V.a. 259, Folger Shakespeare Library. Mountain of Gold: The original quote comes from Adriaen Coenen's *Visboek,* written in the 1570s. On this text, see Christiaan Van Bochove, "The 'Golden Mountain': An Economic Analysis of Holland's Early Modern Herring Fisheries," in Sicking and Abreu-Ferreira, *Beyond the Catch,* 209–43.

20. AHPG-GPAH 3/3354, A:23r–23v; 3/0335, A:49r–v.

21. Olaus Magnus, *A Description of the Northern Peoples (Rome 1555),* 3 vols., ed. P. G. Foote (London: Hakluyt Society, 1998, vol. 3, book 21, chaps. 24–25.

22. Evan T. Jones, "England's Icelandic Fishery in the Early Modern Period," in *England's Sea Fisheries: The Commercial Sea Fisheries of England and Wales since 1300,* ed. David Starkey, Christopher Reid, and John Ramster (London: Chatham, 2003), 3; Public Record Office, *Letters and Papers, Foreign and Domestic, of the Reign of Henry VIII,* vol. 4, no 5101, "Shipping." In 1593, only forty-five ships were registered from the same vicinity. BL, Add MS 34729, fol. 63.

23. On these fisheries, see A. R. Michell, "The European Fisheries in Early Modern Europe," in *The Economic Organization of Early Modern Europe,* ed. C. H. Wilson, The Cambridge Economic History of Europe (Cambridge: Cambridge University Press, 1977). Christiaan Van Bochove, "De Hollandse haringvisserij tijdens de vroegmoderne tijd," *Tijdschrift voor sociale en economische geschiedenis* 1, no. 1 (2004); A. P. van Vliet, *Vissers en kapers: De zeevisserij vanuit hed Maasmondegebied en de Dunkierker kapers (ca. 1580–1648)* (s'Gravenshage: Stiching Hollandse Historische Reeks, 1994); Michel Mollat, *Histoire des peches maritimes en France* (Toulouse: Privat, 1987).

24. Michell, "The European Fisheries in Early Modern Europe," 148; *Calendar of the Carew Manuscripts:, Preserved in the Archiepiscopal Library at Lambeth, 1515–1574,* ed. J. S. Brewer and W. Bullen (London: Longmans, Green, Reader & Dyer, 1867), 81, 422–23. As in the North Sea, these were likely smaller vessels than those that went to Terra Nova. The Irish Sea fishery was especially important for Basque

fishworkers, often those from the same communities that dispatched ships to the northwest Atlantic. Public Record Office, *Letters and Papers, Foreign and Domestic, of the Reign of Henry VIII*, vol. 4, no. 5101; BL, West Papers, vol. III, Add. Ms. 34729, fol. 63: "A True Reporte of All the Shippes and Barkes That Have This Yeare Made Their Voyage into Islande, and Returned and Payed the Compocition of Lynge and Codd." *Mary Rose*: William F. Hutchinson et al., "The Globalization of Naval Provisioning: Ancient DNA and Stable Isotope Analyses of Stored Cod from the Wreck of the *Mary Rose*, AD 1545," *Royal Society Open Science* 2, no. 9 (September 2015).

25. Ramusio, *Navigazioni e viaggi*, 1:261; BSB Codices Hispanici 27, fol. 61; Mary-Elena Carr and Edward J. Kearns, "Production Regimes in Four Eastern Boundary Current Systems," *Deep Sea Research, Part II: Topical Studies in Oceanography* 50, nos. 22–26 (2003); NAW, 1:79; Richard Hakluyt, *The Principal Navigations, Voyages, Traffiques, and Discoveries of the English Nation*, vol. 11: *Africa*, ed. Edmund Goldsmid (Edinburgh: E. & G. Goldsmid, 1885), 86, 131.

26. "Extraict des observations de Nicolay d'Arfeville, daulphinois, premier cosmographe du roy . . ." (1582), BnF Ms. Fr. 20008, fol. 10r.

27. Carmen Mena-García, "Nuevos datos sobre bastimentos y envases en armadas y flotas de la Carrera," *Revista de Indias* 64, no. 231 (2004), 469–71, table on 471. Cites original as "Cargo y data de la cenuta del factor Francisco Duarte," Archivo general de Indias, Contaduria, 288.

28. Chris Otter, *Diet for a Large Planet: Industrial Britain, Food Systems, and World Ecology* (Chicago: University of Chicago Press, 2020); Kenneth Pomeranz, *The Great Divergence: China, Europe, and the Making of the Modern World Economy* (Princeton: Princeton University Press, 2000, 275.

6. Circulations

1. BnF Ms.Fr. 24269, "Guynée," fols. 51r–52v; "Bresil," fols. 53r–55r; Terra Nova, fol. 55r. The manuscript is entitled "Regyme pour congnoistre la latitude de la region et aussi la haulteur de la ligne equinotialle sur nostre orison." It was probably written in the mid-1540s, perhaps 1544, judging by the dates on the last page. We do not know for sure who wrote this text, and while names are written on the last page, we cannot be certain if these refer to the authors. On the vocabularies, see David Dalby and P.E.H. Hair, " 'Le langaige du Bresil': A Tupi Vocabulary of the 1540s," *Transactions of the Philological Society* 65, no. 1 (1966); D. Dalby and P.E.H. Hair, 'Le langaige de Guynee': A Sixteenth Century Vocabulary from the Pepper Coast," *African Language Studies* 5 (1964): 174–91.

2. Peter Bakker, " "The Language of the Coast Tribes Is Half Basque": A Basque-American Indian Pidgin in Use between Europeans and Native Americans in North America, ca. 1540–ca. 1640," *Anthropological Linguistics* 31, nos. 3–4 (1989); Peter Bakker, "A Basque Etymology for the Amerindian Tribal Name 'Iroquois,' " *Anuario*

del Seminario de Filología Vasca" Julio de Urquijo" 14, no. 2 (1991); Peter Bakker, "Language Contact and Pidginization in Davis Strait, Hudson Strait, and the Gulf of Saint Lawrence (Northeast Canada)," *Trends in Linguistics Studies and Monographs* 88 (1996).

3. *Txalupas:* Brad Loewen, "Sea Change: Indigenous Navigation and Relations with Basques around the Gulf of Saint Lawrence, c. 1500–1700." In Greer, *Before Canada.* English voyage: Alison M. Quinn and David B. Quinn, *The English New England Voyages, 1602–1608,* Works issued by the Hakluyt Society, 2nd ser., no. 161 (London: Routledge, 2016), 117.

4. An extremely useful overview of the work on northwest Atlantic Indigenous history prior to 1990, which laid out the basic ideas explored in this section, can be found in Ralph T. Pasture, "Native History in the Atlantic Region during the Colonial Period," *Acadiensis* 20, no. 1 (1990); Bahar, *Storm of the Sea.* A discussion of the evidence and whether or not Corte Real or Sebastian Caboto encountered Beothuk peoples is in Gilbert, "Beothuk-European Contact in the 16th Century," 25–30.

5. Bruce J. Bourque and Ruth Holmes Whitehead, "Tarrentines and the Introduction of European Trade Goods in the Gulf of Maine," *Ethnohistory* 32, no. 4 (Autumn 1985); Marcel Moussette, "A Universe under Strain: Amerindian Nations in Northeastern North America in the 16th century," *Post-Medieval Archaeology* 43, no. 1 (2013).

6. See Brad Loewen, "Intertwined Enigmas: Basques and Saint Lawrence Iroquoians in the Sixteenth Century," in *Contact in the 16th Century: Networks among Fishers, Foragers, and Farmers,* ed. Brad Loewen and Claude Chapdelaine (Ottawa: University of Ottawa Press, 2016). See too Sergio Escribano Ruiz et al., "Basque Fishing Crews' Pottery in Canada: A Transatlantic Evaluation of Ceramic Remains Left by an Early Modern Global Enterprise" (paper presented at the GlobalPottery 1: Historical Archaeology and Archaeometry for Societies in Contact, Oxford, 2014).

7. Matthew McKenzie, "Reassembling the Greater Gulf: Northwest Atlantic Environmental History and the Gulf of St. Lawrence System," in *The Greater Gulf: Essays on the Environmental History of the Gulf of St. Lawrence,* ed. Claire E. Campbell, Brian Payena, and Edward MacDonald (Montréal: McGill-Queens University Press, 2019), 13–31.

8. On Beothuk behavior: Holly, Wolff, and Erwin, "The Ties That Bind and Divide"; Ingeborg Marshall, *A History and Ethnography of the Beothuk* (Montréal: McGill-Queen's University Press, 2014); Pastore, "The Collapse of the Beothuk World"; Turgeon, "French Fishers, Fur Traders, and Amerindians during the Sixteenth Century"; Ralph T. Pastore, "Fishermen, Furriers, and Beothuks: The Economy of Extinction," *Man in the Northeast* 33, no. 3 (1987).

9. Alfonse, *Les voyages auantureux,* fol. 28.

10. For overviews of the Arctic historical context: Howkins, *The Polar Regions: An Environmental History;* William W. Fitzhugh, *Prehistoric Maritime Adaptations of the*

Circumpolar Zone, World Anthropology (Boston: De Gruyter Mouton, 1975); Richard Vaughan, *The Arctic: A History* (Dover, NH: A. Sutton, 1994); Wynn, *Canada and Arctic North America: An Environmental History*. More recently there has been a turn toward the broader polar regions, which include the Antarctic. See *The Cambridge History of the Polar Regions*, ed. Adrian Howkins and Peder Roberts (Cambridge: Cambridge University Press, 2023).

11. Bjarne Grønnow, "The Initial Peopling of the Circumpolar North," in Howkins and Roberts, *The Cambridge History of the Polar Regions*. Conflict: AM Saint Malo BB 11, fol. 78, quote 85v.

12. Lisa Rankin, Matthew Beaudoin, and Natalie Brewster, "Southern Exposure: The Inuit of Sandwich Bay, Labrador," in *Settlement, Subsistence and Change among the Labrador Inuit: The Nunatsiavummuit Experience* (Winnepeg: University of Manitoba Press, 2012); Lisa Rankin, Marianne Stopp, and Amanda Crompton, "Introduction: Les Inuit au Labrador méridional/Introduction: The Inuit in Southern Labrador," *Études/Inuit/Studies* 39, no. 1 (2015); Elliot H. Blair, "Reconsidering the Precolumbian Presence of Venetian Glass Beads in Alaska," *American Antiquity* 86, no. 3 (2021); Michael L. Kunz and Robin O. Mills, "A Precolumbian Presence of Venetian Glass Trade Beads in Arctic Alaska," *American Antiquity* 86, no. 2 (2021). Quote: Lisa Rankin, "Labrador Inuit at the Crossroads of Cultural Interaction," in Greer, *Before Canada*, 193.

13. 1560 mariner: *Europeans in West Africa, 1450–1560: Documents to Illustrate the Nature and Scope of Portuguese Enterprise in West Africa, the Abortive Attempt of Castilians to Create an Empire There, and the Early English Voyages to Barbary and Guinea*, 2 vols., ed. and trans. John W. Blake (London: Hakluyt Society, 1942), 2:430–31, doc. 147. Brasile: NAW, 4:38. Literary reference: excerpt from *Hyckscorner*, c. 1510–12, NAW, 1:128. For a study of very early Atlantic circuits that influenced English interaction with Terra Nova, see Heather Dalton, *Merchants and Explorers: Roger Barlow, Sebastian Cabot, and Networks of Atlantic Exchange, 1500–1560* (New York: Oxford University Press, 2016).

14. Alfonse: Jean Fonteneau and Georges Musset, *La cosmographie avec l'espère et régime du soleil et du nord par Jean Fonteneau dit Alfonse de Saintonge*, ed. Georges Musset (Paris, 1904), 134. Flanders ambush: *Biggar, Cartier and Roberval*, 467. Greenland: Magnus, *Description of the Northern Peoples*, 1:104.

15. Rut: Biggar, *Precursors*, 165–68. Piracy: Olaf Janzen, "The Problem of Piracy in the Newfoundland Fishery in the Aftermath of the War of the Spanish Succession," in *Research in Maritime History No. 52: War and Trade in Eighteenth-Century Newfoundland* (Saint John's, NL: International Maritime Economic History Association, 2013). See the documents in chapter 70, "Privateering and Piracy Become Endemic, 1584–1596," in NAW, 4:45–55.

16. Information on the Norman voyages is taken from two surveys conducted at the end of the nineteenth century: Bréard and Bréard, *Documents relatifs à la marine*

normande; E. Gosselin and Charles de Beaurepaire, *Documents authentiques et in-édits pour servir àl'histoire de la marine normande et du commerce rouennais pendant les XVIe et XVIIe siècles* (Rouen: Impr. de H. Boissel, 1876). Rouen merchants: Gayle K. Brunelle, *The New World Merchants of Rouen* (Kirksville, MO: Sixteenth Century Journal Publishers, 1991). Havre merchants: AM du Havre CC 36. *Perle*: ADC 8 E 6508, fols. 79v, 92.

17. AM Saint Jean-de-Luz 3 EE1, no.1.

18. On return voyages, see ADCM 3 E 1 145(2), notaire Tharazon, March 4, 1567. 1611 reference: Gillian T. Cell, *Newfoundland Discovered: English Attempts at Colonisation, 1610–1630* (London: Hakluyt Society, 1982), 62.

Part 3. Work

Epigraphs: *The Book of the Thousand Nights and a Night*, trans. Richard F. Burton (London, 1888), 1:78; Giovanni Maria Bonardo, *Della miseria et eccellenza della vita humana* (Venice: Fabio, Augustini & Zoppini Fratelli, 1586), fol. 9r.

7. Fishwork

1. FSL L.b. 340, fols. 4v, 9v.

2. The name appears in several forms across different records, including de la Rerreria and de Larerria. AHPG-GPAH 1/2578, I:11v; AHPG-GPAH 1/2567,E:103r–103v; AHPG-GPAH 1/2567,E:103r–103v.

3. ADSM Fonds communales de Rouen, B 1, fol. 11.

4. From transcript in Xosé Manuel Pereira Fernández, "Los mareantes pontevedreses y la pesca de altura en el siglo XVI," *Cuadernos de estudios gallegos* 52, no. 118 (2005): 300.

5. Jennifer Lee Johnson, "Eating and Existence on an Island in Southern Uganda," *Comparative Studies of South Asia, Africa and the Middle East* 37, no. 1 (2017); Jennifer Lee Johnson, "Fishwork in Uganda: A Multispecies Ethnohistory about Fish, People, and Ideas about Fish and People" (PhD diss., University of Michigan, 2014).

6. Quote: Fagan, *Fishing*, 21. See too Fagan, *Fish on Friday*; John R. Gillis, *The Human Shore: Seacoasts in History* (Chicago: University of Chicago Press, 2012); Rozwadowski, *Vast Expanses*; James M. Acheson, "Anthropology of Fishing," *Annual Review of Anthropology* 10, no. 1 (1981).

7. Matthew McKenzie, *Breaking the Banks: Representations and Realities in New England Fisheries, 1866–1966* (Boston: University of Massachusetts Press, 2018).

8. Lauren A. Benton, *A Search for Sovereignty: Law and Geography in European Empires, 1400–1900* (New York: Cambridge University Press, 2010).

9. Thomas Callander Wade, *Acta Curiae Admirallatus Scotiae, 6th Sept. 1557–11th March 1561–2* (Edinburgh: Printed for the Stair Society by R. Maclehose, 1937), 179, 243, case *Schothart v. Quhitheid*. On Scottish piracy and Iceland: on June 2, 1523

a letter between two English royal officials noted that "the Scots are going to set forth six or seven ships to the Islands, to intercept the Iceland fleet on their way home." Public Record Office, *Letters and Papers, Foreign and Domestic, of the Reign of Henry VIII*, 3:3071.

10. *Aberdeen Council Letters*, ed. Louise Barbara Taylor, 6 vols., vol. 1: 1552–1633 (London: Oxford University Press), 68–69.

11. For one history of the relation between maritime work and identity, see Daviken Studnicki-Gizbert, *A Nation upon the Ocean Sea: Portugal's Atlantic Diaspora and the Crisis of the Spanish Empire, 1492–1640* (Oxford: Oxford University Press, 2007).

12. Andreas Hess, " 'Working the Waves': The Plebeian Culture and Moral Economy of Traditional Basque Fishing Brotherhoods," *Journal of Interdisciplinary History* 40, no. 4 (2010).

13. The complete financial records of the *James* are held in the Folger Shakespeare Library, L.b.340. A partial transcript can be found in Ernest R. Cooper, "The Dunwich Iceland Ships," *The Mariner's Mirror* 25, no. 2 (January 1939).

14. Lisa Norling, "Working Women Who Got Wet: A Global Survey of Women in Premodern and Early Modern Fisheries," in *A World at Sea: Maritime Practices and Global History*, ed. Lauren Benton and Nathan Perl-Rosenthal (Philadelphia: University of Pennsylvania Press, 2020); Peter E. Pope, "Fisher Men at Work: The Material Culture of the Champ Paya Fishing Room as a Gendered Site," in *Tu sais, mon vieux Jean-Pierre: Essays on the Archaeology and History of New France and Canadian Culture in Honour of Jean-Pierre Chrestien* (Ottawa: University of Ottawa Press, 2017). Quote: NAW, 4:6.

15. Darlene Abreu-Ferreira, "Fishmongers and Shipowners: Women in Maritime Communities of Early Modern Portugal," *Sixteenth Century Journal* 31, special issue: "Gender in Early Modern Europe," no. 1 (2000); Abreu-Ferreira, "Terra Nova Through the Iberian Looking Glass"; Annette de Wit, "Women in Dutch Fishing Communities: The Cases of Ter Heijde and Maassluis, c. 1600–1700," in Sicking and Abreu-Ferreira, *Beyond the Catch*; Annette de Wit, *Leven, werken en geloven in zeevarende gemeenschappen: Schiedam, Maassluis en Ter Heijde in de zeventiende eeuw* (Amsterdam: Aksant, 2008). See as an example AHPG-GPAH 1/2579,A:5v–6v. Doña Maria Sebastian of Ayçcarnaçabal lent Domingo de Ibarra, owner of *Santa Maria de la Concecion*, a sum of money to outfit his ship in 1564. She was owed 40 ducats and one *grumete*'s share in repayment.

16. Peter E. Pope, "Modernization on Hold: The Traditional Character of the Newfoundland Cod Fishery in the Seventeenth Century," *International Journal of Maritime History* 15, no. 2 (2003); Pope, *Fish into Wine*, 21–32, quote p. 30. On the knowledge of fishwork more broadly, see James M. Acheson, "Anthropology of Fishing," *Annual Review of Anthropology* (1981): 275–316; Rob van Ginkel, "A Texel Fishing Lineage: The Social Dynamic and Economic Logic of Family Firms," *Maritime Studies* 13, no. 1 (2014); Olsen and Thuen, "Secret Places."

17. *The Tangier Papers of Samuel Pepys*, ed. Edwin Chappell (London: Navy Records Society, 1935), 112.
18. Charles O. Frake, "Cognitive Maps of Time and Tide among Medieval Seafarers," *Man* 20, no. 2 (1985).
19. Gísli Pálsson, "Enskilment at Sea," *Man* 29, no. 4 (1994), 920.

8. Killing

1. *The New Found Land of Stephen Parmenius*, 170. Baskets: Biggar, *Precursors*, 20.
2. Dalla Costa and Chilese, *Our Mother Ocean*, 12–20, 30.
3. NAW, 4:6. On fishing techniques: Pope, *Fish into Wine*, 21–31. Long-term overviews in Charles de La Morandière, *La pêche française de la morue à terre-neuve du XVIe siècle à nos jours: Son importance économique, sociale et politique* (Paris: École pratique des hautes études, 1967); and Pope, "Transformation of the Maritime Cultural Landscape of Atlantic Canada by Migratory European Fishermen, 1500–1800." Several scholars have noted that English drying methods differed from those of other crews due to their limited access to salt. Cell, *English Enterprise in Newfoundland*, 21–23.
4. For a description of the green fishery, see Innis, *The Cod Fisheries*, 47–49. Olaf Janzen, "The Logic of English Saltcod: An Historiographical Revision," *The Northern Mariner/Le marin du nord* 23, no. 2 (2013): 128–29. For an example of a voyage mixing wet and dry fish, see NAW, 4:15.
5. Shoemaker, "A Typology of Colonialism."
6. National Archives, HCA, file 45, no. 301. The case is excerpted and translated in part in *Select Pleas in the Court of Admiralty*, vol. 1: 1527–1545, ed. Reginald G. Marsden (London: Selden Society, 1894), 148–49.
7. The numbers herein are rough estimates, given our lack of data on the size and biology of sixteenth-century codfish and how processing would have altered their nutrition. Here I am assuming a ninety-day fishing season, May–July. Seventeenth-century French sources estimated a *morue* as approximately 2.5 kilograms. This is presumably the flesh remaining after trimming and drying, as sold in the marketplace. See Jacqueline Hersart de la Villemarqué, *La pêche morutière française de 1500 à 1950: Statistiques, climat et société* (Plouzané: IFREMER, 1995), 33. Modern commercially available *bacalao* is approximately 50–70 kilocalories per 100 grams, or 500–700 kilocalories per kilogram. A dry-salted codfish as sold in the market may therefore have contained around 1,250–1,750 kilocalories. A thousand codfish would contain something over a million kilocalories. A cargo of 70,000 fish might therefore comprise between 87.5 and 122.5 million kilocalories. This is necessarily a conjecture, and any number of variables would have affected the total calories, but it does indicate the range of possibilities for how much nutrition could be packed into a single ship. On the *Mary Rose*: Douglas McElvogue, *Tudor Warship Mary Rose* (London: Bloomsbury, 2015), 43. Hutchinson et al., "The Globalization of Naval Provisioning."

8. For Normandy, see ships from Granville that appear in the records of Saint Malo in the 1590s: AM Saint Malo BB 8, fols. 21, 37, 177v. See too Mollat, *Le commerce maritime normand*; Charles de la Morandière, "Les ports normands et la grande pêche à Terre Neuve," *Le Mois à Caen* (1967). England: Matthews, "A History of the West of England–Newfoundland Fishery"; Walter James Harte, "Some Evidence of Trade between Exeter and Newfoundland up to 1600" (paper presented at the Devonshire Association for the Advancement of Science, Literature and Art, 1932). French cities: Turgeon, "Pour redécouvrir notre 16 siècle"; Turgeon, *Une histoire de la Nouvelle France: Français et amérindiens au XVI siècle*.

9. In contrast to my own estimates, Brad Loewen believes that "by 1550, the seasonal fishing population had risen to around 20,000 men and boys, and it remained roughly at this level until the end of the century." This estimate assumes five hundred "French" ships sailing by 1550, plus contingents from England, Portugal, and northern Spain. Loewen and Chapdelaine, *Contact in the 16th Century*, 3.

10. NAW, 1:168–71.

11. Seville trade: Huguette Chaunu, Pierre Chaunu, and Guy Arbellot, *Séville et l'Atlantique, 1504–1650*, 8 vols. (Paris: A. Colin, 1955), vols. 2–3 for sixteenth-century statistics, 1565 in vol. 3, 68–75.

12. Patrick W. Hayes et al., "European Naval Diets in the Sixteenth Century: A Quantitative Method for Comparative and Nutritional Analysis," *Historical Methods: A Journal of Quantitative and Interdisciplinary History* (March 2019): 6–7. See too Grenier, Stevens, and Bernier, *The Underwater Archaeology of Red Bay*, 1:58.

13. Holm et al., "The North Atlantic Fish Revolution (ca. AD 1500)"; Holm et al., "Accelerated Extractions of North Atlantic Cod and Herring, 1520–1790." John Nicholls, Bernard Allaire, and Poul Holm, "The Capacity Trend Method: A New Approach for Enumerating the Newfoundland Cod Fisheries (1675–1790)," *Historical Methods: A Journal of Quantitative and Interdisciplinary History* 54, no. 2 (2021): 90.

14. Birds: NAW, 1:116, no. 80. 1502 London: NAW, 1:110, no. 78. Corte Real: Biggar, *Precursors*, 64. Cartier: Biggar, *Cartier and Roberval*, doc. LXXVI, 82. Rouen: NAW, 1:157, nos. 127–28. Abductions in general: Caroline Dodds Pennock, *On Savage Shores: How Indigenous Americans Discovered Europe* (New York: Penguin Random House 2023).

15. A transcript of the letter can be found in *Archives historiques de Saintonge et Aunis*, vol. 6 (Saintes: Librarie de Mme. Z. Mortreuil, 1879), 387–89.

16. On whaling in southern Labrador, there is quite a rich literature. See Grenier, Stevens, and Bernier, *The Underwater Archaeology of Red Bay*, especially vol. 1, for an excellent summary and exploration of whaling ships. See too Michael Barkham, "French Basque 'New Found Land' Entrepreneurs and the Import of Codfish and Whale Oil to Northern Spain, c. 1580 to c. 1620: The Case of Adam de Chibau, Burgess of Saint-Jean-de-Luz and 'Sieur de St. Julien,'" *Newfoundland and Labrador Studies* 10, no. 1 (1994); Barkham, "The Spanish Province of Terranova"; Barkham,

"The Basque Whaling Establishments in Labrador, 1536–1632—A Summary"; Sicking and Abreu-Ferreira, *Los vascos en el marco Atlántico Norte*; Charles A. Martijn, Selma Barkham, and Michael M. Barkham, "Basques? Beothuk? Innu? Inuit? or St. Lawrence Iroquoians? The Whalers on the 1546 Desceliers Map, Seen through the Eyes of Different Beholders," *Newfoundland and Labrador Studies* 19, no. 1 (2003). On a wider Atlantic context, see Cristina Brito et al., "Digging into Our Whaling Past: Addressing the Portuguese Influence in the Early Modern Exploitation of Whales in the Atlantic," in *Environmental History in the Making*, vol. 2: *Acting*, ed. Cristina Joanaz de Melo, Estelita Vaz, and Lígia M. Costa Pinto (Cham: Springer International, 2017); Gordon Jackson, *The British Whaling Trade* (Liverpool: Liverpool University Press, 2005; Vicki Ellen Szabo, *Monstrous Fishes and the Mead-Dark Sea: Whaling in the Medieval North Atlantic*, Northern Worlds (Leiden: Brill, 2008); Nina Vieira, "A Comparative Approach to Historical Whaling Techniques: Transfer of Knowledge in the 17th Century from the Biscay to Brazil," in *Cross-cultural Exchange and the Circulation of Knowledge in the First Global Age*, ed. Amélia Polónia et al. (Lisbon: CITCEM—Centro de Investigação Transdisciplinar Cultura, Espaço e Memória, 2018).

17. Schlesinger and Stabler, *André Thevet's North America*, 23.

18. Brad Loewen, "Historical Data on the Impact of 16th-Century Basque Whaling on Right and Bowhead Whales in the Western North Atlantic," *Canadian Zooarchaeology* 26 (2009). On ovens: Selma Huxley Barkham, "Building Materials for Canada in 1566," *Bulletin of the Association for Preservation Technology* (1973).

19. For a representative example, in his recent survey of Canadian environmental history, James Murton devotes a few paragraphs to fishing and most of a chapter to the fur trade when describing early colonial contact. Murton, *Canadians and Their Natural Environment: A History.* See chapter 3 for the colonial era.

20. Turgeon, *Une histoire de la Nouvelle France: Français et amérindiens au XVI siècle*, 93–96; Jack Bouchard, " 'Gens sauvages et estranges': Amerindians and the Fishery in the Sixteenth-Century Gulf of Saint Lawrence," in *The Greater Gulf: Essays on the Environmental History of the Gulf of St Lawrence*, ed. Claire Campbell, Brian Payne, and Edward MacDonald (Montréal: McGill-Queen's University Press, 2020).

21. Clause "et autres choses et marchandises": Turgeon, *Une histoire de la Nouvelle France: Français et amérindiens au XVI siècle*, 101. Hollander ship: Stadsarchief Amsterdam, Notarial archief, 75/99–101, October 10, 1596.

22. As several scholars have pointed out, mariners on the Terra Nova fishery enjoyed ample provisions compared to other mariners in the early Atlantic or even their families back home. The daily nutrition provided by these provisions for a fishworker or whaler may have been around four thousand calories. A good summary of the diets of fishworkers and whalers in Newfoundland, and their relative nutritional value, can be found in Grenier, Stevens, and Bernier, *The Underwater Archaeology of Red Bay*, 1:56–58.

23. See Jack Bouchard, "Fishwork Is for the Birds: Humans and Birds in the Sixteenth-Century Northwest Atlantic," *Environmental History* 29, no. 3 (2024); Gange, *The Frayed Atlantic Edge: A Historian's Journey from Shetland to the Channel*, 20–22, 70–71. The archaeologist Peter Pope has written an important study on the use of seabirds by sixteenth-century European fishworkers in which he has catalogued the different seabird colonies used in the early fishery. Peter E. Pope, "Early Migratory Fishermen and Newfoundland's Seabird Colonies," *Journal of the North Atlantic*, no. 1 (special volume) (2009).

24. Cartier, *Relation originale du voyage de Jacques Cartier au Canada en 1534*, 1–2. Despite what Cartier says here, *Apponatz* was an Algonkian word for auks.

25. Flayed auks: NAW, 1:207.

26. Elizabeth Kolbert, *The Sixth Extinction: An Unnatural History* (New York: Henry Holt, 2014), 47–69. Fishing near bird grounds: Pope, "Early Migratory Fishermen and Newfoundland's Seabird Colonies," 60.

27. Firewood has only recently received attention, albeit in a later context at Newfoundland, in Arianne Sedef Urus, " 'A Spirit of Encroachment': Trees, Cod, and the Political Ecology of Empire in the Newfoundland Fisheries, 1763–1783," *Environmental History* 28, no. 1, https://www.journals.uchicago.edu/doi/abs/10.1086/722538.

28. Gilbert: NAW, vol. 4, doc. 535. Champlain: Champlain, *Ouevres de Champlain*, 1: 156. Sable Island: Marq De Villiers and Sheila Hirtle, *Sable Island: The Strange Origins and Curious History of a Dune Adrift in the Atlantic* (New York: Walker, 2004).

9. Commons

1. Sources for Gilbert: NAW, vol. 4, doc. 535; and *The New Found Land of Stephen Parmenius*. For this historical context for England, see Kenneth R. Andrews, *Trade, Plunder, and Settlement: Maritime Enterprise and the Genesis of the British Empire, 1480–1630* (Cambridge: Cambridge University Press, 1984).

2. AHPG-GPAH 3/0324, A:117r–118v.

3. In understanding sixteenth-century states as weak and heterogenous systems, I follow Janice E. Thomson, *Mercenaries, Pirates, and Sovereigns: State-Building and Extraterritorial Violence in Early Modern Europe* (Princeton: Princeton University Press, 1994). See too James B. Collins, *The State in Early Modern France* (New York: Cambridge University Press, 1995); Regina Grafe, "Polycentric States: The Spanish Reigns and the 'Failures' of Mercantilism," in *Mercantilism Reimagined: Political Economy in Early Modern Britain and Its Empire*, ed. Philip J. Stern and Carl Wennerlind (Oxord: Oxford University Press, 2014). On the place of urban ports within these states: Kevin C. Robbins, *City on the Ocean Sea: La Rochelle, 1530–1650; Urban Society, Religion, and Politics on the French Atlantic Frontier*, Studies in Medieval and Reformation Traditions (Leiden: Brill, 1997); *Gens de mer ports et cités aux époques ancienne, médiévale et modern*, ed. Eric Guerber and Gérard Le Bouédec

(Rennes: Presses universitaires de Rennes, 2013, 2013); Benedict, *Cities and Social Change in Early Modern France.*

4. AM Saint Jean-de-Luz 1 AA 3, no. 33.

5. Invoking authority: NAW, 4:13–20. Saint Waast: ADSM 1 B Parlement de Normandie, 388, December 23, 1524.

6. On sixteenth-century ship hierarchies: Pérez-Malláina, *Spain's Men of the Sea;* Rediker, *Between the Devil and the Deep Blue Sea; Law, Labour, and Empire: Comparative Perspectives on Seafarers, c. 1500–1800,* ed. Maria Fusaro et al. (London: Palgrave Macmillan, 2015).

7. Ashley Carse, *Beyond the Big Ditch: Politics, Ecology, and Infrastructure at the Panama Canal,* Infrastructures Series (Cambridge: MIT Press, 2014), 94. For state space, see James C. Scott, *The Art of Not Being Governed: An Anarchist History of Upland Southeast Asia* (New Haven: Yale University Press, 2009), especially chapter 2. On information, coercion, and mobile authority in early modern empires, see Benton, *A Search for Sovereignty;* Kenneth J. Banks, *Chasing Empire across the Sea: Communications and the State in the French Atlantic, 1713–1763* (Montréal: McGill-Queen's University Press, 2006); Donna Merwick, *Death of a Notary: Conquest and Change in Colonial New York* (Ithaca: Cornell University Press, 1999).

8. Mawani, *Across Oceans of Law: The Komagata Maru and Jurisdiction in the Time of Empire,* 35–72.

9. Barkham, "The Spanish Province of Terranova."

10. For some of the literature on how historians have understood the premodern commons, see Greer, *Property and Dispossession: Natives, Empires and Land in Early Modern North America;* Donahue, *The Great Meadow: Farmers and the Land in Colonial Concord;* Edward P. Thompson, *Customs in Common: Studies in Traditional Popular Culture* (New York: New Press, 1993); Sean Cadigan, "The Moral Economy of the Commons: Ecology and Equity in the Newfoundland Cod Fishery, 1815–1855," *Labour/Le travail* 43 (1999); Sharika D. Crawford and Ana Isabel Márquez-Pérez, "A Contact Zone: The Turtle Commons of the Western Caribbean," *International Journal of Maritime History* 28, no. 1 (2016).

11. Harold Demsetz, "Toward a Theory of Property Rights," *American Economic Review* 57, no. 2 (1967).

12. John Dee, *General and Rare Memorials Pertayning to the Perfect Arte of Nauigation Annexed to the Paradoxal Cumpas, in Playne: Now First Published: 24. Yeres, After the First Inuention Thereof* (London, 1577), 21. See too Hoffmann, "Economic Development and Aquatic Ecosystems in Medieval Europe"; Richard C. Hoffmann, "Medieval Europeans and Their Aquatic Ecosystems," in *Beiträge zum Göttinger Umwelthistorischen Kolloquium 2007–8,* ed. Bernd Herrmann (Göttingen: Universitatsverlag Göttingen, 2007).

13. Acheson in *The Question of the Commons: The Culture and Ecology of Communal Resources,* ed. Bonnie J. McCay and James M. Acheson, Arizona Studies in Human

Ecology (Tucson: University of Arizona Press, 1987). For a more modern example, see Victoria C. Ramenzoni, "Co-governance, Transregional Maritime Conventions, and Indigenous Customary Practices among Subsistence Fishermen in Ende, Indonesia," *Frontiers in Marine Science* 8 (July 2021).

14. See, for instance, Sandra Pannell, "Of Gods and Monsters: Indigenous Sea Cosmologies, Promiscuous Geographies and the Depths of local Sovereignty," in *A World of Water: Rain, Rivers and Seas in Southeast Asian Histories*, ed. Peter Boomgaard (Leiden: Brill, 2007).

15. Pope, *Fish into Wine*; Pope, "Transformation of the Maritime Cultural Landscape of Atlantic Canada by Migratory European Fishermen, 1500–1800"; Jerry Bannister, "The Fishing Admirals in Eighteenth-Century Newfoundland," *Newfoundland Studies* 17, no. 2 (2001).

16. Parkhurst in NAW, 4:5–7.

17. Colin Scott, "Hunting Territories, Hunting Bosses and Communal Production among Coastal James Bay Cree," *Anthropologica* (1986).

18. Allan Greer, "Commons and Enclosure in the Colonization of North America," *American Historical Review* 117, no. 2 (2012): 366.

19. For numerous examples of English violence, see NAW, 4:45–80; 1593 example on p. 62. La Gran Baya: Biggar, *Cartier and Roberval*, 456.

20. Rouen: ADSM 201 B P, no. 694.Whitehead case: Wade and The Stair, *Acta Curiae Admirallatus Scotiae*, 179–80: "Curia admirallatus Scotie tenta in pretorio burgi de Edinburgh per Davidem Kintor et Richardum trohope vice-admiraldos etc. 7 Dec. 1560." Also summary: xxvii–xxviii.

21. NAW, 4:94.

22. Here I use the updated transcript in José Ignacio Tellechea Idígoras, *Corsarios guipuzcoanos en Terranova, 1552–1555* (Donostia-San Sebastián: Fundación Kutxa, 2000).

23. National Archives, HCA, file 16, no.97: "partibus Izelandie constitutum locum omnino liberum publicumque ac jus piscandi ibidem omnibus commune fuisse."

Part 4. Food

Epigraphs: Desiderius Erasmus. *The Praise of Folly* (1509), trans. John Wilson, accessed via Fordham University Modern History Sourcebook, https://origin-rh.web.fordham.edu/Halsall/mod/1509erasmus-folly.asp; Guy Montgomery, "The A-Z of Healthy Eating," YouTube, August 11, 2020, https://youtu.be/LXSfiBCeR1s?si=ww1tOKKA60-JPQ_A. With permission.

10. *Bourgeois*

1. ADSM 2 E 1, no. 2799, February 1544, supplement, entry for February 23. Entries in this particular register are not numbered by folio. On the de Conihout family and

fishwork in Jumièges, see Jacques Laveque du Pontharouant, *Navires et marins de Jumièges pendant la premiere moitie du XVIème siècle* (self-published, 1997–98). For a study of Norman notarial records and loans that provides useful context for the case of the *Margueritte*, see Francis Brumont, "Les normands à Terre-Neuve au xvie siècle," *Annales de Normandie* 68e année, no. 2 (2018).

2. My thinking about urban centers as loci for Atlantic exchange draws on David H. Sacks, *The Widening Gate: Bristol and the Atlantic Economy, 1450–1700* (Berkeley: University of California Press, 1993). There are several studies of sixteenth-century European ports that include extensive material on Terra Nova voyages and financing. For examples see Etienne Trocmé and Marcel Delafosse, *Le commerce rochelais de la fin du XVe siècle au début du XVIIe* (Paris: A. Colin, 1952); Bernard, *Navires et gens de mer à Bordeaux (vers 1400–vers 1550)*; Amândio Jorge Morais Barros, *Porto: A construção de um espaço maritimo nos alvores dos tempos modernos* (Porto: Universidade do Porto, 2004).

3. A good discussion of the language used in sixteenth-century French maritime contracts, and many features of their basic structure, can be found in Sandrine Kwocz, "Marchands et marins havrais au XVIe siècle. Comment on préparait les expéditions maritimes en 1579," *Études normandes* 41, no. 4 (1992).

4. ADCM 3 E 202, fol. 49v; ADCM 3 E 2149, fol. 7; ADCM 3 E 2147, February 17, 1561; ADCM 3 E 145 (2), n.p.

5. Michel de la Rue is described as an *honorable homme* in a subsequent contract made on the same day, February 23, 1544. For body politic: AM Saint Malo BB 4, 1573, n.p.

6. On Saint Jean-de-Luz, see Barkham, "French Basque 'New Found Land,' " 2.

7. On insurance, see Hilario Casado Alonso, "El mercado internacional de seguros de Burgos en el siglo XVI," *Boletín de la Institución Fernán González* 78, no. 219 (1999).

8. ADSM 2 E 1/489, fol. 490; ADC 8 E 6198, fol. 30.

9. BnF Ms.Fr. 24269, fol. 55v.

10. 1523: Biggar, *Precursors*, 162. Original ADCM, notaire Hémon, fol. 118v, 1562: NAW, 4:99. Charter party for the *Jesus* of Tenby: original in National Archives, HCA, 24, no. 289. Norman ship: *Books of Examinations and Depositions, 1570–1594*, ed. Gertrude Hamilton and Elinor Aubrey, vol. 16, Publications of the Southampton Records Society (Southampton: Southampton Records Society, 1914), 151, no.4. Transition to wages: Pope, *Fish into Wine*, 163–67.

11. For early seventeenth-century records confirming that mariners were older, see ADSM 216 BP Amirauté du Havre, nos. 28, 150, 300. On Innu: Martijn, Barkham, and Barkham, "Basques? Beothuk? Innu? Inuit? or St. Lawrence Iroquoians?" 72. On motley crews and alternatives, see Rediker, *Between the Devil and the Deep Blue Sea*; Marcus Rediker, *Outlaws of the Atlantic: Sailors, Pirates, and Motley Crews in the Age of Sail* (Boston: Beacon, 2014); Daniel Vickers and Vince Walsh, *Young Men and the Sea: Yankee Seafarers in the Age of Sail* (New Haven: Yale University Press, 2005).

12. English quote: Parkhurst in NAW, 4:6. Note on wages: ADCA 1 E 2783. For a study of this problem in a later century, see Romain Grancher, "Fishermen's Taverns: Public Houses and Maritime Labour in an Early Modern French Fishing Community," *International Journal of Maritime History* 28, no. 4 (2016).

13. Robbins notes that in La Rochelle perhaps one-fourth to one-fifth of the population lived directly from the port economy. Robbins, *City on the Ocean Sea*, 56. Rochelais traffic: Trocmé and Delafosse, *Le commerce rochelais de la fin du XVe siècle au début du XVIIe*, 70, table 5. A similar case can be seen in Porto in northern Portugal, whereby in 1558–59, of eighteen ships outfitted in port, six were bound to Terra Nova. Barros, "Porto: A construção de um espaço maritimo nos alvores dos tempos modernos," 616. Saint Malo: AM Saint Malo BB 4, 1573, n.p.

14. *Juliane*: AM du Havre EE 78.

15. Coopers: see example of coopers in Motrico hired to make three hundred new barrels for a whaling voyage in 1547. NAW, 4:93. On Plymouth, see The seventeenth-century example in *Korte Historiael ende journaels aenteyckeninge van verscheyden voyagiens in de vier deelen des wereldts-ronde, als Europa, Africa, Asia ende Amerika*, ed. H. T. Colenbrander (The Hague: Martinus Nijhof, 1911), 23. See too Stadsarchief Amsterdam, Notarial archief 157, fols. 146v–148.

16. See ADSM Fonds communales de Rouen, A 19, entry July 18, 1575. Also ADSM 204 BP Table de marbre de Roue, no. 80.

17. ADCM 3 E 145(2), Tharazon, 1567, n.p. This particular register is badly damaged but has been partly restored by the Archives départmentales de Charente-Maritime.

18. Innis, *The Cod Fisheries*, 34, citing Robert Hitchcock, *A Politique Platt for the Honour of the Prince* (London, 1580).

19. ADSM 2 E 1/409, fol. 191.

20. On notaries, see Merwick, *Death of a Notary. De la Ligurie au Languedoc. Le notaire à l'étude*, ed. Sylvie Desachy and Archives départmentales du Tarn (Albi: Un autre Reg'art, 2012).

21. Richard N. Worth, *Calendar of the Plymouth Municipal Records* (Plymouth: William Brendan & Sons, 1893), 113.

22. ADSM 2 E 1, no. 2799, February 1544, Supplement, entry for February 23. See for another example: ADSM 2 E 2799 (February 1543 Supplement). A contract for several voyages made on February 27, 1544, stipulated that the merchant C. Harmont had to come to Rouen within fifteen days of returning from Terra Nova to repay the loan of 200 *livres*.

23. Storing in Rouen: ADSM Fonds communal de Rouen, B 1, fols. 7, 55.

24. For a discussion of violence at sea and fisheries, see Louis Sicking, *Neptune and the Netherlands: State, Economy, and War at Sea in the Renaissance* (Leiden: Brill, 2004).

25. ADSM Fonds communales de Rouen, A 12, October 22, 1521. Ango: Zeeuws Archief, 243 Admiraliteit te Veere, 1460–1562, no. 7. For another example see ADSM Fonds

communales de Rouen, A 19, entry for July 18, 1575. A call to raise funds to outfit a fleet to protect ships which "vont en Brouage prendre du sel."

26. Ferryman: ANF, notaire Michel de Felin, MC/ET/III/37, January 15, 1550. San Sebastián: this is from the 1850 edition of Isasti's 1625 description of Guipuzcoa. Lope Martínez de Isasti, *Compendio historial de la Provincia de Guipuzcoa*, ed. Ramon de Guereca (San Sebastián: Ignacio Ramon Baroa, 1850), 20–21.

27. NAW, 4:6.

28. A translation of the contract can be found in NAW, 4:99–100. The original is located in AHPG Onate, Partido de San Sebastian, no. 373, fols. 86–86v.

29. John Smyth, *The Ledger of John Smyth, 1538–1550*, ed. Jean Vanes (Bristol: Bristol Records Society, 1974), 36.

30. Here I follow William Cronon, *Nature's Metropolis: Chicago and the Great West* (New York: Norton, 1991). For a study of this regional ecological effect, see Robbins, *City on the Ocean Sea*, 9–60.

31. Biscuit: ADG 3 E, Notaires, Registre Bigot, April 22, 1552. A transcript is found in NAW, 4:94. Calculation: Grenier, Stevens, and Bernier, *The Underwater Archaeology of Red Bay*, 1:56–58, 85, n.273. Ratio of flour to biscuit from Hayes et al., "European Naval Diets in the Sixteenth Century," 3. Yields: Gregory Clark, "Yields per Acre in English Agriculture, 1250–1860: Evidence from Labour Inputs," *Economic History Review* (1991).

11. Eating

1. Alexandre Tollemer, *Journal manuscrit d'un sire de Gouberville et du Mesnil-au-Val, gentilhomme campagnard, au Cotentin, de 1553 à 1562*, Journal de Valognes (Valognes: G. Martin, 1872), 620.

2. For one long-term study of cod eating, see the popular Kurlansky, *Cod*. The most detailed study of cod consumption in the sixteenth century has been done in the French context by Turgeon, first in "Codfish, Consumption and Colonization."

3. French fish: FSL Z.e. 2, "Selection of accounts of the households of various French sovereigns, 1554–1594"; Renée Girard, "Identité alimentaire et frontière raciale en Nouvelle-France," *Revue d'histoire de l'Amérique française* 75, nos. 1–2 (2021).

4. Westminster Abbey: Harvey, *Living and Dying in England, 1100–1540*, 46–47, table A 226. This included all manner of cod, from fresh to dry-salted to pickled. *Accounts of the Priory of Worcester for the Year 13–14 Henry VIII: A.D. 1521–2*, ed. Rev. J. Harvey Bloom and Sidney G. Hamilton (Oxford: Worcester Historical Society, 1907), 53–55; *Comptus Rolls of the Obedientiaries of St. Swithun's Priory, Winchester*, ed. G. W. Kitchin (London: Hampshire Records Society, 1892), 334.

5. Henry VIII: "Edward VI—Volume 15: September 1552," in *Calendar of State Papers Domestic: Edward VI, Mary and Elizabeth, 1547–80*, ed. Robert Lemon (London: Her Majesty's Stationery Office, 1856), 44–45. *British History Online*, http://www.

british-history.ac.uk/cal-state-papers/domestic/edw-eliz/1547–80/pp44–45, AM Saint Malo BB 4, n.p., entry for 1569.

6. Tollemer, *Journal du Gouberville*. For instance, on Thursday, April 8, 1557, Gouberville purchased a variety of fish, including a whole cod, which he sent, along with a mackerel, to his cousin as a gift the next day (341–42). Economic fish days: FSL V.b. 303, no. 1, "Touching the Great Expense of Fleshe."

7. Capitano: Gilbert, "Beothuk-European Contact in the 16th Century," 36, 37. Alfonse: Alfonse, *Les voyages auantureux*, 28r. Fish ponds: NAW, 4:62; Schlesinger and Stabler, *André Thevet's North America*, 72, 228. On varied diets: Donald H. Holly Jr., "Toward a Social Archaeology of Food for Hunters and Gatherers in Marginal Environments: A Case Study from the Eastern Subarctic of North America," *Journal of Archaeological Method and Theory* 26, no. 4 (2019).

8. On the history of stockfish: Sophia Perdikaris, "From Chiefly Provisioning to Commercial Fishery: Long-term Economic Change in Arctic Norway," *World Archaeology* 30, no. 3 (1999); Fagan, *Fish on Friday*; Terje Inderhaug, "Stockfish Production, Cultural and Culinary Values," *Food Ethics* 5, no. 1 (2020); Pal Christensen and Alf Ragnar Nielssen, "Norwegian Fisheries, 1100–1970: Main Developments," *North Atlantic Fisheries* (1996).

9. Nicholls, Allaire, and Holm, "The Capacity Trend Method," 82–84; Thomas Willis, *A Medical-Philosophical Discourse of Fermentation; or, Of the Intestine Motion of Particles in Every Body* (London: T. Dring, C. Harper, J. Leigh, & S. Martin, 1681), 5; Christopher P. Magra, *The Fisherman's Cause: Atlantic Commerce and Maritime Dimensions of the American Revolution* (Cambridge: Cambridge University Press, 2012), 21; Fagan, *Fish on Friday*, 62. In 1558, one half a saltcod was given to four mariners along with a half pound of butter or cheese as a fish day ration. "Spain: April 1558," in *Calendar of State Papers, Spain*, vol. 13: 1554–1558, ed. Royall Tyler (London, 1954), 374–78; *British History Online*, http://www.british-history.ac.uk/cal-state-papers/spain/vol13/pp374–378.

10. Desiderius Erasmus, *The Whole Familiar Colloquies of Desiderius Erasmus of Rotterdam*, trans. Nathan Bailey (London: Hamilton, Adams, 1877), 258–90; Thomas Moffett, *Healths Improvement; or, Rules Comprizing and Discovering the Nature, Method, and Manner of Preparing All Sorts of Food Used in This Nation. Written by That Ever Famous Thomas Muffett, Doctor in Physick: Corrected and Enlarged by Christopher Bennet, Doctor in Physick, and Fellow of the Colledg of Physitians in London* (London: Thomas Newcomb, 1655), 169.

11. Willis, *A Medical-Philosophical Discourse of Fermentation*, 5; Thomas Tusser, *Fiue Hundreth Pointes of Good Husbandrie: The Edition of 1580 Collated with Those of 1573 and 1577*, ed. W. Payne and Sidney J. Heritage (London: Trubner, 1878), 28; Pierre Belon, *La nature et diversité des poissons, avec leurs pourtraicts, représentez au plus près du naturel* (Paris: Charles Estienne, 1555), 122; Glenn Gorsuch, ed., *The Prince of Transylvania's Court Cookbook from the 16th Century*, trans. Bence Kovacs,

2017, http://medievalcookery.com/etexts.html?Hungary; Marx Rumpolt, *Ein New Kochbuch* (Hildesheim: Olms, 1977).

12. Domenico Romoli, *La singolare dottrina di M. Domenico Romoli sopranominato Panunto, dell'vfficio dello scalco, de i condimenti di tutte le viuande, le stagioni che si conuengono a tutti gli animali, vccelli, & pesci, banchetti di ogni tempo, & mangiate da apparecchiarsi di dì, in dì, per tutto l'anno a prencipi* (Venice: Presso Gio. Battista Bonfadino, 1593), 364; Henry Butts, *Dyets Dry Dinner Consisting of Eight Seuerall Courses: 1. Fruites 2. Hearbes. 3. Flesh. 4. Fish. 5. Whitmeats. 6. Spice. 7. Sauce. 8. Tabacco. All Serued in After the Order of Time Vniuersall* (London: Thomas Creede, 1599), n.p. Salt appears under the section "Sauce" in Butts's work.

13. *The Coventry Leet Book; or, Mayor's Register: Containing the Records of the City Court Leet or View of Frankpledge, A.D. 1420–1555, with Divers Other Matters*, 2 vols., ed. Mary D. Harris (London: Early English Text Society, 1907), 651–52; Tusser, *Fiue Hundreth Pointes of Good Husbandrie*, 63.

14. Mark Dawson, *Plenti and Grase: Food and Drink in a Sixteenth-Century Household* (Totnes: Prospect Books, 2009). Even Southampton, itself a significant fishing port, was importing "Scarborowe myllwell" in the 1560s. Merson, *The Third Book of Remembrance of Southampton, 1514–1602: Volume III (1573–1589)*, vol. 2, 71–72; Great Britain, *The Statutes of the Realm: Printed by Command of His Majesty King George the Third, in Pursuance of an Address of the House of Commons of Great Britain. From Original Records and Authentic Manuscripts* (London: Dawsons of Pall Mall, 1810), 964: 35 Henry VIII, chapter 7, 1543–44, "An Acte for the Repealinge of a C[er]ten Statue concerninge the Bringinge in of Salt Fishe and Stockfyshe." Rouen: *Calendar of State Papers Foreign: Elizabeth*, vol. 19: *August 1584–August 1585*, ed. Sophie Crawford Lomas (London: His Majesty's Stationery Office, 1916), February 5/15, 1585, accessed via *British History Online*, http://www.british-history.ac.uk/cal-state-papers/foreign/vol19. Tusser: Tusser, *Fiue Hundreth Pointes of Good Husbandrie*, 133–315.

15. Tollemer, *Journal du Gouberville*, 646; *The Coventry Leet Book*, 1:382–83, 2:632, 646–47, 651–52, 680. Kingdom-level regulations are less commonly found in the sixteenth century, but one example is a 1583 "Edict of the King, for the creation of officers of Sellers of sea-fish fresh, dry and salted" for the cities of the kingdom of France, preserved in the city archives of Le Havre. AM du Havre BB 116, Vendeurs du Poisson.

16. Smythe: Smyth, *The Ledger of John Smyth*, 47, 304. See also ADLA B 705, fol. 17; and AM du Havre BB 116, Vendeurs du poisson. Coventry: *The Coventry Leet Book*, 2:646–47.

17. Newe Fishe Streete: FSL V.a.318, fol. 10r. La Rochelle: AM La Rochelle HH 14, 328, no. 107. Portugal: Abreu-Ferreira, "Fishmongers and Shipowners," 8–11.

18. Flavin and Jones, *Bristol's Trade with Ireland and the Continent*; Tusser, *Fiue Hundreth Pointes of Good Husbandrie*, 134; *The Coventry Leet Book*, 2:634–35; Turgeon, "Cod, Consumption, and Colonization," 41; Moffett, *Healths Improvement*, 148; Tollemer, *Journal du Gouberville*, 644.

19. Staindl: Balthasar Staindl, *Ein Kunstlichs vnd nutz/lichs Kochbuch/vormahlens nie so leycht* (Augsburg: Stayner, 1544), recipe cxxviii, fol. xx.r. Magno: Caroline Barron, Christopher Coleman, and Claire Gobbi, "The London Journal of Alessandro Magno, 1562," *London Journal* 9, no. 2 (1983), 147 gives translation of original Italian. Welseren: A transcription of the full cookbook is found at: https://www.uni-giessen. de/fbz/fb05/germanistik/absprache/sprachverwendung/gloning/tx/sawe.htm. A translation: http://www.daviddfriedman.com/Medieval/Cookbooks/Sabrina_Welserin. html. Recipes 33–34 are for dried cod. Scappi: *The Opera of Bartolomeo Scappi* (1570): *L'arte et prudenza d'un maestro cuoco*, ed. and trans. Terence Scully (Toronto: University of Toronto Press, 2008), no. 112.

20. Barron, Coleman, and Gobbi, "The London Journal of Alessandro Magno 1562," 147; Moffett, *Healths Improvement*, 170.

21. Book of Margery Kempe, BL, Add. Ms. 61823, lines 383–84, 2124–25. Coventry: *The Coventry Leet Book*, 2:632. Southampton: *Court Leet Records*, A.D. 1550–1557, ed. F.J.C. Hearnshaw and D. M. Hearnshaw, vol. 1, Publications of the Southampton Record Society (Southampton: Cox & Sharland, 1905), 213.

22. Quote: Thomas Cogan, *The Haven of Health, Chiefly Gathered for the Comfort of Students, and Consequently of All Those That Have a Care of Their Health* (London: Richard Field, 1596), 149. For some representative cookbooks: Staindl, *Ein Kunstlichs vnd nutz/lichs Kochbuch/vormahlens nie so leycht*; Maestro Martino da Como, *Libro de arte coquinaria*, ed. Emilio Montorfano (Milan: Terziaria, 1990), 73. For a translation: Maestro Martino da Como, *The Art of Cooking: The First Modern Cookery Book*, ed. Luigi Ballerini, trans. Jeremy Parzen (Berkeley: University of California Press, 2005), 103; Robert de Nola, *Libre del Coch* (Barcelona, 1520). Online transcription available through *Biblioteca virtual Miguel de Cervantes*. "Del merluca," in *Een notabel boecxken van cokeryen*, d. Ria Jansen Sieben and Marleen van der Molen-Willebrands (Amsterdam: De Kan, 1994), no. 69; Bartolomeo Scappi, *Opera di M. Bartolomeo Scappi, cuoco secreto di Papa Pio Quinto* (Venice, 1605).

23. Holly, "Toward a Social Archaeology of Food for Hunters and Gatherers in Marginal Environments."

24. Daniel Vickers, "The Price of Fish: A Price Index for Cod, 1505–1892," *Acadiensis* 25, no. 2 (1996); Abreu-Ferreira, "The Cod Trade in Early-Modern Portugal," 141, table 1; Holm et al., "The North Atlantic Fish Revolution (ca. AD 1500)," 8, fig. 6 for data from Germany. For Stourbridge: Dawson, *Plenti and Grase*, 120.

25. In September 1517, for instance, the Breton ship *La Marieu* of Croisic offloaded *morue verte* in Bordeaux. ADG 3 E 9796, September 23, 1517. For some context, Bernard, "Les debuts de la peche a Terre-neuve." On timing, Turgeon, "Pour redécouvrir notre 16 siècle," 533–34; Turgeon, "French Fishers, Fur Traders, and Amerindians during the Sixteenth Century," 594–95.

26. *Descriptions des arts et métiers, faites ou approuvée par Messieurs de l'Académie royale des sciences: Second Parte: Traité général des pesches, et hisoire des poissons*, ed.

Duhamel du Monceau (Paris: Saillant et Nyon, 1772), 73–74; Alison Locker, "The Decline in the Consumption of Stored Cod and Herring in Post-Medieval and Early Industrialised England: A Change in Food Culture," in *Cod and Herring: The Archaeology and History of Medieval Sea Fishing* (Oxford: Oxbow Books, 2016). Biting cod: "La trop trempée n'est pas bonne; et pour ce, qui l'achaitte, doit essaier à la dent et en mengier un petit," Georgine E. Brereton and Janet M. Ferrier, *Le menagier de Paris* (Oxford: Clarendon, 1981), 196.

27. Janzen, "The Logic of English Saltcod," 132. Note, for instance, a century later, the representation of a massive bank fishing fleet on an English map made in 1693. Augustine Fitzhughe, "A Chart of the Coasts of Newfoundland, with the Fishing Districts Marked," *NorFish Platform: Databases & Cartography Hub*, http://cehresearch.org/norfishplatform/items/show/4.

28. For the Basque argument: Brad Loewen and Miren Egaña Goya, "Dans le sillage des morutiers basque du Moyen Age: Une perspective sur l'origine et la diffusion du mot bacalao," in *L'aventure maritime, du Golfe de Gascogne à Terre-Neuve*, ed. Jean Bourgois and Jacqueline Carpine-Lancre (Paris: Editions du Comité des Travaux Historiques et Scientifiques, 1993), 235–50; Joan Coromines, *Diccionario crítico etimológico de la lengua castellana*, vol. 1, Biblioteca románica hispánica (Madrid: Editorial Francke, 1954), 358–59. Coromines notes the first appearance of *cabellauwus* in 1153. An Y. dos Bacalhas appears on a map by Pedro Reinal that is tentatively dated to 1504–5, though exactly when it was made is uncertain. BSB Codices Iconographici, 132. The name *Bacalao* definitely first appears on the 1507–8 Ruysch map, noted above.

29. For example, in 1592 the *Saloman* of London carried dried codfish direct from Terra Nova to Toulon. NAW, 4:116–17. On long-term tastes: Antonio José Marques da Silva, "The Fable of the Cod and the Promised Sea: About Portuguese Traditions of Bacalhau," in *Heritages and Memories from the Sea: 1st International Conference of the UNESCO Chair in Intangible Heritage and Traditional Know-How: Linking Heritage: 14–16 January 2015, Évora, Portugal: Conference Proceedings*, ed. Unesco Chair in Intangible Heritage et al. (2015); José Manuel Sobral and Patrícia Rodrigues, "O 'fiel amigo': O bacalhau e a identidade portuguesa," *Etnografica* 17, no. 3 (October 2013). On the importance of *bacalao* to Caribbean cuisine, see Candice Goucher, *Congotay! Congotay! A Global History of Caribbean Food* (New York: Routledge, 2013), 11–24; Cruz Miguel Ortiz Cuadra, *Eating Puerto Rico: A History of Food, Culture, and Identity* (Chapel Hill: University of North Carolina Press, 2013), chapter 4, "Codfish."

12. Commodities

1. Fécamp: ADSM 7 H 294, fols. 4r, 5r. La Rochelle: ADCM 3 E 3, notaire Hémon, fol. 85.

2. Stefano B. Longo, Rebecca Clausen, and Brett Clark, *The Tragedy of the Commodity: Oceans, Fisheries, and Aquaculture* (New Brunswick: Rutgers University Press, 2015).

3. Adriaen Coenen, *Visboek*, Koninklijk Bibliotheek, fol. 132v; Floris P. Bennema and Adriaan D. Rijnsdorp, "Fish Abundance, Fisheries, Fish Trade and Consumption in Sixteenth-Century Netherlands as Described by Adriaen Coenen," *Fisheries Research* 161 (2015). Coenen's hand-drawn image of the codfish, and much of the text, was copied from Pierre Belon's work, of which more below.

4. "Integrated Taxonomic Information System," https://www.itis.gov/. On cod as fish: Rose, *Cod*; Kurlansky, *Cod*.

5. Guillaume Rondelet, *Libri de piscibus marinis, in quibus verae piscium effigies expressae sunt* (Lyons: Matthiam Bonhomme, 1554); Belon, *La nature et diversité des poissons*; Conrad Gessner, *Historiae animalium: Liber 4. De piscium & aquatilium animantium natura* (Zurich: Apvd Christ. Froschovervm, 1554).

6. In Rondelet, cod was the sixth fish listed under the heading *Aselli*, and is called "*De Molua.*" Rondelet, *Piscibus marinis*, 280. For Belon, "*La Morue*" is "called in Latin *Aselli.*" Belon, *La nature et diversité des poissons*, 122. Gessner assigns the entire fourth part of his book to "*De Asellis,*" of which "*De Molua*" is included with a text and image copied directly from Rondelet. Gessner, *Historiae animalium*, 102; Alfred C. Andrews, "The Codfishes of the Greeks and Romans," *Journal of the Washington Academy of Sciences* 39, no. 1 (1949): 1–16.

7. On names, Eldar Heide, "Stokkfiskr, bakalao/kabeljau og handelsordvandring," *Haloygminne* 96, no. 24; Rondelet, *Piscibus marinis*, 280 (222 in the French edition); Gessner, *Historiae animalium*, 98, 102; Moffett, *Healths Improvement*. On the question of when the work was written, see "Moffet [Moufet, Muffet], Thomas [T. M.] (1553–1604), Physician and Naturalist," *Oxford Dictionary of National Biography*.

8. Cervantes, *Don Quijote de la Mancha*, 40; Thomas Dekker, *The Famous History of Sir Thomas VVyat with the Coronation of Queen Mary, and the Coming in of King Philip. As it was Plaied by the Queens Maiesties Seruants*, ed. John Webster (London: Edward Allde, 1607), n.p.

9. Belon, *La nature et diversité des poissons*, 125.

10. Conrad Gessner, *Fischbuch. Das ist ein kurtze, doch volkommne beschreybung aller Fischen so in dem Meer und süssen wasseren, Seen, Flüssen, oder anderen Bächen ir wonung habden*, trans. Christoph Froschauer (Zürich, 1563), 39, 114; John Maplet, *A Greene Forest; or, A Naturall Historie VVherein May Bee Seene First the Most Sufferaigne Vertues in All the Whole Kinde of Stones & Mettals: Next of Plants, as of Herbes, Trees, [and] Shrubs, Lastly of Brute Beastes, Foules, Fishes, Creeping Wormes [and] Serpents, and That Alphabetically: So That a Table Shall Not Neede* (London: Henry Denham 1567); Biggar, *Precursors*, 18, doc. X, "Second Dispatch of Raimondo di Soncino to the Duke of Milan," December 18, 1497.

11. Name: Stuart Jenks, ed., *London Customs Accounts. 28 Henry VIII (1536/7)–31 Henry VIII (1539–1540)*, vol. 74, part IV, no. 18, Quellen und Darstellungen Zur Hansischen Geschichte (Hansischer Geschichtsverein Lubeck, 2019), 87. "De Roberto Stokefysche, alienigena, pro 7 chestes Burgon glas white. [Precii] 7li"; Laura

Wright, *Sources of London English: Medieval Thames Vocabulary* (Oxford: Clarendon, 1996), 102–5. Ballads: an early version can be found in C. Kerrison, *A Common-
place Book of the Fifteenth Century: Containing a Religious Play and Poetry, Legal
Forms, and Local Accounts. Printed from the Original Manuscript at Brome Hall in
Suffolk*, ed. L. T. Smith (privately printed by A. H. Goose, 1886), 13. A 1719 version,
nearly identical, is in John Blow and Henry Purcell, *Songs Compleat, Pleasant and
Divertive; Set to Musick*, vol. 4 (London: W. Pearson, 1719), 128. Germans: Maplet, *A
Greene Forest*, 114.

12. I have used the 1605 edition of Scappi's *Opera*, held in the Folger Shakespeare Library, but the original was published in 1570. Paolo Giovio, *Libro di Mons. Paolo
Giouio de' pesci romani / tradotto in uolgare da Carlo Zancaruolo* (Venice, 1560), 120.

13. Turgeon, *Une histoire de la Nouvelle France: Français et amérindiens au XVI siècle*.
64–65. Islands quote: Jean Bruyerin. *De re cibaria* (Lyons, 1560), 1059–60. Magno
quote: Alessandro Magno, "Account of Alessandro Magno's Journeys to Cyprus,
Egypt, Spain, England, Flanders, Germany and Brescia, 1557–1565," FSL V.a. 259,
174.

14. Tsing, *The Mushroom at the End of the World*.

Conclusion

1. Richard Whitbourne, *A Discourse and Discouery of Nevv-Found-Land* (London: Fe-
lix Kingston, 1620), 1.
2. *The New Found Land of Stephen Parmenius*, 171; Alfonse, *Les voyages auantureux*,
271.

Appendix A

1. Belon, *La nature et diversité des poissons*, 130.
2. Wright, *Sources of London English: Medieval Thames vocabulary*, 102–5.
3. Great Britain, *Statutes of the Realm*, vol. 3, 35 Henry VIII, chapter 7, 1543–44, p. 964.
4. *Compota domestica familiarum de Bukingham et d'Angouleme, 1443* (Edinburgh: Ab-
botsford Club, 1836), 49.
5. Brereton and Ferrier, *Le menagier de Paris*, 195.
6. *Jacques Cartier: Documents nouveaux*, ed. F. J. des Longrais (Paris: A. Picard, 1888),
201.
7. All Cervantes attestations: Cervantes, *Don Quijote de la Mancha*, 40.
8. "un certo pesco seco . . . che vien a dire in nostra lengua battuto." Magno, "Account
of Alessandro Magno's Journeys," 174.
9. "Scarmo, sorte di pesce, detto ancora Merlusio [*merluccia*]. Hic Asellus." *Dittionario
volgare & latino, nelquale si continene. Come I vocaboli Italiani si possono dire, &
esprimere latinamente per M. Filippo Venuti da Cortona* (1576), 835.

INDEX